RUSSIA AND CENTRAL ASIA

Russia and Central Asia

Coexistence, Conquest, Convergence

Shoshana Keller

UNIVERSITY OF TORONTO PRESS

Toronto   Buffalo   London

© University of Toronto Press 2020
Toronto Buffalo London
utorontopress.com

ISBN 978-1-4875-9435-0 (cloth)   ISBN 978-1-4875-9436-7 (ePUB)
ISBN 978-1-4875-9434-3 (paper)   ISBN 978-1-4875-9437-4 (PDF)

Library and Archives Canada Cataloguing in Publication

Title: Russia and Central Asia : coexistence, conquest, convergence / Shoshana Keller.
Names: Keller, Shoshana, author.
Description: Includes bibliographical references and index.
Identifiers: Canadiana 20190187271 | ISBN 9781487594350 (hardcover) |
    ISBN 9781487594343 (softcover)
Subjects: LCSH: Russia (Federation)—Relations—Asia, Central—History. |
    LCSH: Asia, Central—Relations—Russia (Federation)—History.
Classification: LCC DK857.75.R8 K45 2020 | DDC 303.48/247058—dc23

We welcome comments and suggestions regarding any aspect of our publications—please feel free to contact us at news@utorontopress.com or visit us at utorontopress.com.

Every effort has been made to contact copyright holders; in the event of an error or omission, please notify the publisher.

University of Toronto Press acknowledges the financial assistance to its publishing program of the Canada Council for the Arts and the Ontario Arts Council, an agency of the Government of Ontario.

Canada Council   Conseil des Arts
for the Arts   du Canada

ONTARIO ARTS COUNCIL
CONSEIL DES ARTS DE L'ONTARIO
an Ontario government agency
un organisme du gouvernement de l'Ontario

Funded by the   Financé par le
Government   gouvernement
of Canada   du Canada

Canadä

CONTENTS

ACKNOWLEDGMENTS

I owe a great deal to my colleagues in the field and at Hamilton College for their deep knowledge and generosity. At Hamilton, thanks to Kevin Grant, Lisa Trivedi, Bonnie Urciuoli, Chaise Ladousa, Nathan Goodale, and Sally Cockburn for their careful reading, comments, and help with anthropological theory and Venn diagrams. Scott C. Levi, Gulnara Kendirbai, Alisher Khaliyarov, Alexander Morrison, Sarah Cameron, Marianne Kamp, Russell Zanca, R. Charles Weller, Erika Monahan, and the two anonymous reviewers contributed their scholarship and advice to make this a better book, although all mistakes are my responsibility. The maps were made by Bill Nelson at Bill Nelson – Cartography. My spouse, Deborah Reichler, gets my deepest gratitude for everything.

A NOTE ON SPELLING

It is a truth universally acknowledged in Central Asian studies that spelling is a nightmare. The languages of Central Asia have been written in multiple versions of the Perso-Arabic, Latin, and Cyrillic alphabets. Almost thirty years after the end of the Soviet Union, Uzbekistan, Turkmenistan, and Kazakhstan each use mixed, and still evolving, Latin and Cyrillic alphabets while Kyrgyzstan and Tajikistan use different Cyrillic alphabets. In class I tell my students that any spelling that is recognizably "in the ballpark" will do. That standard, of course, will not do here. I use the Library of Congress system for transliterating from Russian. For Central Asian languages I have opted to use the American standard or most accessible spelling available, rather than the most historically accurate. Hence "Kazakh" as the standard rendering of "Qozoq"; "Kyrgyz" for what could be written as "Kirghiz," "Kirgiz," or "Qyrgyz"; and "Kokand" for the city that is spelled "Khoqand" in pre-Soviet manuscripts and "Qo'qon" in Uzbekistan's current Latin alphabet. An exception is made for the fact that, until 1925, Russians called the Kazakhs "Kirgiz," and the Kyrgyz "Kara-Kirgiz" (Black Kirgiz). In this case I transliterate "Kirgiz" from the Russian to indicate the old nomenclature. For Uzbek words and names I use the current Uzbek Latin alphabet. There are a few letters that need explanation:

G'   a voiced glottal "gh," as in clearing one's throat

J   American pronunciation, as in "July"

Q   a glottal hard "k" sound

O'   a short "u," similar to the German "ö"

X   pronounced as the Yiddish "ch" in "chutzpah"; written as "Kh" from the Cyrillic

PLACE NAMES

REGIONS

Central Asia   the region encompassed by the five "Stans"—Kazakhstan, Kyrgyzstan, Uzbekistan, Tajikistan, and Turkmenistan

Kashgharia   also called Ettishahr, "Seven cities," the group of oasis towns around the Tarim Basin in today's Xinjiang Province of the People's Republic of China

Khurasan   northeast Iran up to the Qara Qum desert

Mawrannahr   Arabic for the region "across the Oxus River," or from the Kopet Dagh mountains to the Syr Darya, and the Caspian Sea to the Pamir mountains

Semirechie   "Seven Rivers" or "Ettisuv" in Turkic. The Kyrgyz and Senior Horde Kazakh lands between Lake Balkhash and the Ferghana Valley. Part of Turkestan 1898–1917

Steppe Krai   the Imperial Russian province of the Kazakh lands, from the Syr Darya to the Orenburg–Omsk fortress line, and the Ural River to the Ili River valley and the border with China, 1881–1920. Semirechie was part of the Steppe Krai, 1881–98

Transcaspia   the Imperial Russian province encompassing the Qara Qum desert and Yomut and Tekke Turkmen lands, between the Caspian Sea and Khiva and Bukhara, 1881–1920

Transoxiana   Greek for the region "across the Oxus River," or from the Kopet Dagh mountains to the Syr Darya, and the Caspian Sea to the Pamir mountains

Turan   ancient Iranian name for the land of threatening nomad barbarians to their northeast across the Amu Darya

Turkestan   the Imperial Russian province from the Aral Sea to the Ferghana Valley, excluding Bukhara and Khiva, 1867–1917

TOWNS AND THEIR MANY NAMES

The Bolshevik love of re-naming towns for revolutionary heroes makes life difficult for students of Soviet history. They never changed the names of the historical population centers: Bukhara, Tashkent, Samarkand, Khiva, and Kokand remained as they were. It was only the newer towns, often founded as Russian forts, and small settlements that were subject to repeated name changes. Here are the ones you will encounter in this book.

Current Name	History
Almaty, Kazakhstan	Founded as Russian Fort Vernoe in 1854. Called Vernyi 1914–29. Re-named Alma-Ata, capital of the Kazakh Soviet republic, 1929–92. Became Almaty in 1992.
Astana, Kazakhstan	Founded as Akmolinsk in 1824. Re-named Tselinograd (grain city) 1961–92. Re-named Aqmola 1992–98. Re-named Astana, capital of Kazakhstan, in 1998.
Qzylorda, Kazakhstan	Founded as Aq Masjid before 1853. Re-named Perovsk 1853–1924. Became Qzil Orda, capital of the Kazakh Soviet republic, 1924–29. Spelled Qzylorda as of 1992.
Bishkek, Kyrgyzstan	Founded as Kokand fortress Pishpek c. 1825. Taken by Russia 1864. Re-named Frunze 1926–91. Became Bishkek in 1991.
Dushanbe, Tajikistan	Built on a crossroads market that opened on Mondays (Dushanbe), 1924–29. Named Stalinobod 1929–61. Re-named Dushanbe in 1961.
Khujand, Tajikistan	Alexander the Great founded a military outpost, Alexandria Eschatae, near this site c. 327 BCE. Known as Khujand by the eighth century CE. Re-named Leninobod 1936–92, then reverted to Khujand.
Ashgabat, Turkmenistan	Founded in early nineteenth century as Ashqabad. Named Poltoratsk 1921–24, then reverted to Ashkhabad. Since 1992, Ashgabat.

MAP 0.1 Contemporary Central Eurasia.

INTRODUCTION

If you look at a map, Central Asia is at the center of everything but is itself nowhere. The region is surrounded by China, India, Iran, and Russia, all influential cultures, yet it is rarely part of our general conversation about modern world history. But if we want to understand what the phrase "modern world history" even means, Central Asia is a terrifically useful place to look. Central Asians have been full participants in global political, economic, and intellectual currents, but because of their location at the center of Eurasia they have participated from an angle oblique to Europe, the Middle East, and Asia. It is precisely their perspective as semi-outsiders that makes the historical experiences of Central Asians essential for understanding how the modern world has developed.

One reason Central Asia has not been a regular part of the conversation is that it does not fit neatly into the familiar boxes we use to categorize the world. This realization should immediately challenge our dependence on those boxes. Central Asians are mostly Muslim, their religious observance shaped by deep Sufi traditions that originated in Central Asia, yet their knowledge and level of practice are quite different from those of people in other Islamic cultures. Most Central Asians are descended from the Turko-Mongol nomadic pastoralists who succeeded the Mongol Empire, and their artistic, literary, and musical forms are rooted in Iranian traditions. The major towns of Samarkand, Bukhara, Tashkent, and Khiva were trade entrepôts along the Silk Road, influenced by merchants and missionaries from India, Iran, China, and the Eurasian steppe. However, the peoples of Central Asia also had connections with Slavs that predated the Mongol Empire. They traded, fought, intermarried, and engaged diplomatically with each other for over eight hundred years. The balance of power slowly tipped in favor of Russia during the seventeenth century; starting in the eighteenth century the Russian Empire and then the Soviet Union ruled Central Asia, directly and indirectly. This experience pushed the development of Central Asian cultures in a different direction from that of Middle Eastern or Asian cultures. Imperial Russia led the modernization of education as well as of some political and economic structures. After 1917 Soviet communism forced stunningly deep and rapid transformations in these areas as well as the realms of religion, family life, living environment, and popular entertainment. Yet, the communists never succeeded in completely remaking Central Asians.

Their complicated heritage leaves Central Asians in a paradoxical position: Muslims who do not easily fit in with Middle Eastern or Asian Islamic cultures; people raised to see the world through a Russian historical lens although they are neither Slavic nor Orthodox Christian; people living in a place that has been part of the Iranian, Mongol, Chinese, and steppe cultural complexes but since 1991 has made few comfortable international ties. This book explores the historical relationship between Russia and the Central Asian peoples, and how that has shaped the Central Asia we see today. In a simplified scheme, I suggest that there have been three phases in this relationship: a period of coexistence when Slavic and Turkic peoples shared the steppe and the burdens of Mongol rule; of conquest, as Russia gradually absorbed the Kazakh steppe lands and then over-ran the settled peoples further south; and of convergence, as Russians and Central Asians both went through communist shock modernization and became connected to global commercial culture. This is not at all to say that these phases were somehow inevitable. There are no laws governing history, however much Karl Marx insisted he had found them. The major events recounted here might have turned out differently for reasons large and small. The task of the historian is to analyze why events happened the way that they did.

WHAT IS CENTRAL ASIA?

One of the many reasons why Central Asia tends to be invisible to the rest of the world is that no one is quite sure where it is. The current popular definition is that it consists of "the -stans": the republics of Kazakhstan,

Kyrgyzstan, Tajikistan, Uzbekistan, and Turkmenistan. However, there are other "-stans"—Tatarstan, Afghanistan, Pakistan—that usually do not get included under the label "Central Asia," although they have plenty of historical and cultural ties with the region. There are Kazakhs, Tajiks, Uzbeks, Kyrgyz, Turkmen, and Uyghurs (close linguistic cousins of the Uzbeks) who live in Iran, Afghanistan, and Xinjiang Province in the People's Republic of China, who can easily be included as "Central Asians" but whose recent historical experiences are different from those of people living in the five "-stans." Then there are the peoples of Mongolia, Tibet, and southern Siberia, who certainly live in the middle of Asia and who are as deeply embedded in the history of the region as any Kazakh or Uzbek, but scholars treat them separately because their languages and religions are different from those found in the "-stans."

To compound the problem, none of the five republics existed before the 1920s, so they are not referred to in historical sources. Iranians 2500 years ago called the land to their northeast "Turan," a region inhabited by frightening, uncivilized barbarians. The Greeks after Alexander the Great (356–23 BCE) called it "Transoxiana," for "across the Oxus River" (today's Amu Darya). The Arabs who invaded in the eighth century CE translated the Greek term into "Mawrannahr." It was part of the Mongol Chaghatay Khanate and then split into successor khanates named for the capitals Bukhara, Khiva, and Kokand. When the Russians took over in the nineteenth century they divided the region into the Steppe Province and the Turkestan Province, for "place of the Turks." For most of the twentieth century Western scholars treated the area as a large blank section of the map between Soviet Russia and China. In fact, that is what sparked my own interest in the region as an undergraduate. I was studying "Soviet" history and realized that what I was really learning was the history of Russia and occasionally Ukraine under communism. We did not talk about the rest of the Union of Soviet Socialist Republics (USSR), even though it spanned from the Ural Mountains to the Pacific Ocean, and from the Caucasus and Kopet Dagh mountains to the Arctic Ocean. Furthermore, I learned in other classes that the histories of India, China, and Iran were influenced by nomadic peoples who invaded repeatedly from Central Asia. Looking at a map, I was somewhat startled to see that this important region was a part of the USSR, but I did not know anything about it. So I set about to learn what was going on with that blank spot on the map.

There are no completely satisfactory solutions to the problem of how to define "Central Asia," but for the purposes of this book I mean the area of today's five Soviet-created "-stans." Since their borders and names have changed a great deal through time, my use of terminology will also have to be flexible. When I am discussing the pre-Mongol period I will use the ancient names Transoxiana or occasionally Mawrannahr; I will use the Russian names for the nineteenth and twentieth centuries. When I discuss the interactions of Kazakhs and Uzbeks with Siberians, Mongols, eastern Turks, or peoples west of the Urals, I call the larger territory "Central Eurasia," meaning the landmass roughly from the Caucasus to Mongolia.

Models for Thinking about Central Asian Identities

Just as the names and definitions of the physical territory of Central Asia have changed greatly over time, so too the names and definitions of peoples have transformed in an ever-turning kaleidoscope, to the great frustration of the modern Western mind that likes to put people in clearly labeled categories. Migration has been the defining feature of human ecology for most of Central Eurasian history, because so much of the area is too dry and cold for settled farming. Nomadic pastoralists followed their herds of sheep, goats, horses, and camels from winter shelter to summer pastures, usually in a south-to-north circular pattern or from lowlands to mountain meadows. The open steppes of Central Eurasia have repeatedly been the platform for large-scale domino cascades, where one group attacks and displaces another, which in turn invades and pushes out its neighbors, who move further to seek new pastures, in waves that have sometimes traveled over 2000 miles. Periodically pastoralists formed tribal confederations that, under a charismatic leader, became empires that controlled most of Central Eurasia and intimidated the agrarian empires of Iran, India, and China.[1] The Huns that terrified Rome in the fifth century CE, the First and Second Turk Empires of the sixth and seventh centuries, and the Mongols of the thirteenth and fourteenth centuries are the best-known examples of these. With all of this movement across huge distances, groups of people did not establish what we would call ethnic identities rooted in a particular place or language. Languages change and borrow from each other, especially when their speakers move around a great deal. Tribal lineage, for which scholars have devoted decades of effort to create taxonomies, turns out to be rather fluid in mobile societies. Tribes break up and merge with other tribes, or when convenient invent a common ancestor to justify an economic or political alliance. What has remained constant in tribal lineage traditions is the universal impulse of elites to maintain their superior status. Tribes could grow or shrink, but the families who traced their lineage back to founding fathers or great spiritual guides made sure that no one could forget their exalted origins.[2]

Even what anthropologists have called the ancient distinction between "the steppe and the sown" was actually a frontier of many shades. Nomads needed to trade with sedentary communities for foodstuffs or items they could not make or raise on their own—to quote a founding scholar of Inner Asian studies, Owen Lattimore, "it is the poor nomad who is the pure nomad."[3] Nomads provided farmers with horses and with goods from their contacts with other peoples at distant ends of their ranges. Semi-nomadic communities developed on the edges of towns, farming part of the year and herding for the rest. Until modern times Central Eurasian nomadic pastoralists looked down on farmers as poverty-stricken servants, and they were right. Sometimes farmers took up nomadizing to improve their lot in life, migrating from one kind of community to another.

Fluidity of identity does not mean absence of identity, however. While in the West the modern concepts of race and ethnicity are the basis of our categorization of peoples, for the Russian, Turkic, and Iranian societies we are concerned with, the fundamental marker of difference was religion. Whether a person was Muslim, Christian, Shamanist, or Buddhist determined where he or she was welcomed as "one of us" and where treated as an outsider. In medieval Muscovy a person of Turkic origin could even marry into the ruling family if he or she converted to Christianity first. This was in notable contrast to Spain or northern Europe, where Jewish or Moorish converts never shook the suspicion of having foreign blood. Within religions people distinguished between nomad vs. settled, one tribal lineage vs. another, and urban vs. rural, but again these categories were never fixed in stone. The great exception to this pattern was the Mongol Empire, which was the only Central Eurasian empire that can truly be called global.[4] The Mongols' indigenous religion can be characterized as Shamanist, centered on the impersonal sky god Tengri, but as rulers they protected every religion under their sway. It was a highly effective tactic for maintaining order. Mongol elites adopted Christianity, Islam, Buddhism, and other religions without endangering their identity as Mongols, as long as they remained rulers.

The idea of race as a permanent identity marker was introduced to Russia from Europe in the eighteenth century and spread eastward with the Russian Empire, but as we will see "race" as a concept operated differently in Russia and the USSR than it did in Europe, much less the United States. For students of Central Eurasia a more useful way of categorizing groups of people, also developed in the eighteenth century, is to look at language. Tracing root languages and their many offspring is a way to sketch out how different groups of people are related to each other and how they have migrated and changed over time. The linguistic tools of analyzing word roots, grammatical structures, and syntax patterns have been particularly helpful in making sense of the far-flung, mobile peoples of Central Eurasia. The two major language families we will deal with in this history are the Altaic (Mongol and the Turkic branch, including Uzbek, Kazakh, Kyrgyz, Karakalpak, and Turkmen) and the Indo-European (the Slavic and Iranian branches, including Tajik). The Semitic language Arabic, as the language of Islamic jurisprudence and philosophy, is also deeply embedded in all Central Asian languages.

It should be clear by now that a history of Central Asia cannot be a history of nation-states in the way that a history of Europe might be, although recent historiography has significantly complicated the model of what a "nation-state" is.[5] This is despite the fact that the USSR created the five "-stans" as part of the most carefully thought-out program to build nation-states in history. There are other theoretical models of how to understand the internal structures of Central Asia that are more useful than the idea of the nation-state. Two models, the "robust ethno-linguistic frontier" and the "cultural complex," are overlapping approaches that emphasize different fundamental structures. The frontier model pays close attention to the interaction of cultures with their physical environment. The cultural complex model defines a culture based on human-created features such as language and religion.

The robust ethno-linguistic frontier model tries to address the factors that have created and sustained the most ancient division of Central Asian peoples, between the nomadic pastoralists of the steppes and deserts and the settled agricultural communities built around oases. The starting point for this analysis is ecological zones: from north to south, forest land shaded into the vast, dry grasslands of the steppe, then changed to hot sand-and-scrub desert punctuated by fertile, well-watered land along the rivers. These zones exist in long horizontal bands across the Eurasian continent, which creates environmental uniformity east to west, but notable changes north to south. The horizontal bands facilitated east-west migrations, while making north-south migrations more difficult. Desert is a prominent feature of Central Asia partly because the Pamir/Karakorum/Himalayan mountain knot to its southeast blocks moisture-bearing winds from the Indian Ocean. At the same time, the region is so far from any major body of water that it has a "continental" climate, with hot summers and cold winters, both dry because so little moisture can reach the interior. The lack of moisture makes rivers crucial to sustaining agricultural communities. The great Amu and Syr rivers, the Zerafshan that waters Samarkand and Bukhara, and the Chu River of northern Kyrgyzstan are all glacial rivers flowing from the eastern mountains.[6] This makes the current shrinking of the glaciers due to climate change of great concern to the region.

Differences in environment have given rise to long-lasting (hence "robust") differences in the lifeways of communities on either side of an ecotone, or ecological frontier, such as that between steppe and river oases.[7] Pastoralist and agricultural peoples regularly interacted with each other, but maintained separate languages and distinct ways of conducting their religious, family, and political lives. These differences could survive for thousands of years and keep similar form, whether the nomadic pastoralists were ancient Iranian-speaking Scythians, early Turks, or the Turko-Mongol Kazakhs, and no matter the ethnic make-up of the settled agricultural communities. In Central Eurasia two persistently opposing "bundles of customs"[8] on either side of the steppe/oasis ecotone can be summarized as the nomadic pastoralist (diet based on meat and milk from the herds; oral culture; more flexible social structures, particularly in gender relations; armies of fast and deadly horseback archers organized according to the decimal system) and the agricultural (varied, plant-based diet; literate with a high intellectual/ artistic culture; more rigid family and social structures). The combination of differing lifeways, ancestry, and language leads to differing ethnic identities developing on either side of the ecological frontier, which then serves as an ethno-linguistic frontier as well.

What makes the model of robust ethno-linguistic frontiers so intriguing for Central Asia is that it explains why nomads who crossed an ecotone to conquer a settled area were absorbed by the cultures they ruled. A pertinent example that will be discussed in Chapter 1 is that of the Uzbeks in the sixteenth century. The Uzbeks were a nomadic tribal confederation that had spun off from the former Mongol Qipchaq Khanate; their language belonged to the Qipchaq sub-family of the Turkic languages. They roamed the steppe east of the Volga River, then in 1500 swept south of the Syr Darya and conquered the agricultural oases of the Timurids. Within a few decades many of the nomads became settled farmers and town-dwellers, adopted the local Oghuz Turkic language (comparable to switching from Italian to Spanish) and carried on the high Islamic intellectual and artistic culture of the Timurids. Older historiography argued that this phenomenon was the completely unsurprising result of an advanced culture swallowing primitive nomads who had no real culture to lose. Rather than attributing the change to a problematic hierarchy of "advanced" vs. "primitive," the ethno-linguistic frontier model suggests that crossing into a new environment required changes in lifeways for survival, and the Uzbeks adapted accordingly. The model also explains why Kazakhs and Uzbeks, who emerged from the same Turko-Mongol confederation, evolved into two distinct ethnic groups, one on the north side of the ecotone and the other on the south.

But wait! This argument threatens to erase human agency in favor of a mechanical "climate = culture" determinism. Nothing is ever that simple with human societies. In the Uzbek case, while the oasis environment did force them largely to abandon pastoralism, and it is likely that the language change can be attributed to a minority population taking up the language of the majority, the Uzbek elites had participated in high Islamic culture before they crossed the steppe/oasis ecotone. Both Uzbeks and the Timurids they displaced were heirs to the Mongol Empire, which in its day had absorbed cultural values from the Islamic Middle East. The ideal Uzbek leader in 1500 wrote exquisite poetry and if possible painted or played the lute when he was not fighting on the steppe. Changes in environment certainly played a role in shaping Uzbek culture after the conquest, but the nomads always had their own contributions to make when they entered a new area.

Russia, and especially the Soviet Union, altered the physical environment of Central Asia and in the process changed how Central Asians lived in that environment. The Soviets built hugely inefficient irrigation canals to spread the planting of cotton, hydroelectric dams across mountain rivers, and dropped thousands of tons of toxic chemicals on the land and water to promote ever-higher cotton harvests. They forcibly settled nomad communities to make them farmers under state control—leading to the 1930–33 famine that killed 1.5 million Kazakhs—and moved entire Tajik mountain villages to lowland collective farms. These economic development policies have resulted in the drying up of the Aral Sea, the largest man-made water crisis in the world, and a host of public health problems from chemical poisoning and community disruption. The Soviets were among the most enthusiastic promoters of the nineteenth-century European idea that technology can overcome all obstacles, and their efforts eroded the ancient steppe-oasis ecotone while replacing it with political boundaries. Central Asian governments today continue an economic instrumentalist relationship to their land and water.

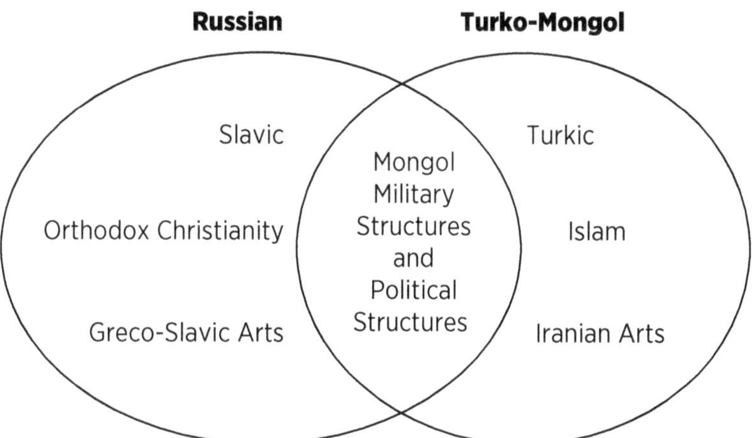

FIGURE 0.1 Venn diagram showing intersections of Slavic and Turko-Mongol cultural complexes.

Another useful model for understanding the relationships of Central Eurasian societies to each other and to Outer Eurasian societies is the "cultural complex."[9] The classic nation-state model posits that individual nations create individual national cultures, an idea that the Soviets promoted quite vigorously. According to the Soviet version of that model, Central Asian peoples had always maintained clear distinctions among themselves, and had little in common with the Russians when they began to live together in the eighteenth century. In contrast, I propose that we look at Central Asian and Russian cultures as expressions of bundles of practices and cultural elements that related to each other as components in a Venn diagram (see Figure 0.1).

The longest-lasting legacy of the Mongol Empire across Central Eurasia was the spread of a Turko-Mongol cultural complex. This cultural complex was characterized by a few fundamental features: Turkic as the dominant language group, Islam as the dominant religion, Iranian modes of artistic and literary expression, and Mongol political and military organization, especially the exclusive right to rule held by the "Golden Kin," direct descendants of Chinggis Khan.[10] Within these broad parameters, some groups lived as nomadic or semi-nomadic pastoralists and some as sedentary farmers; some formed organized kingdoms and some barely had governments in any sense. Russian Muscovy mostly inhabited a different cultural complex: Slavic languages, Eastern Orthodox religion, and Greek artistic roots.[11] No one would place Muscovy within the Turko-Mongol complex, but the two complexes had significant areas of overlap because of the common experience of being ruled by the Mongol Empire. The Russian grand princes used the term "tsar" for the Byzantine emperor and the Mongol khan alike. When Ivan IV "the Terrible" became the first Russian ruler to be formally crowned with the title of tsar in 1547, and then conquered the Mongol successor states of Kazan and Astrakhan, he was making a strong symbolic statement of his status in the Central Eurasian political hierarchy.

Thinking about Central Eurasia in terms of cultural complexes rather than nation-states suggests a way of understanding the effects of Russian rule that emphasizes integration and multi-dimensional development rather than the linear evolution that Imperial Russian and Soviet historians asserted. Russia changed many aspects of Central Asian life, but at the deepest level it took Central Asians out of the Turko-Mongol cultural complex and moved them into a European-Slavic one. Simultaneously, Russia itself became more open to elements from the northern-European Franco-Germanic cultural complex, a process that we usually call modernization or Westernization. Mobile Central Asians had exchanged goods and cultural tropes across Eurasia for millennia; Russia gradually redirected the focus of these exchanges toward Europe. As Russia became more like Europe, Central Asia became more like Russia, joining the modern global integration being driven by new economic and technological forces. Keep in mind that integration never meant erasure: Russians and Central Asians have retained their languages, religions, and cultures in altered but recognizable forms.

QUESTIONS OF COLONIALISM

An obvious way to integrate Central Asia into our current narrative of world history is to discuss the region as a colonial possession of the Russian Empire and Soviet Union, in a similar sense as India was an imperial possession of Great Britain and Algeria a colony of France. There are many points of comparison that match across the three empires: each was structured as a "metropole" (with London, Paris, or St. Petersburg as central) that asserted economic and political dominance over a "periphery." Each metropole governed territories and peoples that dwarfed it in size by a combination of integrating or co-opting local elites and brute force. Each sent settlers to its new possessions, who brought their own cultural habits and acquired local habits. Each tried to "civilize" the colonized peoples with European education, governance, and legal practices. There are a few important differences between the Russian and the British and French colonial empires as well. Great Britain and France drew enormous profits from their colonies, especially the British Raj in India, whereas Russia spent more money and resources on Central Asia than it earned back. For Russian authorities the prestige of being an imperial power was more valuable than the monetary cost, an attitude that arguably contributed to the collapse of the empire in 1917. British and French Christian missionaries built schools, hospitals, orphanages, and other components of a modern social service network, but the Russian Orthodox Church did not make missionary work among Muslims a high priority and Russian governors-general banned missionaries from Turkestan. Government bureaucrats, working cooperatively with Muslim clergy, built a small network of Russian schools that taught in local languages but did not concern themselves with modernizing social services in general. Most importantly, Russia's empire was not across oceans but was part of the same landmass. Russians and Central Asians had hundreds of years of familiarity with each other; the nature of their relationship changed during the eighteenth and nineteenth centuries, but it was not utterly new.[12]

Russian rule gradually spread from the Kazakh steppes in the eighteenth century to the Uzbek, Turkmen, and Kyrgyz lands in the later nineteenth, and so Central Asians experienced and responded to it differently. Nomadic Kazakhs found themselves being progressively penned in and forced to depend on Russian military outposts for food and fodder for their animals. They had the longest exposure to Russian culture of any of the Central Asian peoples, especially the "white bone" aristocrats who lived in Russia as diplomatic envoys or were given Russian educations as royal hostages. The Turkmen and Kyrgyz nomads were the last groups to encounter a permanent Russian presence, in the form of military invasion or Slavic peasant settlers. Their experience of colonialism was more violent, with fewer benefits, than that of other groups. When Russia invaded Transoxiana in 1865 it preserved the khanates of Bukhara and Khiva as protectorates, while it broke up the Kokand Khanate and absorbed it into the Russian-governed province of Turkestan. This gave Uzbeks and Tajiks, neither of which were homogenous communities to begin with, widely varying degrees and kinds of contact with Russians. Some urban merchants learned fluent Russian, sent their children to Russian schools, and got rich from Russian-sponsored industrialization of the cotton and silk trades. Many people in rural areas or the protectorates saw new kinds of goods and technologies but never an actual European. Turkestan and the Kazakh Steppe Province were partially integrated into the Russian legal system, while the protectorates and other nomadic communities were not. One thing that Imperial Russia did not do was to cut Central Asians off from the rest of the Islamic world. On the contrary, Russia facilitated the pilgrimage to Mecca, and a small but highly influential group of intellectuals spent time in the Ottoman Empire and India studying the reformist ideas that were inspiring new political movements across the Middle East. Russian rule gave Central Asians access to a wider range of cultural influences than at any time since the Mongol Empire.

The period from 1905 to 1920 saw astounding political and social upheavals all over the world, in two phases: a series of constitutional revolutions from 1905 to 1911, and then World War I and its diplomatic aftermath from 1914 to 1920. Central Asia participated in both phases from some distance, and emerged into a profoundly different political environment. The wave of constitutional revolutions began in January 1905 in St. Petersburg, the capital of Russia, with a peaceful workers' demonstration for the right to free assembly, free speech, an eight-hour workday, and a body of elected representatives. Instead soldiers gunned them down in droves, which set off empire-wide strikes and riots. By October the tsar was forced to grant most of the strikers' demands.

The revolution of 1905 created opportunities for educated Central Asians to print magazines and newspapers, write plays and pamphlets, to explore and act on a flood of new ideas. Among those ideas were that Central Asia was exploited like India, and that the peoples of the region constituted nations that had a natural right to govern themselves. How to strengthen themselves and reclaim their independence, however, led to sharp arguments between reformist and conservative factions divided by age, education, religiosity, and wealth.

Because the Russian government placed Central Asians in a separate citizenship category from Christians in the empire, they were not called on to fight in World War I. By 1916, however, the government was so desperate for manpower that it instituted a draft of Central Asians to serve in labor battalions behind the lines. This touched off a massive series of riots that, in eastern Kazakh and Kyrgyz areas, turned into bloody rebellion. Hundreds of thousands of nomads fled across the Tien Shan mountains into China, where many died of cold and hunger. Up to a quarter-million others were killed in direct fighting with Russians. The collapse of the Russian Empire began in Central Asia.

Was the Soviet Union a Colonial Empire?

Central Asia would likely have followed a path toward eventual independence from imperial rule as other regions in Asia and Africa did, but the Bolshevik Revolution of October 1917 radically changed its trajectory. The Bolsheviks saw themselves as the vanguard of a global communist revolution that would create a dictatorship of the working class, the proletariat. Their ideal proletarian was a skilled and practical atheist who had no ethnic, tribal, or national identity, believed that men and women were fully equal, and was selflessly dedicated to the welfare of the common state. Creating this "New Soviet Man" in Russia was going to be a tall order, and imposing this new culture on the peoples of Central Asia would seem to be borderline insane. Nonetheless, by 1920 the Bolsheviks had achieved political control over the region and began to build a Soviet socialist government. Among historians, the Soviet creation of modern Central Asia has sparked a debate over whether the USSR was just a particularly brutal colonial empire or whether it was something else, and if so, what.

The case to regard the Soviet Union as a colonial empire is straightforward on the surface. The Soviet Red Army eliminated Central Asian armed resistance by 1930 or so. European communist commissars (mostly Russians but many Jews and Ukrainians as well) took the leading role in creating Uzbek, Kazakh, Tajik, Kyrgyz, and Turkmen communist parties that were all under the supervision of a bureau of the Moscow-based Communist Party's Central Committee. In 1924 this bureau oversaw the creation of the Uzbek and Turkmen Soviet Socialist Republics (SSRs); the Tajik, Kazakh, and Kyrgyz SSRs followed. Under Stalin the Central Asian republics were turned into a huge cotton plantation. Millions of Central Asians were forced to settle on collective farms where they labored for the state rather than for themselves. Millions of Central Asians were killed or sent to prison camps during the purges of the 1930s, often for the "crimes" of being nationalists or religiously observant. After Stalin's death in 1953 Central Asians were increasingly drawn into Russian culture via education and popular entertainment, while the pressure to produce ever more cotton never ceased. Russians who moved to Central Asia usually occupied the skilled technical positions, while Central Asians often kept to the less-skilled sector. By the 1980s the region suffered from deep environmental degradation and social stagnation. It would seem to be clear that Russia imposed itself on and sucked resources out of Central Asia to an even greater extent than Great Britain did with India.[13]

Nonetheless, the Soviet Union operated so differently from the model British and French colonial empires that many historians argue the "colonial" label does not fit at all. To begin with, Vladimir Lenin proclaimed that the Bolshevik Revolution was an *anti-colonial* revolution. Within a week of taking power Lenin issued a "Declaration of the Rights of the Peoples of Russia," which among other things promised "the right of the peoples of Russia to free self-determination including secession and formation of independent states."[14] As it turned out, he meant that he recognized only the right of non-Russian Bolsheviks to secede, since all other political parties were counter-revolutionary by definition. However, no true Bolshevik would want to secede from the workers' state—Lenin had perfected the concept of "catch-22" long before Joseph Heller thought of it.[15] Once the Soviet Union was formally established in 1923 the government embarked on a deliberate program of creating nation-states and national minority spaces within those states where all of the more than one hundred nationalities would be able to govern themselves, teach their children, and build their cultures in their own languages and on their own land. Crucially, the Communist Party relied on its non-Russian members themselves to do the work of drawing borders around the new republics, staffing state and party administrations, and building cultural structures that were "national in form, socialist in content."[16] Russian Bolsheviks found willing Central Asian partners for this project in the small group of people who had advanced educations and wanted to re-shape their societies with the modernizing mold they had seen in Russia, the Ottoman Empire, and India. During the post-Stalin decades Moscow poured resources into education, public health, consumer goods, and recreation and popular entertainment, which substantially raised people's standard of living. Population growth exploded, both from a substantially higher birthrate and decline in child mortality. Most tellingly, in 1991 the Central Asian republics, unlike those in the Baltics and the Caucasus, were not eager for independence. All of the destruction that the USSR inflicted was in the name of making Central Asians fully equal members of the worldwide revolutionary proletariat. As historian Christian Teichmann argues, "Modernization through de-colonization was the *grand projet* of the Bolsheviks in Central Asia, but it has its limitations."[17]

Once again, Central Asia cannot easily be slotted into the familiar categories we use to understand history, which reminds us that these categories are intellectual constructs that reflect historical reality imperfectly. The question remains, if Soviet Central Asia was not a colony of the Soviet empire, how are we to think of it? There is no consensus yet among historians on how to deal with this problem, but several lines of thought seem promising. Political scientist Mark Beissinger suggests that we adopt a more flexible interpretation of the word "empire" and consider it as a way of structuring authority rather than a specific set of political practices. We should acknowledge that the Soviet Union bore a "family resemblance" to other empires even as we analyze how it was different.[18] Historian Adeeb Khalid argues that the Soviet regime had more in common with the authoritarian modernizing states of Turkey and Iran in the 1930s than with the British Raj. These states saw their citizens as tools to be mobilized rather than passive subjects.[19] Historian Botakoz Kassymbekova sees the Soviet state selecting tools from the colonial and the modernizing "repertoires of power" to build a revolutionary society that was greater than both.[20] None of these approaches answers all of our questions, but Kassymbekova's model neatly accounts for the contradictions of Soviet state behavior.

CENTRAL ASIA TODAY

In 1991 the Soviet Union collapsed and its fifteen constituent republics became independent states, whether they wanted to or not. Political and social developments in Central Asia over the last twenty-seven years show how the Turko-Mongol and Slavic-European cultural complexes have converged with each other while also joining the global convergence of cultural complexes being driven by economics and the internet. The three areas where this multi-dimensional evolution shows most clearly are identity, religion, and politics.

Identity

When the five Central Asian Soviet Socialist Republics were created in the 1920s and 1930s they each developed distinct territories, alphabets and languages, political and economic structures, artistic expressions, and historical narratives, in keeping with Stalin's five-point definition of what constitutes a nation.[21] These were all complicated projects, but the trickiest and the last to be completed were the historical narratives. Stalin, who took a personal interest in how history was written, favored a traditional narrative that focused on the actions of the ruler and central state. He added to this narrative his own fixation on the perpetual danger of being beaten by foreign enemies. Stalin's version of Russian history featured centuries of invasion by Germans, Mongols, Poles, Swedes, and the French. This story created a Russian national identity that had clear-cut boundaries from ancient times, formed through bloody struggle against foreigners. The histories of the Central Asian nations, written by Soviet-trained Russian and Central Asian historians, followed the same pattern to create a narrative of long-term national continuity. Whereas in this introduction I have been discussing fluid models for understanding the historical movements of Central Asian peoples, the Soviets developed a fixed model they called *ethnogenesis*, "the process of ethnic crystallization that made it possible to speak of a specific people existing as such through the centuries."[22] This understanding of clearly defined, ancient national identities remains the accepted narrative in the post-Soviet republics, although they acknowledge their mixed, nomadic past. It leads to such oddities as the fact that the medieval philosopher al-Farabi (872–950), born in Otrar along the Syr Darya but who spent his adult life in Baghdad, writing in Arabic and Persian, is claimed by both Kazakhstan and Iran as a great "national" hero, although he lived more than five hundred years before the Kazakh Khanate emerged. The Central Asian states are now firmly invested in their national identities, even though these are rooted in nineteenth-century European political thought that contrasted sharply with Turko-Mongol ways of understanding history.

Religion

Most Central Asians are Muslims: the majority are Sunni, with small Shiite communities including the Ismailis of mountainous Badakhshan in eastern Tajikistan. There are also Jewish and Christian communities, although they are dying out due to emigration. The Soviet Union tried to destroy all religions, but failed and had to settle for putting them under close surveillance. The Soviets did tremendous damage to Central Asian Islam in the process. They destroyed most of the mosques, *madrasas* (religious academies, or higher schools for training clergy and judges), charitable foundations, and the chain of transmitting knowledge from one generation to the next. Then after World War II the state turned around and permitted the creation of a Muslim "spiritual administration" and a small network of mosques and madrasas that cooperated with the Communist Party and the KGB, the political police. In return for cooperation, Muslim clergy were allowed controlled contact with Arab Islamic institutions, which over time brought them closer to Arab thought and practice than they had been in the pre-Soviet period. Simultaneously, the Central Asian republics enshrined local Islamic customs, such as tying strips of cloth to trees to mark sacred places, as part of their permitted national cultural expression. Ordinary Muslims paid little attention to the state-supported clergy, and by the 1970s the majority of Central Asians engaged in religious practice only around major life-cycle events or in old age. They saw no difficulty in celebrating a circumcision or a wedding with plenty of vodka. A small underground of independent clergy taught students, but they also had regular ties with the state-supported clergy.

Mikhail Gorbachev's reform efforts of the late 1980s allowed more open religious expression, and after the Soviet collapse Saudi Arabia, Turkey, and to a lesser extent Iran sent aid to build mosques and schools, distribute Qurans, and revive Islamic knowledge in Central Asia. Independent Islam had a very short lifespan, however. The post-Soviet governments viewed religious expression outside state control with more suspicion than they had when they could rely on protection from Moscow. Their fear that free religious expression posed a threat to their political power was confirmed through the 1990s by several protests in the Ferghana Valley where Islam became a vehicle to express political discontent. The Tajik civil war of 1992–97 and a series of bombings in Uzbekistan turned this fear into terror. Uzbek president Islam Karimov ordered a vicious crackdown on anyone who practiced Islam outside state-controlled institutions, creating one of the worst records of human rights abuses in the world. Meanwhile, Turkmen president Sapurmurad Niyazov, the self-styled *Turkmenboshi* (head Turkmen), imposed a bizarre combination of Islam with his own spiritual guidance in the form of a book, the *Rukhnama* (Book of the Spirit), that was required mass reading just as Mao's Little Red Book or Muammar Qaddafi's Little Green Book had been. The post-Soviet governments pursue a tricky balance of using Islam to legitimize their rule and define their national cultures while also policing Muslims even more ferociously than Stalin did. The convergence of traditional Central Asian Islamic praxis with the Russian belief that religion should serve the state, decades of Soviet militant atheism, and twentieth-century authoritarianism makes this region "a world apart" from any other Islamic culture.[23]

Politics

In the late 1980s Central Asians surprised Gorbachev and the rest of the world with several displays of violent nationalist feeling. In Kazakhstan Gorbachev tried to appoint a Russian, rather than a Kazakh, head of the Communist Party, and Kazakhs loudly protested in response. In Uzbekistan there was open and bitter resentment against Moscow's campaign to end corruption in the cotton industry; Uzbeks saw Russian oppression rather than clean government. Western observers had been warning for some time that the rapidly growing Central Asian population would pose a challenge to Russian dominance. Yet when the USSR unraveled in 1990–91, the Central Asian republics were in no rush to claim independence. When they reluctantly realized that the USSR could not be put back together, the communist parties re-named themselves and the old elites continued governing as before. While they made some concessions to appease nationalist feeling, such as making Uzbek or Turkmen the official state language, the republics discouraged anti-Russian expressions and squashed their small democratic national political movements. At the same time, with the exception of Kazakhstan and Kyrgyzstan, they have held the Russian Federation at a distance. Since Stalin's death Central Asian elites had found profit and protection in the Soviet system. For them, the question was how to hang on to their power, not how to develop their newly independent countries for the benefit of all citizens.

The five republics have had divergent experiences over the last twenty-eight years, but the prevailing political climate has been dictatorial, corrupt, and often violent. All of the republics have been ruled by old communists under new names. Uzbekistan and Turkmenistan rapidly became brutal dictatorships, while Kazakhstan under Nursultan Nazarbaev pursued a softer authoritarianism buoyed by income from oil and gas development. Tajikistan went through a five-year civil war propelled by regional, religious, and political antagonisms and since 1992 has been ruled by Emomali Rahmon, a former Soviet *apparatchik* (bureaucrat). Rahmon is the only Central Asian leader to have ordered that his people de-Russify their names by dropping the ov/ova ending, although Tajikistan is deeply dependent on remittances from migrant workers in Russia. Only Kyrgyzstan has had a democratic type of government, but that has not solved the fundamental problems of poverty and corruption. Since the 2005 "Tulip Revolution" Kyrgyzstan has had many leaders and significant ethnic violence between Kyrgyz and Uzbeks, punctuated by elections that international observers call deeply flawed.

This dismal record is surprising only in the degree of brutality that post-Soviet governments have been willing to inflict on their people. Central Asians never had experience with representative, law-based forms of government. Although the rhetoric of democracy and the rule of law has been adopted globally (see Putin's Russia), the practice requires deep changes in behavior on the part of both ordinary citizens and elites, which would take much longer than a few decades to implement even if the ruling elite were willing to cooperate, which they are not. What we see today is a combination of Soviet political structures, Soviet and Central Asian cultural habits, and the ruthlessness of ruling elites. What is harder to see is the talent and potential of the Central Asian people themselves, which is tremendous, if currently suppressed.

Chapter 1

EARLY COEXISTENCE

When Russians began to incorporate Central Asian lands and peoples into their empire, they were not encountering exotic strangers with unknown customs. There was no Russian equivalent of David Livingstone peering into Darkest Africa, or Britons of the East India Company being boggled by the new cultures they saw. Instead, Russians and the Turkic steppe peoples had lived with each other from the very beginning of Russian and Ukrainian history, in the loose collection of towns called Kievan Rus'. This chapter will outline six hundred years of Slavic-Turkic interactions in war, trade, and marriage. These communities fought each other and cooperated with each other until both were conquered by the Mongols in the thirteenth century. Over two hundred years of Mongol rule created a completely different political landscape across Eurasia, with the Russian state of Muscovy and various Turkic khanates vying with each other for control. New khanates founded by Uzbeks and Kazakhs established themselves in Central Asia around 1500. At the same time, Muscovy had made itself the pivotal power among the Mongol successor states and was eager to expand eastward across the Ural Mountains.

RUS' AND THE STEPPE PEOPLES

The earliest Slav settlers east of the Dniestr River, who arrived in the eighth century of the Common Era, paid tribute to the Turkic Khazar kingdom, which dominated the grasslands north of the Black Sea from the 620s to 965 CE. For the next five hundred years Rus' towns and farming villages lived in fear of raids from Turkic nomadic pastoralists, the Pechenegs (890s–later eleventh century) and their successors the Polovtsy (also called the Kumans, more properly the Qipchaq Turks, 1050s–early thirteenth century). The towns of Kievan Rus' also maintained trade relations with the Turkic Muslim Kingdom of Bulgar (tenth–thirteenth centuries) in the central Volga River region.[1]

Our main source of information for Kievan Rus' history is the chronicles of towns and rulers that were compiled by Christian monks over many centuries. On first reading, the chronicles consistently depict the Pechenegs and Polovtsy/Kumans as pagan devils who do nothing but kidnap and kill. One of the main jobs of Kievan Rus' princes was to defend their towns from nomad raids: princes who lost battles or appeared reluctant to fight were sometimes violently deposed by the people of Kiev. But a closer reading of the chronicle texts reveals more complicated relationships. A chronicle entry from 968 recounts the story of the first siege of Kiev by the Pechenegs. A young Rus' man escaped the city to get help by pretending to be a Pecheneg looking for his missing horse. The chronicler explains that the youth could walk right through the besiegers because "he knew the Pecheneg tongue very well ... And they took him for their own."[2] This level of knowledge must have taken time and close interaction to develop. The Kievan Rus' princes, a dynasty of Scandinavian Viking origin, were prone to fratricidal wars of succession, and never hesitated to enlist Turkic fighters as allies against their brothers. In one of the bloodier tales from the Rus' chronicles, Prince Sviatopolk Iziaslavich of Turov decided in 1097 to have his cousin Vasilko Rostislavich blinded—it was a Turkic servitor who did the deed.[3] We also have evidence of less violent relations. The eleventh-century law code of Prince Iaroslav the Wise, the greatest of Kiev's rulers, punishes any Christian woman who marries a Jew or a Muslim by sending her to a convent while fining her would-be husband. The law is silent about Christian Rus' men who marry non-Christian women, which is just as well since several Rus' princes indeed married Turkic women, starting with the aforementioned Sviatopolk Iziaslavich. The existence of such laws is a good clue as to how diverse Kievan Rus' in fact was, since rulers do not issue laws forbidding things that never happen. The law tells us that Rus' Christians, Turkic Muslims, and Jews (likely Radhanites, long-distance traders originally from Iraq who established a settlement near Kiev) lived closely enough together that occasionally they fell in love, or at least saw each other as good mate material.[4]

The chronicles do indicate that the Turkic brides converted to Christianity when they married Rus' princes.

Polovtsy and Kievan Rus' also developed cooperative economic relationships. Polovets warriors found it advantageous to serve as border guards for Rus' against rival Turkic groups to the southeast. Archeological finds suggest that both Slavs and Turks did well from this relationship:

> Well-armed and numerous, with an elite decked out in silken headgear with silver chains and earrings made by Rus craftsmen, they played a key role in guarding the right-bank approaches to Kiev ... it was their presence which ensured the continuity and intensification of trade along the river, and made possible the development of the large unfortified Slav settlements.[5]

MONGOL CONQUEST

The Rus' and Turkic steppe peoples became interconnected in a formal way when they were conquered by the Mongol Empire founded by Chinggis Khan. Their first encounter with the power of the Mongols came in 1223, when combined Rus'–Polovtsy armies were destroyed at the Kalka River by a small Mongol expedition. The Novgorod Chronicle casually mentions that Rus' Prince Mstislav Mstislavich of Galich was married to a daughter of the Polovets chief, Khotian, although the chronicler always referred to the nomads as "godless Kumans."[6] The Polovtsy ceased to be a serious worry to the Rus' after 1223, and in 1236 Mongol armies destroyed the Turkic Kingdom of Bulgar on the Volga. In 1239 and 1240 the Rus' lands were devastated by a full-scale invasion led by Batu, son of Jochi, who was the oldest son of Chinggis Khan. Batu became the first khan of the Jochid or Qipchaq Khanate, named for his father. In the seventeenth century Russian sources started calling it "the Golden Horde," which became the more widely known name. Turkic, Iranian, and Mongol peoples in the lands between the Aral Sea and the Altay Mountains of today's eastern Kazakhstan were under the Chaghatay Khanate, established by Chinggis's second son. The Rus' and Turkic peoples now found themselves living within the same administrative and economic system.

The Jochid khans had no interest in living in the cold forests of Rus', and so governed the area from a distance, through their own agents and the surviving Rus' princes who were willing to work for them. During the first fifty years of Mongol rule princes in the northeastern town of Vladimir collected taxes, carried out census counts, and drafted peasants for Mongol armies and labor needs. These unfortunate Rus' were shipped wherever in Eurasia their masters wanted them. In 1253 William of Rubruck, a Franciscan monk who was the first European to visit the Mongol imperial capital at Karakorum, reported encountering a Rus' craftsman there.[7] The princes themselves had to make regular journeys to either the Jochid capital at Sarai or all the way to Karakorum, as did Russian Orthodox clergy. The church established a bishopric at Sarai in 1263, and took care to maintain good relations with the khans.

Starting in 1304, the princes of Moscow acquired power by being more efficient and ruthless governors on behalf of the Jochid Khanate than the princes of other towns. These tactics allowed them to establish their dynastic line as supreme and start calling themselves "Grand Prince." Over the next two hundred years, Moscow would absorb the *appanages* (towns and their surrounding countryside) of other princely families into a centralized kingdom called Muscovy. While Muscovy's religious and cultural heritage came from Eastern Orthodox Byzantium and, to a lesser extent, Germanic-speaking northern Europe, much of its fiscal, military, and political structure developed in conformity with Mongol bureaucratic requirements. Russian soldiers fought under Mongol command, Russian treasury clerks collected and paid taxes according to Mongol standards, and Russian *boyars* (upper nobility), princes, and bishops interacted with Mongol ruling elites. Moscow's kremlin, the central fortress of the town, housed a court where envoys from the khans could live.[8] The historical chronicles of Muscovy referred to both the Byzantine emperor and the Mongol khan as *tsar'* (derived from "caesar").

Muscovites began to loosen the grip of the "Mongol yoke" on their necks in 1380, in a battle at Kulikovo Field near the Don River celebrated as the first victory of Christian Russians over Muslim Tatars. The epic tale *Zadonshchina* proclaims: "Throughout the Russian land there was joy and celebration. Russian glory ascended over the brute infidels."[9] Once again, a closer examination of the sources reveals a murkier situation. Moscow had not yet asserted authority over all of the Russian appanages, and not all of the princes thought it worth their while to fight the Mongols. In particular the prince of Riazan', southeast of Moscow and in the most direct line of Mongol attacks, preferred to cooperate with the Mongols while he avoided actual fighting. The Jochid Khanate itself was beginning to fracture (more on that below). The Mongol general that Prince Dmitri Ivanovich "Donskoi" opposed was not a Chinggisid but a usurper named Mamai, who had given Prince Dmitri his *yarlik*, or Mongol certification of rule, in 1371. This presented Prince Dmitri with a sticky problem, since going to battle against Mamai was rebelling against his sworn sovereign. Dmitri resolved this by declaring that he was no rebel, but fought Mamai in the name of the true Chinggisid khan that Mamai had deposed, Tokhtamysh. One year after Kulikovo Field, Tokhtamysh himself defeated Mamai, and then asked all the Russian princes to pay their respects to him at Sarai. Prince Dmitri and a few other princes refused. In 1382 Tokhtamysh led an expedition into northeast Russia and sacked Moscow after Dmitri had run away. Dmitri had to surrender to Tokhtamysh and humbly request that the *yarlik* and the grand princely title be returned to him. Tokhtamysh agreed, on the condition that Dmitri pay much higher tribute than he had paid to Mamai.[10] Two years after Kulikovo Field the Russians were actually under harsher Mongol control, but that fact is not recalled in *Zadonshchina* and other celebrations of the battle. Despite this, Dmitri had laid important groundwork for Moscow's future dominance.

The highpoint of the Jochid Khanate was during the long reign of Uzbek Khan (r. 1313–41), who established secure trade routes across much of Eurasia and led the conversion of the Mongol-Tatars to Islam. Even before Uzbek's reign the khanate had become predominately Turkic in language and ethnic make-up; the bulk of the khanate's inhabitants were the Qipchaq Turks who had lived in the steppe for centuries. The name "Tatar" originally belonged to one of the large Mongol tribes that Chinggis had united in 1206, but came to be applied to the Jochid Khanate and Qipchaq Turks. Europeans called all Mongols "Tartars." The Jochid Khanate was composed of three autonomous camps or *orda* (from which the English word "horde" is derived): the Aq (White), Kök (Blue), and Altan (Golden). After Uzbek Khan's death, the three hordes began to strike out more independently from the control of a series of short-lived khans, giving ambitious non-Chinggisids such as Mamai an opportunity to seize power.[11] Prince Dmitri went to war against Mamai because the fracturing of the khanate multiplied the number of khans or *amirs* (military commanders) who demanded tribute from Russian appanages. Each new leader needed to control territory for his followers' herds, which led to fighting and large-scale movement of people in search of available land. This increased the threat to Russian areas.

Collapse of the Jochid Khanate

Tokhtamysh Khan was not able to re-unify the khanate. Repeated outbreaks of bubonic plague severely weakened the Jochids and contributed to increasing political chaos.[12] Worse, a new and formidable conqueror attacked Tokhtamysh from the southeast, Timur Lang, known to Europeans as Tamerlane (r. 1368–1405). Timur emerged from the remnants of the Chaghatay Khanate, which had never been able to establish a stable government. He was an ethnic Turk born near Samarkand, in today's Uzbekistan, who devoted his spectacularly brutal career to creating a new empire that he intended to equal, if not eclipse, that of the Mongols. Timur, who was not a Chinggisid and so could not call himself khan, protected Tokhtamysh and in 1376 gave him a small khanate along the Syr Darya. This region was held by the Jochid Blue Horde, from which Tokhtamysh had fled as the loser in a contest for rule.[13] The alliance did not last, however, and in 1395 Timur defeated Tokhtamysh and burned the Jochid capital Sarai, including its archives. From that point the decline and break-up of the Jochid Khanate was irreversible.

The Moscow grand princes took advantage of Jochid woes, consolidating their rule over rival appanages and building a solid administrative apparatus. However, in the first half of the fifteenth century new khanates emerged from the rubble of the Jochids: in the 1420s the Great Horde, which roamed the steppes between the Don River and Caspian Sea, and the Crimean Khanate under the Tatar Girey dynasty, were established. The Crimean Khanate quickly became a vassal to the Ottoman Empire; the sultan's backing made Crimean Tatars a grave threat to Muscovy well into the seventeenth century. In 1445 a son of the Great Horde's Ulu Muhammad Khan founded a khanate at Kazan on the Volga River, not far from where the medieval Turkic Bulgar kingdom had been located. A fourth khanate, at Astrakhan on the southern Volga near the site of Sarai, emerged in 1459. The rise of these new khanates coincided with a period of destructive civil war in Muscovy. In the 1430s and 1440s rival Russian princes were traveling to rival Tatar khans to gain the *yarlik*, which now required the payment of large bribes. Despite everything that had happened since the battle at Kulikovo, Russian princes still needed the formal imprimatur of a khan to rule legitimately.

In 1447 Grand Prince Vasilii Vasilievich II (r. 1425–62) emerged victorious from sixteen years of vicious fighting, although one of his cousins, Dmitri Shemiaka, had blinded him in retaliation for Vasilii's blinding of Shemiaka's brother. In need of assistance, in 1448 Vasilii II decided to name his young son

Ivan Vasilievich (Grand Prince Ivan III, r. 1462–1505) his heir and co-ruler. In an unprecedented step, he did not ask for a khan's permission first. This was the first act of true political independence from Mongol-Tatar rule on the part of a Russian prince. Vasilii indicated a further change in the Russo-Tatar balance of power when he accepted into his military service Kasim, another son of the Great Horde's Ulu Muhammad Khan. In 1452 Kasim was allowed to settle in a frontier town on the Oka River that guarded the road between Kazan and Moscow. For two hundred years, he and his descendants held what came to be called the Kasimov Khanate, a Muslim appanage that served Moscow not only to defend the frontier, but as a tool to further Moscow's political interests.[14] Kasimov khans (called "tsars" in Muscovite chancery documents in deference to their Chinggisid status) helped Grand Prince Ivan III conquer the stubbornly independent appanage of Novgorod and repeatedly sheltered runaway princes from all the Tatar khanates so that Moscow could use them as leverage in intra-Tatar fighting.[15]

The Kasimov Khanate gave Moscow's princes a tool, but the reality remained that they had to pay tribute to several Tatar khans simultaneously. Even when this tribute was tactfully disguised as gifts, it cost the treasury thousands of rubles every year until the 1699 Treaty of Carlowitz.[16] The rivalries among the khanates also worsened an old problem, Tatar slave raids. The main source of income for the Crimean Khanate had been protection money extracted from merchants, but in the mid-fifteenth century the Ottomans took control over commerce in Crimea, forcing the Crimeans to find another source of revenue in the slave trade. Muscovite chancery records suggest that 150,000–200,000 people were captured by Crimean and Noghay Tatars between 1600 and 1650 alone.[17] Historian Michael Khodarkovsky estimates that Slavic lands, mostly Russian, were "the second-largest supplier of slaves in the world" after West Africa.[18] The quest to redeem captives and stop further raids was one motivator for Russia's expansion into Central Asia.

Russians considered the formal end of the "Tatar yoke" to be an odd incident known as "The Stand on the Ugra" (1480), when a Muscovite army spent several months staring across the Ugra River at a Tatar army, then both decided to go home. The stalemate was the result of unreliable alliances across western Eurasia. The Crimean Khanate under Mengli-Girey allied with Ivan III against their common enemy King Sigismund of Poland-Lithuania. Meanwhile the main rival to Crimea, Ahmad Khan of the Great Horde, sought a balancing alliance with Sigismund. The new diplomatic configuration may also have been set in motion by Ivan diverting tribute payments from the Great Horde to Crimea.[19] In October 1480 Ahmad Khan led his army to the Ugra River, a tributary of the Volga south of Moscow, and waited for his new Polish-Lithuanian allies to arrive. They never did, and so neither army tried to cross the river. This non-battle was fought between a Tatar-Polish alliance and a Tatar-Russian alliance, and did not change the fact that Muscovy continued to pay tribute to one or more khans and suffer Tatar invasions. The one change, and it was significant, was that no Russian prince ever again needed to ask a khan for permission to rule.

MUSCOVY IN THE MIDDLE

Grand Prince Ivan III and his successors remained involved in Tatar politics, usually as allies of Kazan and Crimea against the Great Horde.[20] The complexities and dangers of navigating relations among three rival Tatar khanates plus the Noghay Tatar horde that held lands east of the Volga River—playing a key role in destroying the Great Horde and damaging Astrakhan in the 1520s—meant that it was vital for Muscovy to cultivate allies, thwart enemies, and deepen its knowledge of the Tatar world as much as possible (see Figure 1.1). In the first half of the sixteenth century, this meant sometimes promising to provide troops to help the Crimean khan, sometimes installing a pro-Russian khan in Kazan to block Crimea, sometimes identifying and encouraging rifts among the Noghays between pro-Russian and pro-Crimean factions. On occasion Tatar princes seeking refuge from the in-fighting were given shelter in Moscow itself. Simultaneously, Muscovy allowed Turkic merchants in horses, slaves, and other goods to trade in its territory, and sent envoys to Istanbul to open direct economic relations with the Sublime Porte and make an end run around the Crimean khan.[21] Among the former Jochid territories west of the Volga, Muscovy had become the pivotal power center. Only Crimea, under the protection of the Ottoman sultan, could still militarily threaten the Russians.

In 1533 Grand Prince Vasilii Ivanovich III (r. 1505–33) died, leaving his three-year-old son Ivan Vasilievich IV (r. 1533–84) in the care of his mother, Elena Glinskaia, and a group of regents. The Glinskii family was of Tatar descent; they had entered the service of Poland-Lithuania in the fifteenth century, then switched to Muscovy in 1509.[22] Elena was Vasilii Ivanovich's second wife, his first marriage having failed to produce heirs. Since Muscovite politics was clan-based, Vasilii III's death left the Glinskii family in the awkward position of being newcomers and somewhat foreign among the elite boyar and princely

В 7044 (1535) году в ноябре
в 25 день Ковгоршад-царевна
и Булат-князь, и вся земля
Казанская великому князю
Ивану Васильевичу изменили,
Яналея-царя убили, которого
им князь великий Василий
Иванович дал царем на
Казань, а взяли себе на Казань
царем из Крыма Сафа-Кирея
царевича.

В лето 7044. Ноября в 25
день, Ковгоршад-царевна
и Булат-князь и вся
земля Казанская великому
князю Ивану Василиевичю
изменили, Аналея-царя
убили, которого им князь
великий Василей Иванович
дал царем на Казань, а взяли
себе на Казань царем ис
Крыма Сафа-Кирея царевичя.

FIGURE 1.1 Young Grand Prince Ivan IV was central to politics in the Khanate of Kazan. The text reads "1535. Tsarevna Kovgorshad and Prince Bulat and the entire Kazan land betrayed Prince Ivan Vasilievich, killed Tsar Ianalei (Jan Ali), to whom Grand Prince Ivan Vasilievich had given rule over Kazan, and Crimean Tsar Safa-Girey took the rule of Kazan for himself." Source: *Litsevoi* Letopisnei *Svod* 19:458 (Moscow: АКТЕОН, 2010).

families, yet central to the power structure. These family-political tensions may have contributed to a difficult childhood for the boy, especially after his mother died in 1538. When Grand Prince Ivan IV reached the age of majority in 1547, his formal coronation marked a new stage in Muscovy's rise: the Russian Orthodox Church Metropolitan Makarii crowned him *tsar'*, the title that Russian princes had used for the Byzantine emperors and Turko-Mongol khans. Historians have argued over the meaning of this act and what it was intended to communicate about Muscovy's European or Eurasian identity. Ivan III and Vasilii III had occasionally used the title, while Ivan IV and his successors accepted either Mongol or European connotations in diplomatic usage, as long as they were recognized as the sole and supreme rulers. Most likely, Ivan IV was claiming to be the successor to both former empires.[23] This was a bold assertion of Muscovy's prestige and power. He acted on his new title within ten years of his coronation, when he conquered the Khanate of Kazan in 1552 and the Khanate of Astrakhan in 1556, bringing both permanently under Russian rule.

Tsar Ivan IV's conquests of Kazan and Astrakhan had profound symbolic and practical importance. The Russian church celebrated them not as triumphs over Jochid khans but as great Christian victories over Muslims, refusing to acknowledge the fact that Turkic Muslims made up part of the tsar's army.[24] The conquests gave Muscovy control over the entire Volga River, from which Russians probed further east into lands held by the Noghay Tatar horde. Bringing non-Slavic, non-Christian polities under Russian rule was the first step in Muscovy's evolution from regional kingdom to Russian Empire.

The conquests also, for the first time, had a direct impact on affairs in Central Asia. The khans of Astrakhan fled east to Bukhara, where they eventually overthrew the Uzbek Shibanid khans and strengthened Bukhara as the dominant power among the oasis states of Transoxiana (see Map 1.1).[25] In the 1580s the frontier guards called Cossacks, authorized by the tsar to protect the interests of the merchant Stroganov family, overthrew the northern Khanate of Sibir'. This opened the vastness of Siberia to Muscovy and brought Slavic Cossacks, merchants, and officials into direct contact with the Kazakh hordes. Finally, the former khanates continued and expanded their role as frontier zones of interaction between the Slavic and Turko-Mongol-Iranian worlds. Astrakhan, located where the Volga River spilled into the northwest shore of the Caspian Sea, had long been a place where merchants from Russia, the Ottoman Empire, Central Asia, Iran, and India traded. Kazan attracted a similar merchant population and added fur traders from Siberia. The importance of these regions as trade hubs was one of the reasons why Ivan IV took them over. Within a few years of the conquest Astrakhan and

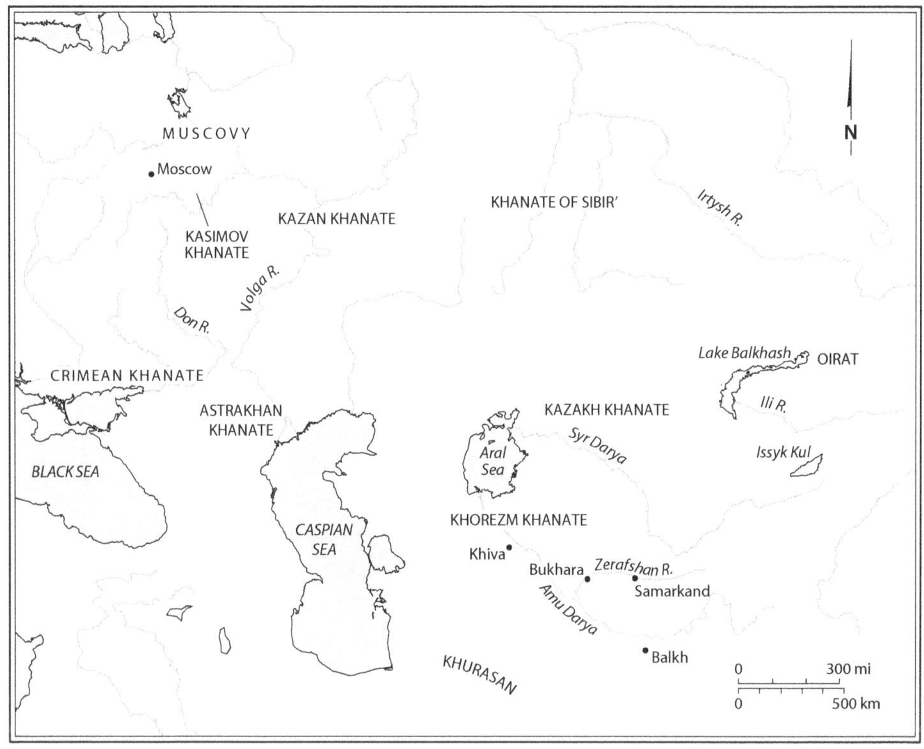

MAP 1.1 Central Eurasia in the sixteenth century.

Kazan became places where Russian customs officers, innkeepers, and soldiers routinely dealt with Central Asian merchants and diplomatic envoys. Russian intervention in Central Asia was a slowly and steadily evolving process, one that later Imperial Russian ministers defended as both logical and natural. The eventual Russian conquest of Central Asia can be interpreted many ways, but it certainly was not an encounter between strangers.

TURKO-MONGOL SUCCESSOR STATES IN CENTRAL ASIA

Long before the rise of the Mongol Empire, the seemingly endless grasslands that stretched from the Danube River to the Altai mountains were dominated by Turkic peoples. Historians came to call this vast part of Eurasia the "Dasht-i Qipchaq," or Qipchaq Steppe. Since the emergence of the First Turk Empire in 552 CE dozens of Turkic-speaking peoples inhabited the steppe in an ever-changing mosaic of political configurations and lifeways. The Pechenegs and Polovtsy, and to an extent the medieval Rus' as well, represented just the western edge of the early Turkic world. East of the Caspian Sea the environment changed from steppe to deserts watered by rivers that originated high in the Pamir mountains. This region, known to the Greeks as *Transoxiana* and the Arabs as *Mawrannahr* (both meaning "across the [Oxus] river") was demarcated by the Syr Darya/Jaxartes River in the north and the Amu Darya/Oxus River in the south. The oldest stratum of population here was made up of Iranian-speakers who lived as farmers or merchants rather than as nomadic pastoralists. Samarkand was the center of Zoroastrian Soghdian culture, whose merchants were important Silk Road traders with China. As the Turks spread from their original homeland in today's Mongolia all the way west to Egypt, they also settled in Transoxiana, inter-mixing with the established Iranian communities. Some Turks settled in villages and towns while others remained nomadic pastoralists. The nomads were the ancestors of widespread tribes that outsiders grouped under the label "Turkmen," or "Turkomans." Arab invaders crossed the Oxus and brought Islam starting in the eighth century, but while Islam replaced Buddhism and Zoroastrianism as the dominant religion, the Arabic language did not displace the Turkic and Iranian languages. Instead a fascinatingly complicated linguistic amalgam developed, with Arabic serving as the language of religion, philosophy, and science, Persian the language of administration and poetry, and Turkic the language of ordinary life and warfare. All three languages, from entirely different linguistic families, borrowed furiously from each other. Turkic languages absorbed large Iranian and Arabic vocabularies, and anyone who could write at all wrote in the Arabic alphabet, regardless of their language.

After the Mongol conquest of the Qipchaq Steppe and Transoxiana in the 1220s–30s, the lands were divided among the Jochid Khanate, the Chaghatay Khanate, and the Il-khanate that governed much of the Middle East. Of the three khanates, the Chaghatay Khanate was the weakest, lacking a stable centralized government and military. The polity spent most of its existence split along an environmental frontier between the steppe and mountainous region that retained traditional Mongol pastoralist and Buddhist or shamanist culture, and the Islamic, Turko-Iranian region of Transoxiana/Mawrannahr. The split became complete in the late fourteenth century, when the Turkic ruler Timur (Tamerlane) established his kingdom with Samarkand as its capital.[26] As noted above, Timur exploited the divisions among the three constituent hordes of the failing Jochid Khanate to extend his own power.

After Timur's death in 1405 his kingdom fragmented among his descendants, with dual capitals developing at Samarkand and Herat, in today's northwest Afghanistan. While culturally brilliant, Timurid Central Asia was open to attack from more organized groups.[27] In the mid-fifteenth century, descendants of the Jochid hordes were poised to exploit Timurid vulnerabilities.

The Jochid Khanate had been based on the White, Blue, and Golden hordes, the history of which is poorly documented. The Blue (Kök) Horde seems to have inhabited lands north of the Caspian and Aral seas in the fourteenth century, extending to Lake Balkhash.[28] The horde itself was composed of several tribes and never developed a central governing structure. A tribe within the Blue Horde claimed descent from Jochi's fifth son, Shiban. Accordingly, the tribe was referred to as the Shibanids or, in Arabic-language accounts, Shaybanids. Another name for the descendants of this Chinggisid lineage was also becoming common: Uzbek or Özbeg. Central Asian historians associated the name with Uzbek Khan, who had converted the entire Jochid Khanate to Islam.[29] Like the rest of the Jochid Khanate, the Blue Horde had become majority Turkic in its population and language, but was Mongol in its political identity. Its rulers called themselves "khan" because they claimed direct descent from Chinggis Khan.

In 1428 the Shibanid-Uzbeks elected an aggressive fighter named Abulkhayr as their khan. Abulkhayr's Uzbeks invaded and occupied a region south of the Aral Sea called Khorezm (ruled by the Qongrat Turko-Mongol tribe) in 1431, and spent the next twenty years raiding as far as Samarkand and Herat, the capitals of the Timurids. Abulkhayr's prestige was severely damaged in 1457, when a new confederation of Mongol tribes invaded from the lands east of Lake Balkhash and defeated him in battle. This was an independent horde that did not claim descent from Chinggis Khan, known variously as the Oirats or Kalmyks or Zunghars.[30] Russian and Turkic writers usually called them Kalmyks, so that is the preferred term here. For steppe warriors like Abulkhayr, one thing could trump genealogy in political legitimacy: success or failure in battle. Defeat by the Kalmyks drove away many of Abulkhayr's fighters and their clans. The leaders of breakaway groups, Janibek and Girey, took their followers east in 1459 to the Lake Balkhash area. They were called or called themselves *Qazaq*, "freebooters," those who had abandoned their community of origin, and they established a new Turko-Mongol horde initially called Uzbek-i Qazaq.[31]

Abulkhayr died in 1468, on his way to attack Janibek and Girey. After a struggle for succession, his grandson Muhammad Shibani Khan (r. 1500–10)

FIGURE 1.2 Portrait of Muhammad Shibani Khan, c. 1507. Source: Portrait by Kamāl ud-Dīn Behzād (1450–1535), Academy of Arts of Uzbekistan. Retrieved from Wikimedia Commons.

tried to restore the fortunes of his line (see Figure 1.2). As Muhammad Shibani looked south from his base on the north bank of the Syr Darya in 1499, he saw Timurid Sultan Husayn Bayqara (r. 1469–1506) presiding over an artistically spectacular court in Herat but unable to control any of the Timurid sub-rulers north of the Amu Darya. In the 1490s Husayn Bayqara's own sons rebelled against him. In addition, the entire region from the Amu Darya to the Ferghana Valley was under continual threat from the khans of Mogholistan, as the eastern half of the former Chaghatay Khanate was now called. In 1485 a Moghol khan had taken the town of Tashkent from the Timurids, who were occupied fighting among themselves. The Moghol khans were no better, having split into three rival sub-khanates in the 1480s.[32]

As a later Central Asian historian put it, "[Muhammad Shibani] at once placed the foot of ambition in the stirrup of enterprise...."[33] Muhammad Shibani Khan gathered Uzbek followers with promises of booty and glory and in 1500 invaded and captured Samarkand. As the Uzbeks proceeded from Samarkand to Tashkent, the Ferghana Valley, and Khorezm by 1505, they drove out the last Timurid sultan, Zahiruddin Muhammad Babur. Babur fled to Kabul and from there, reluctantly, moved eastward into India. Babur always regarded India as an uncomfortably hot, rather barbaric place, but his descendants' creation of the Mughal Empire (1526–1857) overshadowed his dislike. Meanwhile, Muhammad Shibani continued southwest toward Herat, which he claimed in 1507 by right as a Chinggisid. He would soon be pushed back across the Amu Darya by the Turkic Shiite army of Shah Ismail (r. 1501–24), who was in the process of founding the Safavid dynasty of Iran.

The Uzbek Khanates

One way to look at the Uzbek intrusion into Timurid Transoxiana is that one lineage of Turko-Mongol khans displaced another lineage of Turko-Mongol khans (since the Timurids could not call themselves "khan" they ruled as sultans under actual Chinggisids who were captive puppets). This suggests changes among the political elite of the sort that ordinary farmers and herders usually ignore, as long as they know who to pay their taxes to. However, historian Yuri Bregel points out that the Uzbek conquest was not just a matter of thrones changing hands, but was "a mass migration of a part (probably a smaller part) of the nomadic Özbeks from the Qipchaq steppes southward ... according to some (largely hypothetical) modern estimates, the total number of these Özbeks was between 240,000 and 360,000."[34] The Uzbeks spoke a Turkic language of the Qipchaq branch, which was rather different from the Timurid Oghuz Turkic language that was full of Iranian and Arabic loan-words. Uzbeks were still mostly nomadic pastoralists, as opposed to the settled farmers and townsmen of Transoxiana. Muhammad Shibani Khan and the Uzbek elites shared in the Iranian-influenced high culture of the Timurids, but Babur and other Timurid princes regarded them as uncultured outsiders. Babur growled in his memoir that Muhammad Shibani Khan composed "insipid" poetry and did "a multitude of stupid, imbecile, audacious, and heathenish things." Babur was willing to credit Muhammad Shibani with one good deed, however: having an arrogant court musician beaten.[35]

The Uzbek invasion permanently altered the political structure of Transoxiana, replacing the multitude of Timurid sub-kingdoms with Uzbek rule and forcing the remaining Chaghatay Moghol khans to retreat east across the Tian Shan mountains. Muhammad Shibani's extended family formed a dynasty known as the Shibanids, who eventually centered their power in Bukhara. The Shibanids were not the only Uzbeks who founded a lasting kingdom in the region, however. A combination of the disorder created by the last Timurids and the rise of Safavid Iran allowed another Uzbek tribe, the Yadigarids or Arabshahids, to conquer Khorezm in 1511 and establish a khanate based in the town of Khiva. These two small khanates spent the next four hundred years competing with each other for markets and land. They also cooperated to meet common challenges posed by the expanding empires around them: Safavid Iran, China under the Qing dynasty, Mughal India, and Muscovy.

The establishment of the Arabshahid dynasty in Khorezm illustrates the complicated historical juncture in which the Uzbeks found themselves. Muhammad Shibani had conquered Khorezm himself in 1505, but in 1510 he lost a crucial battle to Shah Ismail at Merv, which cost him his life and almost the entire khanate. The Safavids seized Herat and Khorezm, and Babur returned from Kabul to hold Bukhara briefly. The Shiite Shah Ismail sent Muhammad Shibani's scalp to Ottoman Sultan Bayezid II, who had supported the Uzbeks as Sunni champions. Ismail then made the top of Muhammad Shibani's skull into a drinking cup, which was a steppe warrior custom that long pre-dated Islam.[36] Muhammad Shibani's death and the subsequent power struggle between Uzbeks and Safavids allowed the Arabshahids to invade Khorezm from the Qipchaq steppe and establish their own dynasty.

The two Uzbek khanates were the smallest of the new Islamic polities that arose in the early sixteenth century, but even though they were landlocked in an age of great maritime exploration they were not isolated from the rest of the world. The Safavids, who made Shiism the state religion of Iran, blocked Sunni Uzbeks from routes southwest to Iran and the Arab lands. Trade relations on a small scale resumed later in the sixteenth century, even though political and religious hostilities remained. This obstacle was counter-balanced by expanded economic and cultural ties to Mughal India. The Mughal rulers imported large quantities of fruit and other merchandise from Central Asia, in exchange for enormous amounts of cotton textiles, indigo and other dyes, sugar, and Hindu slaves.[37] The Mughals also provided their fellow Sunni Muslims an alternate route to Mecca, by sea. Just as political and religious hostility did not stop Uzbek-Iranian trade, so economic and religious connections did not prevent the Mughals from occasionally trying to take territory from the Bukharans through the sixteenth and seventeenth centuries. Both friendly and hostile encounters allowed Central Asian Muslims to maintain contact with the rest of the Sunni world, although it required arduous travel.

By the mid-sixteenth century borders between the Safavids, Mughals, and Uzbeks were more-or-less settled. They ran from the southeast shore of the Caspian Sea along the northern slopes of the Kopet Dagh mountains and Amu Darya to the knot of the Pamir, Hindu Kush, and Himalayan mountain ranges, which was part of the Mughal Empire. These loosely defined borders corresponded with the ancient Iranian demarcation between "Iran" (land of settled civilization) and "Turan" (land of threatening nomads). Changes in the environment still shaped human frontiers, however. In the 1570s the Amu Darya, which had flowed west into the Caspian Sea for centuries, shifted course north to connect with the Aral Sea. The withdrawal of the river allowed the Qara Qum (Black Sands) desert to expand, and Turkmen nomadic tribes moved in. The larger desert and increased threat of Turkmen slave raids drove out Iranians and widened the ethno-linguistic frontier.[38] While a Turko-Iranian-Mongol cultural complex still extended across the entire region from Isfahan to southern Siberia, environmental barriers weakened Iranian influence.

The Kazakhs and Kyrgyz

The lands north and east of the Uzbek khanates were still fiercely contested among Uzbek, Kazakh, and Kalmyk hordes. While the Shibanid and Arabshahid Uzbeks created settled oasis kingdoms and adopted Oghuz Turkic and Iranian as their court languages, the Kazakh hordes north of the Syr Darya remained nomadic, speaking Qipchaq Turkic. They formed the largest tribal confederation in the Qipchaq Steppe, having spread from the area around the Yaik/Ural River in the west to the Ili River basin in the east. When the Uzbeks left the steppe for Transoxiana, the Kazakhs filled in the gap. The Kazakh khans were also Chinggisids, and repeatedly fought the Uzbeks for control over Tashkent and other valuable properties along the Syr Darya frontier between their domains. At some point in the seventeenth century the Kazakhs split into three *Juz* (or *Zhüz*, literally "hundreds"; in this context "hordes"): the "Junior" or "Little" (*kishi*), "Middle" (*orta*), and "Senior" or "Great" (*ulu*), which occupied respectively the western, central, and eastern lands within their range. Of these three, the Senior Horde in the east fought regularly with Oirats, Uzbeks, and an older group of Turkic nomads called the Kyrgyz. The Junior Horde was the first to be affected by Russian expansion, and the Middle Horde was entwined with the politics and culture of the Bukharan khanate. All three hordes maintained a strong distinction between the *aq suiek* (white bone) aristocracy (people who claimed Chinggisid descent or descent from pilgrims to Mecca or other Muslim notables) and the *qara suiek* (black bone) ordinary Kazakhs.

Yet another group of Turkic pastoralists entered the mix in this period, the Kyrgyz. With virtually no documentation, the origin of the Kyrgyz tribes is poorly understood. They may have been descended from the Turkic horde called Kyrgyz that destroyed the Turkic Uyghur kaghanate of the Tarim Basin in 840 CE, but there is no proof of direct connection. So many Turkic and Mongol groups came, went, and mixed over the next seven hundred years that tracing the lineage of any one group becomes a meaningless exercise. The Kyrgyz of the sixteenth century were Turko-Mongols but did not claim Chinggisid heritage, and so did not have khans.[39] They herded along the northern slopes of the Tian Shan mountains, with their territory centered around Lake Issyk Kul. Their neighbors sometimes called them "those living in felt tents."[40] They were Muslim, following the practices of the Naqshbandiya Sufi order. Kyrgyz tribes absorbed people from the declining Moghol khanates, as did the Kazakhs. Like the Kazakhs, the Kyrgyz split into several sub-confederations of clans. Because they did not create their own written records, we know very little about them before the arrival of the Russians.

EARLY DIPLOMATIC AND TRADE RELATIONS

Muscovy was aware of the establishment of the Uzbek and Kazakh khanates and tried to collect information on them. There are references in chancery archives to notes on the Kazakh Khanate under Qasym (d. 1518), but the notes themselves have disappeared.[41] The Russian conquest of Kazan and Astrakhan in the 1550s caught the attention of the Uzbek and Kazakh rulers in turn, and in 1557 and 1558 Abdallah b. Iskander Khan of Bukhara sent envoys to Moscow to request access and protection for Uzbek merchants.[42] Tsar Ivan IV was similarly interested in expanding trade. In 1555 he granted trading privileges to the English Muscovy Company via the White Sea port of Arkhangel'sk. Three years later he permitted the English merchant Anthony Jenkinson to travel from Moscow to Astrakhan and Bukhara, with the ultimate goal of reaching China. One of Jenkinson's duties was to present personal letters from Ivan to the khans of Khorezm and Bukhara. Upon his return, Jenkinson reported that Russian traders were already active in the area:

> The Russes doe carie unto Boghar, redde hides, sheepeskinnes, wollen cloth of divers sorts, woodden vessels, bridles, saddles, with such like, and doe carie away from thence divers kindes of wares made of cotton wooll, divers kinds of silkes, Crasca, with other things, but there is but smal utterance.[43]

Jenkinson was accompanied on his journey back to Moscow by envoys from Bukhara, Khorezm, and Balkh, an autonomous province of Bukhara in today's northern Afghanistan; trade and diplomatic activity were closely intertwined. In 1573 Ivan IV attempted to send an envoy to the Kazakh Haqq Nazar Khan. However, the envoy was waylaid and killed by a band from the Khanate of Sibir'. Muscovy did not establish stable contact with the Kazakhs until 1588, when an envoy from Tavvakul Khan (r. 1586–98) reached Tsar Fedor Ivanovich (r. 1584–98).[44]

Muscovy and the Central Asian polities approached each other with many, not always compatible, goals. All parties were interested in trade. Muscovy imported an impressive variety of cotton and silk textiles, indigo, Chinese rhubarb (an important medicine), horses, and other goods from Bukharan and Khorezmian traders, who entered the kingdom via Astrakhan or the Siberian gateway city Tobolsk (founded 1587). The khanates were interested in Russian honey, leather goods, furs, hunting falcons, and were especially keen on "fish teeth" (walrus tusks) from the Siberian Pacific coast.[45] However, the khanates also imported and sold large numbers of Slavic slaves, captured in raids on frontier villages or in battle with Cossacks, who served the tsars as frontier guards and settlers. One of the goals of Muscovite diplomatic missions throughout this period was the ransom of Christian slaves.

Life was often uncomfortable for the merchants and envoys who did the actual work of Muscovite–Central Asian relations. Bandits were a ubiquitous hazard, partly because rulers used them as political tools. The khans of Bukhara and Khorezm frequently attacked each other's trade caravans, unless they were in a period of alliance against a common foe like the Safavids. Envoys could spend months stuck in border towns with poor accommodations while officials took their time deciding to allow them to proceed with their missions. Sometimes rulers deliberately held envoys as hostages to guarantee safe passage for their own envoys. Once they arrived at their destination, merchants had to pay fees and taxes for housing and food, for the goods they were selling, and for transit permission, which could put them into serious debt. Russian governors were instructed to treat Bukharan merchants well, but also to interrogate them for information on Central Asian politics. Intelligent rulers ensured that trade was profitable, or else merchants would not deal with them, but governments could be so greedy for funds that they squeezed merchants right up to the margin of profit. Rulers in this period did not much distinguish between the state treasury and their personal expenses, and sometimes merchants suffered because rulers regarded them as handy sources of cash in a pinch. When Jenkinson traveled through the Khanate of Khorezm his caravan was attacked by armed robbers and forced to hand over merchandise and pack animals in exchange for their lives. When he arrived in Bukhara, Jenkinson was pleased that the khan chased after and hanged the thieves and restored some of the caravan's stolen goods. However, the khan also "shewed himself a very Tartar," when he borrowed money from Jenkinson for a battle and then left town without repaying him.[46] Jenkinson's outrage undoubtedly contributed to his dour assessment of the commercial promise of Bukhara.

Jenkinson would not have been mollified to learn that his money helped fund Abdallah Khan's ambitious campaign to make Bukhara a unified state. Like Kievan Rus', the Bukharan khanate was a collection of towns and their surrounding farmland (appanages) ruled jointly by members of the extended Shibanid family, who frequently fought one another. Bukhara had been a famous center of Islamic learning for centuries, and its scholars and *khojas*, leaders of the Sufi brotherhoods, wielded as much political and greater spiritual authority as did the Shibanids. Abdallah b. Iskander, a grandson of Shibani Khan's cousin Janibek, was appointed sultan of the city of Bukhara in 1551 at the age of seventeen. He was elevated not by the "supreme khan" (*khaqan*) of all of Bukhara, who had little real power, but by his own Sufi master, Khoja Islam of the Juybari family of Naqshbandi khojas. This first taste of rule did not last long, but it launched Abdallah on a forty-seven-year career of incessant fighting to expand and unify Bukhara by eliminating most of his relatives. In 1561 Abdallah had his father Iskander elected supreme khan while

Abdallah himself was the real decision-maker. Only when Iskander died in 1583 did Abdallah rule Bukhara directly. By the time Abdallah died in 1598, he had added Khorezm, northeast Iran (Khurasan), northern Afghanistan, the mountainous region of Badakhshan, the Ferghana Valley, and most of the Syr Darya basin to the khanate.[47]

Muscovy Expands Its Influence

Trade, politics, and military needs intertwined in the unsettled conditions of late sixteenth- and early seventeenth-century Eurasia. When Kazakh Tavvakul Khan sent an envoy to Moscow in 1588, he was asking to have his brother Uraz Muhammad, who had been captured by Muscovite troops, sent back to him. Tavvakul had served Abdallah Khan of Bukhara, but broke away in 1583 and took over the khanate of the three Kazakh hordes. He conducted raids into Bukhara and eastward toward Moghul Turfan, which brought him into conflict with the rising Oirat/Kalmyks. Meanwhile, to the north Kuchum Khan of Sibir' was still resisting the Muscovite invasion that had begun under Tsar Ivan IV. Seeking aid against the Cossacks, Kuchum had turned for help to the Noghay Horde (which Kuchum had ruled until 1563). The Noghay were rivals of the Kazakhs. The circumstances are unknown, but Tavvakul's brother Uraz Muhammad had apparently been captured during a battle between Siberian and Cossack units. The Kazakh envoy, Kul Muhammad, also asked Tsar Fedor for firearms, promising to use them against their mutual enemy Kuchum Khan as well as against Bukhara.[48] And yes, there is a connection between the names "Cossack" and "Kazakh." They have a common root in the Turkic word for someone who has abandoned his clan and become a "freebooter," and came to be applied to two groups that occupied similar places in Eurasian social structure.[49] In order to distinguish between the two, Russians referred to Kazakhs as Kirgiz or Kirgiz-Kazakhs until the 1920s.

Tsar Fedor Ivanovich was too feeble-minded to make strategic decisions for his government. Muscovy's expansion to the east was actually directed by Fedor's ambitious regent and successor, Boris Godunov (r. 1598–1605). The Godunovs were a boyar family of Tatar origin, who had been serving the court since the fourteenth century. Godunov found Uraz Muhammad too useful to let go. In 1590 he took Uraz Muhammad formally into the tsar's service, gave him land and allowed this Kazakh "tsarevich" (still acknowledging his Chinggisid status) to fight for Muscovy against the Swedes. It may have been at this point that Godunov allowed Uraz Muhammad's family to join him. A note written by Uraz Muhammad in 1594 thanks the court for giving him one hundred rubles to support him and his grandmother, mother, aunt, and sister during a visit to Moscow. In 1595 Uraz Muhammad sent greetings to Tavvakul from "your mother Azi-tsaritsa, sister Altyn-tsarevna, my mother, your daughter-in-law Altyn-khanym, your nieces Bakhty and Kun tsarevna."[50] An extended Kazakh royal family had taken up residence in Muscovy at the expense of the court; one would love to know how the women spent their time and whether there were any children present.

Uraz Muhammad and his family lived as privileged hostages. He was both a source of intelligence for the tsar on Central Asian political upheavals and a conduit of influence on behalf of Tavvakul Khan. He only met with envoy Kul Muhammad with Godunov's permission, and then translators had to be in the room. Why would two Kazakhs need translators? They did not, of course—the translators' job was to record the conversations and translate them into Russian for the tsar. This gave the Russians valuable insight into the rivalries among the Turko-Mongol hordes and the challenges Muscovy faced if it wanted to extend its power into Central Asia. In one set of conversations, the translators learned that Tavvakul Khan was temporarily at peace with Bukhara and the Noghay Horde, and had one brother held hostage by the Kalmyks, who were pressing from the east. The Bukharan Abdallah Khan had recently ousted the khan of Khorezm and made alliance with the Noghay. Kul Muhammad warned that the Bukharans would help the Noghay recapture territory that Ivan IV had taken from them in 1573, and from there they might threaten Astrakhan. The Kazakh envoy wanted Uraz Muhammad to discourage the tsar from trusting either Bukhara or the Noghay, and to keep asking the Russians for firearms. Furthermore, he requested Russian assistance to arrange a meeting of envoys between the Kazakhs and the Safavids of Iran, bitter enemies of Bukhara.[51]

Boris Godunov was using Uraz Muhammad to learn how best to maneuver among five Turko-Mongol polities (the Kazakhs, Bukhara, Sibir', the Noghay, and Khorezm) that were simultaneously fighting each other for supremacy and tactically allying against common foes, including Muscovy. In addition, involvement with these groups had implications for Muscovy's relations with Iran and the Ottoman Empire. At the same time, the Turko-Mongol rulers were all trying to enlist Muscovite help for their individual military and economic purposes. Uraz Muhammad was not the only high-status hostage being supported by Tsar Fedor's court: the Russians also held Kuchum Khan's son, who wrote to his father: "Here at Court many tsars and princes serve, receiving abundant subsidies."[52] Each also played an intermediary role between his Central Asian and his Russian overlords. Moscow had been able to conquer the Volga khanates because it had become the most organized power in the western steppe and made itself central among the Mongol successor states. Forty years later the fragmented nature of the eastern khanates extended Muscovy's position as the pivotal Central Eurasian power.

Muscovy had only one way of understanding alliances with the non-Christian polities of Central Asia and Siberia: as vassals asking for the protection of the tsar, not as equals seeking allies against common enemies. This was not the working assumption of the Central Asians and Siberians, who were caught off-guard and aggrieved when Muscovy demanded regular tribute payments and other signs of submission. However, while Muscovy could usually enforce its terms against the small and scattered population of Siberia, it was not yet able to do so against the Kazakhs. Tavvakul Khan's repeated requests for firearms were not evidence that the gunpowder revolution was changing the balance of power in Eurasia. His interest is, on the contrary, somewhat puzzling. For millennia steppe warriors had defeated everyone from Romans to Chinese with fast and deadly archers on horseback. Nomad tactics of rapid encirclement, feigned retreat leading to ambush, and the unleashing of storms of arrows that could penetrate armor from hundreds of yards away stymied slow-footed infantries. When harquebuses and cannon arrived in Muscovy in the mid-sixteenth century, they were too immobile and hard to aim to be effective against steppe cavalry. Ivan IV had his first major success using gunpowder against Kazan in 1552, but that was with gunpowder-packed barrels used to blow up the walls of the town. The Muscovite military would not prefer to use gun-bearing infantry until the later seventeenth century, and that was more because of changes in tactical thinking than guns' proven superiority over horse archers.[53] Yet, Tavvakul Khan seemed convinced that firearms would give him an advantage over his enemies, perhaps because he had seen them work against Siberian tribes. This evident desire gave Muscovy some leverage over the khan.

The tsar's letters to Tavvakul used standard diplomatic formulas that recognized no alternative to Russian superiority. While the Kazakh khan was seeking military aid and the return of his brother, Russian documents spoke of "acceptance of the Kazakhs as subjects of Moscow's government," with Tavvakul and his family "under the tsar's hand." Godunov was willing to grant Tavvakul's requests, but only in exchange for an even more valuable hostage, Tavvakul's son and presumed heir Hussein.[54] This was an ancient tactic used by Eurasian and Chinese governments. Royal hostages were educated in the language and customs of their keepers, with the hope that they would guarantee good behavior by their families and promote friendlier relations between the two states in question. In spring 1595 a Muscovite envoy reached Tavvakul himself—this alone was a feat, because the khan was migrating with his herds, and because the Russian party had to avoid capture by bandits or Kuchum Khan. Godunov did arrange a meeting between Kazakh and Safavid envoys, and Tavvakul's family were sent a variety of gifts via their relatives, including a red robe for Tavvakul, knives, boots with gold thread, a mule, and jewelry, but no firearms.[55] For all that, the Kazakhs did not accept Russian rule.[56] In 1600 Tsar Boris Godunov appointed Uraz Muhammad khan of Kasimov; he died in 1610 during the wars of Russia's Time of Troubles.

SUMMARY

For the first several hundred years of their relationship, Eastern Slavs and Turks coexisted in a frontier zone, recognizing clear differences between communities yet crossing marriage and other boundaries regularly. The rule of the Mongol Jochid Khanate, from 1240 to the mid-fifteenth century, created the conditions for the town of Moscow to become the center of the strongest Mongol successor state in the western steppe. Muscovy's centralized administration and the ambitions of its grand princes enabled it to become the mediator among the four khanates that arose in the fifteenth century, even while it still paid tribute to Crimea or the Great Horde and endured sometimes devastating invasions from both. Tsar Ivan IV's conquest of Kazan and Astrakhan in the 1550s marked Muscovy's transition from a strong but not seriously threatening Central Eurasian power to an expansionist state. The Turko-Mongol successor states east of the Volga River, the Kazakh Khanate, and the Uzbek khanates of Transoxiana, noted Muscovy's arrival and sent out diplomatic and trade missions. The khans were interested in Russian firearms, leather goods and hunting falcons, but their attention was mostly focused on battling each other for supremacy or on the threats posed by their great Islamic neighbors, Safavid Iran and Mughal India. Muscovy and Central Asia developed a thickening network of trade points and became familiar with each other, but still inhabited different cultural complexes.

Chapter 2

THE BALANCE OF POWER SHIFTS

The early seventeenth century was a period of dynastic collapse, war, and political chaos from Muscovy to China. Russia and China emerged from these assorted disasters in stronger positions, while the Central Asian khanates did not. The key difference was that Russia and China had centralized administrations that could get the state back to work quickly after a new ruling dynasty came in, while the Central Asian administrations were highly decentralized. As Russia and China extended their power across Eurasia, the Kazakh and Uzbek polities were so preoccupied with fighting internal enemies that they did not even try to coordinate their response. The Kazakh hordes found themselves being squeezed between expanding states from all directions until they were forced to ask for Russian protection in 1730. The Russians, for their part, found that promising protection came with high costs and few appealing options. All the parties concerned were searching for some advantage over their rivals, but the balance of power had shifted decisively toward Russia, allowing it to develop from coexisting with Turkic peoples to conquering them.

INTERNAL FRAGMENTATION, EXTERNAL THREATS

The death of the childless Tsar Fedor in 1598 marked the end of the founding Rurikid Dynasty of Russia. Boris Godunov (r. 1598–1605) was crowned tsar on the basis of election by the boyars, but could not fix the deep fiscal and social crises that were the legacy of Tsar Ivan IV (the Terrible).[1] Godunov spent the last year of his reign fighting an all-out war against an invader from Poland who claimed to be Dmitri Ivanovich, the son of Ivan IV and his sixth wife (of Noghay Tatar descent), who had supposedly died in 1591. Genuine or not, Dmitri's invasion drew strong support from Muscovy's southern and eastern frontier areas. Godunov had been aggressively expanding Muscovy's borders by building lines of fortresses and defensive barriers. These lines protected trade routes and areas that were vulnerable to Crimean slave raids; they also encroached on Noghay and Bashkir pasturelands, even as Turkic soldiers made up a large portion of the expeditionary forces that built them.[2] The fortresses were manned by Cossacks, communities of frontier militias of mixed ethnic and social origin, but predominately Slavic and Orthodox Christian. Cossacks could serve Muscovy or Poland-Lithuania, but were not bound by obligation as they were not subjects of either kingdom. Cossacks needed to work for Muscovy for economic reasons, but also ferociously protected their independence from servitude. Until the late eighteenth century Cossacks were both Russia's vanguard in extending power over Central Asia and the state's most troublesome rebels. They joined forces with Dmitri, the Noghay, and some Bashkirs to destroy Godunov's government and occupy Moscow in 1605. Dmitri was crowned tsar and reigned for eleven months before he was murdered by rival boyars, Poland and Sweden invaded, and the entire state came close to disintegrating in 1610.

The multiple crises slowed, but did not entirely halt, Russia's extension eastward. Even as the famine of 1601–03 killed up to one-third of Muscovy's population, Russian military commanders and their Cossack and Turkic soldiers founded fortress-trading posts across north-central Siberia at Mangezia (1601), Ketsk (1602), and Tomsk (1604). In 1603 Cossacks based on the Yaik/Ural River raided the Uzbek Arabshahid Khanate of Khorezm.[3] The continuing expansion tells us not only that Muscovy had deep resources, but that strong central control was not really necessary to the process. Siberia was economically vital to Muscovy because of the fur trade; Russian officers did not need to be told that securing greater control over the land and people would help themselves and the state, whoever was ruling at the moment. The Cossacks, meanwhile, never waited for permission to raid a place that looked lucrative and vulnerable. Even with a government in turmoil, Russia now posed a direct threat to the Central Asian polities.

The Kazakh and Uzbek Khanates

The Kazakh and Uzbek khanates were vulnerable because of internal disorganization and external pressures (see Map 2.1). In 1598, the same year that Tsar Fedor died, Kazakh khan Tavvakul and Bukharan khan Abdallah also died, both during a Kazakh invasion of northern Bukhara. Tavvakul had sons to succeed him, but they were overwhelmed by Russian and Kalmyk encroachments into their territory. The two Uzbek khanates lost the progress toward centralization that Abdallah had made. When he died the founding Shibanid Dynasty died with him, and the territories he had spent his long reign conquering broke away from Bukharan control. A smaller Bukhara was taken over in 1599 by the Ashtarkhanids, the family of khans who had been booted out of Astrakhan by Tsar Ivan IV in 1556. By 1612 two Ashtarkhanid brothers divided Bukhara into a *de facto* dual khanate, with Imam Quli Khan (r. 1612–42) at Bukhara and Nadir Muhammad Khan at Balkh. Their successors continued the dual structure until the 1680s and were unable to recover permanently any of the lost regions. The Khanate of Khorezm had been conquered by Abdallah late in his reign; after his death the surviving Arabshahid khans vied with each other for control, drawing on Turkmen or Uzbek allies to staff their armies. This turned a family quarrel into a regional series of wars. In the first quarter of the seventeenth century the Arabshahids moved their capital from the town of Urgench to the town of Khiva. People gradually came to refer to the khanate as a whole as the Khanate of Khiva, a name that survived until 1920. The Arabshahid rulers scored some military victories over each other and the khans of Bukhara (causing significant damage to the latter in the 1650s and the 1680s), but over the course of the century they proved to be better at destruction than at building stable administrations.[4] Khiva remained small, poor, and volatile.

Repeated cycles of wars among the ruling elites damaged the Uzbek and Kazakh khanates but did not mean that all cultural development halted. Tourists to today's Uzbekistan are awed and delighted by the azure tile phoenixes of the Nadir Divan Begi *khanqah* (a hostel for wandering Sufis) in Bukhara (see Figure 2.1) and the startling Persianate tiger–sun mosaics of the Shir-Dor madrasa in Samarkand's central *registon* (open plaza). Both were built in the 1620s during the reign of Imam Quli Khan, along with water reservoirs, irrigation canals, and more mundane structures throughout the khanate.[5]

MAP 2.1 Eurasian polities, early eighteenth century.

FIGURE 2.1 Divan Begi Sufi hostel. Source: Author, Bukhara, 2003.

Most of the Bukharan and Khivan khans sponsored art, architecture, and scholarship or engaged in it themselves. Abu'l Ghazi Bahadur Khan of Khiva (r. 1644–66), the strongest of the late Arabshahid khans, spent a fruitful exile in Iran studying historical manuscripts. When he took power in Khiva he decided that it was high time to write updated histories of Khiva and the Turkmen tribes, and did it himself with aims that resonate with modern historians:

> Before us, many words in Arabic and Persian were added to the Turkic histories, and the Turkic was written in rhymed prose in order to show their own skill and mastery to the people. We have done nothing of the sort because the readers and listeners to this book will certainly be Turks and it is necessary to tell the Turk in the Turkic way so that all of them understand. If they do not know the words we have told what is the profit in that? If among them there are one or two knowledgeable readers, they may be able to teach those many who don't know; it is necessary to speak to both nobles and commoners so that it may be acceptable to their hearts. Now, let us write ... [6]

While Russia was pressuring Central Asians from the north and west, the Mongol Oirat tribes launched devastating invasions from the east. Recall that the Oirats/Kalmyks were a non-Chinggisid confederation of Mongol tribes living in the western part of traditional Mongol territory, just north of the Tian Shan mountains and east of Lake Balkhash. Oirat attacks had led to the split between Uzbeks and Kazakhs in the fifteenth century, and they fought regularly with the Kazakhs and the Kyrgyz in the sixteenth. The Oirats fought among themselves as well, which is what drove some tribes west into Kazakh lands and Russian Siberia. The different ways in which Oirats interacted with Russians versus Kazakhs tells us a great deal about who wielded what kind of power in Central Eurasia. The Russian fortress-trading post at Tara reported the first contact with Oirats in 1606. Within two years the Oirats sent an envoy to Moscow to request rights to pasturage and trade. Muscovy at the time was torn apart by the wars of the Time of Troubles. It is possible that the Oirat envoy found himself caught between two rival courts—of Tsar Vasilii Shuiskii and the Second False Dmitri ("the Felon of Tushino")—contending for the loyalty of the boyars. What is remarkable is that, despite Shuiskii's desperate straits, the Russians continued their tradition of treating all non-Christian envoys as though they had been sent to humbly declare loyalty to the tsar, request "the tsar's hand" of protection, and pay tribute. The Oirats had no interest in making themselves subjects of the tsar, much less the Felon of Tushino, but they did succeed in obtaining trading rights. The prospect of Oirat trade was attractive to the Russians in Siberia because the Oirats offered horses, which were hard to obtain and keep alive in the harsh forest environment. In exchange the Oirats took Russian manufactured cloth and paper; they also wanted Russian money, which indicates that the Eurasian economy was partly monetized. Meanwhile, the Oirats had no interest in trade with the Kazakh Senior Horde, since the Kazakhs had nothing to give that the Oirats did not already have. Instead the Oirats repeatedly attacked the Kazakhs, pushing them out of their eastern pastures.[7]

An Oirat tribe called the Torghut inflicted great damage on the Kazakhs in the 1620s–30s, when the Torghut migrated west all the way to the southern Volga. As they arrived in Noghay Tatar lands between the Yaik/Ural and Volga rivers, the Torghut attacked and pushed many Noghay west. In the 1640s–50s they raided Turkmen lands and the Khanate of Khiva. They became embedded in the tangled politics of the southern steppe, allying with Don Cossacks against the Crimean Tatars while repelling attacks from the Bashkirs and Yaik Cossacks. They traded with Russia and attacked Russian towns. In 1654 Russia incorporated Ukraine into its empire, and one year later sought to make its first formal agreement with the Torghut (who they called Kalmyks) to get their military help against Crimea. None of the early treaties between the Russians and Kalmyks lasted long because of Russia's insistence on addressing the Kalmyks as subjects of the tsar, a view that the Kalmyks rejected. Faced with a formidable potential ally who could not be ignored, expelled, or co-opted, by the end of the century Russia offered an agreement that treated the Kalmyks as equals with their own legitimate interests. Thus a Buddhist Mongol people took up residence in the steppe along the southern Volga.[8]

Romanov Russia Reaches the Pacific

Russia's crisis ended in 1613 with the election of a new dynasty of tsars, the Romanovs. Although Tsar Mikhail Fedorovich Romanov (r. 1613–45) was only sixteen years old when crowned, his state began to recover remarkably quickly from fifteen years of devastation. The new government spent the 1630s and 1640s focused on winning back western lands lost to Poland and Sweden, and continued to extend the fortress-trading post line across Siberia.

Cossack expeditions reached the north Pacific Ocean in 1639, Lake Baikal in 1643, and the Amur River by 1650. At this stage Russia was making no attempt to formally administer this enormous territory, although expeditions systematically compiled maps as their knowledge increased.[9] Rather, Russian commanders treated all of the Siberian peoples they encountered as automatic subjects of the tsar and demanded fur tribute, but otherwise did not interfere in their traditional modes of rule. Russian settlers and Orthodox missionaries were present, but in numbers too small to make much impact.

The first direct contact between the Russian and Chinese governments came in 1618, with a Cossack expedition sent from Tobolsk. The connection was made via Altyn Khan of the Khalka Mongols, a new and powerful eastern Mongol confederation located north of the Altai mountains that had diplomatic relations with the Chinese and sought alliance with the Russians against their rivals the Oirats.[10] Cossack commander Ivashko Petlin lacked the proper credentials to be allowed to meet with the Ming Wanli Emperor (r. 1563–1620), but he was able to gather intelligence on the size and wealth of China, trade possibilities, and the trouble the Ming government was having with the rising Manchu kingdom north of Beijing. The Ming court, just like the Russians, assumed that the only reason Petlin would have journeyed to Beijing was to request vassal status for the tsar. Petlin was sent back to Moscow with a letter from the emperor that outlined what tribute the tsar should give. However, since no one in Moscow could translate the Chinese text until 1675, no relationship developed.[11]

In the interim China underwent its own period of political collapse and rebirth, when in 1644 the Manchu kingdom overthrew the Ming Dynasty and established the Qing Dynasty (1644–1911). For the first time since the fall of the Mongol Yuan Dynasty in 1370, the Chinese were ruled by a foreign ethnic group. The Manchus were descendants of the twelfth century Jurchen rulers of northern China. They were distantly related to Mongols and Turks, although their closest relatives were peoples of eastern Siberia. The dynamic and fiercely focused Kangxi Emperor (r. 1654–1722) built an aggressive, centralized state that outgrew the bounds of the old Ming empire by the 1670s. Simultaneously, the Russians were encroaching on ancestral Manchurian lands—the town of Khabarovsk on the Amur River was founded in 1652. Russian relations with the Oirats, whom the Kangxi Emperor regarded as rightfully his subjects, also raised the threat of a conflict that both empires wanted to avoid. The threat was averted with the formal Treaty of Nerchinsk in 1689, which was written in Latin because Jesuit missionaries attached to the Qing court assumed the role of mediators. This agreement fixed state borders in eastern Eurasia for the first time, and required the peoples living there to declare their allegiance to Russia or China. The treaty legally closed a vast frontier zone, although for centuries neither state could really enforce the borders.[12]

Aside from the Jesuits, the true mediators between the Russian and the Qing governments were the Mongol tribal confederations, which benefitted from trade and grew in strength even as they fought continually among themselves and with Turkic peoples. Galdan Khan (r. 1676–97) forged the Oirats and eastern Mongol tribes into the Zunghar state, which dominated the territory between Russian Siberia and China and traded with both. The Zunghars established an economy that combined the strengths of pastoralist and settled lifeways, settling farmers (often Kazakh captives), developing mining and metallurgy, and mixing traditional cavalry tactics with new weapons, such as cannons mounted on camelback.[13] The Zunghars were the biggest regional power in eastern Eurasia until the Qing Qianlong Emperor had them wiped out in 1756–57.[14]

The Russian extension to the Pacific, their generally peaceful relations with the Zunghars, and the establishment of an agreed border with China diminished the importance of the Kazakhs and Uzbeks in the north as economic and political actors. While the tsarist court was occupied with the Time of Troubles, Bukharan traders had been essential for supplying the Siberian outposts, but Romanov Russia's new resources and trade networks eliminated that dependence. Some Bukharan merchants became permanent residents in Siberia, however, occasionally serving as envoys for the Russians.[15] More importantly, as the Uzbek and Kazakh polities were becoming surrounded by states controlled by strong central administrations, they experienced endless wars among their own ruling elites that prevented organized governance except on the local level. The Bukharan, Khivan, and Kazakh rulers expanded their diplomatic and trade networks, but they could not even start to build the centralized administrations that were powering the rising states of the early modern period.

Relations among the Khanates

In Bukhara, Imam Quli Khan, his brother and successor Nadir Muhammad Khan (r. 1642–51), Nadir's son Abd al-Aziz Khan (r. 1651–81), and his brother Subhan Quli Khan (r. 1681–1702) spent most of their time fighting with their sub-rulers (each appanage, such as Samarkand or Tashkent, had its own governor), who were often their close relatives. When Abd al-Aziz acceded to the throne after years of war against his father, it drove Nadir Muhammad to abdicate and seek shelter in Iran, where he died at the age of fifty-nine.[16] Khans were so eager to attack each other that the pattern could look like a deadly game of musical chairs: in 1688 Subhan Quli attacked Khurasan because he was desperate for booty to replenish his treasury. While he was in Khurasan he left Bukhara undefended, and Arang Khan of Khiva (r. 1688–94) attacked. However Arang did not get very far because as soon as he left Khiva the Kalmyks raided and took thousands of captives. Arang complained about this outrage to two new and very young tsars, Peter and Ivan Alexeevich, on the grounds that the Kalmyks were now Russian vassals and should be restrained.[17]

At the same time, Central Asian polities maintained ties with each other on multiple and seemingly contradictory levels. Ever since the establishment of the Kazakh and Uzbek khanates they had fought over who controlled the towns along the Syr Darya; Tashkent changed hands dozens of times over several centuries. In 1642 Tashkent was theoretically part of Bukhara but governed by a Kazakh sultan, Jahangir, whose loyalty to the new Bukharan khan Nadir Muhammad was suspect. To strengthen the alliance the khan arranged for Jahangir's daughter to marry his son Abd al-Aziz. The marriage did not preserve peace, but maintained personal connections among the rivals. The khans of Khiva and Bukhara also married into each other's families.[18] Sometimes they fought as allies against the common Kalmyk enemy, while trade between Uzbeks and Kalmyks was a regular occurrence. Kalmyks also served as mercenary or slave soldiers in Uzbek armies, and some Kalmyk women married into the ruling dynasties.

It appears that the roots of all this family strife were poverty and a too-perfect balance of power. Bukhara and Khiva were continually trying to conquer each other to create a stronger and richer khanate. While Bukhara frequently had the upper hand, the khans could neither permanently defeat each other nor find a route to political merger. Bukharan rivalry with the Kazakhs centered on the Syr Darya basin and the Ferghana Valley. While the Bukharans regularly defeated the Kazakhs in the field, they could never fully conquer nomadic armies that could retreat into the steppe and return to fight another day. Near-constant war drained the treasuries and diverted human resources that might otherwise have gone into administrative and economic development. Because the khans had little control over their governors, who were often potential new khans, there were no incentives to create khanate-wide financial systems. The Bukharan khans regularly debased their coinage by reducing the silver content, sometimes to the point where their own merchants refused to accept the coins.[19] The devaluations, combined with harsh tax demands on merchants and farmers, impoverished much of the population. Poverty then motivated new wars in a self-perpetuating cycle. The medieval Rus' appanages had been in a similar situation, but their Mongol overlords demanded that one prince serve as the central tax collector and enforcer of Mongol will. Mongol imposition of a hierarchy and fiscal structure, not to mention their crushing of rebellious appanages, opened a way for the princes of Moscow to annex their rivals and gradually centralize administration. The Uzbek and Kazakh khanates had no outside power to force them into unity. While the Kazakh hordes were badly weakened by Oirat and Kalmyk depredations, the Mongols showed no interest in conquering and governing the Kazakhs.

Relations between the Khanates and Outside Powers

Under the circumstances it is perhaps surprising that the khans managed to engage in foreign relations at all, but contrary to myth the Central Asian polities were never completely cut off from the rest of the world. Relations with Romanov Russia were distant and inconsistent.[20] Merchants and envoys routinely traveled between Russia and all the khanates; Bukharans made up one of several colonies of foreign traders living in Astrakhan. The imbalance of wealth meant that Central Asians were in the position of importuners, asking for gifts (especially gerfalcons, prized hunting birds and tokens of honor), weapons, aid against the Kalmyks, and improved conditions for their merchants. The Russians continued to be reliable buyers of Bukharan textiles, but they were primarily interested in spreading their political prestige and gathering intelligence about khanate politics and about Mughal India, to which they were seeking an overland route. They also kept an eye on Bukharan–Ottoman ties, since they feared a hostile alliance on their southern border.

The cause of redeeming Orthodox Christian slaves provided one reason for Russian envoys to journey to Bukhara, but the slave trade actually went both ways. Russia wanted to ransom Orthodox captives, but had no objection to slavery as an institution. In some cases envoys were instructed to pay only for male slaves who could be impressed into the tsars' armies, just as much slaves as they had been in Bukhara. Female and child slaves were not worth the price. By the middle of the seventeenth century Russia not only had contract slavery, it had completed the legal process of enserfing its peasants, the vast majority of the population. Russia had its own slave markets where Bukharans sold Kalmyks or bought Tatars or (non-Orthodox) Germans.[21] In 1640 Said, son of Khivan khan Isfendiar, sent Tsar Mikhail a request for gifts including black fox and sable fur, "and a fine Cherkess [Circassian] girl."[22] While there are no systematic statistics, diplomatic documents suggest that Russian envoys rarely freed as many slaves as they hoped to.[23]

The prestige hierarchy between states was expressed in elaborate diplomatic language and ritual. These rituals could reveal sharply differing worldviews. When ambassador Anisim Gribov visited Bukhara in 1643, he expected to be given a fancy ceremonial escort into the town, that Nadir Muhammad Khan would inquire about the tsar's health, and that the khan would stand up when presented with the tsar's diplomatic letter. Instead, not only did Nadir Muhammad fail to acknowledge the tsar's superiority by not performing any of these acts, he refused Gribov's request to free Orthodox slaves and let them return to Russia. He then asserted his equal status in a letter back to the tsar, in which he listed his conquests and demanded that the tsar round up and send all of the Noghay Tatars in Russia to Bukhara in exchange for Orthodox slaves.[24] Tsar Mikhail wanted to maintain friendly relations with Bukhara and did not respond with anger, but the two rulers never achieved a solid understanding of each other. Bukharan envoys were treated with honor in Russia, and Mikhail's successor Tsar Alexei Mikhailovich (r. 1645–76) sent Gribov on a return trip to Bukhara in 1646, but the khanate's internal wars prevented him from reaching his goal. Nadir Muhammad's successor Abd al-Aziz did not receive Russian ambassadors until 1670, by which time they expected the khan to rise at the mention of the tsar's name. He did so.[25]

The Uzbek khans put more energy into trade and diplomatic ties with India and Safavid Iran, although relations with the two Islamic empires may have been more of a net drain than benefit for Bukhara and Khiva. Indian and Iranian rulers invested considerable resources in roads, security, and *caravanserais* (hostels for merchants and their animals) to facilitate trade, but the khans did not match them.[26] The Shibanids and Ashtarkhanids of Bukhara claimed that Khurasan was part of their Chinggisid patrimony and repeatedly fought the shahs over the region. Only Abdallah Khan conquered it, however, and Bukhara lost it after his death. Despite this and the deep religious hostility between Shiite Iran and Sunni Transoxiana, trade never ceased.[27] In the late sixteenth century Shah Abbas (r. 1587–1629) increased trade and diplomacy with the feuding Uzbek rulers partly to exacerbate his enemies' divisions.[28] He was worried about economic competition not only from the other Islamic empires but from the Europeans, and so was open to all possible sources of revenue. When Imam Quli Khan and his brother Nadir Muhammad abdicated at the ends of their reigns (Imam Quli because he had gone blind, and Nadir Muhammad because he lost the war with his son), they were both welcomed in Iran because the shahs felt that friendly relations with Bukhara outweighed theological differences.

Mughal India's enormous economic and political weight motivated Iran and Bukhara to maintain ties despite their many reasons not to. The three powers triangulated their relations depending on who was at war with whom. Bukhara and Iran both had prickly diplomatic relations at best with their giant neighbor, but also depended on trade with it. India was a huge importer of horses and fruit from Transoxiana; it was Bukhara's most lucrative trading partner by far. At the same time, the Mughals had never forgotten their origins in Transoxiana, and periodically took advantage of Bukharan civil wars to try and re-take territory. The most spectacular instance of this was in 1646, when Shah Jahan's son and successor Aurungzeb occupied Balkh. The Mughals also made clear their low opinion of Uzbeks' cultural level, morals, and hygiene.[29] Between outright wars, the khans, their rival relatives and sub-rulers, and other powerful actors such as the Juybari family of khojas, all cultivated connections with the Mughal emperors to further their own factional interests.[30] However, none of these connections resulted in a sustained alliance.

Dynastic Decline

The last two Ashtarkhanid khans (Ubaydullah, r. 1702–11, and Abulfayz, r. 1711–47) lost all pretense of controlling Bukhara as a unified kingdom. Ubaydullah was murdered by his own *emirs* (military commanders).[31] Bukhara's longtime second city, Balkh, broke away under the rule of independent Uzbek emirs. The towns of the Ferghana Valley were functionally independent, being governed by families of Naqshbandi khojas or Uzbek nomadic tribes, of which the Ming tribe was the strongest.[32] In 1709 the chief of the Ming, Shah Rukh, broke the power of the khojas and laid the foundations for what would, two hundred years later, become a third Uzbek khanate, Kokand.[33]

While the ruling family fought, someone had to govern at the appanage level, in the form of collecting taxes, maintaining irrigation works, enforcing just weights and measures in the markets, adjudicating property disputes, and punishing crime. These duties were usually divided between Islamic authorities, who served as the legal experts, and the chiefs of the major tribes that made up the Uzbek confederation. Heads of the madrasas and Sufi *tariqas* (brotherhoods or orders, although there are female Sufis as well) also wielded considerable economic power as the guardians of *waqfs*, lands given as charity to support the upkeep of shrines, khanqahs, madrasas, and institutions that provided for the poor. As disarray increased at the top, local chiefs and khojas took more control in their appanages. They also could gain power by being appointed as *ataliqs*, counselors or viziers who also supervised the khans' sons when they were serving as governors. When the governor was weak or distracted by fighting, the ataliq was in charge. During Abulfayz's reign his ataliq, Manghit tribal chief Muhammad Hakim, gradually acquired the true authority in the khanate.[34]

The Khanate of Khiva was also falling to pieces, but for different reasons. The reign of Arabshahid khan Shir Ghazi (r. 1715–28) began on a positive note when he crushed a Russian incursion. This had been ordered by the preternaturally energetic Tsar Peter I (the Great, r. 1682–1725), who devoted his long reign to making Russia a full and equal member of Europe. One of his many projects was to accelerate the ongoing search for a direct route from Russia to India. He had become convinced that it was possible to locate and secure a passage along the Amu Darya that would allow Russians to reach India by boat. All that would be required, Peter thought, was to send an expedition to Khiva on the pretext of congratulating the new khan upon his accession, persuade local merchants to lead them down the river to the Great Mogul (Peter even instructed the expedition's cartographer to buy ostriches once he got there), scout out where to build to fortresses, divert the river, and essentially take over the khanate.[35] Tragically for the Russian commander, Alexander Bekovich-Cherkasskii, the Khivans saw the expedition as an attempt at conquest and destroyed the group. Shir Ghazi sent Bekovich-Cherkasskii's head to Abulfayz Khan in Bukhara and publicly displayed his stuffed body in Khiva.[36] Undeterred, Peter sent a second embassy to Bukhara (via Iran) two years later. The party was held hostage there until Peter's death in 1725. The incidents became a byword among Russians for tragic loss. They also signaled that Russia's attitudes toward the Central Asian khanates had become more aggressive.

Being able to fend off an ill-prepared Russian force did not mean that Khiva was developing a stronger government—quite the reverse. Shir Ghazi was murdered in 1728 by members of the Qongrat Uzbek tribe that was beginning to challenge the Arabshahids for power. His successor Ilbars (r. 1728–40) could not control the migrations and raids of Turkmen and Karakalpak nomads, who not only dominated lands outside the main towns but took control of the northern half of the khanate.[37] The most devastating blow to the failing Arabshahid and Ashtarkhanid dynasties was delivered by Nadir Shah (r. 1736–47), who invaded both Khiva and Bukhara in 1740, executed Ilbars, and forced the khanates to submit to him. The Iranians did not want to occupy Transoxiana themselves, and so left Abulfayz Khan a puppet and appointed a non-dynastic governor for Khiva. The new governor was still a Chinggisid, but he was a Kazakh: Nuraly, son of the khan of the Kazakh Junior Horde, Abulkhayr.[38] An Arabshahid khan managed to re-take the throne in spring 1742, but over the next several decades the khans became puppets of their *inaqs* (chief ministers). These inaqs were Uzbeks of the Qongrat tribe. By 1803 the Qongrats, who were non-Chinggisids but retained the title of khan anyway, had established a new ruling dynasty that would last until 1920.

Nadir Shah was assassinated in 1747, and in Bukhara ataliq Muhammad Rahim, son of the Manghit chief Muhammad Hakim, took the opportunity to kill Abulfayz Khan and his son, and the dynasty with them.[39] In previous centuries this would have left Muhammad Rahim in a vulnerable position, as he was not a Chinggisid. However, the Chinggisid lineage no longer inspired the awe that it once had, and Muhammad Rahim was comfortable marrying a Chinggisid bride and calling himself emir in 1753. He solidified his legitimacy by re-conquering many of the regions Bukhara had lost, including Tashkent, the town of Yasi (now Turkestan), and the eastern mountain region (parts of today's Tajikistan).[40] The Manghit Dynasty would rule Bukhara until 1920.

While many historians have argued that Central Asia in the eighteenth century was in economic and cultural decline, a newer school of thought suggests that wealth and power were shifting location rather than deserting the region. The rise of Kokand was more a function of the Ferghana Valley's new attraction as a nexus of trade than of Bukharan weakness. In the 1730s Russia founded a new fortress-trading post called Orenburg along the Yaik/ Ural River in the southern Ural mountains.[41] Orenburg was not only a base for Cossacks but a major Eurasian market. Russian goods traveled from there through Kokand to the Turkic oasis towns around the Tarim Basin. Chinese exports such as tea, rhubarb, and silk came through the Ferghana Valley on their way to Russia. Bukhara and Balkh continued to earn a major portion of their revenue by selling horses to India, which required people to relocate from the towns to where horses pastured in the steppe. What could be read as de-urbanization and economic decay may be better interpreted as people moving to new centers of production.[42] Nonetheless, at the start of the eighteenth century the Kazakhs and Uzbeks were surrounded by highly organized and aggressive empires. Within a few decades they were forced to face the fact that they could no longer keep agents of those empires out of their lands.

NOMADIC PASTORALIST CULTURES: THE KAZAKHS, TURKMEN, AND KYRGYZ

The nomadic pastoralist peoples played central political, economic, and cultural roles in Central Eurasia, but historians find them frustrating to study. Few nomads needed to be literate, and those who were did not bother to lug heavy paper across the steppe or up to mountain meadows. That leaves us with virtually no written sources that are not filtered through the eyes of outsiders in one way or another. Archeological sources are more direct, but mute on many of the cultural questions that interest historians. Another difficulty with discussing Central Asian nomadic cultures is our imbalance of information. Because the Kazakhs experienced the earliest and longest contact with Russians and their agents, we know much more about them than we do about the Kyrgyz and Turkmen. Nonetheless, it is impossible to understand Central Eurasian history without engaging with the nomad contribution to cultural and material exchanges across the continent.[43]

The first thing to understand is that, while there are commonalities that can be used to define the term "nomadic pastoralist," nomads' experiences of life varied a great deal, depending on location and historical background. Economically, all pastoralist groups depended on sheep: sheep provided the meat and milk products that made up the bulk of nomads' diets, their wool went into clothing and housing (portable yurts made of felt, wool fibers matted together and often dyed), and they served as a measure of wealth. As the Russians progressively folded Kazakh communities into their legal system in the mid-nineteenth century, local sultans collected tax payments in sheep.[44] The second most important animal in the pastoralist economy was the horse. Horses were the ancient engine of the nomadic military machine, giving armies of archers terrifying speed and flexibility. It was only in the late seventeenth and early eighteenth centuries that gunpowder weapons became mobile enough to be effective against horseback archers who could shoot equally accurately forward or backward (the famous "Parthian shot"). Horses were the Kazakhs' primary export to Russia and to India via Bukhara and Iran until the nineteenth century. They were also an important source of meat and milk, the latter in the form of *kumiss*, a lightly fermented mare's milk drink that had been horrifying or enchanting Europeans since Friar William of Rubruck tried some in the thirteenth century.[45] Double-humped Bactrian camels were highly valued as powerful pack animals (see Figure 2.2), and for that reason expensive and present in smaller numbers in pastoralist communities. Some groups also herded cattle where the land would support them.

Beyond dependence on herd animals, differences become more noticeable than the similarities among the Kazakh, Kyrgyz, and Turkmen tribal confederations. Economically, the Turkmen derived a large part of their income from kidnapping and selling Iranian Shiite or Slavic Christian slaves in the markets of the Uzbek khanates. The Kazakhs and Kyrgyz were themselves sometimes bound into labor by the Mongol Zunghars or Qing or Russian frontier officials, although wealthy Kazakhs could also own slaves.[46] The Kazakhs' early contact with Russia made them a link in the exchange network of goods and culture from the West before the Turkmen and especially the Kyrgyz were so exposed. In 1736 Junior Horde Kazakhs were entertaining European visitors with Russian balalaika music. In 1742 a Russian diplomatic mission gave Abulkhayr Khan (r. c. 1719–48), his sons, and his top retainers gifts of sugar, green and black tea, spices (pepper and a kind of ginger, *inbir'*), and a surprising amount of wine and vodka. These would have been shared with other notables and servitors to encourage loyalty, especially as Abulkhayr's pro-Russian policies were deeply unpopular.[47] This list of gifts provides a striking contrast with diplomatic gifts from a hundred years before, which mostly consisted of internal products such as hunting falcons and Siberian furs. It reflects the changes that Peter the Great wrought when he opened Russia to wider trade with Europe, as well as the global reach of maritime trade. The sugar most likely came from European slave colonies in the Caribbean, while the spices could have come from Dutch holdings in Ceylon (today's Sri Lanka) or Java (today's Indonesia). The teas came from China directly to Russia via border towns in eastern Siberia, which illustrates one of the reasons the Kazakhs were losing control of the steppe: overland trade no longer had to pass through Kazakh lands.

FIGURE 2.2 A Turkmen wedding party, 1924. Photo by Khudaybergan Divanov (1878–1938). Divanov lived in the Khanate of Khiva and became the first Uzbek photographer. He served the government of the People's Soviet Republic of Khiva and became a cameraman in the first Uzbek film studio. He was shot in 1938. Source: Uzbek Journeys: Art, Craft & History Tours to Central Asia, http://www.uzbekjourneys.com/2012/05/khudaybergen -divanov-father-of-uzbek.html. Image courtesy of Andrew Hale, Anahita Gallery, Santa Fe, New Mexico.

Another supposed common feature among nomadic pastoralists, identity via family genealogy, was important to all groups but did not work the same way in all groups. The Kazakhs maintained a strong Chinggisid tradition that only direct descendants of the Golden Kin could rule as khans. The khans and their extended families made up the aq suiek (white bone) aristocracy, a hereditary and clearly marked ruling class. Below them, notable families traced their descent from other Mongol elites or from Muslim notables such as Sufi khojas. The titles *bii* (from the Turkic *bek*, *beg*, or *bey*, "lord," here a tribal judge) and *botir* (warrior) marked high status but were not strictly hereditary. If a botir proved weak or a new tribal configuration eliminated a need for his services, he lost status.[48] The aristocracy enjoyed legal privileges, such as freedom from corporal punishment, not available to ordinary qara suiek Kazakhs. "Black bone" commoners maintained kinship organization that by tradition went back seven generations, but was flexible in response to changing political and economic circumstances.[49]

Some Turkmen tribes also had rulers who called themselves khans, but their connection to the Golden Kin was often questionable. Unlike the Kazakhs, the Turkmen had never existed as a united polity, but as a collection of tribes in the frontier zone between Transoxiana and Iran that claimed descent from a common ancestor, Oghuz.[50] Mahmud Kashghari wrote about Oghuz Turkmen in his eleventh-century dictionary of Turkic dialects, which pre-dated the Mongol Empire.[51] Whether or not the Turkmen tribes had anything that might be called a government has been a matter of dispute among contemporary observers and later scholars. An early nineteenth-century Iranian history depicts the Salir or Salor tribe as being led by a hereditary Chinggisid khan descended from Tolui, Chinggis Khan's youngest son. Because Tolui's son Hülegü invaded through Turkmen territory to destroy the Abbasid Caliphate and found the Il-khanate in 1258, the Salir claim is not implausible.[52] The Hungarian Jewish adventurer Arminius Vambery, traveling through Turkmen lands in 1863, wrote: "The Turkoman himself is wont to say '*Biz bibash khalk bolamiz* (We are a people without a head), and we will not have one. We are all equal; with us, every one is king.'"[53] At the same time, Vambery noted that every tribe had an *oqsoqol* (village elder, literally "white beard") who acted as a "minister" as long as the tribesmen were willing to tolerate him. Western anthropologists have generally agreed with Vambery's description, which was echoed by Russian military observers. Paul Georg Geiss calls the Turkmen community an "acephalous political order"; Anatoly Khazanov argues that chiefdom among the Turkmen was a matter of temporary military necessity.[54] However, David Sneath, in a sharp critique of the use of kinship models developed elsewhere for studying Central Eurasian nomads, points out that Geiss's evidence undermines his own argument when he says that Turkmen recognized titles of high status like beg and botir. Sneath suggests that the Turkmen in fact had a stratum of hereditary "overlord" families, but that their power in the nineteenth century had been weakened by Russian expansion.[55]

Below the elite level, all observer reports say that genealogy was *the* structuring tool of Turkmen society, although lineage traditions could be flexible to the point of being fictive. There were seven major tribes, of which the Tekke and the Yomut were the largest, and dozens of smaller kinship groupings down to the Tekkes' *bir ata* (one father) unit of families that traced their descent from one recent ancestor. One major concern was whether a person came from a *gul* family (descended from freed slaves, usually of Iranian origin) or an *ig* family, pure-blooded Turkmen. The Turkmen also had a *yarimcha* (half-blood) category.[56] All of these sub-groups were recognized as Turkmen, but they occupied different status levels in a social hierarchy. The Turkmen tribes may not have had a government structure that was recognizable to Europeans, but their society was far from a free-wheeling anarchy.

The Kyrgyz presented still a different way of organizing a pastoralist society. The dozens of Kyrgyz tribes claimed no ties to the Mongol khans, but had a hereditary aristocracy of *manaps* (princes), and biis. These manaps and biis ruled over tribes and territories that functioned as political, not kinship, units; obedience to a given manap outweighed genealogy. Their close proximity to the Zunghar and then Qing empires shaped their social-political configuration. Kyrgyz tribes needed clear and stable leaders to negotiate with their powerful neighbors.[57]

Religious Practice

All Central Asian pastoralists regarded themselves as Muslim, but most outside observers were skeptical of that claim. Russian officials and European travelers noted the absence of books and mosques on the steppe, the prevalence of rituals at the shrines of Sufi saints along with healing and divination rituals, and concluded that nomads were at best "lightly acquainted" with Islam. Empress Catherine II (the Great, r. 1762–96) sent Tatar missionaries to civilize the Kazakhs with a more normative form of Islam.[58] The confusion of observers accustomed to the practices of Kazan or Istanbul is understandable. In 1736 a European named John Castle was a member of the expedition that founded the first Orenburg fortress and kept a journal to record his adventures. Abulkhayr Khan had recently accepted vassal status to Empress Anna (r. 1730–40), but most of his followers were resisting any loss of independence. One evening Castle visited a Kazakh camp, and his host shared a lamb with him for dinner. Afterwards the Kazakhs used the lamb bones to ascertain whether or not Castle was an auspicious visitor:

> [T]he lamb's bones … were laid out in the following manner. The bones were heaped together, in a copper pot, with the skull on top. A small stick with a little red flag of red taffeta, like a ship's pennant, hanging from it was inserted in the *sutura saggitali* of the skull, after which lights were placed in the eye holes.
>
> My aforementioned host, called Iungitcha,[59] was wrapped completely naked in a white cloth and then made to lie on his back, with his feet against the doors, without moving at all. 9 burning lights were placed on him, one on his forehead, one on each upper arm, one on each foot, one on each knee, one on his breast and on his stomach, too, there was a light, and these lights were made from the hoof bones that had been struck in half so that each bone produced two lights….
>
> The priest or mulla then performed the ceremony in the Arabic tongue, kneeling on the ground, holding in one hand a whip and in the other a book with strange characters and thus, after much whistling, warning the devils to keep away from all right-minded Muslims by uttering yells and pulling dreadful faces, they sought to discover forthwith whether or not my person and my arrival would bring them good fortune or not?[60]

European Christians, especially after two hundred years of wars generated by the Reformation over the proper status of sacred text, belief, and ritual, saw such wild divination rites as at best an amalgam of shamanism and Islam, with "shamanism" (never a defined religion) in the dominant role.[61] However, more recent scholarship has been less rigid in its approach to religion as actually practiced by believers, which is often notably different from whatever form is advocated by a clerical leadership. No missionary religion, including Christianity in early medieval Europe or Buddhism in fourth-century China, has ever barged into a culture and taken it over whole-sale. A process of integration with and assimilation into the host culture is always necessary for a new religion to generate emotional resonance among potential believers.[62] The Kazakhs were descendants of the Mongol Jochid Khanate, which had converted to Islam in the fourteenth century—they were Muslims before they were Kazakhs, and they clearly considered themselves Muslim, without any caveats.[63]

Castle describes the mulla speaking in Arabic and holding a book "with strange characters"—likely a Quran or a book of Quranic verses and prayers, although it is impossible to know for certain. We should remember that for much of their history the Kazakh hordes controlled towns along the Syr Darya, including the important Islamic centers of Yasi/Turkestan, Shymkent, and Tashkent. The mosques and madrasas in these towns were in turn in regular contact with Bukhara, which was respected throughout the Islamic world as a capital of learning and piety. This chain of connections gave Kazakhs access to a more learned form of Islam, even from a distance. Turkmen tribes in the vicinity of Khiva were served by educated mullas and *qadis* (judges of Islamic law) from the khanate. Some Turkmen studied in Khivan madrasas themselves and then returned to their tribes.[64]

Islam reached Central Asian pastoralists primarily through missionary Sufi mystics, which strongly shaped the way the religion was practiced. Sufism is a path of personal spiritual practice aimed at bringing the believer into a direct experience of God, through special meditations, vocal or silent prayer, or sometimes (as with the famous "Whirling Dervishes" of Turkey), dance.[65] Mystical practices can be traced to the beginnings of Islam, but over time Sufis organized into distinct tariqas founded by charismatic spiritual teachers and continued by their descendants. Three important Sufi tariqas originated in Central Asia: the Yasawiya, founded by Ahmad Yasawi in the twelfth century in the town of Yasi on the north bank of the Syr Darya; the Kubrawiya, founded in thirteenth-century Khorezm by Najm al-Din Kubra; and the Naqshbandiya, founded in fourteenth-century Bukhara by Baha al-Din Naqshband. Upon the founders' deaths their graves became shrines, drawing pilgrims from a wide area to pray for healing—Yasawi's shrine is popular among women suffering from infertility—and other blessings. The graves of their most esteemed followers and other spiritually powerful figures also became shrines, sacred sites which, depending on local custom, would be marked by tying strips of cloth, flags, or horse tails to poles or trees. The importance of saints' shrines made

Central Asian Islamic practice no different from that in India, most of the Middle East, and North Africa.

Tales of how nomadic rulers converted to Islam illustrate the integration and assimilation process necessary for a new religion to take hold. Two types of stories predominate: the missionary convinces because of exceptional strength or exceptional cleverness. In one tale the missionary asks to be allowed to build a mosque in an area the size of a cowhide. When the amused khan gives him the hide, he proceeds to cut it into a long, thin strip that marks out the plot for a sizable building.[66] In other tales the missionary is pitted in a wrestling match against a huge, muscular champion, who he defeats with one blow. In the most colorful tale, the notably hairy Sufi Baba Tukles challenges the magicians of Uzbek Khan of the Jochid Khanate to see who can withstand being baked in a fiery oven the longest. The magicians go up in smoke immediately, while Baba Tukles calmly asks why they opened the oven door so soon.[67] Formal theology plays no role in any of these tales, although proving the superior healing power of Islamic prayer is sometimes decisive. Historian James Millward points out that the missionaries in these stories are re-enacting the feats attributed to Turko-Mongol shamans, and that some stories of conversion to Islam closely resemble older stories of conversion to Buddhism in the same region.[68] The new religion adopts and reconfigures familiar cultural tropes in order to be understood. That does not mean that the Islam practiced by nomadic pastoralists was "really" half pagan, only that religions everywhere reflect as well as shape the cultures of which they are a part.

The Sufi tariqas acquired political as well as spiritual power. Sufi leaders could be called *sheikh* (from the Arabic) or *pir* (from the Iranian), but the term most frequently encountered in Central Asia is *khoja* or *khwaja*, the Arabic term for a direct descendant of the Prophet Muhammad. While some Central Asian communities did maintain a tradition that they were descended from Arabs (the name Tajik comes from the name of an Arab tribe, the Tayy), in practice the word came to refer to the heads of revered Sufi families. The Naqshbandi Juybari khojas appointed Abdallah b. Iskander sultan of Bukhara in 1551, not the formal supreme khan. In towns along the Syr Darya and especially to the east in the Ferghana Valley and out to Kashgharia around the Tarim Basin, khoja families controlled land, wealth, and became hereditary rulers. Khojas were the go-betweens in negotiations between Kazakh and Bukharan rulers in the early eighteenth century.[69] The Islamic cultures of the Kyrgyz and eastern Kazakhs of the Senior Horde were shaped by khoja rule or influence, even during periods when the nomads were vassals of the Zunghars or the Qing.

Since Islam is a law-based religion, outside observers of pastoralists looked to their laws and legal practices as a measure of their Islamicization. The Kazakhs, Turkmen, and Kyrgyz all worked within two deeply intertwined legal systems, *adat* (customary law) and *sharia* (Islamic law). Adat was an unwritten set of principles that the community agreed facilitated general well-being by regulating kinship relations, territorial or livestock disputes, and matters of honor. Adat was adjudicated by clan leaders called biis, who were chosen by communal acclamation of their legal knowledge and high morals. As such, biis were beholden to communal opinion and could rise or fall sharply in status depending on how well people thought they were doing their jobs.[70] Nomads rarely encountered formal sharia courts presided over by madrasa-trained qadis, but when they did they were dealt with according to the Sunni Hanafi school of jurisprudence, which almost all Central Asian Muslims followed. Russian officials, in their codifications of Kazakh law, tried to treat adat and sharia as distinct codes (some even hoped that distributing printed adat collections to biis would undermine Islamic law), but in reality legal traditions could not be separated so neatly.[71] This can be seen most clearly in laws dealing with women, which were rooted in sharia norms but could differ from them. The 1846 investigation of Junior Horde bii courts described standard Sunni practices in the realms of marriage, divorce, and circumcision, although women could not serve as witnesses at all (sharia allows the testimony of two women to equal that of one man) and women could not inherit property from their families (sharia allows women to inherit half of what their brothers receive from deceased parents).[72]

Nomadic pastoralist societies were patriarchal, but not much more so than most other nineteenth-century societies (see Figure 2.3). Marriages were arranged with an eye to enhancing family status, although women technically had a right of refusal. The bride left her household and joined the groom's (patrilocal marriage), and the family of the groom paid *qalin* (bride price) to the family of the bride as part of a complex set of gift exchanges, since marriage was as much about property and family alliances as it was about procreation. A separate gift from the groom, *mahr*, remained with the bride as her personal property and insurance in case of divorce. The goods exchanged in this way might include yurts, livestock, household equipment, and clothing or jewelry, property that the bride could pass on to her children. Polygyny was allowed according to Islamic practice, but as elsewhere only

FIGURE 2.3 Kazakh woman. Source: Alexis de Levchine, *Description Des Hordes et Des Steppes Des Kirghiz-Kazaks ou Kirghiz-Kaïssaks* (Paris: Charriere, 1840).

wealthy men could afford more than one wife. Among the Turkmen it was customary for a new bride in a household to avoid direct communication with her parents-in-law, including covering her mouth, not speaking, and not eating in their presence.[73] In law women's lives were accorded half the value of men's—a murderer's family could pay 1000 sheep in *kun* ("blood payment," usually a penalty paid in money or livestock) in compensation for a man but five hundred for a woman.[74] Nomads were not strict on segregating the sexes, because the rigors of steppe life required everyone's unhindered labor. John Castle not only was granted an audience with Abulkhayr Khan, he was able to meet and converse with the khan's chief wife, Bopai Khanim.[75]

THE BEGINNINGS OF RUSSIAN RULE

The proximate cause for Russia claiming direct rule over the western Kazakh steppe was the disruption caused by Zunghar invasions. The last Kazakh khan who was recognized by all three hordes was Tauke (r. 1680–1715). Upon his death the hordes split into three separate khanates, which were easier for the Zunghars to attack. During a large invasion from 1723 to 1725 the Zunghars captured the Syr Darya basin from Tashkent to Yasi/Turkestan (the main town of the Kazakhs), killing many Kazakhs and causing thousands to flee south into Bukharan territory, where they overran Uzbek towns and drove out many of the inhabitants to starve in the desert. These events so traumatized the Kazakhs that they gave the period a name: the "Barefoot Retreat."[76] Zunghar occupation of the east also pushed Kazakhs further west, where they were exposed to raids by the Kalmyks and brought into closer contact with the Russian fortress line.[77] Over the summer and fall of 1730 Abulkhayr Khan of the Junior Horde sent envoys to negotiate for Russian protection against the Kalmyks in exchange for loyalty, tribute payments, and the khan's sons as hostages. Within three years the Middle and Senior Hordes, as well as the Karakalpaks, also pledged their loyalty.

The initial diplomatic terms followed Russian protocol, which revealed serious differences in perception. Abulkhayr wrote his missive to Empress Anna in Tatar, the *lingua franca* of the steppe, asking "to attain the protection" of her majesty. The Russian translation of the document, which was the real basis for negotiations, read instead "desiring to be completely under Your Majesty's rule."[78] It had already been the case for years that Kazakh khans were expected to show deep respect by removing their hats and standing while inquiring about the tsar's health.[79] Abulkhayr's request went beyond a symbolic show of respect, but fell short of forfeiting Kazakh sovereignty. However, the fact that Abulkhayr and the Russian government had incompatible goals was just the surface problem. Abulkhayr's belief that the Kazakhs could not survive much longer without Russian suzerainty put him in direct conflict with his fellow khans and the vast majority of Kazakhs. When the Russian-Tatar envoy to the Kazakhs, Muhammad Tevkelev, arrived at Abulkhayr's camp in 1731 to receive the oath of allegiance and give the khan Russian insignia of rule, he found that most of the assembled Kazakh aristocracy felt betrayed by their khan and refused to swear allegiance on the Quran. Abulkhayr could only explain that he had no actual control over the fiercely independent Kazakhs.[80] Leaders of the other Kazakh hordes and the Karakalpaks were even clearer in their desire to have Russian protection without the burdens of paying tribute or sending hostages. For their part, the Russians were reluctant to provide military protection to people whose loyalty was so suspect.

None of the participants in these negotiations were happy with what they achieved, but circumstances did not allow any party to disengage from the relationship. The Kazakhs were still not free of Kalmyk and Bashkir attacks coming from their west. The promised Russian protection was not always very good, even after Abulkhayr encouraged the Russians to build the first Orenburg fortress in 1734. On the contrary, the Russians asked for Kazakh raids on the Bashkirs in order to protect their towns and merchants, which opened the Kazakhs to reprisals. More effective Russian protection was dependent on extending the fortress line, which the Russians did through the 1740s, with support from Abulkhayr. The large region around Orenburg was declared a full-fledged province of the Russian Empire in 1744, by which time the Orenburg line had been connected to the older Siberian fortress line at Omsk. Russia now defended a border from the northeast shore of the Caspian Sea to the Altai Mountains (and beyond that to Okhotsk on the Pacific). By the time the Kazakhs realized, as the Bashkirs had before them, that the "protection" offered by Russian fortresses meant that their lands were surrounded and controlled by Russian troops, no effective resistance was possible. This did not stop angry Kazakh bands from attacking fortresses, trade caravans, and Cossack communities.[81]

The Russians found that claiming the Kazakhs as their subjects complicated their relations with the Zunghars and the Qing. In 1727 Russia and China extended their diplomatic and trade relations with the Treaty of Kiakhta. The treaty updated border definitions, as both empires had expanded considerably since 1689. It allowed them to recover fugitives from each other's territories and banned nomads on one side of the border from crossing over to the other side. The complication in this arrangement was that the Qing and the Russians defined their subjects as those who paid tribute, but in this functional frontier zone Kazakh and other groups sometimes changed who they paid, paid both, or paid the Zunghar state. The Qing viewed the Kalmyks on the Volga as properly their subjects who had gotten away, and tried to persuade them to work for Qing interests against the Zunghars. Meanwhile, Abulkhayr secretly promised to send hostages to the Zunghars (making the Junior Horde their tributary) in exchange for the return of Kazakh towns along the Syr Darya.[82] The Russians blocked these moves, but Abulkhayr's scheme reminded them that if they did not make good on their promises of protection the Kazakhs would seek other patrons. However, such promises threatened to enmesh Russia in conflict with the Zunghars, with whom it had always cultivated friendly relations. In 1741 the Zunghars invaded the Ferghana Valley and the Tashkent region, which enabled them to force the Middle Horde to become their tributaries and demand that the Junior Horde do the same. As the Zunghars had been collecting tribute and hostages from the Senior Horde for decades, this was tantamount to claiming suzerainty over all the Kazakhs. The problem was that the Junior and Middle hordes had renewed their oaths of allegiance to Russia just the year before. Neither Russian empress Elizabeth (r. 1741–62) nor Zunghar khan Galdan Tsering (r. 1727–45) wanted war, so they worked out a compromise, wherein the Junior Horde remained solely subject to Russia and the Middle Horde sent hostages and tribute to both sides.[83]

To borrow a term of art from the social sciences, all of the actors in Central Eurasia were bound by path dependence. The choices they had made in the past sharply narrowed the options available to them in the present, regardless of how unpalatable those options were. The Kazakh hordes had some choice regarding to whom they would pay tribute, but genuine independence was no longer possible. If the Russians wanted to claim power over the Kazakhs they had to accept responsibility for their well-being, even when that cost a high price. They could avoid war with the Zunghars, but only by granting more favors to the Kazakhs. The Zunghars could force the eastern Kazakh and Kyrgyz tribes to be their tributaries, but then found that decades of aggression had left them with few friends and powerful enemies. In 1756–57 the Qing Qianlong Emperor smashed the Zunghars and deprived them of the ability to make any choices at all.

Even the elimination of the Zunghar state did not give the Kazakhs a chance at independence, because Zunghar power was replaced by the greater power of the Qing. What the Kazakhs could do was maneuver to create some space for themselves between the two empires. The Qing government accepted tribute from and traded with the Middle and Senior Kazakh hordes, but did not actively subjugate them as it did the Mongol peoples. However, the uncertainty between Russia and China over the boundaries of sovereignty let Middle Horde khans Abulmamet (also spelled Abulmambet, r. 1733–71), Ablai (r. 1771–81), and Ablai's son Wali (r. 1781–1821) suggest to each side that the Middle Horde was more loyal to them than to the other, and thus extract favors.[84]

Policy Disputes

When dealing with Russia, conflicts between military and civil officials allowed Kazakh leaders to use one faction against another to gain some leverage for themselves. This classic tactic might have been more effective if the Kazakhs had been able to unite behind one khan or notable clan. However, not only were the khans of the three hordes in sharp disagreement with each other, they also fought with heads of the notable clans and with their own relatives, while many ordinary "black bone" Kazakhs were finding basic survival more and more difficult. Ultimately, even though Russian officials bickered with each other for years over how best to "tame" the Kazakhs, the strong organization of the imperial state corralled the nomads ever more tightly.

Russian civil authorities argued that the best way to handle the Kazakhs was to soften them by luring them into dependency on Russian grain and goods, encourage the further fragmentation of the hordes by pitting khans and notables against each other, and gradually fold the Kazakhs into the Russian government by ending the hostage system and establishing councils of Kazakh notables appointed by Russia in major towns. The Orenburg governors were even willing to grant an exemption from customs duties to Kazakhs to encourage trade.[85] The Orthodox Church joined with the state to encourage converts to Christianity, who were then settled within the borders of the Russian empire. A few Kazakh notables served as officers in the Imperial Army.[86] These ideas were all congruent with the new model of

Russia as an Enlightened European state that Catherine the Great vigorously promoted until the French Revolution. As in Russia, Enlightenment ideals did not fit well with the harsh realities of the steppe. Most of the converts came to Russia out of economic desperation, not spiritual considerations, but the numbers were large enough to spark bitter complaints from the khans over the loss of population. Many of these new Christians then found themselves enserfed to Russian frontier officials, which did not encourage other Kazakhs to make the leap.[87]

Russian military officers, not surprisingly, favored force over efforts to persuade Kazakhs to become members of enlightened society. They wanted to continue using hostages to keep khans well-behaved and to raise the younger generation under Russian supervision. While the Orenburg governors argued that allowing Kazakhs to graze their herds near the border kept them under Russian surveillance, the military preferred to drive them away in order to protect the growing settlements of Russian peasants and Cossacks. However, the military did not have enough trained soldiers stationed east of the Volga to enforce a hard line consistently.[88]

Two eruptions in the 1770s pushed the Russians into adopting a more systematic approach to controlling the territories of the Junior and Middle Kazakh hordes. In 1771, responding to Russian encroachment on their autonomy and the vacuum created by the destruction of the Zunghars, the Kalmyks left Russia *en masse* for their former homeland in western Mongolia. From the Russian perspective, this was a betrayal of the Kalmyks' rightful ruler Catherine II, but the military was not able to stop the exodus. Indeed, a Cossack unit sent from Orenburg refused direct orders to prevent the Kalmyks from passing.[89] This mutiny was a harbinger of the much more serious crisis created by the large-scale rebellion of Emelian Pugachev (1773–75), which Catherine needed the full imperial army to crush. Pugachev, from the Yaik Cossacks, rallied thousands of enraged Cossacks, Bashkirs, Tatars, and other peoples to rebel against the brutality and oppression they experienced from the Russian government. Nuraly Khan of the Junior Horde (r. 1749–86), which was closest to the fighting, attempted to promise aid to both Pugachev and Catherine while remaining neutral in fact. However, his inability to control the horde made it impossible for him to avoid becoming entangled and damaged. Nuraly had been directly appointed as khan by the Russians in 1749. This act caused most Kazakh aristocracy and commoners to reject Nuraly as a Russian tool, and he was helpless to prevent hundreds of raids on Russian settlements in support of Pugachev. In the aftermath of the rebellion the Russians imposed severe restrictions on where the Junior Horde could graze its herds, which set off more anti-Russian violence by notables who blamed Nuraly as much as they did the government for their plight. In response, Russian governor Osip Ingelstrom chose to support the rebels *against* Nuraly, removing him as khan and accepting an oath of loyalty from Syrym, the very botir who had led major raids in support of Pugachev! Then Ingelstrom allowed the Junior Horde to graze its herds west of the Yaik River (re-named the Ural River by Catherine in an effort to erase the memory of Pugachev) and worked to halt Yaik/Ural Cossack raids on the Kazakhs, which improved their living standards considerably. This startling development reflected a significant change in Russian policy, from supporting khans to supporting the notables in hopes of breaking up the Kazakh hordes further.[90]

The tactic was partially successful. The new Russian favorite Syrym, while not given the title "khan" because he was not a Chinggisid, did attract the loyalty of some notable clans. However, most Kazakhs still refused to take a Russian oath of loyalty, and Syrym found that he was not only as distrusted as Nuraly had been, but also reviled as an illegitimate leader because he was not a khan. Syrym tried to improve his image among the Kazakhs by entering negotiations with Bukhara and Khiva to join forces with the Ottoman Empire, then at war with Russia. This only resulted in his losing Russian trust, and eventually his position. Over the next forty years Russian officials vacillated between using force to divide the Kazakhs and impose rulers loyal to Russia, and persuading the Kazakhs that it was in their best interests to become settled farmers and thus "civilized" subjects of the tsar. The most successful settlement attempt was in 1801, when Sultan Bukey and his followers separated from the Junior Horde and were permitted to live west of the Urals in the "Bukey Khanate," sometimes called the Inner Horde.[91] Neither force nor accommodation succeeded in reconciling the Kazakhs to Russian rule, however.

A New Legal Approach

An underlying cause of this vacillation was that, until the early nineteenth century, the Russian Empire lacked a legal mechanism for incorporating non-Christian subjects into its government structure. Treating non-Christians as distant tributaries even when they functioned fully within the system, like the Volga Tatars and the Kasimov khans, worked well enough until Catherine II tried to make Russia conform to the French *philosophes'* standards of law and political philosophy. Her predecessor Peter the Great liked to use the phrase "well-regulated police state" as a guide for his reforms, but that did not meet the Enlightenment ideal of a state governed by rational laws that Catherine so admired, at least up to the point where rational law might challenge her autocratic authority. Catherine put years of effort into updating and rationalizing Russia's jumble of law codes, including, for the first time, formal legal treatment of non-Christian subjects of the empire. What's interesting about the Russian approach is that Catherine did not simply impose her version of Enlightenment law on the Kazakhs (as she had done with Russians and Poles). Instead, in 1778 she instructed her officials to start by interviewing Kazakh biis and compiling a consolidated code of Kazakh customary law.[92] The project was not completed in Catherine's lifetime, but it was in keeping with her gradualist approach to "civilizing" the nomads by persuasion and education rather than direct force.

It fell to Imperial Russia's most effective administrator, Mikhail Speranskii, to develop a law code that accounted for the empire's increasing number of non-Christians. In 1819 Emperor Alexander I (r. 1801–25) sent a reluctant Speranskii to serve as the governor-general of Siberia with an assignment to clean up the corruption for which Russian officials had become notorious, and to create a comprehensive plan for administering the region.[93] The political and intellectual context in which Speranskii approached his job had changed enormously since the mid-eighteenth century, when Russia was one of three major powers trying to control Central Eurasia for economic and defensive reasons. The Zunghar state had been destroyed, but in the early nineteenth century its destroyer, the Qing Dynasty, had also begun to falter, losing economic ground to European mercantile outposts. Russia now found itself to be the strongest power in Central Eurasia. In the 1770s and 1780s not only did Enlightenment ideas begin to change the way educated Russians thought about themselves, but greater contact and identification with Europe changed how they thought about the Siberian and Central Asia peoples. Internally, Russians no longer saw Eurasian peoples as occasionally difficult trade partners, but as distinctly inferior communities that needed to be assimilated into the empire. Externally, Russians became acutely aware of how Europeans perceived them, which made questions of international prestige more pressing than they had been earlier. Furthermore, the dawn of the revolutionary age in the British American colonies, Haiti, and Latin America showed all the European powers that colonies took a lot of work to hold on to. As Speranskii prepared to leave for Siberia, several of his friends sent him copies of a new book on colonialism—itself a new idea—that argued that imperial centers needed to treat their colonies as extensions of themselves, granting equal political, legal, and economic rights. Otherwise, they invited independence movements.[94] That the Russian government now compared itself directly to the British and Spanish empires shows how much its self-perception had shifted.

Russian officials were encouraging Slavic peasants to settle in western Siberia, but these small outposts did not generate enough revenue to threaten the primacy of the imperial center. What Speranskii saw a great need for was a systematic way to define and regulate the relations of the Russian and non-Russian communities to each other and to the state. This did not require that non-Russians had to abandon their own customs; Speranskii revived the Catherinian project of surveying and compiling Kazakh laws, although this work did not begin until after he issued his code in 1822.[95] The sub-section "Rules on the Siberian Kirgiz" was aimed at the Kazakh Middle Horde, which was still maneuvering between Russian and Qing overlords; the Junior Horde had no rival power to turn to and so was not of immediate concern. Speranskii simultaneously drew the Kazakhs into the Russian system and placed them in a separate legal category from settled Christians. The code abolished the khanate, reorganizing the Middle Horde's territory along Russian administrative lines into defined villages (*auly*), townships (*volosti*), and districts (*okrugi*). Each volost elected a sultan and each okrug elected a "senior sultan" with a board (*prikaz*) that included two Russian assessors, an appointed chief officer, and two elected "honorable" Kazakh representatives.[96] Sultans were granted access to the Table of Ranks, Peter the Great's system that tied elite status to service to the state. If a senior sultan served long enough, he could in principle become a member of the Russian nobility without converting to Christianity, a sharp break from the past.[97] A few Kazakh okrugs asked to have their senior sultans granted the title of "khan" and were turned down, but there was no widespread protest against the abolition of khan-ship. This may have been partly due to exhaustion from decades of multiple and ineffective khans. Another factor in the Kazakhs' general acceptance of this change was that the sultans were still Chinggisids elected by Kazakh aristocracy.[98] Speranskii's gradualist approach allowed the Kazakhs to retain their core political values, which mitigated—although it certainly did not end—resentment of the undeniable reality of Russian rule.

The Russian government was not yet prepared to integrate non-Christians, much less nomads, on an equal footing with Christian subjects. The most significant result of Speranskii's Siberian code was the creation of a new category of imperial subject, the *inorodets* (alien). In Kievan Rus' and Muscovy the key communal boundary marker was religion: only Orthodox Christians were true subjects of the tsar. This was the case even if they had been born Muslim Tatars and converted for the sake of social advancement. As Russia expanded eastward the cultural gulf between Russians and the northern Siberian peoples grew too big to be bridged by religious conversion. Siberians who became Orthodox were relieved of paying fur tribute but were also marked out by the label inorodets.[99] Originally the term was reserved for Siberian herders and hunter-gatherers, but in 1822 it was not a large stretch to add Kazakh and Bashkir nomads to the category. Nomadic *inorodtsy* (aliens) paid the traditional tribute taxes and were directly governed by their own leaders, although Russian officials wielded the ultimate authority over law and governance. Inorodtsy were not subject to military conscription, which spared them from fundamental conflicts during Russia's wars with the Ottoman Empire, but also barred them from one of the great engines of cultural assimilation and advancement. Small numbers of aristocratic Kazakhs continued to serve as military officers, however. By folding the Kazakhs into the Russian administrative system and putting them in a separate legal category from that which regulated the Orthodox population, Speranskii was able to rationalize the Kazakhs' place in the empire while avoiding the danger of creating a colony that might one day demand independence. The imposition of Russian rule in Central Asia began as a negotiated process, but Russia was always in the stronger position.

SUMMARY

The balance of power between Russia and the Central Asian polities tipped toward Russia during the seventeenth century. The three Kazakh hordes found their territories being steadily encroached upon by Russian Siberia in the north, the Mongol Zunghar state in the east, and the Uzbeks in the south. Under this pressure the hordes split into three separate khanates, which weakened them further. The two Uzbek khanates of Khiva and Bukhara combined high levels of artistic and scholarly achievement with near-continuous civil wars that impoverished and fragmented them. Both khanates lost territory, saw dynasties collapse, and were reduced to asking Russian envoys for "presents," sometimes in return for Slavic slaves, sometimes not. As it had with the western khanates, Russia made itself a distant but essential political broker that could command respectful symbolic gestures from the khans. Geographic circumstances made Russia's influence over the Kazakhs much stronger than it was over the Uzbeks. The Uzbeks were not nearly as badly damaged by the Zunghars as the Kazakhs were, and the Uzbeks had an independent source of wealth from their lively trade with India.

Peter the Great declared Russia to be an empire in 1721, but while he was keenly interested in finding a river route to India he did not have serious plans to add Central Asia to that empire. Instead, Russians were drawn by the logic of past decisions into expanding their fortress line to protect the fur trade, making formal border agreements with Qing China and establishing friendly relations with the Zunghars, and so getting entangled in the Kazakh–Zunghar–Qing struggle over control of the eastern steppe. The khans of the Junior and Middle hordes played their larger neighbors off against each other, but Russia was the closest and the strongest power. The Junior Horde pledged allegiance to Empress Anna in 1730, but Abulkhayr Khan was acting out of opportunism and the majority of Kazakhs resented even the pretense of giving up their independence. The Kazakhs found their physical territory and space for political action shrinking as a result of their requests for Russian protection; even the Qing destruction of their old Zunghar enemy did not create an opportunity for real independence. For their part, Russian regional governors wanted greater control over the Kazakhs but were not sure how to achieve it. Attempts in the late eighteenth century to pit khans against aristocracy and split the hordes further weakened the Kazakhs but did not lead to stability and order. Finally in 1822 Russia took the first formal steps toward incorporating the Kazakh Middle Horde into its government. This action set a new train of logical consequences in motion, leading Russia deeper into Central Asia.

Chapter 3

CONQUEST

Why did Russia conquer Central Asia? There is no single, straightforward answer to this question. Russia had enmeshed the Kazakhs within fortress lines and legal regulations by the early 1820s, but still the Kazakhs struggled to preserve their independence and lifeways as much as possible. No tsar or group of ministers made systematic plans to add the Kazakh steppes to the empire, and the government conducted relations with Kazakh leaders through the Foreign Ministry well into the nineteenth century. The process of asserting control over the steppe created its own logic, each action promising but failing to deliver a sense of security, leading to a new action that might finally fulfill its promise. The conquest of the Uzbek khanates by a series of military campaigns unfolded according to several different logical chains, which were not always compatible with each other. A companion question, "How did Russia conquer Central Asia?" also requires a multi-layered answer. Kazakh and Kyrgyz tribes suffered from theft and abuse by fortress commanders and Slavic settlers, but for them conquest was a slow and uncertain process. In the Uzbek khanates people's experiences varied widely: central Bukhara saw no fighting, while Kokand and the Turkmen tribes suffered appalling brutality at the hands of the Cossacks. How Central Asians experienced conquest strongly affected how they responded to Russian rule once it was firmly established.

SETTLED CULTURES: THE UZBEKS AND TAJIKS

In the early nineteenth century three Uzbek khanates governed Transoxiana: Khiva under the Qongrat Dynasty, Bukhara under the Manghit Dynasty, and Kokand, established as a khanate by Alim Khan (r. 1799–1811) of the Ming Uzbek tribe. None of these polities was monocultural; they all contained nomadic and settled populations. The new Qongrat government, established in 1804, staged military campaigns for decades against its neighbors, increasing the size and wealth of the khanate. This resulted in bringing Turkmen, Karakalpak, Kazakh, and independent Uzbek tribes under Khiva's rule. Turkmen made up a large part of the Khivan cavalry, and Muhammad Rahim Khan (r. 1806–26) forcibly relocated Karakalpak tribes from their lands east of the Aral Sea to farm closer to the town of Khiva.[1] The Manghit emirs of Bukhara also significantly expanded their territory south to Merv and east into the mountains of what is today Tajikistan. These conquests, some of which Bukhara had a very tenuous hold on, gave the emirate a highly mixed population of Turki- and Farsi-speaking town-dwellers, nomadic and semi-nomadic Uzbek and Turkmen tribes, Kazakhs in the north, and small communities that identified as Arabs or Jews. The new Khanate of Kokand contained Uzbek, Kyrgyz, Tajik, and Kazakh populations.

The idea of nationalism that was developing in Europe at the time with such empire-shattering consequences had not yet reached Central Asia. People would identify themselves to outside observers most readily by the markers of religion, tribe, where they lived or what their occupation was, but the ethnonyms "Uzbek" or "Tajik" were seldom used.[2] Among the elite Sufi *khoja* families sacred genealogy defined identity and access to economic and political resources.[3] In the towns Turki-Farsi bilingualism was common, along with an ethnonym that would drive later Soviet theorists to distraction, "Sart." Sart derived from the Sanskrit *sârthavâha* (caravan leader), an echo of ancient Silk Road trade.[4] By the nineteenth century it had acquired a broad meaning of town-dwelling merchants or settled people in general, with little regard for language or ancestry. That the term Sart crossed borders of ethnicity and class, central to Soviet Marxist thought, foreshadows the gap between the mental worlds of Central Asians and Russian communists.

The common use of the name Sart reminds us that trade was central to the economies of all the Uzbek khanates. Hindus and Muslims from India had been trading with Bukhara for so many centuries that they had their own permanent caravanserais to live in, where they could protect each other's goods and live according to their own laws.[5] By the 1830s Kokand had made itself an important node for trade between China and Russia, attracting not only goods but also a significant number of people, especially from Bukhara and Samarkand. Kokand's ties with Qing China allowed it to cut into the eastern trade of the Kazakh Senior Horde, at a time when Russian authorities were also limiting Kazakh trade with China for Russia's benefit.[6] Khiva was surrounded by stark desert plateaus that travelers preferred to avoid, but the Qongrat khans countered this by protecting caravans from nomad raids and Bukharan predation. The Bukharan and Khivan rulers recognized mutual benefit in protecting trade routes that ran from Russia through their lands to Afghanistan and beyond, even if they could not always control their subjects. In 1821 Bukharan Uzbeks complained bitterly to the Russian military geographer Egor Meiendorf that Emir Haidar had forbidden them to avenge Khivan caravan raids: "It shames us that we allow such to insult us. We are warriors, we are bold, we have superior horses, if the khan would let us take revenge on those who attack us, we would beat them, destroy the Khivans or take them captive, as we did about ten years ago...."[7] The Qongrats also centralized their administration enough to start collecting steady tax revenue from merchants. Muhammad Rahim Khan founded a mint that struck enough silver and gold coins to allow a sophisticated "venture capital" lending system to develop by the mid-nineteenth century.[8] Khiva thrived economically until the Russian conquest, despite the perpetual state of war in the region.

The majority of Central Asians, like the majority of common people everywhere, were farmers. Irrigation was essential to making agriculture prosper in a desert environment. Two thousand years ago the Iranian-speaking peoples of the region built above-ground canals and sophisticated under-ground irrigation channels called *qanats* or *karez*.[9] When they were not engaged in warfare or hunting, the rulers of Khiva, Bukhara, and Kokand put significant resources into building canal networks in the newly conquered territories, which persuaded some of the nomadic communities to settle and farm for part of the year.[10] Meiendorf estimated in 1820 that Bukhara had a population of approximately 2.5 million people, of whom one million were nomadic or semi-nomadic.[11] Naturally, the khans did not do the hard labor of digging the canals themselves, but levied local villagers to do it. The irrigated lands produced the melons, apricots, grapes, and other fruits that homesick Mughal emperors had imported to India for centuries. The intrepid traveler Arminus Vambery noted, "it is incredible how fertile all the cultivable land is in these three khanats [sic]."[12] He reported an abundance of grain crops everywhere, particularly wheat, barley, sorghum, millet, and rice. Cotton was grown in some areas—Bukhara had a special cotton tax—but the local variety was not as valuable as the finer and whiter Indian cottons.[13] The other important commercial crop was mulberry trees, whose leaves provided food for silkworms. Brightly dyed silk *atlas* and other silk textiles were both exported and used for special-occasion clothing.

Islamic institutions provided the foundations of law, education, and social morality in the khanates. The madrasas of Bukhara were respected throughout the Middle East and India. Their graduates served as judges, scholars, teachers, and guardians of public morality. The *rais* (chief) was notorious among European observers for enforcing proper dress and behavior with his cudgel; the *zakatchi* was charged with collecting *zakat* (the obligatory charitable tithe) in the form of a tax on movable property. There were courts charged with appointing guardians to protect orphans and their inheritances, although orphans had no formal recourse if their guardians were neglectful. Because the Manghit emirs were not Chinggisids, they emphasized their close connections with the *ulama* (scholars) to strengthen their legitimacy. This reliance gave the ulama considerable political power until the Russian conquest.[14] Even so, Bukharans found ways to evade the morality police. Meiendorf, who spoke Turki and Farsi, reported that drinking alcohol in secret was not uncommon, although no one would dare to been seen drunk in the street. Prostitution was punishable by death but never fully eradicated. And in a society that rigorously segregated the sexes, homosexual relations were a common substitute:

> One young Bukharan from a good family, when I asked what he did
> for entertainment, told me that he gives feasts where slaves play musical
> instruments, goes hunting, and finally, that he has *juvoni*, or [young male]
> lovers. I was surprised at the calmness with which he pronounced this word,
> which testified to how accustomed they are here to this most shameful vice.[15]

Women

Most children, girls as well as boys, received their education in the *maktab*, a five-year school that taught rote memorization of the alphabet, key prayers in Arabic, and poetry in Turki and Farsi (see Figure 3.1). The teachers in these schools were local mullas or female religious teachers called *otin* or *khalfa*, whose own level of education was often not far above that of the children

FIGURE 3.1 Children at a maktab. Source: Library of Congress, Prints & Photographs Division, LC-DIG-ppmsca-09951-00194 (digital file from Part 2, vol. 1, pl. 67, no. 194), from *Turkestanskii Al'bom*.

they taught. Later Russian educators and Turkestani graduates of these schools harshly criticized the primitive learning they delivered, although the children of farmers and merchants did not need advanced literacy to fulfill their social roles. There were exceptional pockets of literary creativity, of which the most unexpected was a group of women poets in the Khanate of Kokand. Mohlar-aiim, known by her pen-name Nodira (1792–1842), was the daughter of the *hokim* (governor) of Andjian and wife of Umar Khan (r. 1811–22). When Umar Khan died, she advised her fourteen-year-old son Muhammad Ali Khan (r. 1822–42) during the economic and political high point of the khanate. Nodira wrote hundreds of poems in Turki and Farsi about love and mystical spirituality, supported the Naqshbandi brotherhood, and sponsored mosque-building and other pious works. Her court included a woman named Uvaisii (c. 1779–1845), who also left books of poems. Nodira was executed during an attack by Bukharan emir Nasrulla in 1842.[16]

Nodira's activities were well within the bounds of proper behavior for a woman of her station. Literary circles where elite women wrote and sang poetry for each other were common throughout the larger Iranian cultural sphere, which included Transoxiana. Royal women could and did exercise power via their male relatives. In a seventeenth-century example, the daughter-in-law of Bukharan khan Subhan Quli (r. 1681–1702) had the authority to send a unit of musketeers to quell a fight between rival Sufi groups.[17] In the Khanate of Khiva elite women engaged in money lending for profit through their control of charitable endowments (waqfs).

More unusual was the career of Dilshod, who not only wrote poetry but ran a school for girls. Dilshod was born to an ordinary family in the town of Ura Tepe (today Istaravshan in Tajikistan), which was in the frontier zone contested between Bukhara and Kokand. She was taken prisoner in a Kokandi attack in 1818. Near the end of her extraordinarily long life (1800–1905) she wrote a memoir, *Tarixi muhojiron* ("History of the Displaced"), in which she recounts the attack and her march on foot (with some 1200 other prisoners) to a barren settlement near Andijan. She was taken to the palace as a potential concubine for the khan, but instead of charming him recited a defiant poem. He threw her out onto the streets, where she was taken in by a Sufi lodge and settled with an otin. This woman helped Dilshod learn Turki (at the time she spoke only Farsi) and employed her in the girls' maktab. Dilshod married the woman's son, who was much older than she was, and took over the school when her patron died in 1837.[18] Dilshod taught for fifty-one years, counting among her pupils the notable poet Anbar-oi: "My close friends and confidants were intelligent girl poets. There were always 20 or 30 girls getting an education, from average to superior students. 891 girls became literate, of whom close to one-quarter had a talent for poetry; they were smart girls."[19] Dilshod was part of a community of female poets that was large enough she never met her contemporaries Nodira and Uvaisii face-to-face, although she refers to them in her poetry. Her account serves as a warning that we should not accept later modernizers' dismal descriptions of schools as the whole story.

The lives of settled women were more restricted than those of nomadic women, but the nature of those restrictions was strongly influenced by social class. Women in wealthy families never went out in public on their own. If they needed something, lower-class female merchants would come to them. Keeping one or more wives who did not need to work was a symbol of high status for wealthy men. When upper-class women did venture out to visit friends, they covered their hair with a long-sleeved cloak (*paranji*) and their faces with a long, black horsehair veil (*chachvon*), although it is not certain that women in all areas wore the chachvon before the Russian conquest. Lower-status young girls could run and play uncovered in public, and women could earn income through weaving or raising silkworms. Village women, like their nomadic counterparts, dressed modestly but practically as they worked their fields.[20] Matters of dress aside, women had no independent basis for power. Marriage at a young age was universal and women could initiate divorce only under rare circumstances. People survived as part of family groups, whether happily or unhappily; only the poorest lived on their own. If a woman lived in a family that respected her, all well and good, but if her husband beat her or her in-laws treated her like a slave, she had no recourse.

RUSSIA ENGULFS THE KAZAKHS

You ran and were caught in a trap set by the Russians,
Our brave men, who were born with a strong will,
Raised livestock and slept peacefully,
Are now in the hardship of captivity!

—Shortanbay Qanayuli[21]

During the first half of the nineteenth century the forces surrounding the Kazakh hordes crushed what was left of their independence (see Map 3.1). From the south, the khans of Khiva and Kokand captured land and thousands of people with no effective resistance from the fragmented Kazakh leadership. Kokand, under khans Alim (r. 1800–11) and his brother and successor Umar, seized the Syr Darya basin from Tashkent to the town of Yasi/Turkestan from the Middle Horde, and took considerable territory from the Senior Horde up to the Ili River valley.[22] Khiva conquered Junior Horde territory around the Aral Sea. Many people fled the Junior and Middle Hordes for Bukhara, where the emir took them in as subjects. The Senior Horde concluded a military alliance with Bukhara, which promptly fell apart when Emir Haidar (r. 1800–26) refused to help the Kazakhs against Khiva. In retaliation, Senior Horde raiders attacked Bukharan trade caravans while, in contrast, the Junior Horde had agreed to protect caravans going through their territory to Orenburg.[23]

The disorder strengthened Russian officials' conviction that the Kazakhs needed their protection and control. After ninety years of incremental moves, Russia rapidly expanded its legal and military reach into the steppe. In 1822 Mikhail Speranskii's "Rules on the Siberian Kirgiz"[24] abolished the Middle Horde khanate, divided the horde's lands into Russian administrative districts under the governor-general of Western Siberia, and enrolled Kazakh sultans

MAP 3.1 Central Asia, mid-nineteenth century.

in the Russian bureaucracy, while simultaneously creating a separate legal category for non-Christian nomads, the inorodtsy or aliens. In 1824 the Russian government issued "Rules for the Orenburg Kirgiz," which abolished the Junior Horde khanate and reorganized its lands along tribal lines into three regions, each governed by a Chinggisid sultan in Russia's pay. Re-naming the hordes rhetorically erased their independent identities and gave them new identities that existed only in relation to Russian power.[25] In 1845 the Bukey Khanate was broken up, and the following year half a dozen Senior Horde tribes pledged loyalty to Emperor Nicholas I (r. 1825–55). The Russians abolished the Senior Horde khanate in 1848.[26] The emperor did not rush to annex the Kazakhs formally, however. Russia still dealt with the Kazakhs through the Ministry of Foreign Affairs and military governors-general, not the Ministry of the Interior that governed Russia proper.

Thickening the network of fortresses and the Cossacks that garrisoned them was key to breaking Kazakh autonomy. The ultimate freedom of the nomad was the freedom to move, but open Kazakh lands were being hemmed in from all directions. In 1824 alone Russia built four forts across the northern Kazakh steppe, including Akmolinsk, the site of Astana, today's capital of Kazakhstan. In 1831 Russia established its first outpost in Senior Horde lands, at Ayaguz (Sergiopol') northeast of Lake Balkhash. In 1839–40 General V.A. Perovskii led a poorly planned attack from Orenburg against Khiva, which got stuck in deep snow; half of Perovskii's men and camels froze to death.[27] This disaster impelled Russia to build three forts in a line connecting the Caspian and Aral seas in the mid-1840s. The fortified lines blocked grazing paths for the herds, forcing Kazakhs to buy fodder from Russians or settle part-time and grow their own. With the forts came Cossacks, who were given exclusive fishing rights in the rivers and large tracts of land as theirs to farm. Some 14,000 Cossack fighters and their families settled in Middle Horde lands on the west bank of the Irtysh River just in 1847.[28] Cossacks themselves disdained farming as low-status work that they preferred to avoid. They impressed the local Kazakhs, who now farmed for others land that had recently belonged to them.[29]

These increasing pressures damaged the Kazakhs without delivering the level of control that Russian officials wanted. The new administrative divisions of land into districts (okrugi), townships (volosti), and villages (auly) in some cases split tribes apart and in others forced tribes that regarded each other as enemies to govern together. Where relations were peaceful the tribes began to merge, but in numerous cases tribal leaders refused to relocate or left their assigned territory rather than live with their enemies. Tribes simply ignored orders forbidding them from moving between districts.[30] Resistance worked only up to a certain point, however. By the 1860s new tribal configurations had undermined the authority of the hereditary sultans, and they were mostly replaced by non-Chinggisid leaders. On the Russian side, the Orenburg Frontier Commission, which was under the Ministry of Foreign Affairs but also acted as an arm of the Orenburg governors-general, in 1841 complained: "in the depths of the steppe, where the orders and power of the authorities have not yet been realized, the Kirgiz [Kazakhs] live in almost complete anarchy and therefore they have many opportunities to carry out predation and villainy."[31] This tells us more about the attitude of the Frontier Commission than it does about the Kazakhs: that the absence of Russian rule equaled anarchy, and that Kazakh resistance to losing their lands was "villainy."

The Orenburg authorities also failed to control local Russian officials and the Cossacks, who outrageously abused Kazakh communities by over-taxing, stealing and slaughtering their animals, and beating the people, sometimes to death.[32] Violence was also a government tool. The deep steppe may have been out of Russian reach, but near the fortress lines the military forced back Kazakh groups that tried to migrate to pastures now forbidden to them. The result was sometimes starvation of herds and people.[33] Impoverishment and abuse, unsurprisingly, led to a number of armed uprisings. The largest of these was by Kenesari Qasim-uli, who spent ten years fighting to restore the Middle Horde khanate and drive Russian settlers out. Partly because he was a grandson of Ablai Khan, ruler of the Middle Horde in the 1770s, Kenesari gained broader Kazakh support than had other rebel leaders. On the other hand, he fought against opposing Kazakh tribes almost as much as he did against the Russians. The bitter rivalries among dozens of sultans and their tribes were a major reason that relatively few Russians could dominate such a huge expanse of land. In 1844 Orenburg sent regular troops against Kenesari, and he fled east to the Kyrgyz. He tried to impose himself on them as a sultan, but they rejected and killed him in 1847.[34] A Kyrgyz historical poem about Kenesari vividly conveys their contempt:

Many were the invading Qazaqs, and the princes died in numbers proportional to them. Ormon Khan's trumpets dispersed a number of them early in the fight: what business did the Qazaqs have attacking the Kirghiz if they were frightened by trumpets?! The prince named Seren got a harsh punishment from the Kirghiz when Jantay Baatır got in close and bloodied his lance on him. The Tınay easily captured those princes who invaded with airs of bravery, brought them under restraint to their camp, and cruelly disgraced them: the women killed them, at their ease, one by one. The princes' marrow-bones availed them nothing! Their corpses ended up together on the hill Tekeldirik. The women they had brought along to tend the lambs fell to the Kirghiz in marriage, and dogs ate the [men's] corpses. Why ever did they show contempt for the Kirghiz? ... To hell with such a prince who opposes the Muslims![35]

In the 1830s the Frontier Commission head General G.F. Gens added administrative units called *distantsii* to the system of auls, townships, and districts. Gens charged *distantsiia* chiefs with keeping both the local Russian commandants (*nachal'niki*) and the Kazakhs on their best behavior. Each distantsiia chief had the authority to collect tax payments, enforce ordinances, and expel anyone who did not obey him. On paper, his authority was subordinate to that of the local Kazakh sultan's, but since he reported directly to the head of the Frontier Commission and the Orenburg military governor he had much stronger political backing. This cumbersome system added yet another layer to the bureaucracy, but it enabled Gens to strengthen state control throughout the Kazakh steppe.[36] In 1844 Russia's reach was further extended with a statute that stripped Kazakh traditional (bii) courts of their authority over serious criminal cases and subjected Kazakhs to Russian military courts, which affronted even loyal sultans.[37] In a piecemeal fashion that frequently aggravated Kazakh-Russian tensions, the empire engulfed the Kazakhs.

CHANGE IN THE AIR

One of the factors that made Russian control over the Kazakh hordes difficult was that Kazakhs could find shelter in the Uzbek khanates. This was not because Uzbek rulers were sympathetic to them, but because they sought to use fighters like Kenesari against their rivals.[38] In the mid-nineteenth century the rulers of Bukhara, Kokand, and Khiva were focused first on containing internal enemies and second on attacking each other. Bukhara in the 1820s was torn effectively in two by the rebellion of two Uzbek tribes, the Qitay/Khitay and the Qipchaq. Emir Nasrulla (r. 1826–60) (see Figure 3.2) spent thirty years fighting to regain control over the important town of Shahrisabz, east of Samarkand.[39] In addition he destroyed his rival brothers and attacked Kokand several times, briefly occupying it in 1842—this was when he ordered the poet Nodira and her son the khan to be executed. No sooner had Nasrulla been thrown out of Kokand by a popular uprising when he turned and attacked Khiva, which crushed his army in 1843. He also earned a reputation as a sadistic tyrant whose spies terrorized his subjects.[40] Kokand suffered from internal divisions as well: Nasrulla invaded in part because he was invited to by opponents of Muhammad Ali Khan, who were angered by the high tax burden he imposed and by his egregious violations of moral standards. The khan openly gambled, drank, and worst of all married his father's youngest

FIGURE 3.2 Emir Nasrulla of Bukhara. Source: Nikolai V. Khanykov, *Opisanie Bukharskogo Khanstva* (St. Petersburg: Imp. Akademii Nauk, 1843), between p. 224 and p. 225.

wife, which counted as incest according to Islamic law.[41] Kyrgyz and Kazakh nomads who had only recently come under Kokand's rule eagerly sought opportunities to break away. Kokand never recovered from the Bukharan invasion. In 1844 Qipchaq Uzbeks from Ferghana seized power, to be expelled by the last Ming khan, Khudoyar, whose tumultuous career can be summed up in his dates of reign: 1844–58, 1862–63, and 1865–75.[42]

The Uzbek khanates had been in this self-perpetuating cycle since the seventeenth century. Rulers could not develop effective administrations because they could neither defeat each other nor agree on peaceful coexistence. Or perhaps it was the other way around: they could never achieve lasting victories because internal strife prevented them from properly organizing their governments and economies. Khiva seems to have been a partial exception, since the khanate did develop a solid economic administration, but as the smallest of the khanates it could not assert control over the region. Bukhara and Kokand continued to earn much of their income from international trade, but whereas in the eighteenth century Bukhara had exported its own textiles and dyes to Russia, maintaining a positive balance of trade, in the early nineteenth century Bukhara served more as an intermediary for textiles and dyes moving from India to Russia. By the mid-nineteenth century Kokand was losing importance as a trade thruway, as Russia shifted goods bound for China through the Siberian border town Kiakhta.[43]

The rulers and educated people of the Uzbek khanates were certainly aware of Russian territorial and economic advances, but they did not investigate the causes of the Kazakhs' fall, nor were they curious about the condition of Russia. In 1824 Muhammad Hakim Khan To'ra, a scholar from the ruling family of Kokand, began a seven-year journey through several Russian towns on his way to Iran and ultimately Mecca. When he wrote up his notes almost twenty years later he told his readers it would be bold to describe the thousand things he saw, but he would do it concisely. This is one of the very few travel accounts we have of a Central Asian observing exotic Russians, and it is as valuable for what he did not find notable as for what he did. Muhammad Hakim's trip started in the northern town of Semipalatinsk (today Semei, Kazakhstan). Semipalatinsk had been founded in 1718 on the Irtysh River, and by the early nineteenth century had become a multicultural fortress and trade center. In addition to the Russian Orthodox population, Tatars and Bukharans had built several mosques for the growing Muslim community.[44] Muhammad Hakim described a bustling commercial town where river boats regularly arrived from the direction of China, although he mistakenly thought the Irtysh flowed all the way to the Caspian Sea. Merchants who came from the Uzbek khanates sometimes married local Kazakh women; the resulting children were called "chala" or "unfinished" Kazakhs. Muhamad Hakim thought the people had the most open and cheerful disposition of any people in the world, except possibly "the boys of Shahrisabz."[45]

A visit from an Uzbek of Muhammad Hakim's high rank was unusual. The Russian governor at Omsk notified St. Petersburg, and then traveled to Semipalatinsk to see for himself. There the governor gave Muhammad Hakim a translator (who would also keep their guest under observation) and hospitality. Muhammad Hakim was impressed by the beautiful Orthodox church with its bells and onion domes, although he called it a *butxona*, an idol house. He saw a military drill with thousands of soldiers and horsemen parading on the central square in front of a large crowd of Muslim and non-Muslim (*kofir*, infidel) spectators. His visit coincided with a solemn Orthodox holiday, which led to a tense situation over clashing etiquette codes.

Muhammad Hakim was curious to observe the service, but the governor told him that Russian law forbade Muslims from entering a church. According to Muhammad Hakim, his translator and the assembled congregation of men and women were shocked and dismayed at this disrespectful treatment of such a great foreign visitor. Eventually he was allowed to stand at the door and look in. While as a Muslim he respected Jesus as a prophet, he was dismissive of the large amount of gold and gems decorating pictures of people (Orthodox icons), as though the images might actually speak. His minder told him "this is no place to smile," which Muhammad Hakim obeyed with difficulty.[46] The next day the governor made amends by paying a personal visit to him, which Muhammad Hakim felt showed the appropriate level of respect. They spent the next week in regular conversation, and then came the exciting news of a letter from Emperor Alexander i, who expressed a wish to meet Muhammad Hakim. Since Semipalatinsk could not accommodate a tsar, Muhammad Hakim traveled to Orenburg for their audience.

By 1824 Orenburg had become the commercial and military capital of western Siberia. Muhammad Hakim loved the city, admiring its "magnificent" governor's palace with its gleaming "foreign windows" and the extensive gardens and orchards the Russians had planted.[47] He noted that Orenburg was full of merchants from the Uzbek khanates, and developed a mad passion for a gorgeous Armenian girl. He enjoyed his meetings with Tsar Alexander (he had learned enough Russian to speak a little without the interpreter), but unfortunately could not tell his readers what they discussed, because Russian law banned recording such conversations. Even though Muhammad Hakim wrote his travelogue years after Alexander's death, in Persian, he obeyed the injunction. All he says is that "Many questions were asked about the position of Mawrannahr."[48] He apparently did not have any questions about the position of Russia.

Both the governor of Orenburg and the tsar himself invited Muhammad Hakim to come visit St. Petersburg, but he declined. He does not explain why, although his horror at touring a fetid prison with the tsar seems to have dampened his interest. In any case, the tsar gave him gifts and a letter declaring that he enjoyed the esteem of the Russian government, which guaranteed good treatment for the rest of his journey within the empire. Muhammad Hakim generally liked the Russians he met and admired their towns, but never suggested that Central Asians could learn anything from them. Despite the tsar's apparently close questioning about the Uzbek khanates, Muhammad Hakim saw no threat coming from Russia.

The Uzbek Khanates and the "Great Game"

The Uzbek rulers should also have noticed an increase in the number and kinds of European visitors they were getting. Whereas for centuries they had met with Russian merchants and diplomatic envoys, now their visitors were more likely to be military officers like Meiendorf, who frequently doubled as scientists gathering information on the ethnography and natural history of the region. Another significant change was that some of these officers were British. By the 1830s the British East India Company dominated in eastern India with considerable help from the British government. Both the British and the Russians were increasing their economic and political interference in Iran's weak state under the Qajar Dynasty. Some British officials were convinced that Russia intended somehow to damage their interests in India, and so military agents were sent to the Afghan capital Kabul and Bukhara to evaluate the possibilities for using these small polities as pawns to check the perceived Russian threat. In truth the Russians did not have the resources to challenge the East India Company, and they knew that. Some Russian officials liked the idea of scaring the British, but even that minor thrill led them to promise more aid to Afghanistan's Emir Dost Muhammad than they could actually deliver.[49] Meanwhile the British military agents wrote some stirring accounts of their adventures for the audience back home, but they did not offer anything to convince Emir Nasrulla to take sides in this European rivalry.[50] Arrogance and diplomatic blundering sent two of those agents to very a bad end, which sealed the image of Bukhara as a "blood-smeared part of the world" in the British imagination.[51] In 1838 the East India Company sent Colonel Charles Stoddart to Bukhara with vague instructions to make the emirate friendly to the British. Stoddart's boorish behavior instead insulted Nasrulla so much that the emir had him thrown into the "bug pit," an underground cell filled with ticks and other vermin; the prisoner's hands and feet would be tied so he couldn't defend himself.[52] Stoddart was released from the pit after a few days but not allowed to return to Calcutta. Three years passed, and the Company dispatched Captain Arthur Conolly to rescue Stoddart, who was under pressure to convert to Islam. Conolly traveled very badly disguised as a merchant, which aroused Bukharan suspicions because the British had recently invaded Afghanistan. The Bukharans arrested Conolly in December 1841, just as the Afghans organized a revolt to drive out the British. In January 1842 only one British survivor made it back to India, a brutal defeat that began the legend of Afghanistan as the "graveyard of empires."[53] The timing could not have been worse for the two hapless soldiers. Conolly and Stoddart represented a government that appeared both threatening and weak, and that furthermore had not treated Nasrulla with the respect due to him as emir. They were beheaded in March 1842 after they were caught trying to smuggle letters to India.[54] The incident would have sunk into obscurity were it not for the campaign of a highly eccentric and self-dramatizing British clergyman, Joseph Wolff, to travel to Bukhara in 1843 and rescue these brave sons of Albion or at least learn what had happened to them. Wolff had briefly visited Bukhara in the early 1820s, and used his background to raise funds and publicity, mostly for himself. His published account is not without value, as he had some facility with the local languages and a basic understanding of the khanates' politics. Mostly, however, he laid the foundation for the myth of an unfathomably cruel Central Asia that was in dire need of the civilizing hand of a Christian empire.[55]

MILITARY CONQUEST

The Russian military conquest of the Uzbek khanates unfolded in stages over thirty years. A gradual advance eastward along the Syr Darya began in 1853 with the capture of Aq Masjid (White Mosque, re-named Perovsk) from the Kazakhs. As Kokand weakened, Russia seized land between the Chu and Talas rivers, founding Fort Vernoe (now Almaty, Kazakhstan) in 1854. As with Muscovy's expansion across Siberia during the Time of Troubles, Russia's entanglement in the Crimean War (1853–56) against the Ottoman Empire, Great Britain, and France, slowed but did not stop their advance. The conquest really got rolling during the reign of Emperor Alexander II (r. 1855–81). Commanders extended the fortress line that ran from Semipalatinsk south to Vernoe by taking over a Kokandi fort in 1860 on the site of today's Bishkek, Kyrgyzstan. In 1864 Colonel Mikhail G. Cherniaev resumed the conquest along the Syr Darya, taking the towns of Yasi/Turkestan and Shymkent; this connected the Syr Darya and Semipalatinsk fortress lines. Cherniaev captured Tashkent from Kokand in June 1865, which brought the last of the former Kazakh lands under Russian control. In 1866 and 1867 the army moved south from Tashkent and took some of the mountainous territory of eastern Bukhara. By June 1868 Emir Muzzafar (r. 1860–85) had been forced to surrender most of his lands. The Russians left him ruling over a rump emirate that was entirely dependent on their good will. Five years later it was Khiva's turn: despite Muhammad Rahim Khan II's (r. 1865–1910) efforts to negotiate, Governor-General Konstantin P. von Kaufman reduced Khiva to a Russian protectorate. Finally in February 1876 Kaufman abolished the Khanate of Kokand. By 1884 Russia also controlled most Turkmen lands between Khiva and Iran.

The conquest, after 350 years of generally good relations, raises a number of questions: What motivated the Russians? Why couldn't the khanates mount an effective resistance? How did the Russians expect to incorporate such a robust and different cultural complex into their empire?

To begin with, each phase of the conquest had its own distinct motivations, which depended on the political and military circumstances of the time and the personal priorities of the men in charge. The first serious attempt to invade Khiva had occurred in 1839, in the context of Russian and British maneuvering to protect their economic interests in Qajar Iran and India, with Afghanistan caught in the middle. Russian officials in the foreign ministry and in Orenburg anxiously compared the Russian Empire to the British and French empires, and worried that if they did not assert their honor over "Asiatics" they would look second-rate in the eyes of Europe. Khiva and its Kazakh allies were still capturing Russian subjects and selling them into slavery, a practice that had been going on for centuries. Russia still enserfed the majority of its own population, and in the past had never made a major fuss over Slavic captives. However, in this new context of imperial competition, rescuing Christian slaves became a compelling justification for invasion. The French, the British, and even the new American republic took military action against North African kingdoms that captured their people; Russia would look weak if it did not do the same.

Another layer to this was the personal attitude of General Vasilii A. Perovskii, who greatly exaggerated the number of slaves Khiva held in his effort to convince the government to fund the 10,000 camels and soldiers needed for the campaign. Partly he seemed to be genuinely outraged at the plight of captive Slavs. He also, as his behavior during the disastrous invasion showed, felt insulted that "Asiatics" could dare to treat Christians with anything other than deference. This attitude had developed gradually as European ideas about racial hierarchy were introduced into Russia along with European sciences and higher education.[56] Whereas envoys from Muscovy had certainly disdained Central Asians as Muslim infidels, they respected the sovereignty of the khanates and the intelligence of their Uzbek and Kazakh counterparts. Perovskii, on the other hand, refused to take common sense advice from his Kazakh camel-drivers, leading thousands of men and animals to needless deaths. Instead he complained about how "Asiatics" lied and exaggerated the danger they were in as the entire column got trapped in a blizzard.[57] While many Russians still respected the Central Asians they encountered, as Muhammad Hakim's experience showed, a sense of racial superiority had been added to the traditional assumption of Christian superiority. This marked an important change in Russians' mental landscape. In Muscovy, a person could convert from Islam to Christianity and be fully accepted into society. Race in Imperial Russia, however, was regarded as a fundamental part of a person's nature even before the full development of biological theories of racial differences in the later nineteenth century. Nothing, even religious conversion, could now make an "Asiatic" equal to a Russian.

As Alexander II's reign began the Russian Empire lost significant international prestige, especially in comparison with Great Britain. Russia lost the Crimean War despite having the great advantage of fighting on its own territory, whereas the British and French had to transport men and supplies from 2000 miles away. A major reason for the loss was Russia's technological backwardness: the British built a railroad across the Crimean Peninsula to bring heavy artillery against the fortress at Sevastopol, while the Russians had no rail lines that extended that far south and had to transport their artillery by animal and human power. Great Britain formally incorporated all of India into its empire after the 1857 Indian Mutiny and was extending its economic dominance over Egypt, China, and parts of southeast Asia. Dost Muhammad wrote to Nasrulla in 1857 that he was sure both Afghanistan and Bukhara would become British colonial possessions in the near future.[58] These circumstances have given rise to an extensive literature on "the Great Game," a contest for the dominance of Eurasia between Great Britain and Russia. While some of this literature can make for a gripping read, as an explanation for the Russian conquest of Transoxiana the Great Game narrative falls short.[59]

The central problem with the Great Game story is that it is told almost entirely from the British point of view and does not take into consideration Russian strategic priorities or the actions of the Uzbek khanates.[60] Russia was so humiliated by its defeat in Crimea that Alexander II decided to undertake the fundamental economic and political reforms that Russian elites had known for decades were necessary, but were too afraid of the consequences to launch. The "Great Reforms" began with announcing the emancipation of the serfs and state-owned peasants in 1861, which freed approximately 78 per cent of the empire's population. The actual emancipation was phased in over several years, during which time peasant villages negotiated with their former owners for how much land they would receive instead of simply being given the land they had worked for centuries. The emancipation decrees continued to tie peasants to their villages, because the government feared the consequences of letting sixty million people move freely. The emancipation cost the government a large upfront payment to compensate serf owners for the loss of land, and set off significant unrest among peasants who were angry that they did not receive full and immediate freedom and were expected to pay "redemption dues" for forty-nine years to reimburse the government for the land payments. This hugely consequential reform was quickly followed by reforms that established trial by jury in criminal proceedings, abolished tax farming[61] by gentry vodka producers, set up elected boards for limited local governance, and modernized the military. The Great Reforms brought the Russian government close to being a fully modern, centralized state, although the social and national complexities of an empire that stretched from Poland to Alaska prevented the legal and tax systems from treating all subjects equally.[62] The point is that the Great Reforms soaked up the bulk of Russia's economic and political resources; even if some Russian officials enjoyed tweaking the British, no one seriously planned to attack India. They were, however, interested in securing their southern frontiers.

When Russian armies took control over the entire Syr Darya basin and then Tashkent, they were trying to solve a logistical problem caused by the fact that the existing fortress lines had been built on the ecological frontier between steppe and desert. Cossack settlers could not grow enough grain or trees to feed themselves or provide sufficient building materials; in 1861 it cost almost 1.3 million silver rubles to keep the forts supplied by camel caravan.[63] However, government officials could not agree on how to solve the problem. The governor of Orenburg argued that a new frontier in the well-watered lands further south would be cheaper and easier to maintain. The governor of Western Siberia at Omsk argued that new conquests would cost too much and yield too little, and that the empire would be better off developing the Siberian lands it already had. These disagreements reached into the highest levels of government, where Foreign Minister Alexander A. Gorchakov favored caution and War Minister Dmitri A. Miliutin argued strenuously for pushing the frontier to Tashkent. Some officials even urged the empire to pull its frontier back to where Russians were the majority population. Their opponents argued that if Russia retreated it would lose the money it had already invested and precious international prestige.[64] By 1864 Miliutin prevailed, partly on the grounds that a Russian Tashkent would indeed threaten British India, although given the distance and the mountains between Tashkent and Delhi the threat was symbolic.

From Tashkent to Bukhara

Why didn't the Russians stop there? Cherniaev's seizure of Tashkent unavoidably entangled Russia in the rivalry between Kokand and Bukhara, each of which had ruled the Tashkent region. In 1862–63 Kokand's internal wars flared up, giving Bukhara's Emir Muzzafar a chance to attack and place Khudoyar Khan on the throne as his vassal; the bargain was sealed by Khudoyar marrying one of Muzzafar's daughters.[65] A rival emir, Alim Qul, expelled Khudoyar and the Bukharans in July 1863, but died fighting the Russian advance in May 1865.[66] His death allowed Khudoyar to return to power with Bukharan help. In addition, a pro-Bukharan faction in Tashkent seems to have hoped that Russia would return the city to Bukharan control. However, Gorchakov preferred to make Tashkent an autonomous client khanate as a buffer between Russia and Bukhara. In July 1865 Emir Muzzafar sent an embassy to the tsar to negotiate the matter, but in a stunning change in diplomatic protocol the new governor of Orenburg, Nikolai A. Kryzhanovskii, arrested the embassy and insisted that Bukhara could only negotiate through Orenburg, not with the tsar directly. Given that the tsar had accepted a Bukharan embassy only six years before, Muzzafar must have felt this was a humiliating slap in the face. He responded by arresting a Russian embassy sent from Tashkent in October.[67] In January 1866 Cherniaev attacked the Bukharan town of Jizzax but had to retreat due to a lack of supplies. The Bukharans interpreted this as a sign of Russian weakness. Muzzafar marched his troops toward Tashkent, only to be crushed at Irjar by General Dmitri I. Romanovskii (who had replaced Cherniaev) in May. Romanovskii then proceeded to take Khujand, which cut off the direct connection between Bukhara and Kokand and prevented a coordinated resistance. In January 1868 Kaufman concluded a separate treaty with Kokand that gave Russian merchants free trade rights in the khanate and Kokandi merchants reciprocal rights in Turkestan. Because the Russian economy was so much larger, this in effect made Kokand Russia's economic vassal.[68]

Bukhara could not hope to win this game of tit for tat. The Bukharan armies were divided along regional and ethnic lines and their commanders did not always cooperate with each other. Even when faced with a foreign invasion, some tribes and towns within Bukhara continued to rebel against the emir. A few military units actually had professional training, courtesy of fugitives from the Russian army, but it was not sufficient.[69] They were also completely outgunned, pitting matchlocks and brass cannons against Russian rifles and rockets. The Bukharans' guns were so limited in power and accuracy that Russian soldiers could simply stay out of range while firing at will, which resulted in very lop-sided casualty rates.[70] Despite the enthusiasm of the ulama for declaring *jihad* (holy war) against the Russians, which Muzzafar did in April 1868, it was no surprise when he was forced to surrender in June. The 18 July 1868 peace treaty between Bukhara and Russia restored Muzzafar's sovereignty but deprived Bukhara of its second city, Samarkand. Muzzafar agreed to allow Russian merchants to conduct business in Bukhara on the same terms local merchants did, and to pay a war indemnity as compensation for Russia's expenses.[71] Technically this was a treaty between two independent states, but by controlling Samarkand Russia also controlled the Zerafshan River that was Bukhara's major water source. Bukhara now had very little room for independent action.

Whereas the conquest of the Syr Darya basin and Tashkent had been subject to debate and approval by the ministers in St. Petersburg, the Bukharan war was carried out by officers on the ground against Foreign Minister Gorchakov's explicit instructions. Displeased with Cherniaev's aggression, St. Petersburg recalled him in early 1866 and replaced him with Romanovskii, only to see Romanovskii attack Khujand. To be fair, the ministers' instructions could be ambiguous, both forbidding the acquisition of more territory and stating that "the Asiatic respects only armed force."[72] Romanovskii preferred to act rather than wait the necessary two months for clarified orders to arrive from the capital. In July 1867 Romanovskii was replaced by Kaufman, who would serve as the first governor-general of the new Russian *oblast* (province or district) called Turkestan.

The self-reinforcing logic of imperialism was more powerful than the will of ministers in determining the fate of Transoxiana. While even the hawkish War Minister Miliutin criticized the generals for disrupting the peace and stability they claimed to protect, once territory had been acquired Miliutin and Gorchakov agreed that retreat would be an intolerable insult to Russian dignity.[73] The ministers' conviction that any concession to "Asiatics," such as treating them with the respect due to sovereigns, would fatally compromise Russia's standing among the European powers gave the generals a free hand.

One result of the haphazard nature of the conquest was that plans for administering the new territories lagged well behind the Russian army. In early 1865 the government declared that the lands Cherniaev took from Kokand were now the Turkestan Oblast, under the governor-generalship of Orenburg. Tashkent was annexed to Turkestan in 1866. In 1867 Turkestan became a stand-alone oblast under Governor-General Kaufman. The "Temporary Statute for the Administration of Turkestan" divided Turkestan into two sub-regions (also called oblasts): the Syr Darya basin to the Aral Sea and Khiva; and Semirechie (seven rivers), the Kazakh and Kyrgyz territory between Lake Balkhash and Lake Issyk Kul. In 1868 Kaufman added the Zerafshan okrug when he took Samarkand from Bukhara. Tashkent became the administrative capital of Turkestan. The new oblast brought Uzbeks, Kazakhs, and Kyrgyz, who had all lived in separate polities, together under Russian governance. Because Turkestan was so little understood and so far away, St. Petersburg gave Kaufman more independent power than the governors-general of Orenburg or Siberia enjoyed. He could organize his administration as he saw fit, declare war against the khanates and conclude agreements with them, and assess local fiscal resources and decide how to tax and use them.[74] The people of Transoxiana took to calling him "Yarim Podshoh," the Half-Emperor.

Crushing Khiva and the Turkmen

Muhammad Rahim Khan II of Khiva now faced a serious military threat from Turkestan to his east and new encroachments to his west. Russia had completed its conquest of the North Caucasus in 1859, after decades of grinding guerilla warfare. In November 1869 a military expedition crossed the Caspian Sea from Daghestan to establish a new fortress-trading port called Krasnovodsk (today Turkmenboshi in Turkmenistan) about 200 miles west of the khanate. The port allowed goods from Transoxiana and points south to ship directly to the Volga River, by-passing the long and dangerous caravan routes from Khiva to Orenburg.[75] This cut into Khiva's income and into the livelihoods of the Turkmen tribes that had either protected or raided the caravans. Muhammad Rahim had learned from watching Bukhara's defeat, and repeatedly tried to send embassies to the tsar to negotiate peaceful terms while also asserting his sovereignty. He released the Russian captives in Khiva to deprive Russia of its main justification for war. Kaufman had no interest in accommodating Khiva, however, even though he could have gotten substantial concessions without a military invasion. In this case the reasons for conquest were a combination of the logic of imperialism and personal ambition. Kaufman refused to allow Muhammad Rahim to negotiate directly with the tsar, just as Kryzhanovskii had downgraded Bukhara's diplomatic status. The khan responded in kind, communicating with Kaufman only through his viziers rather than directly. The Russians had made a minor cult of the failed expeditions of Perovskii and Bekovich-Cherkasskii, and wanted revenge. Turkmen raids, which Khiva could not control, were a continuing threat. Kaufman, although he supported the creation of Krasnovodsk, was annoyed that his rival from the Caucasus command got the credit for it and wanted further opportunities for glory for himself.[76]

In December 1872, after many complaints from Kaufman about the "insolence" of Khiva and the threats it posed to Russian merchants, Alexander II agreed to allow a military expedition to punish the khanate, with the proviso that Kaufman must then withdraw.[77] In the spring Kaufman led an elaborate invasion of four columns, comprised of over 12,000 men and tens of thousands of camels and horses, that attacked Khiva from three directions (the column from Krasnovodsk got stuck in the desert and was forced to turn back). The Uzbek Khivans offered minimal resistance, to the great disappointment of some Russian officers who had looked forward to a good fight.[78] The Turkmen in contrast fought ferociously, and inflicted most of the battle damage Russians suffered. On 14 June Muhammad Rahim surrendered in person to Kaufman, who required him to govern under the control of a Russian-led *divan* (council) for the ten weeks of direct occupation. Kaufman treated Khiva as his personal prize, shipping the khan's throne to Moscow as a trophy for the Armory and his library to St. Petersburg. On 12 August 1873 Muhammad Rahim was forced to sign a much more onerous peace treaty than Muzzafar had agreed to five years before. Whereas Bukhara was legally—if not in reality—still an independent state, Khiva became a legal protectorate of the Russian Empire, the khan acknowledging that he was the "obedient servant" of the tsar. Disobeying the tsar's instructions, Kaufman seized all of the Qyzyl Qum desert from the Syr Darya to the Amu Darya delta and built Fort Petroalexandrovsk (today's Turtkul, in Uzbekistan) 40 miles east of Khiva. Khiva had to grant Russia control over navigation on the Amu Darya and extensive privileges to Russian merchants. The khan abolished slavery and agreed to pay Russia a war indemnity of 2.2 million rubles over the course of twenty years.[79] These terms destroyed the bases of Khiva's economy, but the subjugation of Khiva did nothing to restrain the Turkmen.

For reasons that seem to have been a mix of real security concerns and a desire to give more Russian officers a chance at battle glory, Kaufman created a pretext to attack the Turkmen in July. He imposed an impossible indemnity of 600,000 rubles on all of Khiva's Turkmen tribes, half of it to be paid by the Yomut, and gave them two weeks to deliver. Kaufman's generals did not think further fighting was a good idea, but obeyed when Kaufman ordered them to destroy the Yomut. The campaign was witnessed by American journalist Januarius MacGahan, who had been embedded with Kaufman's troops since May on behalf of the *New York Herald* newspaper. MacGahan spared nothing in describing the sort of "glory" Cossack units earned for themselves against the Yomut:

> This was war such as I had never before seen, and such as is rarely seen in modern days.... I follow down to the marsh, passing two or three dead bodies on the way. In the marsh are twenty or thirty women and children, up to their necks in water, trying to hide among the weeds and grass, begging for their lives, and screaming in the most pitiful manner. The Cossacks have already passed, paying no attention to them. One villainous-looking brute, however, had dropped out of the ranks, and levelling his piece as he sat on his horse, deliberately took aim at the screaming group, and before I could stop him pulled the trigger. Fortunately, the gun missed fire, and before he could renew the cap, I rode up, and cutting him across the face with my riding-whip, ordered him to his *sotnia*.[80]

Many other Turkmen were not so lucky, although there is no way to confirm MacGahan's story of his personal heroism. There are no counts of the Turkmen dead and wounded, but all sources agree that casualty rates were high and the Cossacks burned every village and farmstead they found. By the end of July the Turkmen had agreed to pay; Kaufman extended their deadline.[81]

Breaking Up Kokand

Kokand was by now under Russian economic control but by no means under Russian political control. The khanate posed an extremely complicated problem to Russian officials because of its location, political reach, and many factions. Directly northeast of the khanate was Kashgharia, a series of oasis towns around the western edge of the great Tarim Basin that today are part of Xinjiang. Kashgharia's population was also mostly Turkic and Muslim; it had been governed by Qing China since 1759, after the Qing destroyed the Zunghars. The khans of Kokand intervened in Kashgharia throughout the nineteenth century, seeking commercial advantage or political control as the Qing Dynasty weakened.[82] In 1864 Kashgharia rebelled against Qing rule, and Emir Alim Qul sent a military commander, Yaqub Beg, to seize what he could in the chaos. Yaqub Beg exceeded expectations and conquered all the towns of the southern Tarim by 1871.[83] Yaqub Beg's new emirate lay between an expanding Russia and a faltering China, and attracted Russian and British agents to the region; Yaqub Beg signed treaties with both empires. The British were interested not only because Kashgharia was close to British Kashmir, but because they were also busily carving up China into "spheres of influence" and did not want Russia to gain a toehold. Russia did take the Ili River valley from China and occupied it until 1882, which fueled British fears. The "Great Game" in Transoxiana was more good story-telling than action, but in Kashgharia Russians and British directly engaged with each other. Many of these encounters were cooperative, between scientists mapping the land and its resources, but always with an edge of rivalry.[84] For Kaufman, Kokand's ties to this deeply contested region meant that any plan to take over the khanate had to take possible British and Qing reactions into consideration.

Alim Qul's death allowed Khudoyar Khan to return to rule. For ten years he cooperated with the Russians, who in turn supported his efforts to consolidate power. However, his ties with Russia in combination with his oppressive methods of rule led to a new revolt by Kokandi Kyrgyz notables, who drove Khudoyar out in August 1875. Russian troops installed Khudoyar's son Nasruddin, who agreed to pay three million rubles and cede the northern section of the khanate to Turkestan. However, Kokandi anger against the khan and the Russians was so hot that barely two months later Nasruddin had to flee. The khanate was deeply fractured: pro-Russian merchants opposed anti-Russian clergy, Kyrgyz fought Uzbeks, and Ming tribal leaders battled Qipchaq chiefs. Some Muslims now fought on the Russian side and earned medals for their valor. Kaufman worried that the chaos might allow Yaqub Beg or Muzzafar or the British to gain influence, and asked St. Petersburg for a line of credit to fund a military campaign to impose order.[85]

The multiple armies involved made Kokand particularly difficult to subdue. There were notably bloody fights at the towns of Mahram and Oshoba, where women attacked Russian troops with knives, rocks, and anything else that came to hand.[86] The casualty rates were as lopsided as they had been in Bukhara and Khiva, but in addition Major-General Mikhail D. Skobelev made a point of murdering civilians to crush all possible resistance. Vladimir P. Nalivkin was a young officer who served under Skobelev and spent the rest of his life in Turkestan, learning Turki and writing deep studies of rural life. Thirty years after the conquest he described a horrifying incident as Russian troops rode their horses toward Namangan in late November. Villagers were fleeing ahead of them, some with carts full of possessions and some just running in panic. Skobelev ordered "Swords out! Charge!" The Cossacks broke into a gallop, while Nalivkin's division commander Nil N. Kuropatkin counter-ordered, "Don't you dare touch your swords! Trot!" Ahead Kuropatkin saw an unarmed man carrying a child, with two Cossacks bearing down on him. He shouted to Nalivkin to chase after. Nalivkin recalled:

With a cry "leave him alone! leave him alone!" I rushed toward the man (*sart*), but it was already too late: one of the Cossacks brought down his sword, and the unfortunate two or three-year-old child fell from the arms of the dumbfounded, panic-stricken man, landing on the ground with a deeply cleft head. The man's arms were apparently cut. The bloody child convulsed and died. The man blankly stared now at me, now at the child, with wildly darting, wide eyes.

God forbid that anyone else should have to live through the horror I lived through in that moment. I felt as though insects were crawling up my spine and cheeks, something gripped me by the throat, and I could neither speak nor breathe. I had seen dead and wounded people many times; I had seen *death* before, but such horror, such abomination, such infamy I had never before seen with my own eyes. This was new to me.[87]

The fighting ended in January 1876 after the bombardment of Andijan, during which thousands of townspeople died (in his own description of the campaign Skobelev called it a "pogrom").[88] Kaufman decided that Kokand was far too volatile to maintain as an autonomous Russian protectorate. He formally declared the khanate abolished 19 February, as a gift to Alexander II on the anniversary of the tsar's accession to the throne. Kaufman annexed the region to Turkestan, calling it the Ferghana district. He rewarded Skobelev for his services by naming him governor of Ferghana.[89]

The final phase of the conquest was the subjugation of the Turkmen Tekke tribes who lived around the oases of the Qara Qum desert between Khiva and Iran, an area the Russians called Transcaspia. There was no military or economic reason to control Transcaspia; indeed the harsh conditions made Russian troops' presence there expensive and insecure. The motivations here were a combination of diplomatic maneuvering and the personal rivalries and ambitions of Russian officers. In 1878 Russia defeated the Ottoman Empire in a short war and demanded that the Ottomans grant the Balkan provinces of Serbia, Romania, and Montenegro independence while making Bulgaria an autonomous state under Russian influence. Some Russian nationalists even asked the tsar to seize Constantinople/Istanbul for Orthodoxy. These ambitious plans were blocked by the northern European powers, led by Great Britain, with the Treaty of Berlin. During the Berlin conference War Minister Miliutin ordered Kaufman to mobilize armies in Turkestan to pressure the British by threatening to invade India. This negotiating bluff involved mobilizing 12,000 troops to march in three columns toward Afghanistan and Kashmir, partly through Bukhara and Khiva. A fourth column set off from Krasnovodsk toward the town of Kelif on the Amu Darya, through Tekke Turkmen territory. The Krasnovodsk army was commanded from the Caucasus, not Tashkent, under General N.P. Lomakin. Even though Miliutin called the whole thing off a week after the troops set out, Lomakin continued south to establish a line of forts along the border of Iranian Khurasan. These small and poorly supplied forts were vulnerable to Turkmen attacks, which was damaging to Russian prestige. Any defeat by "Asiatics," even when the new fortress line had no defined purpose, could not be tolerated. In September 1879 Lomakin lay siege to the Turkmen fortified town of Gök Tepe, where some 20,000 people, including women and children, had taken refuge. Russian artillery prevailed until Lomakin ordered his infantry to storm the town, at which point the Turkmen routed the Russians in fierce hand-to-hand combat. Even so, the Turkmen suffered thousands of casualties, many of them civilian, to the Russians' hundreds.

If attacks on small forts were intolerable, out-and-out defeat was unimaginably insulting. The revenge campaign was put under Skobelev's command, which provided the additional satisfaction of allowing the Turkestan military to show up their counterparts in the Caucasus. Skobelev applied overwhelming force and his own taste for killing to besiege Gök Tepe in November 1880, finally blowing up the walls in January 1881. He ordered his Cossacks to pursue and cut down everyone who fled, killing over 14,500 people, mostly non-combatants.[90] As intended, his attack shattered the Tekke Turkmen for decades. This was the last major military action of the Russian conquest of Transoxiana.

SUMMARY

The Russian conquest of Central Asia proceeded from multiple motivations. Russian government officials and military officers agreed that the empire's international prestige had to be upheld at all costs, and that a Russian must never be seen treating an "Asiatic" as an equal. Beyond that, Russia could not develop a coherent, unified policy to guide why and how it should impose its rule over Central Asians. For their part, the Kazakhs were too divided among themselves and too weakened by a century of military and settler encroachment on their lands to do more than try to protect the authority Russia allowed them to have at the local level. The three Uzbek khanates were losing economic ground to the new trade networks of the Russian and British empires, and a fatal combination of internal rebellions and wars amongst themselves left them highly vulnerable to outside attack by a modern army. War Minister Miliutin and Russian military officers invaded the khanates to secure resources for the southern fortress line, to protect themselves from Bukharan and Kokandi counter-attacks, to display their might to the British, and to earn medals and public praise for their valor. Having conquered, the Russian government now had to take responsibility for governing peoples whose lifeways, languages, religion, and worldview differed profoundly from its own.

Chapter 4

IMPERIAL RULE

The Russian Empire reached its full size with the addition of Transoxiana, stretching across half the planet from Poland and Finland to the Kamchatka Peninsula, from the Qara Qum desert to the Arctic Ocean. The empire encompassed almost 14 million square miles and more than a hundred different nationalities. The majority of its peoples were Christians of one variety or another, but adding the peoples of the Kazakh steppes and Transoxiana significantly increased the weight of Islam as Russia's second religion. While the conquests kept up Russian prestige in the European imperial competition, they presented the government with difficult questions: How would the new regions be integrated into Russia's legal and economic structures? Should Central Asians be "civilized" to become more like Russians, and if so, how? And, in a period when the interactions between people and state were undergoing deep transformation in Russia proper, how should Central Asians expect to interact with the state? Even starting to think through these issues was difficult because the government knew very little about its new subjects. Russians had more than a hundred years of close interactions with the Junior and Middle Horde Kazakhs before they started formally incorporating them with the 1822 law code. In comparison, centuries of irregular contact with Uzbek merchants and diplomatic envoys was poor preparation for the nuts and bolts of governing, and the workings of Kyrgyz and Turkmen societies were a black box. It would have been impossible for Russian officials to implement a fully considered colonial policy even if they had been able to agree on one. Turkestan and the Kazakh lands were gradually brought under governance systems that were similar to each other, but still legally distinct from the rest of the empire. Russian officials depended on cooperation from Central Asians, who played a subordinate but active role in the areas of economic development, education, and social dynamics. Some Central Asians prospered under the new regime and some became poorer, but for better or worse Russian rule began a slow process of cultural convergence.

GOVERNANCE

It is necessary to understand the basics of the governing apparatus in order to understand the power and the limits of the Russian colonial regime (see Map 4.1). Turkestan and the Kazakh regions were both governed by the military, and both were run for decades on the basis of "temporary" legal statutes. The 1867 Turkestan statute gave Governor-General Konstantin P. von Kaufman enormous freedom to govern as he chose. Kaufman developed his own draft of a permanent legal statute in 1873, but when that failed to get St. Petersburg's approval he went ahead and implemented it in the new Ferghana district, while other districts were under yet different vintages of law. Turkestan did not get a consolidated law code until 1886, when a permanent legal statute that limited the power of the governor-general was approved.[1] The Kazakh steppe was given its own temporary statute in 1868, which divided the land into four oblasts, the western two governed from Orenburg and the eastern two from Omsk, not including the two Kazakh-majority regions that were now part of Turkestan. The Kazakh oblasts were not united under a single governor-general until 1882, when the Steppe *Krai* (frontier region) was formed.[2]

Effective governance depended on knowledge and money, both of which were in short supply in Turkestan. Kaufman hired ethnographers and other scientists to compile information about the people, environment, and natural resources under his sway, which provided a wealth of knowledge but led to complaints about the cost from the Ministry of Finance. He engaged the painter Vasilii Vereshchagin, who had served as an officer during the Bukhara campaign, to depict Central Asian life for Russian viewers in St. Petersburg and Moscow. Vereshchagin's 1874 exhibition of paintings and drawings was a sensation, although it caused controversy because of his brutal depictions of war.[3] Kaufman also commissioned the 1872 *Turkestanskii Al'bom*, a collection

MAP 4.1 Central Asia under Russian imperial administration.

of thousands of photographs of the people and lands of Transoxiana.[4] The Ministry of Finance was eager to make Turkestan self-supporting, especially since the costs of the continuing conquests had not been budgeted for, and this required that Kaufman's government take over and modernize the tax systems from the khanates. The process and results of this project illustrate not just the steepness of the challenge for Russia, but how drawing Central Asian society into the Russian fiscal structure began to alter that society, even though that was far from Kaufman's intent.

The khanates' tax laws were rooted in Islamic law, but there were differences between medieval legal texts' prescriptions and how the tax system had actually developed in response to changing local conditions. Russian officers started to collect tax revenue from the Zerafshan district (Samarkand) immediately after they acquired it in 1868, but they were confounded by the contradictions between their understanding of Islamic tax law and what local people told them about what kinds of taxes were levied against what kinds of property. Rather than follow established practice, Russian officers imposed their own interpretation of what Islamic tax regulations required, sometimes inventing "Islamic" terminology in the process! Furthermore, Kaufman in his desperate search for revenue went after the people who claimed to be tax exempt based on their status as khojas or *sayyids* (descendants of the Prophet). He demanded that these holy families produce written genealogies to prove their status or prepare to pay property taxes. In doing so Kaufman imposed a modern, document-based standard for determining who could claim high religious status where customary practice was based on flexible oral traditions. Kaufman was well aware of this, and likely wanted to use the process to cut down on the number of khoja families. This would not only increase tax revenues, but weaken potential opposition to Russian rule. The documentary standard also made elite families conform to a European way of legitimizing personal identity.[5]

One of the permanent realities of governing Turkestan was insufficient personnel. Russian military officers were poorly educated and had no special training in governance.[6] They had to work with local authorities, although they usually banished the beks and in their place elevated oqsoqols, local *mirzas* (military commanders), and other lower-level notables as the intermediaries between people and state. In the late 1870s, as Turkestan absorbed the Kokand Khanate, Kaufman hoped to use an amalgamation of Russian and Kokandi tax assessment methods both to maximize revenue and to show villagers that Russia treated them more fairly than the khans had. Russian officers still found local tax practices confounding. Since Ferghana was governed under a different legal statute from that of Zerafshan, they could not simply transfer taxation methods to the new district. Instead, the governor of Ferghana[7] employed Russian and Kokandi surveyors to measure taxable farmland using both Russian and local methods. Kaufman again wanted to use documentation to fix accurate measurements of agricultural production and to change the system from taxing entire villages to taxing the individual households within villages. However, scientific measurement took a tremendous amount of time and labor, so after one year the Ferghana administration allowed traditional assessment methods to return under the supervision of local notables. The notables in turn could use their new power to acquire wealth; in one case an enterprising township administrator quadrupled his land holdings in ten years.[8] Whereas in Zerafshan Kaufman used modern documentation to undermine the social hierarchy, in Ferghana modern methods proved to be unworkable and the government had to accept Kokandi methods.[9] Developing a functioning colonial government required give-and-take between Russian and Central Asian ways of doing things.

The 1886 permanent "Statute on the Administration of the Turkestan Krai" described significant changes in how Turkestan was organized and governed. Kaufman had retired because of illness in 1881, dying in 1882, and the statute stripped his successors of his almost unlimited authority. The governors-general were still military officers, but they were to be supported by a council that included civilian bureaucrats. In reality, the Ministry of War and a dozen other agencies in St. Petersburg made decisions on resources and policies, so the governor-general remained the central coordinator.[10] The 1867 statute had divided Turkestan into Russian administrative units, and the permanent statute re-divided it into new oblasts, *uezdy* (counties), volosti, towns, and villages. These paralleled the way the 1868 temporary Steppe Statute had divided the Kazakh lands. As in the Kazakh lands, the new divisions brought together and divided tribes and communities in new arrangements. The counties were governed by Russian nachal'niki, while Turkestanis governed below that level. Township and village leaders were stripped of some of their traditional authority, however. Only Russian military courts could adjudicate major crimes such as murder, leaving minor offenses and family law to local sharia courts.[11] This again paralleled the Kazakh situation.

The other major governance question that Russian officials wrestled with was how much to preserve local structures and values. Russia could impose its military will on Central Asia, but just did not have the personnel or the funds to replace Central Asian governments wholesale. Logistical issues were not as important as philosophical ones, however. Many Russian officials, especially in the military, were convinced that integrating such culturally alien populations was impossible, even dangerous. They argued for maintaining military control but allowing Central Asians to run their own communities according to local customs. In part these officials were genuinely afraid that installing Russian governance in Central Asia would set off mass revolts among the Muslim "fanatics," as they routinely called all observant Muslims. Other officials believed in a "civilizing mission" that obligated Russia to mold Central Asian societies, especially the nomadic ones, according to Russian values and practices. Some proponents of the civilizing argument thought that allowing Central Asians to govern themselves under benign Russian supervision was the right tool to get Central Asians to acknowledge and adopt superior Russian ways on their own.[12] Others thought that forcing integration was the only way they were ever going to become civilized. This debate played out most fully over the question of the Kazakhs and law.

Recall that Russian governors since the 1820s had encouraged Kazakhs to follow adat instead of Islamic sharia in their tribal courts, and that Kazakh biis adjudicated all but serious crimes, which were handled by military courts. As officials were preparing the 1868 temporary Steppe Statute, the Russian court system was also being modernized as part of the Great Reforms. For the first time Russian citizens could have their cases defended by lawyers and heard by juries at different levels of courts in a system designed to be "quick, just, merciful, and equal."[13] Not all Russians, though: the newly emancipated peasants were shunted to a separate court system until such time as the government decided they were civilized enough to enjoy the privileges of full citizens. Russian officials saw Kazakh nomads as only somewhat more alien than Slavic peasants, and some hoped that bringing the Kazakhs closer to the Russian courts would speed up the civilizing process. The governor of Orenburg sent expeditions to consult with Kazakh biis and tribal chiefs on their views of the legal system. They seemed open to reformed procedures but also keen to protect their own traditions and authority. What they got was more state control without the liberal judicial reforms. The temporary Steppe Statute's prescription for the court system amounted to "someday, but not yet." The statute folded Kazakh biis into the imperial bureaucracy and allowed Kazakhs to bring some disputes to new courts that served both Kazakh and Russian inhabitants of the steppe, but did not introduce jury trials or a court system independent from the administration. An independent court system did not arrive in the steppe until 1898, sixteen years after the three Kazakh hordes had been brought together under one governor-general in the Steppe Krai. By that time, however, the Slavic settler population had increased significantly, and the new courts only served Kazakhs when they were in disputes with Russians. The tribal courts remained in place until the end of the empire.[14] For those officials who had hoped to use the courts to bring Kazakhs closer to Russian civilization, the results were quite disappointing. The Kazakhs were also unhappy, because they lost more independence without gaining the benefits of a modern court system.

ECONOMIC DEVELOPMENT

During World War I Vladimir Lenin argued that European colonial domination of the world was driven by capitalist corporations seeking more resources and profit.[15] That may have been a reasonable description of the "scramble" to cut up Africa in the 1890s, but it did not fit how the Russian Empire conquered the Uzbek khanates. For one thing, Russia did not have powerful corporations at the time of the conquest. For another, Turkestan not only ran a budget deficit every year, its deficit grew larger every year. By 1881 governing Turkestan had cost Russia 86–100 million rubles, an enormous amount given that the budget for the entire empire in 1855 had been estimated at 206.8 million rubles.[16] Nor did military officials make economic development in Central Asia a high priority until after they had consolidated their conquests in the 1880s. Kaufman collected taxes and encouraged agriculture, but he was better at sketching out ambitious development plans than executing them. A major barrier to increasing trade between Russia and Central Asia was the lack of railroad connections; it took six to eight weeks to travel from Tashkent to Orenburg by camel caravan. Russia built its first Central Asian rail line in 1880–81, through the Qara Qum desert from Krasnovodsk to Qzyl Arvat, 124 miles ending in sand. The railroad was to move soldiers to control the Turkmen, not trade goods, which illustrates the priorities of Turkestan's military government. The Transcaspian line was extended to Ashkhabad in 1885, and Merv in 1886. The decision to extend the line northeast toward Samarkand was again made for military reasons rather than economic ones, after a skirmish between Russian and Afghan soldiers in March 1885.[17] The extension had to go through Bukhara, which required the permission of Emir Muzzafar, particularly since Russia hoped to persuade the emir to pay for some of the construction or at least donate the land. The line reached Samarkand in 1888, and did not connect to Tashkent until 1898. A railroad connecting Tashkent directly to Orenburg was not built until 1906.

Building the railroad through Bukhara inevitably opened the way for a permanent European presence in the emirate, despite Muzzafar's reluctance and strong opposition from the ulama. Muzzafar had agreed to allow a telegraph line to go through Bukhara in 1883, but the railroad was a more serious threat to Bukhara's autonomy. Thousands of Bukharan peasants performed the unskilled labor under Russian supervision, while engineers built railroad and repair stations that were staffed by Europeans. At Muzzafar's request the rail line passed south of the city, but within a few years the train station there had become the hub of a Russian settlement, known as New Bukhara. In 1895 Bukhara was absorbed into Turkestan's customs regime, and by 1897 more than 10,000 European civilians and soldiers lived in the emirate. A significant number of Bukharan merchants obtained Russian citizenship so they could conduct business on equal terms.[18] The last two emirs of Bukhara, Abdul Ahad (r. 1885–1910) and Alim Khan (r. 1910–20), while proclaiming to their subjects that they staunchly defended Bukhara from Russian predation, in fact became savvy investors in the new economic order. They acquired millions of rubles in wealth, primarily from trade in Astrakhan wool, and gave generously to Russian charitable causes to keep relations sweet.[19] In 1898 Abdul Ahad was able and happy to pay for a branch of the railroad to go directly into the city, partly because it was so popular with Bukharans.[20] In contrast, no railroad went through Khiva, which kept Russian settlement very small but also deprived the khanate of economic development.[21] Bukhara gained new connections and wealth from the Russian protectorate, while Khiva dwindled in importance.

Despite its military origins, the railroad became an economic force soon after the Samarkand extension was completed. Textiles were one of the earliest sectors of the Russian economy to industrialize, which caused traditional trade relations between Russia and Transoxiana to reverse. Bukhara had been famous for centuries for its dyed cottons, but by the 1850s Russia was exporting factory-made cottons to Central Asia.[22] Demand for cotton textiles grew across the empire, but supplies of cotton from the United States became less reliable as American domestic demand was also growing.[23] In the 1870s Kaufman imported seed stock for a long-staple American variety of cotton that he hoped would grow well in the long, hot summers of Turkestan. Russian planters began growing it on rented land with hired local labor, and requested tax breaks from the state, but faced skepticism and slow action from officials.[24] Turkestan did not start to produce industrial quantities of long-staple cotton until the 1880s, although once the process began it grew rapidly; the new railroad strained to keep up with demand. Some Turkestani and Bukharan landowning and merchant families also took advantage of the new cash crop regime, not only planting their own cotton but building ginning mills to clean the cotton for export. They learned enough Russian to help their businesses and developed relationships with agents from the Russian textile industry as well as government officials. They began to deposit their money in Russian banks that paid them interest.[25] A future leader of Soviet Uzbekistan, Fayzulla Xo'jaev, was born in 1896 to a wealthy Bukharan merchant family who sent him to Moscow to complete his education.[26] Russian colonial authorities avoided deep interference in Turkestani cultures, but the force of economic transformation was irresistible.[27]

The Kazakhs had a much more negative experience of modern economic development. The lands that could produce a cash crop, such as grain or cotton, were increasingly being taken by Slavic settlers. As Kazakhs lost grazing lands, they came under pressure to become settled farmers themselves. The government declared that all nomad land, in both the Steppe Krai and in Turkestan, was state property that nomads were allowed to use but could not own.[28] Most Slavic settlers were technically illegal, but in 1889 the state passed a Resettlement Act that allowed peasants to move to the northern Kazakh lands legally. So many Slavic families flooded in that state surveyors could not measure out enough allotments of land to keep pace with demand. The program had to be suspended in 1891, a terrible year of disease and famine in European Russia. Settlement resumed shortly after, supplemented by a new law that allowed the state to take land that was "surplus" to nomad needs. A 1904 decree allowing freedom of movement throughout the empire increased rates even more. Between 1890 and 1917 almost three million Slavic settlers moved to Kazakh and Kyrgyz lands.[29] As good pastureland grew scarcer, disputes between Kazakh tribes over access to what was left increased. These disputes were exacerbated by the 1868 temporary Steppe Statute, which re-drew the earlier administrative divisions and re-disrupted tribal relations. The only Kazakhs who benefitted from these changes were the locally elected aul and volost heads, who could use their positions to take the best available land for their families.[30] That in turn generated resistance and contributed to the breakdown of Kazakh political and social order, as ordinary Kazakhs refused to tithe the customary sheep and camels to tribal biis who they regarded as Russian tools.[31] The one positive economic development was that the growing Slavic population had an appetite for Kazakh meat, and some herders switched to raising beef cattle for the new market.[32]

EDUCATION

Perhaps the biggest difference between Russian colonial imperialism and that of the British or French was the role of Christian missionaries. In British and French colonies missionaries were enthusiastic builders of schools as a way to lead Muslims and Hindus toward Christian civilization. The Russian Orthodox Church hierarchy—which had a monopoly on elementary education until the 1860s—saw schools as being for Christians only, and largely preferred conversion by force rather than by persuasion.[33] This may be one reason Governor-General Kaufman banned missionaries entirely from Turkestan.

Kazakh aristocrats were the earliest group of Central Asians to learn in Russian schools. In the seventeenth and eighteenth centuries these were mostly royal hostages who were raised to be loyal servants of the tsar. The hostage system created a small cohort of pro-Russian Kazakh families, which by the nineteenth century contributed to the political fragmentation of the Kazakh leadership. Just how tangled elite family dynamics could get is nicely illustrated by the life of the first modern Kazakh scholar, Chokan or Shoqan Valikhanov (1835–65). Chokan was a descendant of the eighteenth-century Middle Horde ruler Ablai Khan and his son and successor Wali (from which the family name Valikhanov derived). Wali Khan's wife, Chokan's grandmother, was an educated, staunchly pro-Russian woman named Aiganym who enrolled her son Chingis in the Russian military academy at Omsk.[34] Chingis was a senior-rank sultan and an officer in the Siberian army, and in turn enrolled his son Chokan in the academy in 1847. Chokan's notable intelligence led him to be recruited to a military-geographical expedition to the Lake Issyk Kul area, a Kyrgyz region that Russia was in the process of conquering. There Chokan drew maps and made extensive notes on the resources and animals of the region. He also made the first notation of *Manas*, the Kyrgyz historical epic poem. Upon his return, Chokan became friends with the great Russian novelist Fyodor Dostoevsky, who was in exile in Semipalatinsk for the "crime" of reading unauthorized philosophy (see Figure 4.1). Chokan led a second major expedition into Kashgharia in 1858; in 1860 he delivered the expedition report in person in St. Petersburg. Tragically, he also contracted tuberculosis, and died five years later at the age of twenty-nine.[35] Chokan and Chingis Valikhanov represented just one branch of Ablai Khan's numerous descendants, however. At the same time that they were serving Russia with distinction, their cousin Kenesari Qasim-uli was leading the largest Kazakh uprising of the entire nineteenth century. Ten years after

FIGURE 4.1 Chokan Valikhanov and Fyodor Dostoevsky. Source: Photo by N. Leibin, 1858. Retrieved from Wikimedia Commons.

the Kyrgyz murdered Kenesari, Chokan brought them literary fame with his transcription of *Manas*.

Despite the Orthodox Church's lack of interest in educating Muslims, the governors-general realized that providing a basic Russian education to Kazakhs could give them a pool of local administrators that they desperately needed. In 1858 a new school in Orenburg brought together ten Kazakh children with ten children of Russian bureaucrats, in hopes that day-to-day socializing would give the Kazakhs good command of Russian. Two years later the Orenburg administration got more ambitious and opened five secular schools designed not just to educate bureaucrats, but to raise the level of Kazakh culture and impart European civilization to them. These schools were available to interested adults as well as children, but they were located in the fortress towns of the western steppe and only reached those Kazakhs who were already open to Russian acculturation.[36]

An important dissenter to Orthodox Church rigidity was Nikolai I. Il'minskii, who was a lay (non-clerical) member of the Orthodox missionary society in Kazan. Il'minskii, a professor of Turkic languages at the Kazan

Theological Academy, in 1872 founded schools that taught baptized Tatars a Russian curriculum in their own language, rather than alienating them further with Russian-language classrooms. As the school system grew larger some baptized Kazakh parents sent their sons, and Il'minskii accommodated them by printing the first Cyrillic-alphabet books in the Kazakh language.[37] Governor-General Kryzhanovskii in Orenburg was interested in opening native-language schools for Muslim Kazakhs and Bashkirs as well, partly to separate them from Tatar influence. Whereas Catherine the Great had sent Tatar missionaries to the Kazakhs to teach them how to be better Muslims, a hundred years later Russian officials in the Steppe Krai feared that Tatars were teaching Kazakhs to become religious "fanatics." In 1882 Ibrahim Altynsarin, a Muslim Kazakh who worked closely with Il'minskii, opened a Kazakh-Russian elementary school in each Kazakh oblast, as well as a trade school and a teachers' academy. In 1888 he opened six schools at the volost level, and in 1889 added a few mobile schools to educate nomadic children. The number of students was small—in 1883 the four oblast schools taught 118 boys, of whom almost one-third were actually Russian, and the volost schools included all of ten seats reserved for girls, although two more sections for girls had to be added to meet demand. The schools taught elementary reading, writing, and arithmetic in Kazakh as well as Russian, and promised parents that no Christian religious instruction would be included.[38] The surprising fact that Russian children studied in the Kazakh-Russian schools suggests that practical considerations over-ruled Church sensitivities. Outside of the towns access to any school was rare, and parents took whatever educational opportunities came their way. This also indicates that Kazakhs and Russians were living together closely, although that tells us nothing about whether interactions were friendly, hostile, or (most likely) a mix.

Russian-language schools that were open to Kazakh children also expanded to the eastern steppes. The cohort of Kazakhs who were comfortable speaking Russian or who wanted their children to learn Russian grew as the reach of the imperial state grew. By the 1890s more Kazakh children attended Russian schools than attended the Kazakh-Russian schools, especially in Russian towns such as Vernoe (today's Almaty). In 1890 an eleven-year-old boy named Mukhamedjan Tynyshpaev enrolled in the preparatory course for Vernoe's *gimnazium* (secondary school), and ten years later earned a gold medal for academic excellence and the chance to study engineering in St. Petersburg. He went on to become the first Kazakh railroad engineer, but he was not alone: his classmates included a future lawyer, a mathematician, and a doctor.[39] In a largely illiterate society, this tiny number of educated people would have a disproportionate impact on future developments.

In Turkestan, Bukhara, and Khiva, early interest in Russian-language education came from families who wanted to prosper under the new government, not from Russian officials. Kaufman's approach to local cultures was a policy of *ignorirovanie* (ignoring Islam), or not bothering with an active civilizing mission on the assumption that mere contact with superior Russian culture would cause local Islamic practices to wither and die. He barred the Muslim Spiritual Assembly at Orenburg, which Catherine the Great had created in 1788 to regulate Muslim communities, from extending its authority to Turkestan. The policy reflected not just Kaufman's arrogance but his real fear of the power of settled Islamic cultures—he did not want to spark a backlash. He put priority on Russian schools for the nomadic Kazakhs and Kyrgyz of Turkestan, who he believed were not deeply Muslim. Kaufman's one lasting action to promote Russian education was to found a teachers' academy in 1879, which taught in Russian and Kazakh.[40]

When Kaufman's successor as governor-general, N.O. Rosenbach, started a small set of *Russko-tuzemskii* (Russian-native) schools in 1884, most of the money and the students came from wealthy merchant families that already had ties to Russia. The schools did not draw much interest from ordinary Turkestanis until after 1905, and even then there were just under one hundred schools in the oblast, as opposed to thousands of traditional maktabs.[41] Russian officials were inclined to blame the "fanaticism" of the ulama for this apathy, despite the fact that Muslim clergy taught in the Russian-native schools. Conservative religious opposition was only one factor, however. A more important problem was that parents did not believe that the schools taught well or taught subjects that were useful for their children's economic prospects.[42] Similarly in Bukhara it was wealthy merchant families that pushed to start one Russian-native school in the 1890s; no such schools operated in Khiva.[43] Except for these small pockets of activity, the traditional maktabs remained unchallenged until the upheavals of 1905 opened the door to reformist ideas from the Ottoman Empire and India.

SOCIAL DYNAMICS

The process of incorporating Turkestan into imperial government structures brought more than 200,000 European soldiers, businessmen, bureaucrats,

Table 4.1 1897 census data on Europeans in Turkestan

OBLAST	Russians	Ukrainians	Poles	Germans
Syr Darya	31,900	12,853	2,825	1,887
Samarkand	12,485	1,391	1,531	440
Ferghana	8,140	1,698	1,535	369
Transcaspia	27,942	5,151	3,812	1,026
Semirechie	76,839	18,611	185	–
TOTAL	157,306	39,704	9,888	3,722

Source: "Demoskop Weekly," Institute of Demographics at the Higher School of Economics (census data), accessed 1 February 2017, http://demoscope.ru/weekly/ssp/emp_lan_97 _uezd.php?reg=799.

and peasant settlers, who by their very presence changed the social dynamics of the region. In 1897 St. Petersburg conducted a comprehensive census of the Russian Empire, which was its first (and as it turned out, last) attempt to count and organize the entire population. The census workers did not use race or ethnicity as ways to distinguish among peoples; they used language, asking people what their "mother tongue" was. When it came to counting the major European groups in Turkestan, this method yielded the results shown in Table 4.1.[44] "Mother tongue" was an ambiguous guide (someone born in Poland to Ukrainian parents might have spoken Ukrainian, Polish, or a local mix of dialects at home), but it provided a pretty good approximation. The numbers suggest that most Europeans were in Turkestan either to serve the state, or to farm. Syr Darya Oblast included the capital city Tashkent, which had a total population of 155,673, and 40 per cent of all the Europeans in the oblast concentrated in the New Tashkent quarter of the city. The largest group of settlers were the peasant farmers attracted to the grasslands of Semirechie, although this statistic was recorded just as their numbers started to explode with the recent completion of the Trans-Siberian railroad. In contrast, the fertile Ferghana Valley attracted fewer settlers than did desert Transcaspia, because the Turkic and Tajik population there was already so dense.

Counting and categorizing that population was much more difficult to do, and the criterion of "mother tongue" yielded highly ambiguous results. Many Turkestanis, especially in the Ferghana Valley that had seen such brutal fighting in the 1870s, believed that being counted made them vulnerable to some future state-inflicted harm. This was certainly a reasonable fear, and they avoided census workers as much as possible.[45] To try and win

Table 4.2 1897 census data on non-Europeans in Turkestan

Ethnonym	Population Estimate
Tajiks	114,081
Persians	1,465
Kara-Kirgiz	201,579
Kipchaks	7,584
Karakalpaks	11,056
Sarts	788,989
Uzbeks	153,780
Kashgharis	14,915
Other Turks	261,234
Chinese	1,640

Source: "Demoskop Weekly," Institute of Demographics at the Higher School of Economics (census data), accessed 1 February 2017, http://demoscope.ru/weekly/ssp/emp_lan_97 _uezd.php?reg=930.

trust, Russian officials trained locals to carry out the census. This yielded the most comprehensive count yet, but also a categorization nightmare. Table 4.2 shows the main native populations that the 1897 census recorded in Ferghana Oblast.[46] Some puzzles posed by this table are easily solved: "Persians" were people from Iran as opposed to the local Farsi-speaking Tajiks, although Hindus might also have been included in this category. *Kara-kirgiz* was the name Russians used to distinguish today's Kyrgyz from the *Kirgiz-kaisatskii*, now called Kazakhs. The Karakalpaks and Kipchaks were Turkic tribes with distinct lineages. But "Uzbeks," "Sarts," and "other Turks"? These groups were largely created by the census workers, who recorded "mother tongue" answers idiosyncratically. The category "other Turks" was based on workers writing down "t" or "tu" for language, which could have meant half a dozen possibilities. The biggest group, Sarts, were people who said they spoke the Sart language, which was most likely some mix of Turkic and Farsi that varied from town to town. The census illustrates the wide gap between how Turkestanis thought about themselves and the clear ethnic categories that Russia desired. The census compilers used language as a rough proxy for race, which was a meaningless concept in Central Eurasia. However, the 1897 census would become a first step toward the Soviet introduction of clearly defined ethnicity as an organizing principle for Central Asian peoples.[47]

Table 4.3 1897 census data on the Steppe Krai

OBLAST	Russians	Ukrainians	Poles	Germans	Kazakhs[48]	Tatars
Uralsk	160,894	2,959	250	–	460,173	17,809
Turgai	453,416	30,438	–	–	410,904	3,197
Akmolinsk	174,292	51,103	1,142	4,791	427,839	10,819
Semipalatinsk	65,062	3,257	195	–	604,564	9,940
TOTAL	853,664	87,757	1,587	4,791	1,903,480	41,765

Source: "Demoskop Weekly," Institute of Demographics at the Higher School of Economics (census data), accessed 1 February 2017, http://demoscope.ru/weekly/ssp/emp_lan_97 _uezd.php?reg=0.

The Muslim population in the Steppe Krai was less diverse than that in Turkestan, so categorization was simpler. The statistics here are useful for seeing the geographic distributions of the European and Turkic populations (see Table 4.3).[49] The European population was larger in the western oblasts—Slavs actually outnumbered Kazakhs in Turgai. The Kazakhs were heavily dominant in Semipalatinsk, where the European population was smallest, which raises the possibility that Kazakh tribes had migrated east in their search for open grazing land. Meanwhile, a German colony had taken root in Akmolinsk.

Russians and Turkestanis lived in the same region but did not live together. In the major towns Russians built separate neighborhoods with streets and architecture that reminded them of home. Kaufman took great pride in the wide boulevards, gardens, and stately government buildings he commissioned for Russian Tashkent in the 1870s. The new quarter was modeled on St. Petersburg, with its spoke pattern of streets radiating from a central park. The street layout also enabled Russian troops to deploy quickly against outside threats. Most people in both communities preferred to live separately, although several hundred Muslims, mostly merchants, built homes and shops in the Russian quarter.[50]

Everyday Life

Kaufman's assumption that contact with superior Russian civilization would lead Turkestanis to adopt it voluntarily was frequently undermined by the behavior of the ordinary soldiers, railroad workers, and peasants who moved to Turkestan in the late nineteenth century. Soldiers made up a large part of the Russian population, and most of the time they had little to do. The soldiers' favorite cure for boredom and homesickness was alcohol, and by 1883 a Russian observer expressed shame at the dozens of distilleries and hundreds of taverns in the Tashkent district. This was especially conspicuous in a larger community of non-drinking Muslims. Indeed, in Tashkent a stereotype developed of lazy, drunken Russians who were economically exploited by clever Turkestani merchants. This reversal of the expected colonial relationship revealed Russians' sense of insecurity in an alien land.[51]

Relationships based on friendliness and mutual curiosity also developed between Turkestanis and Russians. In 1870 Kaufman sponsored a Turkic-language newspaper, *Turkiston vilayotining gazeti*, to communicate government intentions to educated locals. Originally a weekly dedicated to translations of new decrees, under the editorship of Nikolai P. Ostroumov the paper evolved into a forum for discussion of local issues, new technology, poetry, and news of Russia and Europe. Ostroumov had learned Turkic in the anti-Islam division of the Kazan Theological Academy, but in Tashkent he was barred from missionary work and instead cultivated long-term friendships with the men who wrote for him. Several of these young men used the newspaper to debate ideas for reforming their society. These included the poet Zakirjon Furqat and education reformer Mahmudxo'ja Behbudiy.[52] No Russians dove more deeply into Turkestani culture than Vladimir and Maria Nalivkin, who in 1878 made the extraordinary decision to purchase a house and land in a small village in the Ferghana Valley and live there with their children for six years. After Vladimir's horrific experiences during the conquest of Kokand, he dedicated the rest of his life to learning local languages and writing about Central Asian history and culture. Maria also learned the village language and lived as her neighbors did, wearing the paranji in public and doing farm work. She added tremendous depth to the couple's ethnographic studies, since as a woman she could observe aspects of life from which Vladimir was excluded.[53]

The Nalivkins provide information on aspects of ordinary life that few literate Turkestanis thought were worth writing about, such as children's street games and rhymes or the etiquette of visiting friends. Life in their village was precarious: a bad harvest or the death of a husband could destroy a family. Life was also marked by joyful celebrations of holidays and weddings, and arguments between spouses that neighbors tried to help patch up. The Nalivkins' writings, which were aimed at a popular Russian readership, showed ordinary people doing their best to get by. This was a sharp contrast to the depiction of faceless hordes of Muslim "fanatics" that was so prominent in the memoirs of military or government officials. Their work is problematic for modern readers, however, because the Nalivkins never lost their fundamental belief that Turkestani society was inferior to Russian. They genuinely liked the people they lived among, but could treat them condescendingly.

There are a number of Turkestani memoirs of the late Imperial period, but most of them were written by political or religious elites and do not consider daily life. An exception is the childhood memoir of Tajik educational reformer Sadriddin Aini, who was born in a small Bukharan village in 1878. His father and grandfather were literate craftsmen who made mill wheels and did general carpentry while farming; his grandfather was also a village imam. Aini wrote his memoirs in 1949, in a very different world from where he had grown up, but he gives his readers a vivid and affectionate view of village life. People lived on small farms fed by irrigation canals, where they struggled against sandstorms that choked the water supply and wild jackals that stole chickens (see Figure 4.2). Aini opens his book by recalling the wonderful party his father threw for him when he turned seven. There was a great cauldron of *pilau* (pilaf), the traditional rice, mutton, and vegetable dish for feasts, musicians played, and little Sadriddin had a new set of white linen clothes his father had made. Then suddenly his grandfather grabbed him—this was his circumcision feast, but no one had told him why he was the star of the day. He certainly remembered the searing pain between his legs, but wrote that it was mitigated by the love and joy of his family.[54]

Aini also wrote extensively about his schooling, which in his account mostly consisted of memorization and avoiding being beaten by the teacher, who kept a collection of canes soaking in water so they delivered maximum pain.[55] The boys' maktab was so chaotic that after a year Aini's parents removed him and placed him in a more orderly girls' school. At the elementary level girls and boys studied the same curriculum. After memorizing the names of the letters of the alphabet, children recited from collections of short Quranic verses and instructions on ritual and prayer. Texts in Arabic or Farsi were not translated, however, and teachers did not care whether children understood what they were saying. When children learned poetry selections they recited along with the teacher as she pointed to the words. Aini recalled that he could "read" any poem he had learned in school, but was dumbstruck in front of texts he had never seen before because he had never learned how to sound out new words phonetically. After learning the required books, the most promising

FIGURE 4.2 Turkmen maintaining a canal. Source: Photo by Khudaybergan Divanov. Courtesy of Andrew Hale, Anahita Gallery, Santa Fe, New Mexico.

boys could go on to the madrasa, but girls ended their formal education after five years in the maktab.[56] Aini's memoir is delightful, but should be read skeptically because he wrote it toward the end of his life at the high point of Stalinism. In his book rich men are always villains and imams are out to fool gullible peasants, as required by Soviet censors. Comparing his entirely negative depiction of traditional education with Dilshod's account reveals that the maktab experience varied.

Religious Culture

A maktab education prepared children to perform the correct prayers and actions at the correct times in a world that was defined by Islam. Contrary to Russian stereotype, this world changed through time as much as any other human society did. The political and economic forces that imperial rule introduced rapidly accelerated that change in directions that neither Russians nor Central Asians anticipated. For the first time since the Mongol Empire fractured in the late thirteenth century, Eurasian Muslims from the Volga River to the western Pamir and Altai mountains lived within the same empire. This facilitated greater and faster contact between Tatars and Central Asians. Tatars had dominated religious institutions among the western Kazakhs since the eighteenth century; Russian expansion allowed Tatar merchants to travel along the fortress lines, funding mosques and madrasas where they settled. By the 1880s Semipalatinsk had nine madrasas, an exponential leap in access to formal education for the eastern Kazakhs. Bukharan merchants also built mosques in trading towns, which were administered separately from those of the Tatars.[57] Some Russian officials fretted that these contacts would lead to a "pan-Islamic" confederation against the empire, but greater interaction did not lead to greater liking among the various Turkic-Muslim communities. Between this institutional growth and the spread of Kazakh-language books printed by Altynsarin, Kazakh religious knowledge increased and their practice conformed more closely with that of Muslims in Kazan.[58]

Russia facilitated connections with the larger Islamic world intentionally and unintentionally, by making it easier for their subjects to make the *hajj*, the required pilgrimage to Mecca, and by inspiring mass unauthorized emigration to the Ottoman Empire. Hundreds of thousands of Crimean and Volga Tatars fled real and feared oppression in the late nineteenth and early twentieth centuries, but some of them were able to move back and forth between empires. In 1902 a Volga Tatar who had become an Ottoman subject successfully petitioned to return to Russia because he had been offered a teaching job in Tashkent. He would have introduced his pupils to a much larger view of Islam than what Aini had been able to see in his village school.[59] Because most routes to Mecca went through the Ottoman Empire, Russian military officers worried that allowing the hajj posed a security risk, but attempts to bar Muslims in the Caucasus from the pilgrimage created the very hostility that officials feared. Instead, in the 1840s Russian consulates began to sponsor and protect pilgrim caravans as a way to control them.[60] Central Asian Muslims had usually made the pilgrimage by trekking through Afghanistan and sailing from Mughal India, a route that took many months and posed many dangers. Becoming part of the Russian Empire allowed them to take safer routes across the Caspian and Black seas to Istanbul, although Russian security concerns never entirely disappeared. In the 1890s *Turkiston vilayotining gazeti* was running articles on how to make the hajj, while steamships and railroads made it faster and easier for Central Asians than ever before.

Russian assistance allowed thousands of Central Asians to travel to Mecca, and thousands more made the journey without legal authorization.[61]

Russian rule weakened the Muslim clergy's bases for authority, while the widening of Central Asians' worlds led to challenges to clerical power from new groups. The 1886 Turkestan statute stripped most charitable waqf lands of their tax immunity, which reduced the income of many Islamic institutions. The growing Russian court system gave enterprising Turkestanis the ability to appeal sharia court decisions that did not go in their favor, and reduced the need for a bevy of professional scribes who had made a living by writing out legal petitions in archaic formal language.[62] In Bukhara, the emirs split the ulama into rival factions and made them more dependent on the emirs' good will for favorable appointments. The ulama tried to secure their incomes by charging more money for services such as certifying documents, which stoked popular resentment and cynicism.[63]

New internal pressures and outside influences provoked resistance from those who wanted to preserve the old ways. The prospect of violence from mobs of Muslim "fanatics" was the nightmare of every Russian official, but in fact the late nineteenth century saw few significant uprisings, and fewer still that were clearly rooted in religious feeling. In the western Kazakh oblasts enforcement of the 1868 Steppe Statute, which increased taxes and restricted access to grazing lands, was met with widespread violence in the form of destroying telegraph lines and roads and attacking tax collectors. The Russians sent thousands of troops to crush the rebels and destroy their herds.[64] A more overtly religious conflict arose in Tashkent in 1892 when a cholera epidemic ravaged the city. Cholera is a water-borne disease that requires intercommunal cooperation to contain, but the crisis exacerbated already tense relations between the Russian and Asian sections of Tashkent. The Russian section got its water from canals that ran through Old Tashkent and were maintained by Turkestani engineers, since Russian engineers had embarrassed themselves in the 1870s by proving unable to build and manage their own canal.[65] When the cholera hit in June, Russian city officials required that the Muslim dead be buried outside city limits in a special cemetery without the standard ritual washing. This violated Muslim families' need to treat their loved ones with dignity, and angry Asian Tashkent residents blamed their own elected oqsoqols for not standing up to the Russians. Their rage, which was also based on older grievances that had built up over time, culminated in a brawl with Russians that left more than a hundred Turkestanis dead.[66]

The incident that most powerfully invoked Russian fears of Muslim fanaticism was a rebellion in spring 1898 lead by a Naqshbandi Sufi *ishan* (teacher or master) named Muhammad Ali, known as Madali or Dukchi Ishan. Dukchi Ishan planned attacks on Russian soldiers in Andijan, Osh, and Margelan, reportedly showing his followers a letter or a gold ring "from the Ottoman sultan" pledging support for a religious war.[67] He was captured after a brief battle and hanged with five other leaders, while hundreds of their followers were exiled to Siberia and a Russian settlement of 260 families was imposed on the area.[68] However, the level of organization and determination Dukchi Ishan showed frightened the new governor-general, S.M. Dukhovskoi, into abandoning Kaufman's policy of ignoring Islam. He called for strict supervision of Islamic institutions and greater military control, but the ministers in St. Petersburg preferred a cultural assimilation approach. They instructed Russian officials to study local languages and Islamic history and beliefs. The Ministry of Education started a program to inspect maktabs, while Dukhovskii encouraged the growth of Russian-native schools and the addition of Russian history and literature to their curriculum, including translations of works by Alexander Pushkin and Lev Tolstoi into Turki.[69] As with many government instructions, these remained largely on paper because there was neither the personnel nor the budget to implement them effectively. A lack of stability in the governor-general's office also caused ambitious plans to fizzle and die. Dukhovskii was in place for less than two years, and after him eight more men held the position from 1901 to 1917.

SUMMARY

For all of the Russian Empire's deserved reputation as a stifling autocracy, colonial Central Asia was shaped as much by the actions of local people as by ministers in St. Petersburg. Kaufman was the most important and dynamic of the Turkestan governors-general, but found that he had to cooperate with local leaders and their legal and taxation procedures because he did not have the personnel to impose new systems. Allowing elected qadis, biis, and oqsoqols to run local affairs for Kazakhs and Turkestanis was efficient and largely kept the public peace, but also created a cohort of people who knew how to use Russian government to enrich themselves and their families. The military built the railroad, but it was Russian and Turkestani cotton growers and merchants who turned it into a vital economic artery. Central Asians both resented Russian rule and wanted to benefit from it; they pushed more than Russian officials did for Russian-language education and for assistance in making the hajj. The colonial relationship also yoked Russians and Central Asians together at a time of accelerating change. Tsar Alexander II's Great Reforms unleashed enormous economic and social forces that made Russia an industrializing power like the states of Europe. Central Asians were caught up in the modernizing process, and both societies split between people who embraced and grew rich from these changes and those who rejected them or lost out. Up to this point, the political and social dynamics within Central Asia were similar to what other colonial societies experienced. No one could have guessed the scale of the changes that the dawn of the twentieth century was about to bring.

Chapter 5

REVOLUTIONS

From 1905 to 1920 revolutions and wars destroyed empires and shattered societies around the world. First, revolutionary constitutional movements erupted in Russia, Iran, Turkey, Mexico, and China, unprecedented challenges to the rule of emperors and aristocrats. These were minor crises compared to the Great War (World War I) of 1914–18, which destroyed the Austro-Hungarian, Ottoman, and Russian empires, and enabled the British and French to divide the Middle East between them. Meanwhile the new republican government of China could not unify the former Qing Empire, which fractured into dozens of enclaves run by warlords. Initially the Central Asian peoples watched these movements from a distance, but post-1905 Russia allowed new venues for expressing new ideas, and educated Central Asians jumped in to debates about what their societies were and where they should be going. While they experimented with new forms of education, literature, and political organization, the state encouraged millions more Slavs to settle in the Ferghana Valley and Semirechie, displacing Central Asians and causing great hardship. When the war weakened the tsarist government, Central Asians needed little provocation to explode with anger.

THE REVOLUTION OF 1905 AND ITS EFFECTS

The Great Reforms of the 1860s raised expectations among Russia's subjects for more just and responsive government, but some groups thought the reforms were not enough. Serfs were angry about the terms of the emancipation; in 1861 university students joined them by rioting in St. Petersburg. In 1862 a group calling itself "Young Russia" circulated a proclamation in St. Petersburg that mocked religion and family, incited people to assassinate the tsar, and to destroy the ruling classes. In March 1881, after many attempts, a revolutionary group called "The People's Will" killed both Emperor Alexander II and his wife. Their son Alexander III (r. 1881–94) tried to crush the revolutionaries by hanging, flogging, and exiling them to Siberia, but only succeeded in hardening their commitment to violence.

The revolutionary groups did not all share the same goals or use the same tactics, but they were all reacting to how industrialization was changing Russia. The Great Reforms freed capital resources and encouraged the growth of private enterprise. Cities grew as new factories attracted peasant employees, who started as seasonal workers but became permanent urban residents. The government expanded higher education to women and Jews, who flocked to professions such as medicine and law. The new local governing boards called *zemstvos* hired young doctors and teachers to work in the villages, which introduced modern ideas into rural areas. Peasants and young professionals alike were often horrified by what they encountered, whether atheism and revolution or ignorance and poverty. The revolutionaries agreed that tsarist oppression and industrial capitalism were crushing the mass of ordinary people, but they did not agree on how to fix the situation. Their arguments were really about Russia's future: should Russia remain a community of agricultural villages where peasants owned and worked the land in common, or should it embrace capitalism and work for the day when industrial workers seized control of the factories and banks?

The first strain of revolutionary thought was called "populism." The populists idealized the peasant communal village and wanted to preserve it from industrialization. They were better at random assassinations of government officials than at organization, but in 1902 they formed a political party called the Socialist Revolutionaries. The second strain of revolutionary thought was inspired by the ideas of Karl Marx, a German political economist who argued that the future belonged to industrial workers, who he called the proletariat. In 1848 Marx and his close collaborator Friedrich Engels wrote "The Communist Manifesto," which sketched out in ringing prose how and why the proletariat would take control over the enormous productive power of industrial capitalism. Since Russia was just barely beginning to industrialize, Marx and Engels themselves did not pay much attention to it, but a small group of Russian revolutionaries thought that their future lay in industrial cities, not in agricultural villages. They believed that Marx's "iron laws of history" prescribed industrialization as the inevitable future for the entire world. The only question was who was going to control that future, the current ruling class or the workers. In 1898 this group founded the Russian Social Democratic Labor Party, which in 1903 split into two rival factions: the Mensheviks, and the Bolsheviks led by Vladimir I. Lenin.

The revolutionaries were just a small part of the Russian population and had nothing to do with starting the Revolution of 1905. Russia was losing a war to the Japanese, earning the humiliating distinction of being the first European power to be defeated by an Asian power. One of the reasons that Russia lost was that the government kept its best troops in the capital to put down worker unrest. As public anger against the government rose, an Orthodox priest in St. Petersburg organized a peaceful protest march for factory workers. Father Gapon and his allies hoped to ameliorate working conditions, not overthrow the state. Their procession on Sunday, 9 January humbly asked Emperor Nicholas II (r. 1894–1917) for an eight-hour workday, the right to strike, and a representative assembly, among other things. Tragically, Nicholas believed that his God-given duty was to preserve autocracy unchanged and at all costs. This created a terrible mismatch between the government and a society that was changing rapidly. Nicholas, who was not in St. Petersburg that day, ordered soldiers to disperse the procession. They opened fire on the unarmed workers. Hundreds of people died, and the survivors were arrested and exiled. This gave them the opportunity to tell a wide audience how the tsar had murdered his innocent subjects on Bloody Sunday. Riots and strikes broke out in more than two dozen other cities; the workers were supported by many in the professional and even aristocratic classes, who were out of patience with a government that covered up incompetence with brutality. So many different segments of society staged strikes and protests that the empire largely ground to a halt for the summer. Finally the unrest forced Nicholas to issue a capitulation called the October Manifesto, which provided for "genuine inviolability of the person, freedom of conscience, speech, assembly and association" and the election of a representative body, called the Duma.[1]

Two Central Asias

Two Central Asias responded differently to Bloody Sunday. Russian Central Asia did not hear about Bloody Sunday until February, but when it did workers went on strike and the Socialist Revolutionary (SR) and Social Democratic

(SD) parties coordinated with each other to organize anti-government actions. The revolutionary parties had members in Tashkent because of the tsarist policy of exiling troublemakers far from the Russian center. In this way the government itself helped to spread revolution. Railroad workers and engineers led a unified labor action in October, which was attacked by Cossacks wielding clubs. By the end of the year the strikes abated, but more because of worker disorganization than satisfaction with the October Manifesto.[2]

Islamic Central Asia did not see the upheavals of 1905 as its fight. There are no recorded strikes or protests led by Muslims over Bloody Sunday. Russian officials attributed this indifference to the conservative influence of the ulama, which led them to view Islamic institutions as possible allies against revolutionary forces. They were misreading the situation, however. Some Kazakh and Kyrgyz nomads agitated against the Slavic settlers who were driving them into ever-smaller areas while calling them "dogs."[3] In 1905 and 1906 Tatars convened empire-wide congresses of Muslims, but few Turkestanis or Kazakhs attended.[4] The true impact of 1905 lay in the new freedoms that the government had been forced to grant. These principles were limited: newspapers no longer had to submit articles for prior censorship, but the state could punish them post-publication. Nevertheless, the October Manifesto opened up one of the greatest periods of free expression in Russian history, and Central Asians fully participated in it.

A small group of Turkestani intellectuals founded the first independent Turki-language newspapers in 1906. These lasted barely eighteen months before being shut down, but they printed important discussions of the new ideas that were rattling Islamic societies from Cairo to the Dutch East Indies. The first issue of *Taraqqi* (*Progress*) printed a cry of frustration on its front page:

> Are we Muslims becoming free? No! Kinsmen, a hundred times no!
> During these two years all peoples have argued and struggled. The Muslims
> have been asleep. In Petersburg, Moscow, and other places people argue
> and the workers grab for justice. Our children see this and call us savages.[5]

The image of sleeping Muslims who need to wake up and fight for themselves can be found in reformist writings throughout the colonized world.[6] Educated Turkestanis were joining an international conversation about how Islamic societies had become so weak and what to do about it. For the young men behind *Taraqqi*, awakening the Muslims began with reforming education.

Since Napoleon invaded Egypt in 1798, some Muslims had argued that the best way to resist European encroachment was to adopt European science and technology, which required adopting some European ways of thinking as well. This was a dangerous proposition because it threatened traditional ways of understanding the world and traditional authority structures. By the 1880s there were robust movements in Egypt and India to modernize Islam, and robust opposition to those movements. The most important Russian Muslim to spread knowledge of these debates was the Crimean Tatar Ismail bey Gaspirali, who founded a reformist newspaper called *Terjuman* (*The Translator*) in 1883. The core of Gaspirali's program was to create a unified Turkic language and teach that language phonetically. This would free Muslims throughout the empire to read and write about new ideas in a language that all could understand. By the mid-1880s a few hundred people in Turkestan were reading *Terjuman*. By the turn of the century newspapers from the Ottoman Empire, India, and Kazan also circulated widely.[7]

Schools were the key to realizing Gaspirali's vision. The first Jadid ("new method") school in Turkestan opened in Samarkand in 1893. By 1903 around twenty new-method maktabs were operating in Tashkent; similar schools opened in Kokand and even Bukhara by 1910. These schools were open to girls as well as boys, and incorporated a new idea of childhood into their curriculum by using textbooks aimed at children's level of understanding rather than expecting children to memorize adult texts by rote. The schools taught geography and basic arithmetic in addition to phonetic literacy and religion.[8] The organizer of the Jadid schools in Tashkent, Munawwar Qori, explained his motivations to readers of the newspaper *Khurshid* (*The Sun*) as follows:

The Europeans, taking advantage of our negligence and ignorance, took our government from our hands, and are gradually taking over our crafts and trades. If we do not quickly make an effort to reform our affairs in order to safeguard ourselves, our nation, and our children, our future will be extremely difficult. Reform begins with a rapid start in cultivating sciences conforming to our times.[9]

What "nation" was Qori addressing in his essay? The word *vatan* (homeland) was not new to his audience, but it did not have a universally accepted definition. Qori and his fellow reformists thought in terms of "the Muslims of Turkestan," a community bounded by religion and the approximate borders of the old Uzbek khanates. This loose definition excluded the nomadic Turkmen,

Kyrgyz, and Kazakhs.[10] It also excluded the Farsi-speaking Jewish community, which had lived in the region for a thousand years, and of course the millions of Slavs who by now thought of Central Asia as their home. The Jadid reformers' "nation" at this point was a distant ideal. They focused their energies on expanding their school network and writing essays and theater dramas that exhorted Muslims to abandon encrusted customs and embrace new thinking.

The Jadids consisted of small groups in Turkestan and Bukhara. Other groups had different ideas about how to fix their society, or did not consider that it needed fixing at all. Wealthy merchants in Tashkent, who had benefited the most from Russian colonization, sponsored their own newspaper called *Tojjar* (*The Merchant*). This was a moderate publication that advocated for political rights for Turkestanis within the empire, criticizing both worker and police violence.[11] The few hundred men who had studied in Russian-native schools had direct access to Russian political debates. Ubaydulla Xo'jaev was born in 1880 in Tashkent; after school his first job was as a translator in a Russian law office there. His hunger for learning impressed his employer, who brought the young Xo'jaev along to a new job in Saratov in 1905. There Xo'jaev began doing his own legal work and made contact with members of the populist SR and Marxist SD parties, whose ideas intrigued him. He also wrote an admiring letter to the writer and Christian social philosopher Lev Tolstoy, which shows his curiosity about a wide range of Russian thought. When Xo'jaev returned to Tashkent in 1913 he became involved in some of Munawwar Qori's Jadid theater productions, and edited the reformist newspaper *Sadoi Turkiston* (*Voice of Turkestan*).[12]

It is tempting to divide Turkestani intellectuals into clear-cut "reformist" or "conservative" categories, but we need to resist the lure of a simple story. While Russian agents in Bukhara complained about ulama who rejected modern medicine, even those clergy who opposed the Jadids were not a uniform block. Most Jadid reformers were graduates of madrasas, and some traditionalist scholars bewailed the low state of local Islamic culture in the same terms that Jadid publications used.[13] Too much focus on the views of the few who were educated and politically engaged also allows us to forget that we simply do not know how the majority of ordinary Turkestanis felt about the state of their society. The poet Dilshod, one of the few non-elites who left a written record, commented:

After Kokand passed into the hands of Russian governors I had the opportunity to take the train to my hometown O'ratepe three times. [On my first] trip, my days under siege, the exiled prisoners of O'ratepe who were

driven on foot along the narrow path of terrible suffering into the desert
wasteland, the battle on the square, the chains of torment, and the hanged
[men] passed one by one before my eyes. God's truth, I was grateful for
the loving care of the Russian master road-builders. I had learned about
thousands of denunciations of Moghul and Qipchaq officials, who were
Bukharan troublemakers. Now looking at the scenes of life in O'ratepe under
the Russian office, I concluded that the situation of the people of Istravshan
is a thousand times better than it was before for the Muslim community.[14]

Dilshod could only represent her own experience; the man who had seen a
Cossack murder his child would have had something very different to say.
Turkestanis' understanding of their situation cannot be reduced to a simple
formula of resistance and reaction.

Educated Kazakhs also discussed ideas of cultural revival and nationhood,
and promoted Gaspirali's new method of teaching. In addition to publishing
newspapers and forming literary circles, in late 1905 they organized a nationalist movement called Alash Orda.[15] The Kazakhs faced a deeper cultural crisis
than the Turkestanis did because Slavic settlers had pushed nomadic life to
the brink of collapse. The reformers, led by Alikhan Bukeikhanov, were "white
bone" elites who had attended Russian or Russian-Kazakh schools.[16] They
were searching for a viable way to be Kazakh in a world that prized literacy,
technology, and economic power. They believed that nomadism had no future
and could not agree on the role that Islam should play in a modern Kazakh
nation. They were able to unite around educational and language reforms that
would allow Kazakh to become a creative literary language and the core of a
new national identity.[17] While Turkestanis could not participate in the first
Duma and had minimal representation in the second, Kazakhs including
Mukhamedjan Tynyshpaev served as active deputies. After the second Duma
was disbanded in June 1907, however, all Central Asians lost representation.[18]
Bukeikhanov also worked to make Alash a political movement for Kazakhs
of all tribes, a difficult task that pitted him against his fellow aristocrats.

THE GREAT WAR AND THE GREAT UNRAVELLING

World War i began in June 1914 with a Serbian nationalist assassinating the
heir to the Austro-Hungarian throne in Sarajevo, Bosnia, a region that had
belonged to the Ottoman Empire but was annexed by Austria in 1908. The

complexities spiraled out from there, soon engulfing not only Europe but also the European powers' colonies. The Ottoman Empire had undergone its own constitutional revolution in 1909 and was ruled by a party of nationalist modernizers, who sought economic and political aid from an alliance with Germany. This alliance drew the Ottomans in to a fatal entanglement, as Austria (backed by Germany) presented unacceptable demands to Serbia (backed by Russia), which led to the Germans and Russians mobilizing their massive armies in July. When the Ottoman government entered the war on the German side in late October, Minister of War Enver Pasha personally led the Third Army in an attack on the Russian Caucasus. Enver's quest for glory turned into a catastrophe that cost the Turks some 60,000 men, the first in a series of disasters.[19]

By 1914 the Russian Empire contained almost as many Muslims as the Ottoman Empire, and Russian officials worried about their loyalty. When the Turks marched on the Caucasus, Russia deported Muslims in the border areas on suspicion that they would collaborate with the enemy. Beyond that action, the Russian government found it more valuable to project the image of a multi-ethnic empire united by loyalty to the tsar than to publicly doubt Muslim trustworthiness. While some Muslims were sympathetic to the Ottoman side, half a million of them did fight for Russia.[20] These included few Central Asians, however. As inorodtsy (legal aliens) the nomads were exempt from the military draft, and the Russian military believed that settled Turkestanis were not acculturated enough to serve.

The war was far away from Central Asia, but it exacerbated tensions that had been building up for years. A law passed in 1909 gave land in Turkestan deemed "surplus" to nomad needs to Slavic settlers, and expanded irrigation works created more arable land out of former steppe and desert. Much of this new farm land was planted with cotton: between 1902 and 1913 the acreage under cotton more than doubled to 550,000 desiatinas (1.3 million acres), making Turkestan dependent on grain imports from Russia.[21] Settlers who abused Turkestanis did not fear government punishment.[22] Settler migration dried up when the war began, but in place of settlers the war brought the first prison camps to Turkestan. These held around 200,000 prisoners of war in appalling conditions; camp commanders paid locals a bounty for capturing escapees.[23] Urban Turkestanis suffered under higher taxes, inflation, and worsening food supplies as the war dragged on.

Russia's role in the war, at least according to Britain and France, was to supply an infinite steamroller of soldiers that would overwhelm the Central

Powers with sheer numbers. This fantasy evaporated when the Germans destroyed the Russian First and Second armies in August and September 1914. Russian soldiers fought bravely but were poorly fed and equipped, and coordination among commanders was unreliable.[24] All the combatants entered the war expecting a short conflict, but this war definitively proved the proposition that the war you plan for is never the war that you actually get. While soldiers on the Western Front were trapped in the bloody stasis of the trenches, in the east the war sent millions of people on the roads along a thousand-mile frontier as soldiers marched west and Poles, Jews, and other civilians were forced to abandon their homes and walk east. The Russian military was decimated by millions of casualties and prisoners of war, and in the chaos hundreds of thousands of soldiers deserted.[25] By 1916 manpower and supplies were dangerously low. The criminal incompetence and corruption of Tsar Nicholas's government enraged and disgusted the public. The Council of Ministers tried to fix the crisis by drafting Central Asian men to serve in labor battalions behind the front lines.

The Colonial War of 1916

The announcement of the draft in early July created confusion and then anger in Turkestan. The government did a poor job of explaining the purpose of the draft to a population that had little understanding of the war. Russian officials ordered local oqsoqols to draw up lists of who would be drafted; often oqsoqols demanded bribes to keep names off the lists. The first riot broke out in Khujand in the Ferghana Valley, where a crowd attacked a police station. The violence spread quickly to Samarkand, Tashkent, and Jizzax, and turned murderous: rioters killed Russian officials, oqsoqols, and their families. Women played a notable role, often in the front ranks of protesting crowds. Some were enraged because the draft threatened to take away the men who supported them, others did not want to sacrifice for the colonial occupier. Russia had to use troops that were desperately needed elsewhere to crush the violence, which subsided after a few weeks.[26]

The draft ignited an all-out war in the eastern Steppe Krai and Semirechie, which cost hundreds of thousands of lives. The unraveling and collapse of the Russian Empire began here, when Kazakhs and Kyrgyz exploded in rage after decades of settler encroachment. As in Turkestan, the violence began with angry crowds lynching local officials charged with implementing the draft.

Within about six weeks fighting groups organized themselves in the steppe to attack Russian telegraph and railroad lines and Russian villages. This was open anti-colonial warfare, and the Russian military and settlers responded with savage violence of their own. In the area of Semirechie around Lake Issyk-kul, Kyrgyz and Slavic settlers fought to exterminate each other, both sides using terror against civilians as a major weapon. Early Kyrgyz attacks killed 3500 settlers, and in reprisal Russian troops systematically slaughtered Kyrgyz. By the fall hundreds of thousands of Kyrgyz, with their animals and households, were fleeing across the Tien Shan mountains into China. Winter had come early in 1916; the passes were slippery with snow and food was scarce. At least 200,000 Kyrgyz died of cold, hunger, and Russian bullets.[27]

Even here, however, people acted out of complicated motivations. For some nomad aristocrats the insult was not in being drafted, but in being drafted to dig ditches rather than fight. Kanat Abukin was a Kyrgyz manap who had been born in Semirechie in 1856, making him fifty-eight years old when the war broke out.[28] He had worked with Russian officials for years in his capacity as a village chief, but watched the lives of his people worsen as settlers moved in. In 1914 he and his son tried to enlist in the army and were upset when they were refused. In August 1916 Abukin dictated a letter to Russian authorities on behalf of a group of Kyrgyz men who were willing to fight for the tsar in positions that accorded with their sense of dignity.[29] Rejected again, in October Abukin was captured while leading his people into China. The Russians hanged him in January as a supposed leader of the entire uprising. In April the new Provisional Government rescinded martial law and the draft for Central Asians, although that did not halt the fighting.

Overthrow of the Tsarist Regime

After ninety years of revolutionary agitation, the last threads holding the tsarist government together snapped. In a fit of patriotism, in 1914 the capital St. Petersburg had been re-named Petrograd, and Petrograd in early 1917 was a cold and hungry city. Food riots broke out 23 February/8 March after women who had been waiting in line all day for bread were told there was no more.[30] This was not so unusual, but what turned a riot into a revolution was that soldiers guarding the warehouses decided to side with the crowd against government orders. Once a government loses the support of its army, there is nothing it can do to protect itself. Tsar Nicholas abdicated with a whimper on 1/15 March at the demand of two new bodies that were vying for control in Petrograd: the Provisional Government and the Soviet of Workers' and Soldiers' Deputies.[31]

The Provisional Government consisted of ministers and Duma deputies who banded together to stabilize administration until an elected body could convene to draft a constitution. The Soviet was a more complicated entity. The word *soviet* means "council" in Russian; soviets of workers had first appeared during the 1905 revolution. In 1917 they reconstituted themselves as councils of representatives of workers and soldiers without a fixed party affiliation. Initially SRs dominated the soviets, but Mensheviks and Bolsheviks also participated. The Petrograd Soviet was the most organized and powerful due to its close ties with rank-and-file men in the Petrograd garrison and the Baltic Fleet. For most of 1917 a situation of "dual power" prevailed, wherein the Provisional Government and the Soviet exercised authority in different spheres. Neither side paid much attention to what the many non-Russian peoples of the empire were doing.

Russian and Muslim Central Asians alike greeted the February Revolution with joy, but the fall of the tsar did not bring the two Central Asias together. In fact removal of the common enemy revealed deep divisions within each community, not just between them. All of the major political parties were represented in the Russian population, but none was dominant. Russians in Tashkent could not organize a branch of the Provisional Government until April, while Russians in the Steppe Krai never organized a regional government. Russian soldiers and workers set up soviets of their own, reflecting their distrust of upper class Russians. The new Turkestan government was headed by a member of the centrist Constitutional Democrat (Kadet) party. It was almost entirely a Russian enterprise, and as such its power was confined to Tashkent, Samarkand, and a few other towns. The lawyer Ubaydulla Xo'jaev was one of four Muslims on the Tashkent Executive Committee, but he had little authority. Members of the soviets were openly hostile to Muslims.[32]

Divisions among Central Asians reflected multifarious tensions along lines of status, age, education, tribe, and political ideals. Leaders of the Kazakh Alash Orda movement were affiliated with the Kadet party, which represented the views of the intellectual and professional class in favor of a constitutional, democratic regime. Bukeikhanov, Tynyshpaev, and the writer and linguist Akhmed Baitursunov joined local Provisional Government organs but were suspicious of the Bolsheviks. They and other Kazakhs participated in several empire-wide congresses of Muslims, but the congresses were dominated by Tatars. The Alash party's major concern was restoring Kazakh control over the land. They favored uniting all Kazakhs within a federal republic of Russia, which would have destroyed the remaining tribal structures. The Alash party list received a majority of Kazakh votes for the Constituent Assembly in November, but that was nullified by Bolshevik actions. The assembly was elected as a representative body to draft a constitution, but the SR party won a plurality of votes. The Bolsheviks had seized power just before the election, and shut down the assembly at gun point 6/19 January 1918. In any case, with ongoing war between nomads and settlers and an unstable situation in Petrograd, no group had the resources to implement a political program.[33]

Muslims in Asian Tashkent organized their own governing council, the Shura-i Islamiya (Muslim Council), which then organized councils in other cities. Turkestani politics was divided between the older ulama and oqsoqols and the younger reformers who challenged their authority. Jadid reformers dominated the First Turkestan Muslim Congress, held in April, and approved a political program similar to that of Alash, including support for Turkestani autonomy within a federal Russian republic. The congress created a Turkestan National Council to coordinate with Alash, headed by Mustafa Choqay, a Kazakh Turkestani with Russian legal training.[34] The ulama picked up the modern tool and formed their own political party, the Ulama Jamiyati (Society of Ulama). Anger between the factions flared when Petrograd gave women everywhere in the empire the right to vote. The Jadids were eager to enroll women as voters for their reforms, while the ulama rejected any possibility that women and "youth" (*yoshlar*, as they dismissed the reformers) could have a say in governance.[35] Not much action came out of these arguments, not only because governing organs were so primitive but because food supplies had been disrupted and preventing starvation became the top priority. Hunger exacerbated tensions between Russians and Turkestanis, as insecure Russians were convinced that Turkestanis were hiding food from them.[36]

People in the protectorates of Bukhara and Khiva were also happy to see the tsar go, but the two polities were in very different positions. Khiva had been weakened by the Russian conquest and saw few benefits from railroad and cotton development. Meanwhile the Yomut Turkmen of Khiva had recovered their military strength, and in 1915 a Yomut leader named Junaid Khan occupied Khiva and made Khan Isfendiyar (r. 1910–18) his puppet. The Russians drove him out, but the revolution allowed him to return in 1917 to rule through Isfendiyar and then his brother Sayyid Abdullo (r. 1918–20).[37] Khiva became so chaotic that no one group could assert real control over the area for some years. In Bukhara Emir Alim Khan tried to balance the Russians, the ulama, and an active Jadid group against each other. In April he issued a proclamation promising fiscal reforms that the Russians wanted and educational reforms that the Jadids liked, but within the limits of sharia. Some reformers, including Fayzulla Xo'jaev and a young writer named Abdurauf Fitrat, organized a demonstration to demand more from the emir. Conservatives mounted a counter-demonstration, and the emir used the unrest as an excuse to arrest and expel as many Jadids as his police could catch. Sadriddin Aini suffered seventy-five lashes of the whip in the emir's prison.[38]

In Petrograd the Provisional Government was flailing. Great Britain and France were desperate to keep Russia in the war, and Russian ministers were determined to honor their commitments to them. The soldiers and most civilians, however, saw no reason to keep dying for the abstract cause of national honor. Peasant soldiers deserted from the front to return to their villages and join the mass peasant confiscation of land from the nobility. The Provisional Government was powerless to stop them. The moderate socialist SR and Menshevik parties that dominated the soviets cooperated with the government, but their support of the war caused many workers and peasants to lose trust in them. Vladimir Lenin, leader of the Bolsheviks, played to public exhaustion with a slogan promising what everyone wanted: land, bread, and peace. Lenin had returned to Russia from exile in April, and startled his fellow Bolsheviks by proclaiming that Russia was ready for a full communist revolution in which the working class would wield all political and economic power. As the Provisional Government's authority leaked away over the summer, the Bolsheviks gained popular support in Petrograd and in Moscow. On the evening of 24 October/6 November, despite the qualms of many of his comrades, Lenin ordered the party's muscle, the Military Revolutionary Committee headed by Lev Trotsky, to seize control of communication and transportation centers and occupy the Winter Palace where the Provisional Government met. In Petrograd the government folded as quickly as the tsarist government had, but in Moscow it took several weeks of fighting for the Bolsheviks to establish their control. Nonetheless, in a tumultuous meeting 8 and 9 November, the All-Russian Congress of Soviets declared a new, socialist government to be run by a Council of People's Commissars, chaired by Lenin.

MARXISM, BOLSHEVISM, AND EMPIRE

The Bolsheviks' greatest advantage over rival parties was that Lenin laid out a political program that guided concrete actions, whereas other parties and the Provisional Government were disorganized and more reactive than proactive. Lenin's first two decrees withdrew Russia from the war and abolished private property, enacting two-thirds of the Bolsheviks' summer slogan. Another way in which Lenin's political thought stood out was that he was the only leader who had seriously considered how the revolution should affect Russia's multi-national empire.

Karl Marx and Friedrich Engels taught that proletarians all over the world would seize control over factories, land, and other means of economic production. Then, because nations were the product of capitalist economic processes, proletarian class solidarity would override national loyalty and nations would cease to exist. Marx and Engels did not, however, spend time imagining the details or how the transition would work. In the early twentieth century, communists from the Austro-Hungarian Empire and Russia argued over two models of how revolutionary, multi-national societies should be structured. Their main concern was how best to guarantee equality to national minorities during the transition to full communism. The Austrians proposed "national-cultural autonomy": small nations had the right to develop and preserve their cultures in a communist society even if they lived in widely scattered communities. Lenin hated the idea of grafting nationalism onto Marxism, and commissioned a young Georgian Bolshevik named Joseph Djugashvili (writing under the *nom de guerre* Koba Stalin) to write a counter-argument. Stalin's essay "Marxism and the National Question" (1913) would provide the theoretical basis for a profound re-shaping of Central Asia after the Bolsheviks took power.

Stalin structured his argument in clear stages. First, that a nation can be defined as "a historically constituted, stable community of people, formed on the basis of a common language, territory, economic life, and psychological make-up manifested in a common culture."[39] Second, that the owners of the means of production (the bourgeoisie) whip up national prejudices to oppress minority workers: "One cannot speak seriously of a full development of the intellectual faculties of the Tatar or Jewish worker if he is not allowed to use his native language at meetings and lectures, and if his schools are closed down."[40] Therefore, even though nations were invented by the bourgeoisie, it is the duty of conscious proletarians to fight against national bigotry and oppression. The best way for Marxists to purge the poison of bigotry is to support the right of self-determination for all nations, but Stalin adds an important caveat:

> While combatting the coercion of any nation, [Social Democracy] will uphold only the right of the *nation* itself to determine its own destiny, at the same time agitating against harmful customs and institutions of that nation in order to enable the toiling strata of the nation to emancipate themselves from them.[41]

Early Bolshevik nationality theory makes a neat package: the communist revolution will be a global revolution, but national minorities that have been oppressed by Russians have good reasons to be suspicious of a revolution led by Russians. In order to allay these suspicions, the revolution guarantees the right of national self-determination to all peoples who fit Stalin's definition of "nation." However, communist economic structures will inevitably destroy the idea of "nationhood," and to that end the Bolsheviks also claim the right to undermine cultural practices that they determine to be harmful to the working class. These practices include religion and patriarchal family structures.

When Stalin wrote this, no one expected the revolution to happen soon. A mere four years later, Lenin named Stalin his Commissar of Nationalities in the new government, and together they began to apply theory to the real world. Soon after seizing power they issued a proclamation that promised national self-determination, including the right of nations to secede from the Bolshevik state. Their next proclamation was specifically addressed "To All Toiling Muslims of Russia and the East." It promised:

> Henceforth your beliefs and customs, your national and cultural institutions are declared to be free and inviolable. Establish your national life freely and without hindrance. You have the right to do this. Know that your rights, and the rights of all the peoples of Russia, are guarded with all the might of the revolution and its organs, the soviets of workers', soldiers', and peasants' deputies.[42]

They had not yet begun to grapple with the reality that many of the non-Russian peoples of the former empire did not meet Stalin's criteria for nationhood, in particular the mixed societies of Central Asia. In fact Lenin saw these proclamations as slogans to persuade non-Russian peoples to pledge loyalty to his government, not as the bases for a new state. He believed with absolute faith that the Bolshevik Revolution would set off the world-wide communist revolution, and that the workers of Europe would come to impoverished Russia's aid to build a global proletarian society. Instead, by early 1918 the Bolsheviks had real control only in the core Russian regions of the former empire. Ukraine, Georgia, Finland, and other territories had proclaimed themselves independent nations, and "White" armies led by former tsarist officers were gathering to crush the "Red" communists. The ensuing civil war would kill approximately ten million people.

CENTRAL ASIA SHATTERED

For Central Asians the Bolshevik Revolution was about hunger and communal violence, not class conflict. Soldiers seized control of Russian Tashkent in the name of the soviet for the first time in September 1917; their goal was control over the railroad station and food warehouses. They retreated then, but returned permanently on 1/15 November. The Ulama Jamiyati, which governed Asian Tashkent independently, offered to work with the new government, but the soviet flatly rejected Muslim participation on the grounds that there were no Muslim factory workers.[43] Within a month the Tashkent soviet was conducting food requisition raids in the Asian city, motivated by the old Russian suspicions that wily locals were hiding grain stocks. The Tashkenters followed the Petrograd Bolsheviks' lead in banning private trade and confiscating large land holdings, which not coincidentally put much of the food infrastructure under Russian control.[44] The soviet distributed grain to the Slavic population without regard for Turkestani needs. These actions hastened the approach of famine for everyone, since they disrupted farming and markets. In January 1918 commissars searching for grain in Orenburg noted, "At Chust, 10–12 people die every day, in the uezd of Aulie-Ata the bodies of famished and frozen Kazakhs lie along the roads." Then anti-Bolshevik Cossacks at Orenburg cut the railroad line between Turkestan and Russia until October 1919, which certainly did not help matters. By 1921 famine and disease would kill approximately 1.6 million Central Asians, most of them in the already hard-hit nomad population.[45] The Slavic minority covered their anxiety with communist rhetoric, but their revolution was a colonialist power grab.

Those Central Asians who were not struggling just to stay alive suddenly had multiple routes for political action, but all of them were fraught with danger. At the end of November 1917 a congress of Muslims in Kokand voted to set up their own autonomous government, with a ruling commission led by Kazakhs Choqay and Tynyshpaev from the Alash party and Turkestani modernists like Ubaydulla Xo'jaev. The Turkestan (or sometimes Kokand) Autonomy government was run by Muslims but included places for Russians and Jews as well. The government aligned itself with anti-Bolshevik parties, but it probably would have been doomed for logistical reasons even if the Tashkent soviet had not attacked Kokand in January. Kokand alone did not have the financial or food resources to survive. More importantly, it had no army. Nonetheless, this brief bid for a new kind of government drew enthusiastic support from people who wanted to see Turkestan become a modern nation that was respected in the world. The young reformers Fitrat and Cholpon (Abdulhamid Sulayman Yunus) lauded Turkestan Autonomy as a new dawn that should warm the blood of Central Asian Turks.[46] Their poems illustrated how the idea of nationhood had taken root in reformist thought, although they could not yet define what the Turkestan nation might be. The Turkestan Autonomy leaders were hoping to participate in a federal Russian government created by the Constituent Assembly, but the Bolsheviks closed down the assembly by force. Three weeks later, 29 January/11 February, soldiers from the Tashkent soviet stormed the gates of Kokand and destroyed the government and much of the city.[47] The leadership survived (Tynyshpaev returned to Semirechie, Choqay died in Germany in 1941), but no new viable movements for Turkestani independence developed.

Early Communist Government

Despite the fact that the Bolsheviks were largely cut off from Central Asia, they were able to send an extraordinary agent for the party, Petr A. Kobozev, to Tashkent in April 1918 to implement communism. Kobozev shocked all sides by his actions. He forced the Tashkent soviet to accept Muslim members, and in June pushed them to establish a formal Communist Party of Turkestan (KPT) that was subordinate to the Russian Communist Party. In 1919 the KPT authorized the establishment of a Muslim bureau within the party staffed by communist Turkestanis, of whom Turar Rysqulov was the most prominent. Kobozev strengthened earlier land decrees by setting up "committees of the poor," encouraging them to take land from Slavic settlers and large Muslim landowners and distribute it to poor Muslims. This included the arable land that belonged to waqfs, Islamic charitable endowments. The Bolsheviks were especially keen on seizing control of the cotton fields. Even before Kobozev arrived, the Turkestan government had claimed a monopoly on all aspects of cotton production. Lenin dedicated fifty million rubles to developing irrigation in Turkestan.[48] The land seizures enraged settlers and clergy, who said that they violated Islamic property laws. Many poor Muslims did not want to see themselves as thieves, and refused to cooperate. Kobozev was backed by soldiers, but resistance was so widespread that all he succeeded in doing was creating instability and contributing to the famine.[49]

The revolutionary years in the Kazakh lands were even more chaotic. Soviets organized in the towns but there was no administrative center equivalent to Tashkent. Alash leaders negotiated with Lenin and Stalin in March 1918 to have the Bolsheviks recognize Alash as the Kazakh government, but neither side trusted the other.[50] By May that became irrelevant, as the White Army of Admiral Alexander Kolchak swept across Siberia and the northern Kazakh areas, Cossacks seized control in Orenburg, Vernyi, and Akmolinsk, and an army of stranded Czech prisoners of war fought to return home. The Red Army occupied the Syr Darya basin and parts of Semirechie and worked with a small pro-Bolshevik Kazakh party. Political authority became communal rather than territorial: Kazakhs were governed by Alash, Russians by Kolchak, and Cossacks by their local hetmans (Cossack commanders). Ordinary people were beset by hunger and disease and were targeted by armies of all sides; murder, rape, and pillage were common.

In this fluid and dangerous situation, the Alash leadership managed to organize a bare-bones government in Semipalatinsk. While they were negotiating with Lenin he had sent them funds for organizing a congress, and they acquired more money "under the table" from a White officer group.[51] This was enough to print a newspaper and start raising their own militia. When the Whites took over in June, Bukeikhanov co-opted the former tsarist administrative apparatus to collect taxes, run schools, and found a Kazakh officer academy. Under the circumstances this was impressive, but still the government was too poor and weak to come close to meeting Kazakhs' needs. A bigger problem was that Kolchak had no more respect for the Kazakhs than Lenin did, and so while several thousand Kazakh soldiers fought the Bolsheviks, Alash and White leaders argued over who had the authority to command and pay them. In July Kolchak's government announced that it would grant the Kazakhs cultural autonomy, but not political independence.

The Kazakhs angrily protested, and the result was a stalemate where the Alash government was neither independent nor fully subordinate.

Lenin moved the capital to Moscow in March 1918, and over the course of 1919 the Bolsheviks' central location and superior organization turned the war in their favor. In March Red commander Mikhail Frunze connected the Turkestan Army with the Fourth Army of the eastern front to create a united line that threatened White control in Orenburg and Uralsk oblasts. By July the Fourth Army reached the Ural River; in October they pushed out the Cossack government at Orenburg. The Alash government had split into western and eastern sections in September 1918, and fragmented further under Red pressure. In March 1919 Baitursunov brought his military forces to join the Soviet of Worker, Peasant, and Kazakh Deputies in Turgai. In July Stalin gave him a nominal position on a new proto-governing board, the "Kirgiz" [Kazakh] Revolutionary Military Committee.[52] Once the Bolsheviks controlled Orenburg they started to woo the western Alash chiefs Jagansha and Khalel Dosmukhamedov, and the brothers joined the Reds in November after the Bolsheviks had declared an amnesty for Alash members.[53] By December the Reds were in Semipalatinsk planning how to absorb Alash's assets, including the small oil industry. In March 1920 the Bolsheviks formally dissolved the Alash government. In August they created the Kirgiz [Kazakh] Autonomous Soviet Socialist Republic (ASSR) within the Russian republic, its capital at Orenburg. The Bolsheviks honored their amnesty pledge, and Bukeikhanov, Tynyshpaev, and the Dosmukhamedovs went to work for the new government. While Alash was always an anti-Bolshevik party, in fact Lenin and Stalin had a similar vision for the future of the Kazakh nation: no longer divided into tribes, united on the basis of language and territory, in possession of their own land, with modern education available to all. Baitursunov argued that for this reason the Bolsheviks offered the best hope for true Kazakh liberation. In any case, they had no choice.

After the Turkestan Autonomy government fell in February 1918 there were four governments operating in Transoxiana: Bukhara, Khiva, Turkestan, and an anti-Bolshevik Russian government in Ashkhabad. In addition, dozens of small bands known as *basmachi* fought against the Bolsheviks, the emir, and the Shura-i Islamiya. The Council of People's Commissars (Sovnarkom) of Turkestan, chaired by the former railroad worker Feodor I. Kolesov, was convinced that Emir Alim Khan of Bukhara was itching to attack Tashkent with help from Ashkhabad and the British, who still controlled India, Iran, and parts of Afghanistan. This fear was overblown; the emir stayed neutral and waited to see who would win. Nonetheless, Kolesov made contact with the Bukharan Jadids, most of whom had fled to the Russian "New Bukhara" settlement after the emir expelled them.

The "Young Bukharans," as the reformers now called themselves, were eager to ally with the Bolsheviks not only to remove their common enemy the emir, but to implement their dreams of modernization. Kolesov's help instead came close to destroying them all. He arrived in Russian Bukhara in March 1918 with weapons for the Young Bukharans and the few hundred Russian soldiers stationed there, and they demanded that Alim Khan surrender to Young Bukharan-Bolshevik joint rule or fight. The emir played for time by agreeing to the demand but asking for a few days to disarm his troops. Kolesov gave him only one day, but that was all the emir needed to cut the railroad and telegraph lines behind the Russians and trap them. A mob massacred the delegation that Kolesov sent to accept the emir's surrender. The Russians spent a day and half shelling Old Bukhara, but somehow managed not to hit anything. Then Kolesov started to retreat on foot, accompanied by Russian settlers and the Young Bukharans. The emir demanded that Kolesov hand over Xo'jaev, Fitrat, and other Jadids, but Kolesov refused. The column was rescued after several days by troops sent from Tashkent, and Alim Khan was delighted to find that he had rid himself of the Young Bukharans and many Russians with minimal effort. The frustrated Young Bukharans dispersed: Xo'jaev went to Moscow to secure more Bolshevik support, and the rest moved to Tashkent or Samarkand.[54]

One might be wondering at this point why the Bolsheviks did not just let go of Central Asia, which was nowhere near the level of economic development that Marx and Engels deemed necessary for communism. The answer lies in their assumption that the communist revolution by definition must be a global revolution. Stanislav S. Pestkovskii, chair of the Kazakh regional Revolutionary Military Committee, wrote in 1919:

> It is now that Turkestan is ordained to be the gates from Europe to Asia: from Soviet Russia, the current center of the world revolution, the idea of social and political freedom for the long-suffering working masses of the East—from the native as well as from the newly-arrived enslavers—must be transfused through Turkestan to Asia.[55]

Pestkovskii's comment succinctly reveals Bolshevik thinking and the staggering scale of the gamble that Lenin and Trotsky took with the

October Revolution. They believed that Marx's exhortation "Workers of the world unite!" meant just what it said: either all workers unite, or global capitalism would crush them. That included workers in India, Iran, and China, who were going to need help from more advanced European proletarians to reach their revolutionary potential. Note that Pestkovskii lists unspecified "native" as well as colonial oppressors from which Asian workers will be freed. The revolution would define who the "native enslavers" were. Those who disagreed would automatically be considered counter-revolutionaries.

To that end, the Bolsheviks set up new governing committees that would bring Turkestan under tighter central control. In addition to the Turkestan Communist Party and its Muslim Bureau, in October 1919 the Communist Party in Moscow formed the Turkestan Commission, a council of commissars who represented Moscow directly in Turkestan. Initially the commissars were all Slavic, but Rysqulov, Nazir T. Turakulov, Abdullo R. Rakhimbaev, Sultanbek Xo'janov, and Kaigisyz S. Atabaev joined in 1920. These multiplying layers of government were not only confusing, they clashed with Turkestani communists' assumption that they would be governing themselves with Bolshevik assistance. In January 1920 Rysqulov proposed to re-name Turkestan the Turkic Soviet Republic, governed by the Turkic Communist Party, based on his belief that national identity was equivalent for colonized peoples to class identity for European communists. The Muslim Bureau went so far as to propose creating a Muslim Red Army.

Rysqulov was among a number of Muslim communists, the best known of whom was the Tatar Mirsaid Sultangaliev, who argued that being colonial subjects was their version of being proletarians, and that developing their national cultures was just as revolutionary as establishing the dictatorship of the proletariat. For them the enemy to overcome was not so much bourgeois capitalism as *kolonizatorstvo* (colonizerism)—the oppression of Turkic Muslims by European settlers, regardless of political ideology. The Russian members of the Turkestan Commission also wanted to end settler abuses, but they made clear that Bolshevik ideological terms could not be changed or challenged. Turkic and Slavic communists took their fight all the way to Lenin in Moscow, who sided with the Slavs on the commission. Lenin ordered new elections to be held for all party and government offices, which resulted in the expulsion of thousands of Slavic officials for "colonizerism," but also cost Rysqulov and his allies their positions. The Muslim Bureau was disbanded and any talk of Turkic or Muslim nationhood as equivalent to

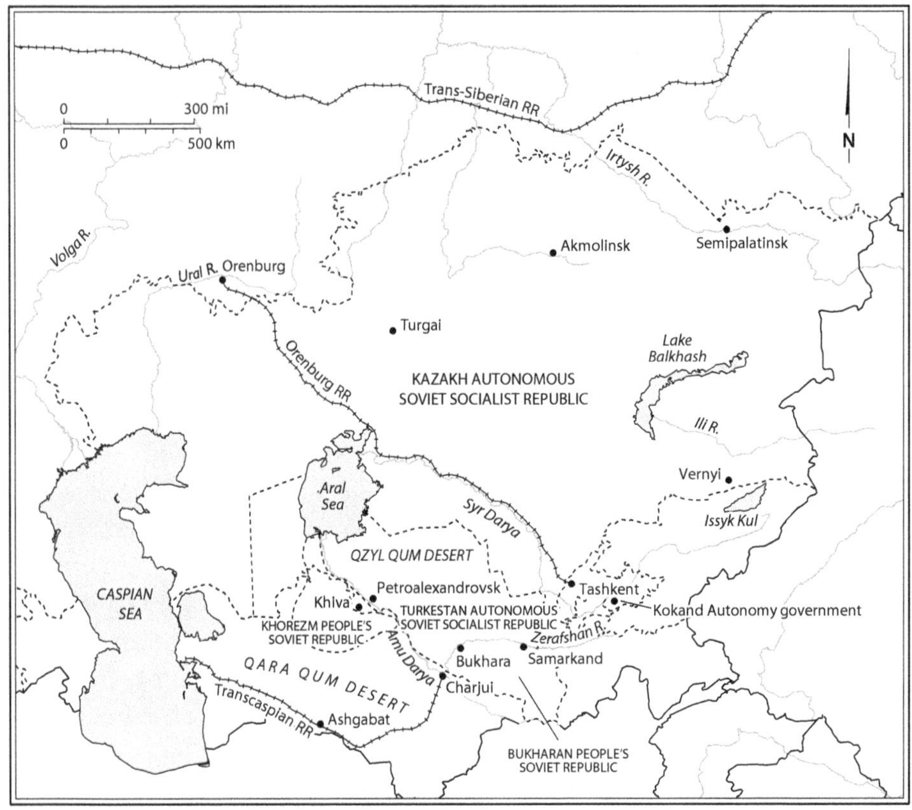

MAP 5.1 Central Asia in 1920.

proletarian class status was labeled counter-revolutionary.[56] The Turkestan Commission was replaced in July 1920 by the more powerful Turkestan Bureau of the Communist Party, one of six bureaus established to act as agents of the Central Committee in the far-flung regions of the former empire. The Kazakh ASSR was also put under a regional bureau in 1922.[57] Turkestan became an ASSR in September 1920. Central Asians would be allowed to govern themselves through the Turkestan and Kazakh communist parties, but only under terms set in Moscow and supervised by the party bureaus (see Map 5.1).[58]

As the Turkestan Commission settled in Tashkent and the Red Army gained control in the Transcaspian region in the fall of 1919, the Bolsheviks turned their attention to Khiva, where the Yomut Turkmen warlord Junaid

Khan was fighting all opposition to his rule. This included the Khivan old guard, rival Yomut chiefs, the Russian garrison at Petroalexandrovsk, and a tiny group of Uzbek Jadid reformers. The reformers fled to Tashkent, where the Turkestan Commission organized them into a Young Khivan party to mirror the Young Bukharans. The Red Army invaded Khiva in late December 1919, but it took a month of fighting before they drove out Junaid Khan. In February the Turkestan Commission forced Sayyid Abdullo Khan to abdicate and replaced him with a military revolutionary committee made up of Turkmen and Young Khivan representatives, although as a concession to local feeling the committee included a mulla. The committee quickly asked the Bolsheviks to help them set up a soviet of workers and peasants. In April 1920 this soviet formally proclaimed the end of the four hundred-year-old Khanate of Khiva and the founding of the Khorezm People's Soviet Republic (khNSR).[59] That did not mean that the Bolsheviks now had firm control of the situation, however.

In Bukhara Emir Alim Khan spent the months after Kolesov's failed putsch expanding his army and executing hundreds of opponents, from reformist clerics to peasants protesting tax increases. He also strengthened diplomatic relations with Afghanistan, newly independent under King Amanullah, and with the British in Iran, which greatly alarmed the Turkestan Commission. By July 1920 Frunze was preparing a new invasion of Bukhara, but Bolshevik policy required that this not appear to be a Russian colonialist attack under a red banner. The Bolsheviks had two Bukharan parties willing to cooperate with them, but inconveniently the parties hated each other. The first was the Young Bukharans, who did not support the dictatorship of the proletariat but understood that the Bolsheviks provided their only real chance at ousting the emir and instituting their reforms. The second was a Bukharan Communist Party that had formed on its own in September 1918, but most of its members were not actually from Bukhara.[60] In early August the Bolsheviks forced the two to merge, and 28 August Turkmen near Charjui started a "spontaneous" revolt against the emir that provided cover for the Bolshevik invasion. Militarily the campaign went smoothly, although Red Army shells did major damage to the old city (see Figure 5.1). The emir escaped; in an echo of medieval Muscovite practice his sons were sent to Moscow as hostages.[61] The emir's top officials were executed, and in September 1920 the united Bukharan Communist Party announced the independent Bukharan People's Soviet Republic (BNSR).

FIGURE 5.1 The Kalon minaret in Bukhara with repaired shell holes. Source: Author, 2003.

SUMMARY

Over the course of fifteen years Central Asians saw their governments and much of their societies collapse. They played active roles in the 1905 and 1917 revolutions and World War I, even though the origins of these upheavals were far away. The intellectual class seized on exciting new philosophical and political opportunities, and many ordinary people used the new freedoms to fight for their land and prosperity. An active role was not a controlling role, however. As much as current scholarship likes to emphasize the agency of colonized peoples, the best that Central Asians could do was to create small areas in which they could govern or at least try to survive. Over 1.5 million of them could not survive, and those who did found themselves in a new landscape governed by political principles of which they had only a hazy understanding. The new rulers were simultaneously declaring Central Asians free and telling them that they were too backward to define what freedom meant for themselves. Whether encouraged or afraid, no one could be certain what Soviet Central Asia would bring.

Chapter 6

FOUNDING SOVIET CENTRAL ASIA

After the war everyone dreamed of building a better world. Kyrgyz and Kazakh nomads hoped to re-gain their pastures. The Turkmen hoped for freedom from all outside authorities, Muslim or not. Uzbek modernizers dreamed of creating independent countries with enlightened citizens. Most people just wanted to get their normal lives back. The Bolsheviks were a party of revolutionary dreamers, but they dreamed of a world most Central Asians could not imagine.[1] In 1921 Soviet Central Asia was made up of the Kazakh and Turkestan ASSRs and the "people's soviet republics" of Khorezm and Bukhara. Over the next eight years the Communist Party replaced Turkestan with the Uzbek, Turkmen, and Tajik soviet socialist republics, added a Kyrgyz ASSR, and altered the Kazakh ASSR's borders and population. The new republics provided the administrative structures to support fundamental cultural, social, and economic changes. In order to make Central Asians into communists, everything had to be done at once: all children needed access to elementary education, which required native-language textbooks, which led to switching from Arabic to Latin alphabets to facilitate reading (and make it hard to read Islamic texts). The court system needed to be secularized and Soviet law codes translated into local languages, once linguistic experts agreed on how to define what local languages were. These profound changes all required more money and personnel than the state had. The 1920s was a period of many decrees and few results: traditional institutions existed alongside Soviet ones, administration was disorganized, and efforts to change family structure or settle nomads were limited. Nonetheless, the Soviets laid down the foundations for cultural transformation.

AUTHORITY AND CREDIBILITY

Lenin and Stalin were serious about their promises of self-determination to the national minorities of the former Russian Empire, as long as the nationality governments were Bolshevik. This was a tricky balance even in theory, and practice was inevitably loaded with contradictions. The major problem was that the state needed educated functionaries to implement its program of modernization, and in Central Asia educated men were almost by definition class enemies: graduates of madrasas, like Abdurauf Fitrat, or bourgeois Russian schools, like Akhmed Baitursunov. As the Tashkent soviet had never tired of pointing out in 1917, there were no Central Asian proletarians that Marx would have recognized. The remaining option was to hire unqualified, often illiterate people (including women) and train them to run a government. The state initially took on anyone who was willing to work with it, but placed them under the supervision of the Turkestan and Kazakh bureaus of the Central Committee of the Russian Communist Party (bolshevik).[2] Simultaneously, it established schools to teach basic literacy and office skills and sent promising candidates to study in Russia to create cadres (a favorite Bolshevik term) of Central Asian communists. The Soviet government needed to establish both its authority as the only source of political and moral ideas, and its popular credibility as the giver of independence and opportunity to Central Asians.

A first step in establishing communist credibility was to evict Slavic settlers from Semirechie. In late June 1920 the Politburo, the highest party committee, ordered that land should be confiscated "immediately" from the settlers and redistributed to nomads for use as pasture and farm land. Refugees from 1916 would have preference, and Kyrgyz farmers would get subsidies and expert advice. The settlers, especially former tsarist police or officials, were to be sent to "concentration camps" in the Volga region.[3] This decree encapsulates what many Central Asians initially found attractive about the new government and what went wrong. The Soviet state was always in a hurry, more excited about smashing corrupt old ways than steady reform. In order to remove the approximately 300,000 settlers in Semirechie "immediately" the party sent in not only dedicated cadres, but a new entity in Turkestan, the Cheka or political police. The eviction was carried out with horrendous brutality: settlers were beaten bloody and threatened with execution, while the commissars commandeered food and the services of "young women or girls to do the laundry"—likely more than clean shirts was expected.[4] For the Kyrgyz, the promised subsidies did not materialize, and those few who were able to read the original decree might have noticed its emphasis on encouraging nomads to settle and farm. The party did not remove all of the settlers, and it was less aggressive in de-colonizing Kazakh lands. It passed two decrees early in 1921 on returning "unoccupied land" to Kazakhs, but did not have the means to enforce them. It also banned new immigration by settlers in the mid-1920s, but the flow never stopped completely.[5] The party promised more than it could deliver and caused great suffering in the process.

"National self-determination" meant that the non-Russian peoples would govern themselves. This was central to the Bolsheviks' insistence that they were not a colonial power, but they could not create fully fledged local communist parties overnight. The Turkestan, Kazakh, and Bukharan parties were full of members who did not agree with or understand communist principles, while the Khorezm party was barely functional. In 1922 the Turkestan Bureau of the Communist Party was replaced by a stronger body that answered directly to General Secretary Stalin, the Central Asian Bureau (Sredazburo). The top Sredazburo positions were held by Russians, but from the beginning the bureau included Turkestanis such as Fayzulla Xo'jaev of Bukhara. The bureau recruited younger men and a few women into the KPT who were trained in brand new Communist Party schools and looked to the party as a source of income and power. Moscow ordered that all decrees and other information be issued in local languages as well as in Russian, although they did not have the translators needed to realize this ambition. But the party purged new members almost as quickly as it trained them. The *chistka* ("cleansing") was built in to a system where ideological obedience was just as important as legal obedience. In 1923 the KPT purged "great power chauvinists" (code for Russian supremacists) and "local nationalists" (code for Turkestanis who were too independent) from the government. Most of the Turkestanis were quickly re-hired, however, because they could not be replaced.[6] Purges were almost continuous until Stalin's death in 1953, making stable government impossible.

THE PEOPLE'S REPUBLICS

The brief history of the "independent" people's republics of Bukhara and Khorezm illustrates how complicated and difficult building a communist Central Asia was going to be. The KhNSR was governed by a Communist Party and a Council of Nazirs (ministers) staffed by a mix of communists, Uzbek Young Khivans, merchants, Turkmen tribal leaders, and ulama. Not one of them was genuinely loyal to the Soviet cause. They were so fractious that in 1921 the Red Army moved in and forced elections for an entirely new government, and even that did not bring order. The fundamental problems were the lack of governing experience combined with bitter hatred between Uzbeks and Turkmen. The republic's location amid deserts, hundreds of miles from any Soviet center, made oversight difficult. By 1923 over half of the KhNSR government was made up of Russians and Tatars rather than locals.[7] The Bukharan People's Soviet Republic (BNSR) presented quite a different problem. The combined Young Bukharan/Communist government was also fractious, but its leaders Fayzulla Xo'jaev, Abdurauf Fitrat, and Abduqodir Muhitddinov had well-developed, independent ideas of what the revolution was for. They envisioned Bukhara as the center of an expansive, republican Turkestan governed by and for Turkic Muslims. The Jadids were focused on building a modern society, "bourgeois" in Marxist terms, but its Turkic national character was much more important to them than any notions of class struggle. This vision put Jadids in the Turkestan ASSR and Bukhara in an untenable position, however. Not only were their goals incompatible with Soviet communism, they were unacceptable to most of the Turkic Muslims that the Jadids held so dear. The Young Bukharans owed their political power directly to the Red Army, which made them collaborators with Russian infidels in the eyes of Bukhara's people even as the Soviets barely tolerated them. The modernizers were a minority under siege, dependent on hostile powers to realize their vision.[8]

Other groups of Central Asians were pursuing their visions equally vigorously, most famously the guerilla insurgency known as the basmachi or qurbashi.[9] This was not an organized "Islamist" resistance movement, much less a Turkic nationalist one, but a conglomeration of dozens of local warlords and their bands, some more powerful than others, who fought against Bolsheviks and Turkestani modernizers with equal zeal. Their main goal was to drive all outside authorities from their lands, although some qurbashi thought in broader political terms. The two centers of basmachi activity were the Ferghana Valley and eastern Bukhara. The Soviets treated both regions as active war fronts into the late 1920s, employing extrajudicial killings and other methods of "Red Terror" as they did in the civil war.[10] The fighting was savage, involving thousands of soldiers on both sides with civilians caught in the middle. The basmachi threatened the Soviets not only because they disrupted government in the affected areas, but because they regularly crossed Turkestan's borders with Afghanistan and China, which triggered Moscow's fears of British invasion. Ibrahim Bek, the strongest qurbashi in eastern Bukhara, was able to establish a functional government for several years partly because his ties to the former emir Alim Khan gave him popular legitimacy. When Red Army pressure grew too great in 1926 he moved into Afghanistan, where the emir and his court lived. Ibrahim Bek's war against the Soviets lasted until his capture and execution in 1931.[11] Other qurbashi attended a 1922 conference of the short-lived Turkestan National Unity organization, with the aim of establishing a new independent Turkestan government. These loose coalitions could not seriously threaten the power of the Soviet state, however.[12]

Armed force was the Communist Party's most direct tool for establishing its authority, but control over the economy was the party's very reason for existence. The 1920s were a period of creativity and economic chaos, due to Lenin's institution of the New Economic Policy (NEP) in March 1921. The policy restored free markets at the retail level while the state maintained control of the "commanding heights" of heavy industry, communication, and transportation. In Russia the NEP era was the high point of Soviet social and artistic freedom, but in Central Asia NEP meant the withdrawal of state subsidies and loss of local economic control.

Even when it was not at all clear that the Bolsheviks would win the civil war, Lenin had invested in secular schools as an essential step toward building communism. Between 1917 and 1920 the Bolsheviks set up approximately 1500 schools in Turkestan and some in the Kazakh lands, which did not come under Bolshevik control until 1920. These ramshackle schools depended on central funding, but NEP's demands for budgetary discipline eliminated the money and most of the system crashed. The Islamic maktabs remained the backbone of education until the late 1920s.[13] From Moscow's perspective the most important sector of the Central Asian economy was cotton, which had been devastated by years of war. In 1921 the government levied thousands of peasants into labor battalions to clean and repair irrigation canals and distributed land taken not only from Slavic settlers but from a new enemy, "feudal *bais* and *manaps*" (wealthy landowners and notables). As long as the state paid low prices for raw cotton, however, hungry Central Asian farmers were reluctant to grow it. In early 1923 Moscow gave up its monopoly on cotton production to let prices rise, but that concession had minimal effect because seeds and other components of the production chain remained in state hands. The only incentive that farmers responded to were payments of 1.5 gold rubles per desiatina of cotton.[14] If the state wanted a reliable supply of cotton it was going to have to either spend more money or gain direct control over agriculture.

The independence of Bukhara and Khorezm was also a barrier to economic control. The two republics circulated their own currencies in addition to Soviet ones, and while they depended on money and resources from Turkestan to survive, they resisted adopting Soviet laws and taxes.[15] Their leaders were intent on protecting their power from Turkestan and from each other. Xo'jaev and Muhitddinov came from rival merchant families whose great wealth had been confiscated by the emir in 1917. While jockeying against each other for power under the new regime, both men also reclaimed as much of their family assets as they could. Muhitddinov even moved into the emir's palace and greeted a Soviet agent in the traditional courtly manner, although he was a member of the Communist Party himself![16] In 1923 the Central Asian Bureau forced Bukhara and Khorezm, over their vociferous objections, into an economic union with Turkestan. The union meant merging currencies, credit and banking structures, irrigation and transportation resources, and more. It was accompanied by a purge of uncooperative ministers like Fitrat from Bukhara and the conversion of Khorezm into a Soviet Socialist Republic, which meant that Young Khivans and other non-communists could be summarily expelled from the government.[17] The stage was set for a complete re-making of Transoxiana.

THE CREATION OF UZBEKISTAN AND TURKMENISTAN

Lenin had considered dividing Central Asia into national areas as early as June 1920. He commissioned an ethnographic map with sections marked for "Uzbekiia, Kirgiziia, and Turkmeniia," although he stressed that the division was only a suggestion. The Politburo affirmed that the Turkestan ASSR should create political administrations for these three nationalities.[18] Lenin had promised the "toiling Muslims of Russia" in 1917 that they had the right to establish their national cultures; according to Stalin's definition of "nation" this required a fixed territory. The Communist Party turned this sketchy Bolshevik nationality theory into comprehensive policy at the XIIth Party Congress of April 1923, one of the most important in Soviet history. This was the first congress that Lenin did not preside over. In December 1922 he had a stroke that weakened him considerably. He tried to remain active in the leadership, but he was isolated "for the sake of his health" in a dacha in Gorkii (now Nizhnii Novgorod) with limited contact with the outside world. In March 1923 Lenin had a massive stroke that left him partly paralyzed and unable to speak. He lived on until January 1924, but was helpless. While Lenin was struggling to stay involved, Stalin quietly pushed for his own ideas of how the Soviet state should be structured.

By 1923 it had become clear that Lenin and Trotsky had lost their gamble that the premature Bolshevik Revolution would be rescued by revolutions in Europe. Germany crushed its communists after a failed putsch in 1919, and the communist parties of France and Great Britain were small and weak. The Soviet state was going to have to figure out how to build communism on its own, in "conditions of capitalist encirclement," with no guidance from Marxist theory. Lenin favored a federal system of autonomous regions and republics to fulfill his promises to the non-Russian nationalities and gradually convince them to exchange their national identities for class-based identities. Stalin, a Georgian who had a more realistic sense of the power of nationalism, argued that this arrangement would open the door to local national chauvinisms tearing apart the state. He preferred that Russia have a strong central government within which the nationalities could have autonomous areas. Trotsky does not seem to have had strong opinions on nationality policy, but he was appalled by the abusive behavior of Bolsheviks in Georgia, where Stalin ally Sergo Ordzhonikidze slapped a local communist and then had a fit of hysterics.[19]

Even though Lenin could not contribute directly to the XIIth Congress proceedings, his views carried tremendous authority. The congress ratified a compromise structure: the Union of Soviet Socialist Republics (USSR) would be built on an intricate nesting system of national regions, autonomous republics such as the Kazakh and Turkestan ASSRs, and full soviet socialist republics that technically were independent states joined in a voluntary union. Each nationality would get its own government, consisting of a Communist Party branch and a state branch. As a corollary, each nationality would be governed by its own people (*korenizatsiia*, or "indigenization"). Each nationality had the right to governance, education, and cultural development in its own language and according to its own traditions, within limits defined by the Communist Party. The party and state commissariats in Moscow provided the strong central structures that held the whole thing together. The party Politburo and Central Committee made executive decisions that the lower-level party organs were not free to disobey. The state commissariats decided how to distribute resources and to what extent national republics were responsible for funding themselves. The four original republics of the USSR were Ukraine, Belorussia (today's Belarus), the joint Transcaucasian republic of Georgia, Armenia, and Azerbaijan, and the Russian Soviet Federated Socialist Republic (RSFSR). The massive RSFSR included Russia, the north Caucasus, the Volga basin, Siberia, the far east, and the Kazakh and Turkestan ASSRs. All of these peoples were given their own national governments except the Russians themselves, who were tacitly assumed to have their national identity merged into the Soviet state. No empire in history had ever tried such a paradoxical experiment: in order to reach the international proletarian promised land, the USSR was going to create nations where they had not existed and modernize them to the point where they were ready to give up their nationhood and embrace true communism.[20]

Applying this policy to Central Asia meant first marking out territories that could be labeled exclusively "Uzbek," "Turkmen," and "Kirgiz [Kazakh]." This was going to be a complicated task, because the populations were so mixed and the idea of "nation" so foreign to most Central Asians. Fortunately, the Soviets had eager allies for this project among the educated modernizers. The Jadid writer Fitrat had organized a literary circle in 1918 called *Chaghatay Gurungi* (Chaghatay Conversation) that was devoted to creating a "pure" Turkic language purged of Arabic and Iranian vocabulary. The group researched and recorded history, folklore, and music that they attributed to Turks of Transoxiana. Fitrat went so far as to declare that the Farsi-speaking Tajiks were really Turks who had been corrupted by Iranian court culture. They also decided that "Sart," the old name for town-dwellers that had no particular ethnic connotation, was not only inaccurate but insulting to Uzbek national dignity.[21] The Kazakh Alash movement had been working along similar lines since 1905, combining early Kazakh mythology with visions of a modern nation based on Kazakh rather than Turkic unity. By 1922 there were even a few Kyrgyz communists who argued that the Kyrgyz required a national territory separate from both Kazakhs and Uzbeks.[22]

The Central Asian nation builders and the Communist Party were drawing on a common source, European Romantic nationalism. European ideas of nationhood began with scholarly studies of linguistics and folklore, which inspired an intellectual elite to demand political rights based on common language and history, followed by this demand being taken up by the general public.[23] The Soviet nation building project in Central Asia was not a case of communists brutally imposing a "divide and rule" principle, as some older historical accounts argue, but rather a convergence of goals that developed as Russia and Central Asia came into contact with the European cultural complex. This alignment of interests made the national delimitation of Central Asia possible, but still not easy.

The first steps were taken by ethnographers shortly after the revolution. One of the greatest Russian scholars of Central Asia, Vasilii V. Bartol'd, used a "complex" method of recording data on languages, kinship, physical type, religion, and lifeways to draw up ethnographic maps of the region. This was a considerably more sophisticated way of defining nationality than the "mother tongue" criterion used for the 1897 census. The information was combined with detailed studies of economic resources and lists of ethnonyms and turned over to the Central Asian Bureau in January 1924.[24] Sredazburo set up a Commission on the National-Territorial Delimitation, headed by Fayzulla Xo'jaev, which floated a proposal for an Uzbek republic past the Bukharan Communist Party in late February. The Bukharans promptly came back with their own proposal that looked a lot like a Greater Bukhara, encompassing Khorezm, Ferghana, Samarkand, and Syr Darya oblasts but with its capital at Samarkand. At all stages the delimitation would be a contest of wills between the Central Asians, who wanted real independence, and the government, which wanted union republics that served the needs of the revolution.[25]

The Khorezm SSR presented a different problem. Yomut chief Junaid Khan re-invaded in January, this time sparking a mass anti-government uprising. Even observers from Sredazburo were sympathetic to the rebels, writing that the Khorezmian government had no authority and was merely presiding over the "economic ruin" of the people. It took weeks to drive the Turkmen out, and then Sredazburo officials learned to their dismay that the republic was so poor and anarchic it was not capable of basic governance.[26] They also discovered that the Khorezmians were hostile to joining an Uzbek republic that would erase their distinctive identity. Sredazburo had run out of patience, however, and in March forced the Khorezm government to agree to be broken up along national lines, in this case Uzbek, Kazakh, Turkmen, and Karakalpak.

Drawing the Borders

Once Sredazburo approved a general scheme, it created a territorial commission in July that would oversee Uzbek, Kazakh, Turkmen, and Kyrgyz national bureaus draw borders by September. The commission was largely composed of Communist Party members from Bukhara and Turkestan, including Xo'jaev, Muhitddinov, Abdullo Rakhimbaev, Kaigisyz Atabaev, and Sultanbek Xo'janov. They faced enormous challenges: first, in the Syr and Amu river basins and in the Ferghana Valley it was impossible to separate the nationalities neatly; second, drawing national borders meant breaking apart common economic zones, such as the irrigation networks of the Amu delta; and third, inevitably some groups would gain resources at others' expense, which was going to create tension along national lines. In fact, the disagreements between groups that arose as a result of the delimitation contributed directly to the early formation of national identities.

The desert-steppe frontier zone between the Aral Sea and Tashkent had been contested between Kazakhs and Uzbeks for centuries, and was the subject of bitter fights and many petitions to Moscow in 1924. A major concern was that, no matter where the border was drawn, Kazakh and Uzbek communities would be stranded as minorities in republics dedicated to the interests of the majority nationality. To solve this problem Xo'janov, a Kazakh nationalist with a hot temper, argued that it would be better to make Central Asia a federation like the Transcaucasian republic, with cultural autonomy guaranteed.[27] Another point of contention was Tashkent, which both Kazakhs and Uzbeks claimed as their own, with equal historical basis. The city itself was majority Uzbek with a substantial Slavic settlement, but the villages surrounding it had almost equal Uzbek and Kazakh populations.[28] Xo'janov's federation proposal had some support from other Sredazburo members, but the Uzbeks and Turkmen believed that they had more to gain from having their own republics than from promoting cooperation across ethnic lines. Stalin, who was the ultimate authority over the delimitation, did not support a federation because of his commitment to defining nations based on territory. Stalin's view prevailed, leading Xo'janov to accuse the Bukharans of "sabotage" and Sredazburo of supporting Uzbek interests:

> It remains unknown to us why we decided to examine [the issue] and
> to send [an opinion] to the commission, when the question had been
> predetermined. Who are we fooling with this on the diplomatic front?

Perhaps the leader of Sredazburo did not have the competence and the courage just to say that investigation and conversation about autonomy was unnecessary....

I am communicating these facts to you not so much for information, but as notification that we Kazakh workers (*kirrabotniki*) do not consider ourselves more interested in and responsible for the Kazakhs than Sredazburo is and speak about the interests of the Kazakhs according to the authorization and invitation of Sredazburo. Therefore do not cheat us, for we are not foreigners within the party and do not require actions for outward show.[29]

Xo'janov strongly asserted Kazakhs' rights as equal party members, although he lost the argument. When the borders were announced in October, Uzbekistan received the Tashkent region and Kazakhstan received the area from the Syr Darya to the Amu delta and almost the entire Aral Sea coast. In 1925 the land just east of the Aral became the Karakalpak Autonomous Oblast within the Kazakh ASSR.

The putative border between Uzbekistan and Turkmenistan posed an economic problem. Turkmen communists, led by Atabaev, were enthusiastic about a republic where their people could rule after centuries of living on the outskirts of the Uzbek khanates.[30] However, not only were the Turkmen and Uzbek populations of southern Khorezm highly mixed, the irrigation networks that they depended on could not be split up without disrupting agriculture. In July the Khorezm government rejected the partition plan it had been forced to accept in March precisely on these grounds. They made a counter-proposal to increase Khorezm's territory and natural resource base by adding the Amu Daria oblast (the future Karakalpak Autonomous Oblast). While the Turkmen and Uzbek Bukharans were happy to have republics based on nationality, the Khorezmians were much more concerned about economic viability.[31] They were over-ruled.

The act of asking local communities to consider how to divide what had always been shared quickly led to fierce fights and to a new conflation of national identity with access to water. Since the point of placing the border was to demarcate "Uzbek" and "Turkmen" communities, in some areas villages chose a national identity based on what they thought would give them the greatest advantage in resources. The national principle did not apply in all cases, however. The Turkmen areas around Termez and Karakul went to Uzbekistan to keep economic zones together.[32]

The eastern Ferghana Valley was so complicated that the Uzbek and Kyrgyz commissions jointly agreed that Sredazburo should make the actual border decisions. Sredazburo drew some of the lines around Namangan and Andijan, and required that Uzbekistan guarantee water rights to the Kyrgyz where they shared sources. However, when it came to the region around Osh, Sredazburo passed the decision-making buck on to the new Uzbek and Kyrgyz governments, once they were organized. This delay was built in to the process, which provided for future reconsideration of borders. The ability to modify borders did not stave off ethnic hostilities, however, because the act of declaring an area "Kyrgyz" or "Uzbek" generated hostility against the minority population, just as Xo'janov had feared it would. In a series of angry petitions in 1925 Uzbeks in a region assigned to the Kyrgyz ASSR complained that Kyrgyz discriminated against them in education and employment. Sredazburo officials agreed that their complaint was just, but decided that they could not give the region to Uzbekistan because giving more territory to the Uzbeks would further anger the Kyrgyz and Kazakhs. They compromised by creating a tiny Uzbek national territory within the Kyrgyz ASSR. This kind of complicated nesting of territories within territories would multiply over the next several years.[33]

The Soviet Socialist Republics of Uzbekistan and Turkmenistan, along with the Kara-Kirgiz [Kyrgyz] ASSR (within the RSFSR), were announced with great fanfare on 27 October 1924 (see Map 6.1). Samarkand was the first capital of Uzbekistan; in 1930 the capital was moved to Tashkent. A Tajik Autonomous Oblast was formed within the Uzbek SSR in 1925. The capital of Turkmenistan was Poltoratsk (re-named Ashgabat in 1927), that of the Kyrgyz ASSR was Pishpek (re-named Frunze in 1926). Later in 1925 the Soviet government finally stopped referring to the Kazakhs as "Kirgiz," and re-named the two autonomous republics the Kazakh and Kyrgyz ASSRs within the Russian federated republic. The Kazakh capital was moved from Orenburg to Qzyl Orda (Red Horde), the former Perovsk on the Syr Darya; in 1929 Alma-Ata (the former Vernyi) became the capital.

The new republics may have erased Bukhara and Khorezm as political centers, but they were replaced with an Uzbekistan that contained the largest population and claims to resources in all of Central Asia. The Uzbek SSR included almost all the major towns within Transoxiana, as well as the wealthiest and most highly educated population. This reflects the influence of the Jadid nationalists, who were able to have Sarts, Qipchaqs, and other Turkic-speakers considered as Uzbeks, whether they recognized themselves

MAP 6.1 Soviet Central Asia, 1925.

Table 6.1 Balance of populations in the new republics

New Republics	Population from Turkestan	Population from Bukhara	Population from Khorezm	TOTAL
Uzbekistan	2,323,764	2,319,498	320,023	4,963,285
Tajik AO	135,665	603,838	–	739,503
Turkmenistan	350,000	313,101	192,013	855,114
Kazakh ASSR	1,468,724	–	–	1,468,724
Kyrgyz ASSR	714,648	–	–	714,648
Karakalpak AO	91,098	–	128,008	219,106
Disputed regions	170,682	–	–	170,682
TOTAL	5,254,581	3,236,437	640,044	9,131,062

Note: The total population for Uzbekistan has been corrected from the original 3,963,285. The total population for Bukhara has been corrected from the original 2,236,437. The grand total has been adjusted accordingly. The Kazakh figures reflect the number of people acquired from Turkestan, not the total population.
Source: RGASPI F. 62, op. 1, d. 34, l. 7.

by that name or not. Table 6.1 shows the Central Asian Bureau's estimates of the new population balance. Sredazburo officials freely admitted that these figures were rough guesses. Censuses of Turkestan had been carried out in 1920 and 1923, both with large gaps. In 1920 not all nomadic groups could be located, and census takers focused on the farming population. The 1923 census asked people what their *natsional'nost'* was, but many if not most Central Asians did not understand the term.[34] Now that these republics provided the national form for Soviet Central Asia, the government faced a much more complicated task: filling the form with socialist content.

NEW GOVERNMENTS

The Soviets organized or re-organized the Central Asian communist parties at the same time that they formed the new republics. First, they sidelined uncooperative nationalists. The stubborn Xo'janov was replaced as secretary of the Kazakh Communist Party in 1925 by Filipp Goloshchekin, whose previous claim to fame was participating in the murder of Tsar Nicholas II and his family in 1918.[35] Alash leaders Tynyshpaev and Bukeikhanov were shunted off into non-political jobs, while Baitursunov was placed in the Kazakh educational department, grandly named the Commissariat of Enlightenment (Narkompros). Turar Rysqulov was transferred to the Comintern (the coordinating body of international communism), and from there sent to Mongolia as a representative.[36] Very few Uzbek Jadids were willing to work for the government. The Central Asian Bureau named Xo'jaev chair of the Council of People's Commissars of the Uzbek SSR in 1925 while a Tashkent communist named Akmal Ikramov became secretary of the Uzbek Communist Party. Ikramov was part of a younger cohort of Uzbeks who were the earliest beneficiaries of Communist Party training and looked to the Soviet state to make their careers. Ikramov had a "class enemy" background in that he was from a prominent religious family, but the party was so desperate for Uzbek members that this did not hamper his rise.[37]

The Turkmen and Kyrgyz communist parties had barely existed before 1924, and there was no Tajik party. The problem in these republics was to find enough warm bodies to make the claim of local governance plausible. The Central Asian Bureau drew on people from the national border delimitation commissions, favoring those who had strong Russian-language skills and appeared to support the party's goals. These preferences, while understandable, set up conflicts in the infant republics. In Turkmenistan the early leadership came mostly from the western tribes, which left eastern Turkmen under-represented. Since the Turkmen had never in their entire history been united under a single government, this caused resentment at the possibility that the Yomut or Tekke might claim to rule all Turkmen.[38] Leaders of the Kyrgyz Autonomous Oblast were split by a bitter rivalry that combined personal, political, and regional/tribal differences. The first "Kyrgyz" Communist Party secretary was a Russian who was supposed to balance the factional fighting but who was drawn in himself, prolonging the instability.[39] The Tajiks had never had a nationalist movement and were completely unprepared for their new status. Turki-Farsi bilingualism was so common in Bukhara and Samarkand that ordinary people did not connect their "native language" with their "national identity." This not only confounded the core assumption of Soviet nationality theory, it made it easy for Uzbek nationalists to claim these cities for their republic. The ethnonym "Tajik" was seldom used; more common were "Farsi" (Iranian-speaking) or "Eroni" (which meant "Shiite," as opposed to the Sunni majority). The only territory that was predominately "Tajik" was the mountainous region of Eastern Bukhara, which was so poor it did not have any towns. Under these highly unpromising circumstances the Soviets scraped together a government from the materials at hand. A settlement at a weekly market became the "capital" Dushanbe (Monday), and Xo'jaev arranged to have his rival Muhitddinov re-identified as a Tajik and sent to head the new government, effectively a political exile. Amid this weakness and fractiousness the Central Asian Bureau, with its mostly European staff, remained the top political authority. The final authority rested with the political police and their guns.[40]

Modernizing Cultures

The Communist Party did not wait for new governments to start modernizing Central Asian cultures. Already in 1918 the party had sponsored "physical culture circles" for adults and children, involving games, calisthenics, and track and field exercises. The first Central Asian *olimpiada* was held in 1920, featuring boxing, wrestling, weightlifting, soccer, and equestrian events. The same year Red General Mikhail Frunze sent a telegram to Lenin and Trotsky about organizing theater and cinema on barges floating on the Syr and Amu rivers.[41] The goal was to give indigenous activities, such as wrestling and horse games, new meaning rooted in the communist value system. Simultaneously, the Bolsheviks wanted Central Asian cultures to express themselves through European modes of art and leisure. They faced two main obstacles: the local intellectuals, who the government depended on to produce a new high culture, had competing ideas of its purpose and meaning. Secondly, Soviet ambitions vastly outstripped the available resources.

If any one thing was key to this enterprise, it was education. Estimates of literacy among Central Asians were all very low, although the statistics are unreliable because questioners did not employ a common definition of literacy. The Soviets targeted women as a population that was in dire need of basic literacy and should be grateful to the government for providing it. The Bilim Yurt (Knowledge House) in Uzbekistan was supposed to train the first generation of secular female teachers, but while it enrolled hundreds of students, by 1926 it had graduated all of fourteen. Its most influential graduates had entered with prior training at Jadid schools.[42] To reach nomads (men as well as women) the governments of Kazakhstan and Turkmenistan organized mobile "red yurts" to provide intensive "liquidation of illiteracy" classes. Many nomads did not see any practical reason to learn how to read, however. In 1929 an ethnographer studying a Yomut community reported that not one girl was in school, although workshops on carpet weaving were popular.[43] In Uzbekistan traditional Islamic schools predominated because there was not enough money to build a Soviet school system. In 1926 the government moved to reform Islamic schools with the aim of re-making them into Soviet schools, which opened a way for non-communist Jadids, including reformist clergy, to get some state support for their projects. The state had no way to measure the reform's effectiveness, because it could not complete a count of schools of any type.[44]

Some Jadids argued that a major reason for mass illiteracy was the Arabic script, which did not accurately represent Turkic sounds and included letters for sounds not found in Turkic languages. Orthography and language reform was one area where Central Asians led, since the party showed little interest in the issue. In 1921 Fitrat got a proposal to Turkicize vocabulary and orthography approved at a Bukharan conference on developing a modern Uzbek language. His simplified Arabic script encountered strong resistance from language conservatives, but provided the basis for a burgeoning Uzbek print culture until the end of the decade.

In 1926 a conference in Baku, Azerbaijan, on Turkic languages and cultures voted to adopt a unified Latin alphabet for all Turkic languages in the USSR. The conference proceedings show how much the environment for nationalist modernizers had changed in just five years. The Republic of Turkey, founded out of the ashes of the Ottoman Empire in 1923, was considering Latinizing its script in the name of promoting rapid modernization. Some Russian communists proposed creating a Latin alphabet for Russian for similar reasons, which may be why Moscow did not pull out the old imperial bugbear of "pan-Turkism" against Turkic Latinization. The Baku conference was organized and hosted by Azerbaijani scholars who had already developed a Latin alphabet for their language, although Russian linguists also played a prominent role. The unified Turkic Latin alphabet transformed the Uzbek Jadids' project of national culture construction into a union-wide effort that had the potential to homogenize Turkic languages. Nevertheless Fitrat, Xo'jaev, and Ikramov joined the commission to develop a Latin script, perhaps because they realized resistance was pointless.

What saved the Jadid project was that Soviet nationality theory also demanded the establishment of distinct nations in each republic. Latinizing Turkic orthography required decisions about how to express vowel sounds that provided opportunities to shape Central Asian languages in ways that emphasized differences among them. The party wanted national languages to reflect the culture of the common people rather than intellectual elites, which meant elevating rural dialects over the literary language called Chaghatay.[45] Fierce arguments over how to reach these goals with a Latin alphabet continued into the 1930s, but were not fully resolved. Uzbek publications were written in unstable variations of a Latin alphabet until 1941, when all Turkic languages were forced to adopt a Cyrillic alphabet. The irony is that a reform that was originally intended to promote mass literacy instead impeded it. The Jadids had written textbooks in their simplified Arabic script, but these had to be scrapped when the Latin alphabet was introduced in 1927. People who had just learned how to read had to re-learn with Latin letters, and then start all over again with the introduction of Cyrillic. Language modernization was just one of many areas where Soviet policy tripped over itself.

The Challenge of Islam

Soviet communism aimed to be a complete system, providing people not only with economic and social justice, but a moral philosophy by which to live. So did Islam. The Tashkent Ulama Jamiyati warned of this conflict as soon as the Bolsheviks took power, writing: "Regarding the Bolsheviks ... for them the *din* [religious law] consists merely of things related to faith, rituals, and other matters of this sort. But they do not consider that trading, penal laws and matters regarding land are also related to the din."[46] Marx had declared that religion was an illusion foisted upon workers by the ruling classes, and would be destroyed by communist economic relations. However, in Central Asia Islam had a significant advantage over communism in that it formed the basis of legal and social structures while the Soviets did not have the resources to build robust alternatives, as in the case of schools. Soviet attempts to replace or undermine the courts that adjudicated Islamic sharia and nomadic adat law and the waqf endowment system did not gain traction until the late 1920s, but they did signal the party's vision for Central Asians' future.

Kazakh courts had been stripped of their authority over serious crime by Imperial Russia but retained control over family law. They also mediated property and honor disputes via the practices of kun and *barïmta* (reprisal raids on livestock) that Russian authorities had tried unsuccessfully for decades to stamp out.[47] For communists, these practices were unacceptable not only because they were outside state control, but because they were "primitive," not European. Customary law was one area where Bolshevik promises to allow national cultures to flourish were trumped by their conviction that Europe, for all of its capitalist flaws, was still the only model for any "advanced" society. This assumption was so deeply embedded in the minds of the Bolsheviks that they never questioned it. As a corollary, communists saw the ways that Islamic and customary law limited the freedom and equality of women as a terrible injustice that they should correct immediately.

In the fall of 1920 the new communist Kazakh government issued plans to replace traditional courts with Soviet courts and gradually ban bride price, polygyny, levirate marriage, kun, and barimta.[48] They passed laws formally banning these practices over the next year. In 1924 the Kazakh Commissariat of Justice complained that, while Islamic courts had largely disappeared, adat courts still operated in the "remote steppes."[49] The government passed laws banning the courts again in 1925, and in 1928 imposed a hefty fine for using them. Why couldn't the Soviet state sweep away these primitive practices? First, passing laws was fairly easy, but in 1921 the Kazakh government did not have a press to make and distribute copies. The only way to locate nomadic communities to tell them about the new laws was to send out mobile "red yurts" and "red caravans" to explain the laws orally, but that required hiring and training personnel who would be willing to travel the steppe for months. Kazakhs who were educated enough to explain law preferred office jobs with a regular food supply. On a deeper level, the Soviets discovered that Kazakhs believed their customs to be proper and necessary, and telling them how Marxist theory disproved their belief did not cut much ice. Baurdzhan Momysh-uly, who grew up to be a decorated officer in World War II, recalled how his formidable grandmother Qyztumas reacted to the idea of abolishing qalin:[50]

> "Qalin is the road paved by our fathers and mothers. They took qalin for my mother, they took qalin for me, my daughter and son were married off with qalin. How could we live without qalin now? What about the bride coming without payment into a strange house? What kind of respect will they have for her? The husband took her for free and will drive her away for free? If qalin is not taken, that means there will be no dowry, no *toi* [celebratory feast]. Who benefits from this?" she lamented. "No, while I live no woman will marry without qalin. Do it my way. When I die, you can do whatever you want."

The Soviets saw bride price as the purchase of a woman just like the purchase of livestock, but for Momysh-uly's grandmother a generous bride price was a mark of the esteem that the groom's family held for the bride's. It was precisely the exchange of gifts between families that gave value to the marriage, because marriage was embedded in Kazakh family relations. The idea of marriage as a private agreement based on the personal feelings of two people was a recent European development that made little sense to Central Asians. This kind of gap in cultural understanding proved to be a more formidable obstacle to realizing the Soviet dream than logistics and language barriers.

The waqf system provided financial support for mosques, schools, madrasas, shrines, and the teachers and mullas who staffed them. During the civil war the Bolsheviks had tried to seize control of waqfs, only to encounter such fierce resistance and social chaos that they had to give them back. In December 1922 the state created an administration under the education department to register waqf property and channel its funds toward schools, but it was run by local Muslims.[51] Waqfs sat at a nexus of competing interests: the Soviets wanted to seize them in order to undermine the clergy and bring all land under state ownership. Central Asian reformers wanted to control waqf assets to further their modernization program, and the ulama who had traditionally overseen waqfs wanted to maintain their income and authority. The ulama lost the contest first, but that did not mean the other two parties won. Local governments were desperate for funds, and regularly diverted waqf income that was supposed to go to schools for other purposes. In 1925 the Central Asian Bureau launched a land and water redistribution campaign in Uzbekistan, Turkmenistan, and Kyrgyzstan that was intended to break the old system of land tenure and the tribal social structures that rested on it.[52] The state absorbed most waqf assets during this campaign, with the significant exception of waqfs that supported mosques. The party did not yet feel secure enough to attack mosques directly, although it did close the madrasas in Tashkent by the end of 1926. The land was supposed to go to poor peasants who would be encouraged to grow cotton, but the reform was carried out so quickly and chaotically that it disrupted farming and did little for the poor.[53] The party left the remaining waqfs alone until 1928, when it confiscated them in the context of destroying Islamic institutions and collectivizing farming.

Agricultural development worked differently in Tajikistan. The government of this new autonomous oblast was the least secure and most impoverished in Central Asia. Government offices were housed in buildings of unbaked clay bricks that disintegrated in heavy rain. Three agencies shared one typewriter. Then somebody broke it.[54] The qurbashi Ibrahim Bek regularly invaded from his base in northern Afghanistan, and over 200,000 people, mostly Turkic pastoralists, fled over the porous border in 1926 alone. Here, taking land from waqfs and bais was less important than moving people. The government wanted to resettle Tajik communities from the mountainous north to the more fertile lowland south, both to grow cotton and to secure a region dominated by Turkic tribes with more pliable and "advanced" Tajik farm villages. In 1925 and 1926 over 15,000 Tajik households were re-located to land formerly inhabited by Turkic tribes.[55] This was just the first stage in a process that would see hundreds of thousands of people unwillingly re-settled in the name of building a nation that would serve Moscow's purposes.

Within a few years these migrations allowed the Tajik government to claim that the balance of its population had changed to favor Tajiks over Turks. In keeping with the policy of self-government (korenizatsiia), the Central Asian Bureau had been recruiting more Tajiks into the Dushanbe government, and these men were becoming impatient with what they saw as their unfair subordination within the Uzbek SSR. They had many reasons for grievance: the Uzbek government claimed that a 1926 census showed the Tajik population of Bukhara, Samarkand, and Khujand had dropped precipitously, and refused to fund Tajik-language schools for children it regarded as really Uzbek. Tajiks thought that the Uzbeks had rigged the census.[56] Tajik communists believed that the Uzbeks were diverting economic development funds that should have gone to Dushanbe. Finally, they argued that the towns of Khujand, Samarkand, and Bukhara were in fact majority Tajik and should be transferred to the Tajik oblast.[57] In 1929 this turned into a demand to become a full soviet socialist republic. The Uzbeks were outraged by Tajik claims, and while Central Asian Bureau agents agreed with the Tajiks' demographic arguments, they did not want to give Bukhara and Samarkand to Tajikistan on that grounds that the towns were not geographically connected to it. Khujand, in the western Ferghana Valley, was added to the new Tajik SSR when it was formally announced in October 1929. This calmed, but did not eliminate, the ethnic antagonism. The eruption of fierce anger between peoples who had lived with each other for centuries demonstrated a truth about nationalism that Soviet nationality policy had overlooked: "A nation is a group of persons united by a common error about their ancestry and a common dislike of their neighbors."[58]

SUMMARY

The tenth anniversary of the Bolshevik Revolution was celebrated with parades and speeches all over the Soviet Union, but in Central Asia communists must have viewed the festivities with a sense of hollowness. They had accomplished much: the emir, the khan, and much of the old notable class were gone. Each Central Asian republic had a government, a communist party, a secular law code and court system, secular schools, a new Latin alphabet, a native-language press, and even an embryonic film studio. Everywhere they looked, however, these accomplishments were shabby and fragile. The courts were few in number and did not command the obedience of ordinary citizens; in many areas Soviet law was ignored because no one could read it. The government and party organizations were so poor they could only gesture at fulfilling orders from the Central Asian Bureau or Moscow. Soviet schools were vastly outnumbered by reformist and traditional Islamic schools, and efforts to liberate women had barely scratched family life. Most importantly from the perspective of the man who already dominated the leadership in Moscow, the state's ability to command obedience and the production of commodity crops was weak. Central Asian communists were too prone to putting the needs of their republics before the needs of the USSR, and even when they did obey instructions they routinely failed to meet quotas and deadlines. Not that Central Asia actually occupied a lot of Stalin's time; these were the same problems that he saw all over the country. However, the region would be one of the first in the Soviet Union to experience Stalin's brutal shock methods of gaining the absolute control he craved.

Chapter 7

BREAKING AND BUILDING— THE STALIN ERA

In 1927 the Soviet government began a violent campaign to overturn Central Asian society. Central Asians had never before had to live under a state that ordered them to stop praying and believing in God, to collectivize their farming and stop following their herds, and told women to take off their veils or feel free to ask their husbands for divorce. The Communist Party's forced sedentarization of Kazakh nomads alone killed approximately 1.5 million people. The women's liberation campaign, the near-elimination of Muslim clergy, and the political purges of the mid-1930s destroyed hundreds of thousands more lives. At the same time, Joseph Stalin's government invested resources in the region, building the bases for educational and healthcare networks, agriculture, and some industry. Kazakhstan and Kyrgyzstan became full soviet socialist republics, and thousands of Central Asians found employment in growing state bureaucracies. Central Asians also learned to adapt the Soviet system to their own values and needs. As the 1941 German invasion devastated the USSR west of the Urals, Central Asians willingly served in the Red Army and gave shelter to refugees in their cities. Stalin agreed to create a state-controlled Muslim religious administration in 1943. Central Asians took pride in their patriotism, and in 1953 they mourned Stalin's death with the rest of the Soviet population.

THE GREAT BREAK

Since Lenin's death in 1924 the Soviet Union had been led by the members of the Politburo, who argued over economic policy and took every chance to undercut each other. They fought over how long to continue with the compromise of the New Economic Policy (NEP), which gave the state control over heavy industry but left retail marketing in private hands. The partial restoration of a free market under NEP alleviated the terrible famines of the civil war period, but many communists felt that it betrayed their revolutionary ideals. Stalin, who served as the General Secretary of the Communist Party, preferred to keep a low profile and watch his rivals battle each other. While they argued, he did his job of staffing party organizations, promoting and demoting people, and allocating resources. The Commissariat of Nationalities had been closed in 1923, but the many disputes and questions from the non-Russian regions still came to him for mediation. By steadily conducting everyday business, Stalin made himself the practical head of the party as far as its rank-and-file members were concerned. In 1925 the first issue of the Uzbek Communist Party journal *O'zbekiston Kommunisti* featured a drawing of Stalin with the caption "The Russian central party's head secretary Comrade Stalin" (see Figure 7.1).[1]

The Soviet Union was still largely agricultural, and it was the lone communist country in the world. To create the conditions for Marxist prosperity and justice, it had to find a way to build simultaneously the productive engines of industrial capitalism and a revolutionary moral culture, all on its own. Politburo members debated whether they should live with NEP for decades while they modernized the country, or leap into rapid communist economic and social development. In 1926 the faction in favor of marching to communism as quickly as possible gained the upper hand and approved a plan for increased investment in industry. Stalin took their side, with the support of many party members who longed for the excitement and sense of purpose they would get from building communism as opposed to managing the disappointing halfway measures of NEP. The catch was that rapid industrialization depended on capital to build factories and buy equipment, which the Soviets certainly were not going to get from Europe. The money was going to have to come from squeezing the peasant farmers, which could only be done by asserting state control over agriculture. In the fall of 1927 Stalin extracted cheap grain from the Urals with a carrot-and-stick method: he sent trainloads of scarce manufactured goods to persuade farmers to sell their grain in exchange, but accompanied the goods with thousands of young communists who were

FIGURE 7.1 "Rusia markazi firqumining bosh kotibi o'rtoq Stalin." Source: Cover of *O'zbekiston Kommunisti* 1, no. 1 (1925): 1.

authorized to seize grain and cash reserves by force if the peasants balked. Some Politburo members were horrified, but Stalin had enough support in the party to ride roughshod over their objections. With this act he became the USSR's supreme leader.

Moscow's priorities were communicated to Central Asian communists via instructions and speeches from the Sredazburo, local-language party publications, and direct action by the political police (OGPU). In the mid-1920s the party's program was already clear: the "titular nationalities" were to govern their own republics (the policy of korenizatsiia) but put the USSR's needs first, communism was to replace Islam as the sole legal and moral system, family structure and the place of women in society would conform to Russian patterns, and cotton production would be the top economic priority. What changed over 1926–27 was that party rhetoric became much harsher, warning of enemies everywhere, and that the party stepped up demands for decisive action on social and economic goals. A younger generation of Central Asian communists picked up quickly on the new aggression, and used it to muscle their predecessors out of the way. Despite the fact that Sredazburo was actively pushing korenizatsiia, Jadids in and out of the government were attacked for "nationalism" and "elitism," code words for promoting national instead of class identity and high culture over worker and peasant cultures. These attacks had real consequences: some people were sentenced to prison or lost their jobs. Abdurauf Fitrat changed his writing to conform to party demands, even though he had never been a communist. Fayzulla Xo'jaev was publicly vilified for his wealthy background and lost influence to the Uzbek party head Akmal Ikramov, despite the fact that Ikramov himself came from a clerical family.[2] Ikramov was quicker to demonstrate his obedience than Xo'jaev was, but that does not mean he was purely toadying to Stalin. These hot-headed young communists were motivated by a mix of eagerness to realize the party's promises, to achieve a level of power that only the destruction of the old order would give them, and to act on personal resentments.

Stalin's "Great Break" with the past was enacted by the First Five Year Plan, carried out from 1928 to 1933. In Russia and Ukraine the Plan meant building heavy industry on a massive scale at a breakneck pace and collectivizing agriculture, accompanied by a violent anti-religious campaign and continuous public attacks on external, and especially internal, enemies. In Central Asia industrialization was not nearly as prominent a part of the Plan, although the state built the Turkestan-Siberian railroad from Semipalatinsk to Kyrgyzstan and the large coal-mining complex at Karaganda.[3] Instead of factories, the Plan brought an attack on the pillars of traditional society called the *hujum* (assault) to unveil women and liberate them from other traditional strictures, and a campaign to eliminate not only the Islamic social infrastructure, but the mosques and clergy themselves. Farmers were collectivized and ordered to grow enough cotton to make the Soviet Union independent of world markets. For nomadic pastoralists the Plan meant a brutal campaign to sedentarize them and collectivize herding. Across the USSR the Plan resulted in the deaths of millions.

Attack on the Social Order

The hujum and the anti-Islamic campaign were intertwined; local people played a prominent role in both. In Uzbekistan some women, usually from educated families, went out in public without their paranjis before 1927, but they were a small group and attracted little attention. Tatar women in Central Asia had never covered their faces, and the few people who wrote about women's status considered the paranji more a symbol than a cause of oppression.[4] As Sredazburo began to discuss a women's liberation campaign in late 1926, its focus was on education and child marriage. The idea of women publicly casting off their veils appealed to party activists' sense of drama, however. The campaign formally launched on 8 March (International Women's Day) when thousands of women tore off their veils, threw them on bonfires, and marched while shouting party slogans (see Figure 7.2).[5]

The demonstrations served notice to all that the old sources of morality and authority were going to be torn down, but what they would be replaced with was much less clear. Unveiling was just the beginning. Uzbekistan introduced a legal code in 1926 with a new category of crime, *bytovye prestupleniia* (crimes of everyday life), that made sexual intercourse with minors, the payment of qalin, forcing women to marry against their will, and male homosexual sex illegal. Secular marriage and divorce replaced Islamic rites in 1928, and polygyny was banned in 1931.[6] The law was not changed uniformly throughout Central Asia; Turkmenistan did not formally ban qalin until 1928, while Kazakhstan and Kyrgyzstan were part of the Russian republic and conformed to its laws, which banned qalin earlier but did not outlaw male homosexuality until 1934.[7] The hujum was a shock campaign, intended to deal a swift and decisive blow to traditional customs. Shock tactics, combined with a lack of planning for Central Asians' reactions, resulted in the beating, rape, and murder of thousands of women over the next three years. There were no shelters for women who were expelled by their families, and law courts were often indifferent to this new category of crime. Many women who unveiled one day re-veiled the next in order to avoid social ostracism. Male Central Asian communists often refused to allow liberation within their own households.

Much of the violence was not a spontaneous response to a woman's unveiling, but was planned in advance. Historian Marianne Kamp compares it to lynching in the United States around the same time, which was a display of ritualized mutilation and murder intended to enforce the power of the dominant group.[8] While no agency kept reliable statistics on the violence

FIGURE 7.2 Poster for International Women's Day, 1930. Source: "8 марта—Международный женский день," *Russian Perspectives on Islam*, http://islamperspectives.org/rpi/items/show/10058.

and its causes, it appears that a woman asking for divorce was particularly likely to be attacked. Women who accepted positions of authority on local soviets were also frequently targeted.[9] With the hujum the party demanded that people abandon overnight what they regarded as core moral values: the primacy of patriarchy and family honor. Even women who actively supported the hujum had trouble changing their behavior so quickly. During meetings of the Uzbek Union of Militant Godless men and women sat in separate rooms and shouted to one another; the idea of sitting together to discuss atheism was just too uncomfortable.[10]

The Union of Militant Godless was a communist anti-religious propaganda organization that was almost comically ineffective among Muslims. There was nothing funny about the destruction wrought by the anti-Islamic campaign, however. Soviet laws that recognized only secular marriage and divorce and that banned the sanctioned practices of polygyny and child marriage undercut the authority of Islamic law. Opposing women's liberation became a reason to arrest Muslim clergy. As the hujum unfolded, the Uzbek Communist Party ordered that all Islamic courts be closed by October 1927 (the tenth anniversary of the Bolshevik Revolution), that maktabs be closed by 1928, and that the remaining waqfs be liquidated by the beginning of 1929. None of these institutions was in fact fully eliminated by the deadline, but the waqfs and courts were reduced to underground remnants by the end of the Plan. Maktabs hung on longer because the Soviet school system was still underfunded and weak.[11]

OGPU agents reported with satisfaction that they observed widespread impoverishment and despair among Muslim clergy. Sufi *ishans* were losing followers and many clergy fled to Afghanistan or Xinjiang. An imam in Andijan lamented, "We have begun to live badly, everywhere you look; everywhere they oppress us … and everything has become tighter."[12] In the Kulob region of southern Tajikistan thousands of people decided that suppression of Islam meant the end of the world had come, and refused to eat or work in the fields.[13] Steady degradation of the clergy was not enough, however. In 1927 a minor spat with Great Britain became a serious war scare in Soviet newspapers, which helped fuel the anti-Islamic campaign by promoting fears that clergy were conspiring with agents from British India. The party also became convinced, falsely, that Muslim clergy across the USSR were uniting to organize a counter-revolutionary movement. While in public the party insisted that scientific education and propaganda were the only legal anti-Islamic tactics, in a closed meeting the Uzbek Central Committee directly ordered nighttime arrests of clergy, the collection of punitive taxes from Sufis to destroy their brotherhoods, and the surveillance and arrest of anyone who protested against these measures.[14] It was violence carried out by the OGPU, not "scientific education," that destroyed Islam as a foundation of Central Asian societies.

Violence against clergy was accompanied by violence against mosques and sacred shrines. This part of the campaign rapidly escaped the party's control; how and why this happened reveals how severe state pressure was shaping new power dynamics in local communities. Mosques first became vulnerable not because they were Islamic centers, but because they were made of bricks and wood. Local governments were always frantically hunting for building materials to fulfill the continuous rain of orders to build schools, medical clinics, workers' clubhouses, and other facilities for which they had no resources. Small village mosques and large madrasa complexes were equally vulnerable to this kind of predation, which was carried out by local Central Asian officials, not Russian agents. In a number of cases Russian OGPU agents punished the locals because the destruction of Islamic buildings stirred up serious anti-government unrest. One of the worst of these cases occurred in 1928 in Bukhara, where a neighborhood soviet closed a three hundred-year-old mosque, promised but failed to convert the building into a club, and finally allowed an OGPU mounted detachment to use it as a stable for their horses. Muslim protests triggered an investigation by Sredazburo, during which Akmal Ikramov erupted:

> If someone wants an uprising in Uzbekistan, all that is needed is a
> few outrages like this.... I consider this situation intolerable. Comrade
> Zelenskii noted in his report that there is counterrevolutionary behavior
> in connection with this.... There is a problem here—in some places the
> population no longer believes in the Soviet government. I have read a
> report from the OGPU concerning another mosque. They closed one
> mosque. Several religious people met and said that they needed to send a
> petition to a higher Soviet authority, but then the majority declared that a
> complaint to the Soviet government was not needed—better still was an
> uprising. This situation is completely intolerable....[15]

In other cases local communists physically abused believers while destroying their buildings; in G'ijduvon the village oqsoqol was forced to climb the minaret and urinate during prayers.[16]

That European communists would abuse Muslims is not surprising, but how do we explain outrages committed by Central Asians? It is not that Central Asian communists were atheists; the majority of them believed and observed religious rituals in private. Islam had clearly lost its public authority, but these local officials were also disobeying Sredazburo's instructions on how to close mosques peacefully. The explanation lies with the zealotry and terror generated by Stalin's Plan, which was now the most powerful force in Central Asia. Mosques that were not torn down for their materials were commandeered to provide storage for grain that was being requisitioned as part of the collectivization campaign. As a Bukharan communist told Ikramov's investigating committee:

> [M]osques were closed by decision of party cells, Komsomol cells, by decision of village soviets, committees of the poor or simply without any decision at all.... It was established by a commission that in 1928 there was a definite directive ... that the mosques had to be closed. The mosques were closed, especially at the time of the grain procurement campaign, when mosques were used for storage. Something like a competition to close mosques sprang up between the raion departments....[17]

The Plan put immense pressure on local cadres to fulfill and over-fulfill quotas and to demonstrate maximum enthusiasm for destroying the old way of life. A communist was more likely to be punished for hesitating than for committing abuses, so safety lay in quick, brutal action. It was also the case that some Central Asian communists genuinely wanted to destroy the old social structures.

The hujum and the campaign to destroy Islam hit Uzbekistan harder than other areas, because that republic contained most of the Islamic institutions in Central Asia and the settled women who wore the paranji. In Turkmenistan, Kazakhstan, and Kyrgyzstan nomadic women did not cover their faces, so the liberation campaign focused on changing family structure and women's public roles. The results were less violent than in Uzbekistan, but in all areas people reacted to attacks on their culture by clinging more tightly to the customs in question.[18] The above quotation also points toward the way in which the insatiable economic demands of the Plan were rapidly swallowing the hujum, the anti-Islamic campaign, and all other party projects. These demands were the main driver of Central Asia's social transformations.

COLLECTIVIZATION AND THE KAZAKH TRAGEDY

Absolute control over the food supply was vital to fulfilling the Plan's industrialization targets, which were raised and raised again to fantastical heights. Across the USSR millions of people were moving from rural villages to new industrial sites such as Magnitogorsk, the huge steel complex in the Urals, where they worked twelve-hour shifts with primitive tools and lived in drafty barracks. Because the state took over the retail markets when it abolished NEP, it made itself responsible for feeding industrial workers. Stalin promised workers cheap food, which he obtained by stripping *kulaks* (wealthier peasants) of their assets, deporting them, and moving the "middle" and "poor" strata of peasants onto large farms where land, equipment, and animals were held in common, all under the ownership and direction of the state. Peasants resisted these *kolkhozes* (collective farms) with all their might, slaughtering their animals, destroying their tools, and refusing to plant for the state. They learned that Stalin was prepared to see them starve, as long as in the end he could send the food they produced wherever he needed.

Agriculture in Kazakhstan existed in two inter-linked sectors: European settlers who grew grain and Kazakh pastoralists who raised cattle, sheep, goats, and camels. Despite almost a hundred years of Russian pressure on Kazakhs to settle and farm, only 23 per cent of Kazakhs were fully sedentary; the rest led nomadic or semi-nomadic lives. The nomads regularly traded cattle to settlers in exchange for grain, which made up a large part of their diet. A symbiotic relationship with farmers was an ancient pastoralist method of survival in a harsh and unpredictable environment. The effects of late spring frosts (*jut*), which decimated herds by icing over grass just as the new lambs were starting to graze, could be mitigated by such trade. Another vital symbiotic relationship was between the bais, aristocratic owners of large herds, and the poorer members of their tribes. In times of hunger bais were obligated to lend animals to the poor, who would tend them on behalf of the bai while consuming their milk and wool for themselves. This guaranteed broader survival and strengthened tribal bonds.[19] To the communists, however, bais were simply the Kazakh equivalent of kulaks who were exploiting the poor and should have their "excess" cattle confiscated. Party planners also decided that since Kazakhs ate so much grain that they did not themselves grow, it would be more efficient to remove "excess" animals from them and make them grow their own grain. The confiscated cattle would be slaughtered to feed workers in Moscow and Leningrad, to which

Kazakhstan was linked in one of the economic zones that the USSR had recently been divided into.[20]

The Kazakh famine happened because of the decisions made by economic planners, but the planners did not intend to cause famine. Stalin demanded that his Plan's targets be met at all costs; if fulfilling those targets killed large numbers of people, then so be it. In the fall of 1927 party cadres began requisitioning grain from Slavic settlers and cattle from Kazakh bais. They also deported about seven hundred bai families. This disrupted the reciprocal obligations between bais and poorer Kazakhs, as intended, but caused greater suffering than expected because the jut frosts were severe that spring. The requisitions also provided an opportunity for local officials to steal Kazakh cattle for themselves under the guise of "collectivizing" them. Both Kazakh and Slavic officials engaged in this thuggery, but bald bigotry on the part of Slavs was an important factor in turning what might have been a period of hardship into an absolute disaster.[21] They viewed Kazakh nomads as primitives whose needs were not worth considering. The cattle confiscations were accompanied by a massive increase in taxes and often brutal treatment of Kazakhs. In 1928 the party resumed allowing European settlers to move to Kazakhstan, which took away more land.[22] Europeans also suffered in this process, but damage was disproportionately inflicted on Kazakh pastoralists.

Stalin demanded a 100 per cent collectivization rate throughout the USSR over the winter of 1929–30. In Kazakhstan that extended confiscations of herds from bais to all pastoralists. Kazakh Communist Party chair Fillip Goloshchekin instructed that cadres should not be "afraid of excesses," meaning that any level of violence that got the job done was acceptable. Cadres sent as many animals as possible to the kolkhozes, which often did not have adequate food or shelter for them.[23] Then in 1931 a new population of more than 200,000 settlers arrived, but in contrast to previous generations, these people did not come voluntarily. The "dekulakization" campaign in Russia and Ukraine took approximately 1.7 million people, many of them children, packed them into freight trains, and sent them to special settlements in Siberia, Kazakhstan, and the far north. A large percentage of them died. In Kazakhstan kulak families were dumped onto open steppe and told to start by building their own housing. With few tools, families ended up living in holes in the ground, sometimes for years.[24]

After years of talk, the state tried to sedentarize Kazakh pastoralists in 1932 by sending them to kolkhozes, but the collapse of the seed-grain supply and mass die-off of animals caused by earlier phases of collectivization made the kolkhozes death traps. Already in April 1930 Moscow bureaucrats noted how blind demands for production caused immense, pointless destruction:

> [T]he burden of meat production fell on *seredniaks* [middle farmers] and *bedniaks* [poor farmers], not only seizing the surplus, but the pitiable remainder ... seized meat, especially in the Jangilan raion, has been stored carelessly, so that the stench, arising from the meat as a result of putrefication, prevents anyone from getting near.... [I]n December 1929 and January 1930 local authorities assessed a compulsory [levy] of wool from the population. Then the people sheared their sheep and camels, despite the hard frost, and because of this cut down a considerable quantity of cattle, since the animals, deprived of their natural protection, could not withstand the winter severe cold and died.... Thanks to these excesses, which were tolerated by local authorities for the procurement of bread, wool, and meat, the number of cattle has fallen by 75%.[25]

People began dying of hunger and disease in large numbers in 1931, one year before the better known and equally man-made famine struck Ukraine. Kazakhs who had been deprived of all other sources of food took to eating grass, cats, dogs, and occasionally resorted to cannibalism. Typhus, scurvy, and smallpox epidemics may have killed as many people as did starvation. By 1934 approximately 1.5 million people, 1.3 million of them Kazakhs, had died, as well as 90 per cent of herd animals. Another one million Kazakhs fled to Xinjiang and to other parts of the USSR. The death toll constituted approximately one-third of the entire Kazakh population.[26] Conditions only began to ease in 1933–34, when Goloshchekin was removed and the state started to send grain to Kazakhstan instead of stripping it bare.

Resistance and Rebellion

Kyrgyz and Turkmen also suffered in this period, but they did not experience such complete devastation. Both groups put up ferocious armed resistance to collectivization. In Turkmenistan collectivization meant forcing pastoralists to give up herding and farmers to grow cotton instead of grain. This left the Turkmen dependent on food imports from the rest of the USSR, but since most of the country was going hungry those imports were inadequate to nonexistent. Collectivized herds died of neglect as they did in Kazakhstan;

by the fall of 1930 women complained that their children were swelling from hunger. Even before then large mobs, often led by women, were ransacking party offices and beating up any Soviet officials they caught. Their demands included not only dissolution of the kolkhozes, but expulsion of all Europeans from Turkmenistan. Armed bands of horsemen began to attack OGPU outposts and collectivizers in late 1930. The broad crisis led rival tribes to unite against the greater foe; by 1931 almost half of Turkmenistan was in open revolt. Thousands of households fled to better lives in Afghanistan.[27] Kyrgyz tribes, under similar pressure, also rioted and tried to murder communists whenever they could. Surviving bands of basmachi fighters re-grouped and added many eager recruits. For a while the basmachi managed to completely halt collectivization in southern districts of Kyrgyzstan.[28]

The rebellions forced collectivization to slow down, although they did not stop the process. In border zones the government granted tax relief to peasants, lowered cotton quotas, and permitted a looser form of collective farm called a TOZ, where only land and some equipment was held in common. Armed resistance alone does not explain why the Turkmen and Kyrgyz fared relatively better than the Kazakhs did, however. Kazakhs also put up violent resistance where they could.[29] The Kazakhs' location in the center of the steppe made it harder for them to pressure authorities by mass emigration; only people living in the east could escape to China, whereas a larger percentage of Turkmen and Kyrgyz lived near a border. The most important factor seems to have been that Kazakhstan was yoked to the Russian economic zone, while Kyrgyzstan and Turkmenistan were part of the Central Asian economic zone. In 1928 Soviet planners divided the USSR into twenty-four zones, each with a designated economic specialization. These zones had no relation to political borders. Kazakhstan was considered a food-producing region for workers in major Russian cities, while Turkmenistan and Kyrgyzstan were supposed to turn most of their arable land over to cotton production. Planners shipped food to the cotton producers, however inadequately, and took food from the grain and meat producers. While almost all Kazakh herd animals were slaughtered for Russia or died of disease and starvation, the Turkmen and Kyrgyz herds declined by only 12–13 per cent during the most intense phase of collectivization.[30] Turkmen and Kyrgyz still suffered from severe hunger, but they avoided famine.

For Uzbeks collectivization meant cotton. While violence also accompanied the process here, Uzbeks and Tajiks did not react with organized uprisings. Exploring why not can help us understand why the entire USSR did not collapse from self-inflicted damage during the First Five Year Plan. Cotton is an expensive crop because it needs a lot of water and labor to thrive. Any hope of making the Soviet Union independent of world cotton markets rested on expanding the irrigation networks, which cost money, which the state never had enough of. The need to cut costs to the bone clashed with the party's policy of promoting local self-governance, which raised tensions between Uzbek and Russian communists. The Uzbek government wanted to hire poor peasants to oversee water distribution on collective farms, partly to create a local governing cohort who had good reason to support the party. Moscow refused to pay the cost, which was not only a matter of money, but also of relinquishing strong central control over water. This heavy-handedness offended Uzbek leaders Ikramov and Xo'jaev, who were dedicated to making Uzbeks into the modern nation that Soviet leaders promised. They pushed cotton—Xo'jaev was willing to withhold grain and water from farmers who refused to plant it—but they wanted the Uzbek party to have greater authority over the process. Because the USSR government lost local cooperation in expanding irrigation canals, the amount of irrigated land actually declined until the later 1930s. The OGPU tried to force better results by expelling thousands of Uzbek kulaks even as dekulakization campaigns slowed down elsewhere, but increased oppression did not produce more water. In the gap between Moscow's impossible demands and its inability to enforce them, Uzbek collective farm leaders found ways to benefit, or at least stay alive, by diverting water to their family gardens and submitting false reports on cotton harvests.[31] These indirect methods of resistance eased the hardship, whereas other groups felt their only recourse was to fight.

Another factor that allowed Uzbeks to accommodate themselves to collectivization was that Europeans had a less direct hand in the process than they did in Kazakhstan and Kyrgyzstan, and Uzbek kolkhoz organizers were able to persuade many families that they would benefit from the new way of life. Contrary to Soviet news reports from the time, no one joined a kolkhoz because they were eager to fight for the USSR's cotton independence. Instead, while non–Uzbek-speaking Russians gave general instructions from the rear, local organizers promised that families would get grain and cooking oil, exemptions from taxes, and possibly a few cows. Poor families saw a real chance to improve their standard of living via the kolkhoz, whereas wealthier families were more likely to resist collectivization. Some poor people also openly enjoyed the sight of their richer neighbors being stripped of their land.[32]

Collectivization was still a coercive, violent process: some who refused the kolkhoz were beaten or shot. Thousands of kulak families were rounded up and deported, many to southern Russia and the north Caucasus. The headless corpses of communist organizers turned up in ditches.[33] Abdullo F. was around ten years old when he was accused of being a class enemy in 1928. He recalled:

> I was a little child ... and it hit me hard: [they said] his father is a mulla, he recites *namoz* [prayers], he gives the call to prayer, he is a cattle thief, and they would point to the child. It is this child, and if they pointed at me, then they got together and drove me out, and then I wandered around for a month or two. There was no room for me. I got dirty on the street ... what else could I do? They all went to school, but even though I had the desire I had no opportunity....[34]

Abdullo's father was able to make a personal petition to Uzbek president Yo'ldosh Oxunboboev and the boy was eventually allowed to return to school. Overall, the perception that collectivization was mostly being run by Uzbeks, in combination with the release of pressure that local disobedience provided, prevented all-out rebellion. It was already clear in the early 1930s that the only way the Soviet planned economy could function at all was by breaking the law. The system was incapable of providing the necessary resources for either factories or families to do the jobs the state assigned to them. The kolkhoz bosses who made sure that their people had enough to eat by "stealing" water from the cotton fields and padding the harvest records to ward off punishment for not fulfilling the Plan were in fact doing the government a favor by making it possible to live with communism. Areas where local agents were unable to divert resources and connect with the black market not only suffered enormously, they could not even come close to fulfilling their production quotas. If some of these agents acquired considerable local power and even wealth through their activities, that gave them all the more reason to support the regime.[35]

In Tajikistan collectivization was deeply tied to the older policy of forcibly resettling people in order to change the ethnic balance of the area, secure the border, and bring the mountain communities within the state's reach. Soviet planners saw Tajik culture as especially backward and were daunted by the steeply mountainous terrain. The fact that southern Tajikistan was open to Ibrahim Bek's basmachi raids until 1931 increased government caution. The republic was put on a slower schedule, with only the north destined for mass collectivization, and less of its arable land was dedicated to cotton. Tajiks still resisted by selling or slaughtering their animals, by fleeing to Afghanistan, and by joining Ibrahim Bek. The OGPU arrested and exiled thousands of people.[36]

THE CONTRADICTIONS OF STALINIST MODERNIZATION

For all of the fathomless suffering and effort that went into the First Five Year Plan, it failed to achieve its production goals. Furthermore, the chaos and destruction caused by collectivization had brought Soviet agriculture to the brink of collapse, which even members of the Politburo acknowledged. The Second Five Year Plan (1933–38) established more realistic production targets and a better organized approach to governance. At the same time, the only explanation for failure that was acceptable to Stalin was that enemies were conspiring to destroy the Soviet Union, and the only way to deal with enemies was to exterminate them. Stalin's great purges wiped out the founding generation of communists and sent millions of ordinary citizens into the Gulag camp system or to their deaths.[37] The later 1930s were a confusing and contradictory period for Central Asians. Moscow gave the republics greater political autonomy, but destroyed their leaders. Central Asians' labor was firmly roped to Moscow's needs, but the central state also put significant resources into developing schools, healthcare, and modern infrastructure.

In 1934 the Communist Party's Central Committee closed its Central Asian Bureau, removing the middle layer of supervision between the republics and Moscow. From now on Central Asian party leaders would answer directly to the central government, although their roles in the government were limited. Uzbekistan's Akmal Ikramov was the only ethnic Turk to hold a full membership on the Central Committee.[38] For all of the USSR's loud proclamations of equality among the nationalities, its central governing organs were entirely in the hands of the "more advanced" European nationalities. The tsarist legal category of inorodtsy (aliens) had been abolished, but in practice people from former inorodtsy backgrounds were still barred from the ruling elite. At the same time, republic leaders did gain real power: they now decided questions of personnel and resource allocation, albeit within the limits set by the center. The network of village soviets and district administrations thickened, which provided more reliable tools for governance and created new opportunities for local actors to wield economic and political authority. In late 1934 republic leaders were given the authority to hand out death sentences for political and economic crimes: the Uzbek tribunal tried fifty-five people and sentenced thirteen of them to death for failing to meet cotton production quotas.[39] These tribunals could potentially have allowed republic leaders to eliminate their enemies and build independent political blocs. To guard against such an outcome, the tribunals had to include Politburo member Valerian Kuibyshev. This was a poisoned gift—the new authority drew them into Stalin's killing machine, which would soon grind up the Central Asian leadership.

In 1936 the Soviet Union approved a new constitution which, on paper, gave its citizens unprecedented freedoms, including freedom of religion. In Uzbekistan the anti-Islamic campaign noticeably relaxed; public observances of the Ramadan fast and reports of women re-veiling themselves were not uncommon.[40] As part of the celebration of the "Stalin Constitution" Kazakhstan and Kyrgyzstan became full soviet socialist republics, although their communist parties were still headed by Europeans. The Transcaucasian Republic was split into the Georgian, Armenian, and Azerbaijani SSRs in the same year, which brought the total number of Soviet republics to eleven.

Most Central Asians saw improvements in their daily lives during the Second Five Year Plan, although years of fighting and hunger set the bar for "improvements" at an extraordinarily low level. The party was still committed to re-molding Central Asian cultures to fit a modern European Marxist template, which required increased investment in social and cultural institutions. Once Stalin had broken the peasantry with collectivization, he was willing to spend the money. The path to modernity was winding and full of potholes, however, not the shiny straight line depicted in party propaganda. In 1930 the USSR passed a law providing for universal compulsory primary education, a hallmark of the modern, centralized state. In Central Asia this was to be implemented first in collectivized areas and gradually extended from there, but it was precisely collectivization that made building stable schools impossible. The number of schools increased over the next three years, but statistical tables said nothing about the quality of those schools. In fact, published statistics showed a drop in the number of children in school in Kyrgyzstan and Uzbekistan from 1932 to 1935, although by the end of the decade certainly many more children were in Soviet schools than had been at the beginning. What this suggests is that many of the schools built during the First Five Year Plan frenzy, like the kolkhozes, existed on paper only and vanished as soon as the pressure relaxed.[41] Throughout this period, getting parents to allow their daughters to attend school along with their sons was a hard-fought battle with few successes.

What were the children who were actually in school learning? Most teachers had barely completed elementary school themselves, and textbooks and other teaching materials were in short supply. School buildings were often unheated, unfurnished, and dirty, although some schools were well-equipped. Under the circumstances, the best that teachers could do was to impart basic arithmetic and literacy in the new Latin alphabet. They read aloud to classes from the few available textbooks and continued to rely on rote memorization, although now children memorized party slogans and secular facts rather than Quranic verses and poetry.[42] Stalin personally oversaw the creation of a sovietized traditional Russian curriculum in the mid-1930s, which included teaching Russian history and Russian language in all schools.[43] This provided the basis for a uniform narrative of Soviet identity for students, although it would be years before the new curriculum was broadly available. In 1935 the republics set up stable teacher training academies, which improved the supply and expertise of teachers. Personal connections were often the most important factor in determining a student's success. The young Kazakh Mukhamet Shaiakhmetov suffered enormously because he came from a kulak family, but a teacher saw his intelligence, encouraged and tutored him, and arranged a Komsomol job so that he could stay in school and still support his family. Even though the Soviet government had exiled Shaiakhmetov's father, he felt grateful for the opportunity to learn and considered himself a loyal Soviet citizen.[44] Many other Central Asian children were learning to feel the same way.

The Soviet government invested considerable funds and personnel in building a modern healthcare system in Central Asia. The sight of professional doctors curing ancient scourges like *rishta* (Guinea worm) and midwives delivering healthy babies was a natural showcase for the benefits of scientific communism, while improving workers' health would increase production, always the state's highest priority. This high-profile project also encapsulated core contradictions embedded within Soviet policies.

On paper, the state spent 853,000 rubles on healthcare in Uzbekistan during the First Five Year Plan and increased the percentage of Uzbek medical students from 8 to 48 per cent of the total. Kyrgyzstan increased its number of hospital beds from 100 in 1914 to 2458 by 1938; its total healthcare budget went from 5 million to 48.2 million rubles by the end of the 1930s. Turkmenistan and Tajikistan more than doubled their numbers of hospital beds from 1929 to 1935. In Kazakhstan the state founded medical vocational schools that trained pharmacists, nurses, and midwives; by 1939 these schools were graduating over 1200 healthcare workers a year.[45]

These impressive numbers did not translate into radical improvement of everyday healthcare, however. The Soviet policies of korenizatsiia and proletarian dictatorship were on collision course with each other in Central Asia. Workers were always first in line for places in medical schools and access to care, but the few Central Asians who were literate enough in Russian for medical training were pretty much by definition class enemies. Class preference automatically turned into a national preference for Europeans over Central Asians. Korenizatsiia required that instruction be conducted in local languages, which would have corrected this problem except that Europeans flatly refused to learn Central Asian languages, and there were no Central Asian healthcare textbooks or teachers. In order to fulfill korenizatsiia quotas, schools graduated people who had understood very little of the medical curriculum. That was not as disastrous as it might have been, because supplies of modern drugs and surgical equipment were so low that the rural clinics Central Asians were most likely to encounter relied heavily on traditional herbs. Even so, the number of Central Asians who graduated from these programs peaked in the mid-1930s somewhere below 50 per cent of all medical students and then declined, so that by the beginning of World War II Kazakhs had dropped from 17 to 4 per cent and Uzbeks from 48 to 20 per cent in their republics.[46]

Medical resources devoted to maternity and infant care were second only to resources devoted to care for industrial workers. Many of the Central Asians who became doctors and nurses were women with a personal interest in this area. Kazakhstan developed mobile maternity clinics that could include a midwife or a doctor (rarely both, and sometimes neither), cow's milk for infants, and educational materials on healthy child-rearing. Most medical workers preferred to work in the cities, however, so the rural majority of Kazakhs rarely saw doctors of any kind. By 1938 there were over 17,000 day-care centers, vital since the state wanted mothers to work. Kolkhoz bosses were expected to fund and staff these centers out of their own scant resources, but fulfilling production quotas always took priority over such orders. When the requirement to help mothers clashed with the requirement to bring in the harvest, bosses forced women on the verge of giving birth to work in the fields.[47] Considering that there was no modern medical system in Central Asia before 1917 the investments of the 1930s did improve the situation, but not nearly as much as they might have if government policies did not continually undercut each other.

Purges and Deportations

The most fundamental contradiction within Stalinism was between the campaigns to build modern societies and what Western historians call the "Great Terror." No sooner did a cohort of trained Central Asian bureaucrats, doctors, engineers, or artists appear than most of them promptly disappeared into the camps and killing grounds. The intellectuals whose activities we have discussed since the late Imperial period, and who shared a dream of modernization with the Bolsheviks—Nadirbai Aitakov, Kaigysyz Atabaev, Akhmed Baitursunov, Alikhan Bukeikhanov, Cholpon, Abdurauf Fitrat, Akmal Ikramov, Abdullo Rakhimbaev, Turar Rysqulov, Mukhamedjan Tynyshpaev, Fayzulla Xo'jaev, and Sultanbek Xo'janov—were all executed in 1937 or 1938. Ubaydulla Xo'jaev and Munawwar Qori were arrested in the 1930–31 round of purges; Qori was shot and Xo'jaev's fate is unknown. Abduqodir Muhitddinov was executed in 1934. The only Jadid to survive the 1930s was Sadriddin Aini, who went silent and retreated from public life.[48]

When historians talk about "the purges, camps, and terror," we are referring to intertwining, complex phenomena that happened for multiple reasons. Purges were built into the communist system from the beginning. The party regularly purged members who stole money, drank too much, abused their power, and were either ignorant of party policies or disobeyed them. The korenizatsiia directives made purging non-Russians for "nationalist deviations" less common, but during the First Five Year Plan this charge became useful for blaming locals for the anger roused by collectivization. The central state was not the only actor that used accusations of nationalism to protect itself. In late 1929 writers in Uzbekistan went through a spasm of accusing each other of nationalism, pan-Islamism, pan-Turkism, and serving the long-defunct Khanate of Kokand. The OGPU arrested over one hundred Uzbek writers and government officials in a widening spiral of trials and executions that did not peter out until 1931. A similar wave engulfed the tiny intelligentsia of Turkmenistan in 1932.[49]

Purges also served to scapegoat local "wreckers and saboteurs" for failures to meet production quotas or for the damage caused in trying, as in the 1934 trial of kulaks for not producing enough cotton. Here the scope of the purges widened beyond Communist Party members to include workers in high-priority industries, which were increasingly entangled with the Gulag camp system. "The Gulag" was a vast complex of different kinds of forced labor camps. There were "special settlements" for deported kulak families like those who were dumped in the Kazakh steppe in 1931, labor camps devoted to gold mining or tasks like building the White Sea Canal, and prison camps for punishment of political and common criminals. Stalin decided that slave labor would be a cheap way to industrialize, and went so far as to arrest engineers so he could send them to specific projects.[50] Many Central Asians who were arrested or exiled were sent far from home, but there were camps in Central Asia as well. Over 30,000 prisoners worked in Uzbekistan in the mid-1930s, growing cotton or digging new irrigation canals.[51] The most significant slave labor camp in Central Asia was the Karaganda coal mining complex in Kazakhstan. Karlag, as it was called, was itself a system of camps that sprawled over 16,000 square kilometers from Akmolinsk to Lake Balkhash, incorporating coal mines, farms, fisheries, glass and sugar factories, and prisons. The camps were a major driver of industrialization in Kazakhstan, although most of the prisoners were not Kazakhs. Approximately one million men, women, and children passed through Karlag from 1931 to 1959; its population peaked at 65,673 in 1949. The number of people who died there cannot be accurately determined.[52]

In the later 1930s Stalin spent much of his time on diplomatic maneuvering to stave off war with Nazi Germany and Imperial Japan. Russo-Japanese relations had been cool since Japan defeated Russia in 1905. In 1910 Japan annexed Korea, and then in 1931 invaded Manchuria and created a puppet state called Manchukuo. The USSR had been active near this region since the 1920s, providing military aid and commercial trade to governments in Xinjiang and sponsoring a communist satellite state in Outer Mongolia. As hundreds of thousands of people fled Soviet Central Asia for Xinjiang the OGPU worried that they would become a reservoir for invaders, especially when Uyghurs formed the short-lived Eastern Turkestan Republic in 1933.[53] Furthermore, the deeply aggrieved refugees appeared to be potential allies of an aggressive Japan. Soviet political police arrested or killed suspected anti-Soviet agents in Xinjiang; as early as 1930 they claimed to have caught basmachi guerillas armed with Japanese rifles.[54] Meanwhile Stalin became increasingly concerned that the Poles, Germans, and religious sectarians who lived in the western Ukrainian and Belorussian SSRs might betray the state to Nazi Germany, even as he was secretly sending diplomatic feelers out to Hitler. These fears, which were not entirely paranoid, led Stalin to quietly abandon the communist principle that class identity always overrides national identity and assume that these and other ethnic groups along Soviet borders should be treated as enemy populations. That logic, combined with Stalin's profound fear of the generation of Old Bolsheviks and his conviction that all of the problems associated with the five year plans were the work of hidden saboteurs, led to the climactic phase of the purges in 1937–38 known as the Great Terror. This phase affected Central Asia in two waves: a new wave of forced resettlement and a wave of mass killing that drowned ordinary citizens as well as communists.

The Kazakh population had been so depleted by famine that much of the steppe was uninhabited. That is why it was relatively easy to build the Karlag camps; there was no one there to displace. There was still plenty of empty land for cultivation, and in 1936 Moscow deported over 100,000 Soviet Poles and Germans to central Kazakhstan. As usual, the "special settlers" were expected first to build their own homes with only the tools they had been allowed to bring with them, if they were lucky enough to arrive before winter had frozen the ground. Families spent years living in semi-underground dug-outs. The NKVD (the new acronym for the political police in 1934) was pleased enough with the results that it made Kazakhstan the designated dumping ground for almost two million people being deported from border areas around the USSR: Daghestanis and Chechens from the north Caucasus, Turks from southern Georgia, Kurds and Armenians from Azerbaijan, and Koreans from the border with Japanese-occupied China and Korea.[55] By the end of the 1930s Kazakhs had become a minority within their own republic, a situation that would not change for fifty years.[56]

Kazakhstan was the primary, but not the only, destination for deported peoples.[57] Kyrgyzstan received settlers from the Caucasus, while the 175,000 or so Koreans (the entire population of the Soviet far east) were distributed across Central Asia. The biggest group of Koreans went to Uzbekistan, where unlike other special settlers they were able to integrate themselves into Uzbek society. Initially most of them were sent to grow cotton on kolkhozes, but this resulted in ethnic hostility and low productivity, because the Koreans spoke Russian but not Uzbek. The settlers insisted that they should be able to set up their own kolkhozes to grow rice, as they had done in their home territory.[58] Koreans found a ready local market for their rice among the Uzbeks, who used it in their traditional *pilau* (pilaf with meat and vegetables). Having created a niche for themselves, Koreans eventually became accepted and even prosperous citizens.[59]

Table 7.1 Order no. 00447's quotas for Central Asia

Republic	First Category	Second Category
Kazakhstan	2,500 (plus 10,000 Gulag prisoners)	5,000
Kyrgyzstan	250	500
Tajikistan	500	1,300
Turkmenistan	500	1,500
Uzbekistan	750	4,000

Sources: J. Arch Getty and Oleg V. Naumov, eds., *The Road to Terror: Stalin and the Self-Destruction of the Bolsheviks, 1932–1939* (New Haven: Yale University Press, 1999), 475–76; Vladimir N. Khaustov, Vladimir P. Naumov, and N.S. Plotnikova, eds., *Lubianka: Stalin i glavnoe upravlenie gosbezopasnosti NKVD 1937–1938* (Moscow: Mezhdunarodnyi fond Demokratia, 2004), 274–76.

The deportations overlapped with the dozen or so "mass operations" initiated from July 1937 to November 1938 by Stalin and his new NKVD director Nikolai Ezhov. Whereas the deportations removed potential traitors away from the borders, the mass operations aimed against Poles, Germans, Afghans, Finns, Iranians, and other groups were arrest and execution campaigns. The largest mass operation of all, No. 00447 against former kulaks, White soldiers, SRs, and members of national independence movements from the civil war period, was launched in August 1937. These juggernauts of murder worked on the basis of blind quotas, which were rapidly exceeded by local party officials. Order No. 00447, for example, specified the numbers shown in Table 7.1 for arrests in Central Asia. People assigned to the First Category were "subject to immediate arrest and, after consideration of their case by the troikas, to be shot." People in the Second Category were "subject to arrest and confinement in concentration camps for a term ranging from 8 to 10 years."[60] In total Order No. 00447 demanded the executions of 75,950 people, mostly Slavs, but the true toll was much higher because local officials were well-attuned to Stalin's signals that the quotas were suggestions and over-fulfilling the plan was always encouraged. The Tashkent troika alone sentenced 5161 people to death or the Gulag in July and another 1122 to death in September. The total number of executions from all of the mass operations has been estimated at 700,000.[61]

The frenzy of killing swept up the entire Central Asian leadership and many ordinary citizens in a storm of outlandish accusations. In August 1937 the NKVD issued a follow-up order to arrest the families of "enemies of the people," which swelled the numbers of victims exponentially. The order included instructions for the distribution of children as young as one year old to state childcare centers. At the beginning of 1939 the NKVD estimated that it held 57,069 Central Asians from all five republics in the Gulag.[62] One of the peculiarities of the Terror was Stalin's insistence on observing the letter of the law: victims had to be formally charged and tried, however perfunctorily. Stalin also required that the accused had to confess to the charges before punishment began, which in 1937 meant the widespread use of tortures such as sleep deprivation and beatings. The charges tell us more about Stalin's paranoid fantasies than about the actual political situation. In 1935, before the mass operations, a group of Muslim clergy in Tashkent was arrested and confessed to spying for Japan, allegedly saying "Japan is the single country which is defending the interests of Muslims." The following year all the leading imams of Ufa (in the Bashkir region) were arrested as Japanese spies.[63]

Fayzulla Xo'jaev was arrested in June 1937 for being part of an "Anti-Soviet Turko-Tatar nationalist organization," along with many other Central Asians. Akmal Ikramov was arrested several months later.[64] Ikramov, Xo'jaev, and former chair of the Central Asian Bureau Isaac Zelenskii became bit players in the last of the great Moscow show trials, the "Case of the Anti-Soviet Bloc of Rights and Trotskyites," broadcast to the world in March 1938. The stars of this trial were Nikolai Bukharin and Alexei Rykov, who had opposed Stalin's radicalism, and Genrikh Iagoda, who, as the former chief of the OGPU, had directed earlier purges. Xo'jaev and Ikramov, who had always been bitter rivals, now confessed to running a bourgeois-nationalist conspiracy together, supported by England, that was responsible for all the horrors of collectivization and other economic failures.[65] They were shot a few days after the trial.

The Great Terror wiped out not only the leaders, but roughly one-half to two-thirds of the members of the Central Asian communist parties along with their families.[66] Stalin did not accomplish their destruction single-handedly, of course. The NKVD included a small number of Central Asian agents, but those agents found "enemies" to arrest on the basis of denunciations by other Central Asians, both those who had been arrested and those who feared arrest. During the months between Xo'jaev's arrest and Ikramov's, Ikramov was eager to proclaim Xo'jaev's guilt.[67] While it is clear that there was no love lost between the two men, Ikramov did not join in the denunciations purely out of spite, but because that was the murderous logic of the Terror. The best way to prove that you were an honest communist was to demonstrate your vigilance in ferreting out hidden enemies. Denouncing someone else was a pre-emptive strike against their denunciation of you. In Ikramov's case, he had to be worried that his failure to denounce Xo'jaev earlier would be used as evidence that he was part of Xo'jaev's conspiracy, as indeed it was. Finally, confessions always involved naming more co-conspirators, so that the cycle of arrest and denunciation became self-perpetuating. By late 1938 Stalin decided that the killing had to stop, although even he struggled to halt the machine he had set in motion.[68]

One of the reasons Stalin ended the Terror was that the Soviet government was threatening to break down because so many experienced people had disappeared. On the other hand, the Terror now enabled him to appoint a new generation of party officials who owed their careers entirely to him, and who did not have competing ideas of what "national in form, socialist in content" should look like. In Uzbekistan the new First Secretary of the Communist Party was Usman Iusupov. Iusupov had joined the Communist Party after the national delimitation, and was rapidly promoted to Third Secretary of the Uzbek party. He married a Tashkent-born Ukrainian woman and lived comfortably among Slavs, which was an important, if unspoken, criterion for political success—Ikramov and Xo'jaev had also had European wives. It was Iusupov who pushed through the large-scale irrigation canal building that Xo'jaev and Ikramov had been reluctant to pursue without greater control and financing. Iusupov drafted hundreds of thousands of manual laborers to dig 1332 km/827 miles of canals, including the Great Ferghana Canal of 1939, a showpiece of high Stalinist industrialization that was poorly planned and wasted huge amounts of water, like most shock campaigns of the 1930s.[69] In the other republics Stalin found fewer Central Asians he was willing to entrust with leadership. Kazakhstan had a Russian First Secretary and Kazakh Second Secretary until 1946, and Turkmenistan was run by paired European-Turkmen co-first secretaries. This new generation of leaders had little time to establish themselves, however, before the entire USSR was consumed by the greatest crisis of its history, the German invasion.

WORLD WAR II AND AFTER

After years of publicly fighting fascism as the number one enemy of communism, Stalin shocked the world in August 1939 by signing a mutual non-aggression treaty with Nazi Germany, the Molotov-Ribbentrop Pact. The pact gave Stalin the freedom to extend his western borders by invading and annexing the independent Baltic states of Estonia, Latvia, and Lithuania, eastern Poland, and the region of eastern Romania called Bessarabia/Moldavia. He also engaged in a brief "Winter War" with Finland and won territory immediately north of Leningrad, although the Finns exposed just how weak and disorganized the Red Army was as a result of the purges. Stalin's understanding with Hitler was short-lived. The German military built up a huge invasion force near the Soviet border in the spring of 1941 while Stalin ordered his officers to take no defensive measures and ignore German reconnaissance missions. When "Operation Barbarossa" began early on 22 June 1941, the USSR was almost completely unprepared. Within a month the Germans had encircled Leningrad and penetrated deep into southern Ukraine, while panic and chaos reigned at all levels of the Soviet government.

"The Great Fatherland War," as the Soviets called it, was the defining experience of Soviet history. It became the lens through which people understood everything that came before and after: industrialization, collectivization, and the purges were harsh but necessary measures that enabled the USSR to re-build and start pushing the Germans back by 1943. For decades afterward, all poverty and hardship could be explained as a result of the war. Above all, the war forged a new meaning of Soviet citizenship that centered on a Russian national victory over fascism rather than an international proletarian victory over capitalism. Where Central Asians fit into that sense of citizenship was a complicated question, since they had fully participated in the victory but were relegated to the position of Russia's "younger brothers."

Whereas the Russian Empire had reluctantly drafted Central Asian men for labor battalions in the middle of World War I, in 1941 the Soviet Union quickly mobilized over 1.5 million of them into the military and another 95,000 into labor battalions in the Urals. On the home front, Uzbekistan hosted around one million evacuees from occupied territories, including 200,000 children.[70] Central Asia suffered much less direct damage in this world war than it had in the previous one, but total war for the very existence of the USSR affected it profoundly (see Figure 7.3).

Small numbers of Central Asian men had fought in the Red Army during the civil war, and in 1926 the government established a Central Asian Military District in Tashkent served by locally recruited soldiers. Military service opened the road to upward mobility only to a very few who were fluent in Russian, however. Soviet military units were segregated by nationality until 1938, which was in keeping with korenizatsiia principles. However, military needs and korenizatsiia were incompatible. A union-wide military

FIGURE 7.3 A Kyrgyz kolkhoz chairman gives instructions, 1941. Source: Sovinformbiuro. Kyrgyz Fotoarkhiv. http://www.foto.kg/galereya/3758-predsedatel-kolhoza-oktyabr-zachityvaet-kolhoznikam-soobschenie -sovinformbyuro.html.

could not function in one hundred languages, not to mention the potential threat that giving unhappy non-Russians military training might pose. In practice, Central Asian soldiers were limited to local border patrol, and did not have access to the level of training or equipment that regular (that is, European) army units received.[71] When they were drafted *en masse* in 1941, non–Russian-speaking Central Asians suffered not only from poor training, but because they were unable to understand instructions. As a result, their frustrated Russian officers neglected and abused them, leading soldiers to desert or mutilate themselves to escape the front. The situation was even worse for men in the labor battalions, who were both abused and given the taint of treachery by association with the exiled "enemy nationalities" they were forced to work alongside.[72] The military could not come up with effective ways to engage Central Asians until 1942–43, after the initial panic subsided and the Germans were turned back at Stalingrad. They issued local-language training and propaganda materials and recruited bilingual "agitators" to talk to, train, and inspire non-Russian soldiers. The agitators also occasionally helped soldiers get compensation for poor treatment.[73] The agitators helped turn alienated Central Asians into valuable soldiers. More than one hundred

Central Asians earned the title of "Hero of the Soviet Union" by 1945, although discrimination kept their numbers disproportionately low.[74]

As the Germans raced through Soviet territory in 1941, thousands of factories, artworks, and millions of people were packed into trains and sent east of the Urals. This astounding feat of evacuation was chaotic and brutal. At its peak in late 1941 Tashkent was receiving two hundred children a day, most of whom had been separated from their parents.[75] In addition, Tashkent became home to dozens of factories and the cream of the Soviet academic and artistic elite, including the composer Dmitri Shostakovich, the poet Anna Akhmatova, and the theater director Shlomo Mikhoels. Food and housing were in desperately short supply, and tensions between residents and evacuees often ran high. Despite the hardship and rancor, the situation gave Uzbeks a place in the Soviet war epic as exemplary citizens who opened their hearts and homes to orphans. Caring for children was a rare point of agreement between communist and traditional Uzbek values; Usman Iusupov and his wife adopted a girl from Leningrad in late 1941, and many other government families imitated them. The Shamakhmudovs, a kolkhoz family, were celebrated all over the USSR for adopting fourteen orphans. Like all war tales, the story of Tashkenters as loving, selfless protectors of evacuees was a truth heavily coated in myth, but the myth helped define a new kind of Uzbek Soviet citizenship.[76]

The war killed approximately twenty-seven million Soviet citizens and destroyed towns and infrastructure throughout the lands west of the Urals. Central Asians certainly suffered their share of casualties—three-quarters of Uzbek soldiers were injured or killed—but the region's role as an evacuation zone left it with more modern infrastructure than three five year plans had built.[77] An entire industrial complex was transferred from Russia to Uzbekistan, including large aviation, chemical, and metallurgical plants. These factories needed workers and power to function. Hundreds of thousands of local people, mainly women and teenagers, were drafted to build and work in the plants and to build five new hydroelectric dams, largely with hand tools.[78] The biggest dam, Farhodstroi on the upper Syr Darya, was not completed until 1949, but it became an important source of electricity for Uzbekistan and Tajikistan. Like women in all the combatant countries, Central Asian women had to fill in for absent men on the kolkhozes and in other jobs, which gave them a greater sense of capability and independence than traditional custom had allowed. For their part, many of the returning men had new technical and Russian-language skills that had previously only been available to the educated elite. Their war experiences drew millions of ordinary Central Asians toward the Russian-European cultural complex. They were more comfortable with it than their grandparents had been. On a deeper level their actions on the front and at home made them not just recipients of, but contributors to, a Soviet culture that was still predominately Russian but now also theirs. The returning *frontoviki* (veterans of the front) claimed leadership roles in government, industry, and on kolkhozes that they believed they had earned with blood. They brought with them a breadth of experience that no previous generation of Central Asians had had, and they used that experience to shape a society that was becoming Soviet and Central Asian in equal measure.[79]

The war made the Soviet Union second only to the United States in power and influence. When it tested an atomic bomb in 1949 near Semipalatinsk in Kazakhstan it joined the US as a "superpower." High international status did not mean that Stalin relaxed pressure on Soviet citizens, however. In 1943 he had berated Iusupov for not producing enough cotton and demanded that he step up troika trials of shirkers; over the next two years almost half of Uzbek party members were purged. Iusupov himself was removed from the Uzbek party leadership in 1949. Immediately after the war levies of workers to dig new irrigation canals resumed even though food was in such short supply that people were dying of hunger in some areas.[80] A new wave of forced migrants put further strain on resources: in 1944 and 1945 Stalin accused Chechens, Ingush, Crimean Tatars, and other nationalities of collaborating with the Nazis and brutally expelled them from their homelands. Uzbekistan agreed to take 70,000 Crimean Tatars and actually received twice that many, leading to numerous deaths. The North Caucasians, Germans, and Georgian Meskhetian Turks sent to Uzbekistan and northern Kazakhstan fared no better.[81]

The one great concession that Stalin made during the war was to end the campaign against Islam. In 1943 he allowed imams to set up a state-supervised administration for all of Central Asia, modeled on Catherine the Great's effort to control Muslims by folding them into her government. The Spiritual Administration of the Muslims of Central Asia and Kazakhstan (SADUM) tried to serve the state and believers equally, a difficult balance. Nonetheless, SADUM would exert noticeable influence on Islamic thought through the postwar decades.[82] It was not responsible for an increase in public religious observance such as wearing the paranji or polygyny, however. Although party activists wrung their hands over the confounding *perezhitki* ("survivals" of Islam) that seemed to surge right after the war, mostly what was happening was that people sought comfort in tradition after the shocking upheavals of the previous fifteen years.[83]

Despite the continuing hardship and repression, Central Asians also carved out space to assert their own desires and needs, even to the point of direct disobedience to party orders. When Stalin had criticized Iusupov for tolerating "lazy" kolkhozniks, he was not inventing the problem. During the war kolkhozes had imported children, members of the Komsomol, and prisoners to do the hard and poorly paid manual labor in the cotton fields. After the war kolkhoz men saw no reason to discontinue the practice, and the growth of rural administrative offices gave them plenty of opportunities to take desk jobs instead. In the late 1940s as many as 40 per cent of male kolkhozniks refused to work in the fields despite direct criticism from the Uzbek party. Kolkhoz bosses and party officials took advantage of postwar state weakness to plant food crops for private sale rather than cotton, to steal money, and to submit fraudulent harvest records. Furthermore, Central Asians started to demand services from the state such as care for wounded veterans, poor families, and even regular access to such luxuries as soap and decent housing.[84] They were beginning to behave like citizens, even though the state still preferred to treat them as subjects.

SUMMARY

When Stalin died on 5 March 1953 Central Asians went into shock and public mourning along with their fellow Soviet citizens. Despite the enormous suffering he had inflicted on them, he was the only leader that most of them had ever known, and there was no guarantee that a new leader would be any more merciful. Twenty-five years of Stalin's dictatorship had broken down or destroyed most of the social elements that had structured Central Asian cultures for centuries: nomadic pastoralism, small village farming, private trade, governance by Islamic law and elite elders, patriarchal rule over private life, and religion as the source of morality and knowledge. At least two million Central Asians were dead out of a 1926 population of roughly 10.5 million, not including war casualties. Tens of thousands had been exiled to other republics or the Gulag and thousands more had fled over the borders, tearing apart families and communities. Stalin's rule had also built at least the foundations for new structuring elements: state-controlled collective farming and trade, textile and extractive industries, governance by secular law, and a new elite educated according to European standards. Thanks to two million "special settlers," the republics had more ethnically diverse populations than ever before. Most Central Asians did not have a good understanding of communist ideology and would not have agreed with it if they had, but enough of them benefitted from the new economic and political arrangements that they not only accepted them, they began to adapt them to their own values and needs. They were learning to think of themselves as Kazakhs, Uzbeks, Tajiks, Turkmen, and Kyrgyz, within the larger context of the Soviet Union, rather than as members of particular tribes. This is not to say that everything about the old Central Asia was dead. Religious belief, traditional gender relations, loyalties to family and locality, foodways and artistic expressions were changed but still easily recognizable. In broader terms, however, Central Asia was starting to resemble Russia and Ukraine more than Afghanistan or Kashgharia. The years of relative calm after Stalin's death would extend and deepen that resemblance.

Chapter 8

STABILITY AND GROWTH

A Central Asian teenager in 1960 had a number of options when deciding how to spend his or her leisure time. Summer camps offered sailing on Lake Issyk Kul, sports contests, hiking in the mountains, book clubs, and sewing circles. The politically ambitious could attend Komsomol camps where they studied Marxism-Leninism and learned how to set up "atheist corners" in their schools. Schools sponsored all sorts of extracurricular clubs, for model airplane enthusiasts, folk dancers, or "young historians." Older teens and adults could go to dances at workers' clubs, see movies, or root for their local team in the new professional soccer league. By the 1970s teenagers were annoying adults with a new kind of entertainment: rock bands. After all the suffering and upheaval of the Stalin period, the appearance of "normal" society in Western terms seems sudden, almost shocking. Some of these activities in fact began in the 1930s or 1940s, but it was the relaxation of political terror and a new recognition in the 1950s that citizens had their own legitimate needs that allowed Soviet modernity to flourish in the Central Asian republics.

The Soviets enjoyed their own version of Europe's *trente glorieuses* (the thirty glorious years of economic growth) after Stalin's death, but the period was a golden age only in comparison with what came before and immediately after. While children on collective farms had more access to schools and leisure activities, they still spent much of their time doing manual labor in the fields. The republics' economies and populations grew rapidly, but production of food and basic consumer goods lagged behind citizens' needs. Perpetual *defitsit* of everything helped create a class of political and economic elites who had access to scarce goods and used their *blat* (pull) to form a new kind of clan based on patronage and kickbacks rather than tribal loyalty. Higher education and arts institutions fostered a Central Asian *intelligentsia* in the Russian style, but the party line still constrained what they could think and do. It was the best time to live in the Soviet Union, but the promise of a communist paradise receded before a shabby reality.

CHANGING RELATIONS BETWEEN MOSCOW AND THE REPUBLICS

In his late years Stalin deliberately kept his Politburo members at daggers drawn with each other. Immediately after his death the younger men, led by Nikita Khrushchev and Georgii Malenkov, moved to strip the older ones of power. They arrested and executed the feared political police chief Lavrenti Beria at the end of 1953. Stalin's long-time henchmen Lazar Kaganovich and Viacheslav Molotov stayed on, but did not have the energy to out-maneuver the upstarts. The Politburo chose Khrushchev to be the First Secretary of the Communist Party nine days after Stalin died because they thought the excitable motor-mouth would be fairly easy to control. They were repeating the mistake of 1922, when Trotsky and Bukharin did not imagine that the plodding General Secretary Stalin could pose a threat to anyone. Khrushchev's real rival for power was Malenkov, who as new Premier of the Council of Ministers was the head of the state side of the government.[1] One thing that all the surviving Politburo members agreed on was that the punitive taxes, arrests, and general misery of Stalin's last years had to stop. For a change, Soviet citizens benefitted from political rivalry at the top as Malenkov and Khrushchev vied with one another to reduce taxes on farmers, release prisoners from the Gulag, and invest in increased food and consumer goods production. By late 1954 Khrushchev bested Malenkov in the contest for influence, which freed him to start economic reforms that he had been dreaming about for years.

Khrushchev was the Politburo's designated agricultural expert. Even before Stalin's death, he had proposed combining small collective farms and moving their inhabitants to "agrotowns" to improve efficiency and make it easier for the state to supervise them. Khrushchev really believed that the

USSR could fulfill its promises of abundance under full communism if he corrected Stalin's "mistakes." He saw the steppes of northern Kazakhstan as a vast potential grain basket that only needed enough people to start producing that abundance. In November 1953 Khrushchev ordered Kazakh party leaders to prepare plans for intensive farming in the region around Akmolinsk. By opening up these "Virgin Lands," Khrushchev also altered Moscow's relationship with Kazakhstan and Kazakhstan's internal political and social dynamics.

By 1939, between the famine and the influx of forced settlers, ethnic Kazakhs accounted for only 38 per cent of the inhabitants of their titular republic, while Russians and Ukrainians made up 51 per cent. During the war Stalin deported additional hundreds of thousands of North Caucasians and other "collaborator nations" to Kazakhstan, of which more than 60,000 were sent to the Akmolinsk region.[2] Khrushchev wanted Akmolinsk officials to draw up ambitious plans that would require many more people, and much more investment, than the region had ever had before. The chair of the Akmolinsk oblast party committee, a Russian, assured Khrushchev that his hopes for grain production would be fulfilled and over-fulfilled. However Jumabai Shaiakhmetov, First Secretary of the Communist Party of Kazakhstan, told his subordinates to underestimate the amount of arable land in Akmolinsk to dampen Khrushchev's expectations.[3] Shaiakhmetov had joined the party in 1927 and risen through its ranks entirely under Stalin, including ten years in the interior police confiscating property from kulak families. He was named Second Secretary in 1939—a beneficiary of Stalin's Terror—and became the first ethnic Kazakh to serve as First Secretary in 1946.[4] His reluctance to endorse Khrushchev's scheme was rooted in practical concerns, but he also represented the Stalinist *apparat* that Khrushchev wanted to undermine. Khrushchev decided to work with the Akmolinsk oblast party directly and push Kazakhstan's ostensible leader off to the side, blithely ignoring Soviet political principles concerning the sovereignty of the national republics. In 1954 Khrushchev dismissed Shaiakhmetov from his post and replaced him with a Russian who was more cooperative. For the next ten years Khrushchev treated the Virgin Lands region more as a satellite of Russia than as a part of Kazakhstan, although this was because of his focus on maximum harvests rather than ethnic prejudice. In 1960 he was just as quick to dismiss an unsatisfactory Russian first secretary and replace him with Kazakh Dinmukhammed A. Kunaev, whose career would long outlast Khrushchev's.[5]

Treating the independence of the national republics as fictional was nothing new, but it is notable that Khrushchev and the central leadership were now so far removed from the original Bolshevik debates over how a multi-national communist government should function that they did not see the republics as having even symbolic autonomy. In fact Khrushchev would make his own contribution to Soviet nationality theory by declaring in 1957 that the nationalities were simultaneously "blossoming" and "drawing together" to create an entity that neither Marx nor Lenin had ever envisioned, "the Soviet people."[6] The new formulation had a paradoxical effect: it allowed Khrushchev to ignore the wishes of the Kazakh Communist Party when convenient, but it also freed him to give more power over local affairs to the republics without worrying about the threat of national chauvinism as Stalin had done. If the republics were truly drawing together, then there was no national chauvinism to fear. Nuriddin Mukhitdinov, the only Uzbek ever to serve as a full member of the Politburo, opposed Khrushchev's idea, but Khrushchev did not listen to him.[7] In this way Khrushchev inadvertently created conditions that enabled the Central Asian republics to develop real political autonomy, the direct opposite of his vision of a unified Soviet people.

The Virgin Lands campaign and de-Stalinization together led to new demographic changes in Kazakhstan. Politburo members began quietly releasing a trickle of Gulag prisoners soon after Stalin's death, but once some families welcomed their people home, others began to agitate on behalf of their relatives. Large-scale riots by prisoners at the Kengir camp added to the pressure, and in 1954 the Politburo began to ease restrictions on the North Caucasian and German special settlers.[8] The North Caucasians began to leave immediately, although legally they could not return home until 1957. The Germans could move within Kazakhstan but were not allowed to go home, and most of them stayed put. They were joined by some 300,000 new volunteer Virgin Lands settlers from poor rural Slavic areas. The Virgin Lands volunteers had a very high turnover rate during the first years of the campaign, but enough of them stayed to form the basis of a highly mixed society. In 1959 over forty religious communities were active in the area, including German Mennonites, Kazakh Muslims, and a new Sufi order founded by a local sheikh.[9] The giant Karaganda camp complex was closed in 1959, but the coal mines and related industries stayed open and many of the former prisoners remained in Kazakhstan because they had nowhere else to go.

The Akmolinsk region was not the only part of Kazakhstan that the central state appropriated for its own use. Beginning in 1947 Beria developed an 18,000-square-kilometer "polygon" between Akmolinsk and Semipalatinsk as the USSR's main test site for nuclear weapons. The Soviets exploded their first atomic bomb there in 1949, and their first hydrogen thermonuclear bomb in 1953. Between 1949 and 1989 approximately 450 nuclear tests were conducted in the polygon, including 116 above ground. The area was sparsely populated, and Beria had seen no reason to evacuate the few thousand people who lived there, aside from removing them from the immediate ground zero site. In some tests the military apparently used local Kazakhs as guinea pigs to test the effects of radioactive fallout. The nuclear facilities did not attract large numbers of settlers as the Virgin Lands did, but they made what once had been Kazakh land off-limits to most Kazakhs.[10] In 1955 Moscow blocked off a small region on the Syr Darya near the village of Toretam to build a launching pad for ballistic missiles and space rockets. In October 1957 the very first satellite, Sputnik, was launched from there; by the 1960s the area had been named the Baikonur Cosmodrome.

These developments left Kazakhstan in an anomalous position within the Soviet Union. It was the most diverse republic in the country except for the Russian Soviet Federated Socialist Republic; it was the only republic where the titular nationality was a minority; and it was the only republic where large sections of its territory were not controlled by its own administration. The other Central Asian republics also had minority populations, but there the titular nationalities all held solid demographic majorities. The Bolsheviks had formed national territories in order to create modern national identities as a necessary step on the road to international communism, but later government actions effectively disconnected Kazakh identity from citizenship in Kazakhstan. Kazakhstan had been set on a social and political trajectory that made it distinct from the rest of Central Asia.

Khrushchev appointed new leaders in all the Soviet republics, causing a great deal of governmental churn. The most influential Central Asian was Nuriddin Mukhitdinov, a war veteran and chair of the Uzbek Council of Ministers as of 1951. Mukhitdinov met Khrushchev in 1953 and made enough of an impression that he found himself included in the first Soviet trade delegation to Finland. There he was deeply embarrassed when the Finnish president took off his clothes and invited the delegation to join him in a sauna, then jump into a cold pond, but he gamely went along—probably the first Uzbek ever to do so.[11] In 1955 Mukhitdinov hosted Khrushchev for the first visit to Uzbekistan by a Soviet leader and was rewarded with the position of First Secretary of the Uzbek Communist Party. In 1956 Khrushchev elevated him to the Politburo. Around the same time Khrushchev promoted Tursun Uljaboev to head the Tajik Communist Party. Khrushchev changed personnel as rapidly as he changed his mind, however. Mukhitdinov was replaced as head of the Uzbek party by Sobir Kamalov in 1957, who in turn was replaced by Sharaf Rashidov in 1959. Turkmenistan went through three first secretaries in three years. In 1961 Khrushchev replaced the Kyrgyz first secretary Ishak Razzaqov (served 1950–61) with Turdakun Usubaliev, removed Uljaboev from the Tajik leadership and installed Jabbor Rasulov, and demoted Mukhitdinov from the Politburo. Mukhitdinov would be named Soviet ambassador to Syria in 1967, where he served for ten years.

While at first it may appear that Central Asians were still powerless before Moscow, Khrushchev turned over personnel so frequently because republican leaders were resisting and countering his economic demands. Khrushchev invested tremendous resources in increasing cotton production, but the republics wanted expensive projects like hydroelectric dams that would benefit them in return. Local officials also grew bolder in manipulating production quotas: Khrushchev demoted so many people in 1961 because Tajik farms were caught padding their totals of harvested cotton so they could collect undeserved bonuses from the state, a practice from which Uljaboev personally profited.[12] Central Asia's recovery from Stalin's Terror was visible in the new leaders who were administering their republics with confidence and a sense of their own rights under the Soviet constitution. From 1940 Uzbeks formed the majority in the Uzbek party leadership, although Russians retained key positions heading local political police and military units. The first Turkmen first secretary, Sukhan Babaev, made Turkmen a majority of his party's apparat.[13] The process of Central Asians becoming true governors of their republics was just beginning in the 1950s, but Khrushchev's repudiation of Stalinist violence meant that generations of trained administrators were no longer being destroyed. Governance began to stabilize after the 1961 upheavals: Kunaev in Kazakhstan, Rashidov in Uzbekistan, Usubaliev in Kyrgyzstan, and Rasulov in Tajikistan all stayed in office into the mid-1980s.[14] Turkmenistan's Muhammadnazar Gapurov was in place from 1969 to December 1985. These men would gradually extend their own authority over every area of local life except cotton production.

COTTON MONOCULTURE, COTTON MONOMANIA

It is impossible to exaggerate the role of cotton in Soviet Central Asia. Most central state investment in the region was intended to increase cotton production in one way or another. Expanding networks of irrigation canals and dams, resettling tens of thousands of people, building factories to make agricultural equipment, and fulfilling the old promise of comprehensive education and medical systems were ultimately all about cotton. People sang songs about cotton, celebrated holidays about cotton, and waited for buses at stops decorated with cotton motifs. A kolkhoz director invoked an Islamic shrine to inspire his farmers to increase production.[15] In Uzbekistan soccer fans cheered for the national team *Pakhtakor*, the Cotton Growers. The obsession with cotton entrenched Central Asia in the role of raw commodity producer for the industrialized European parts of the USSR. It also led to the biggest man-made water crisis in history, as over-irrigation and the uncontrolled use of agricultural chemicals began to dry up the Aral Sea and damage the health of millions of people.

Globally, the 1950s and 1960s saw explosive growth in agricultural productivity due to increased mechanization and the use of fertilizers, herbicides, and insecticides derived from petroleum and minerals. Cotton posed a difficult challenge to enthusiasts of this "Green Revolution." American engineers struggled for years to figure out how to mechanically separate the soft cotton boll from its tough, prickly capsule. It was not until 1949 that they developed the first commercially viable mechanical cotton picker. The Soviet Union started to manufacture its own mechanical picker in substantial numbers in 1950.[16] Khrushchev welcomed competition with the West; he said both that he wanted to pursue "peaceful coexistence" and that "we will bury you." Behind his boasting, Khrushchev discovered that raising Central Asian cotton production to meet the new global standards entailed much more than inventing a new machine.

The Hungry Steppe

The initial success of the Virgin Lands campaign in Kazakhstan inspired Khrushchev to start similar projects in the steppe and deserts further south. The Hungry Steppe was a dry, largely uninhabited plateau shared between Uzbekistan and Kazakhstan.[17] A big cotton kolkhoz, staffed mostly by non-Central Asian prisoners, had been operating in the region since the 1920s. In 1956 the central state ordered that 300,000 hectares of Hungry Steppe should be irrigated and cultivated by dozens of new *sovkhozes* (state farms), all built as quickly as possible. Two years later Moscow planners added another 80,000 hectares to the target. In terms of production statistics, the opening of the Hungry Steppe was impressive. By the mid-1960s eleven water reservoirs were constructed in Uzbekistan alone, plus major hydroelectric dams and reservoirs in Tajikistan and Kazakhstan. A cadre of engineers from all over the USSR built a main Hungry Steppe Canal and tributary canals and founded seven sovkhozes within five years, overseen by a bureaucracy of some 18,000 people. The Hungry Steppe project was also where a cohort of young Central Asian engineers and agronomists gained crucial professional experience.[18]

Speed inevitably caused damage, however. Soviet engineers adapted French techniques for building concrete canal liners, but laid them so quickly and cheaply that almost half the water leaked or evaporated before reaching its destination. Extensive seepage into naturally arid soil and farmers' practice of flooding cotton fields as an easy method of irrigation caused groundwater to rise. The groundwater brought up salts that contaminated the topsoil and made it harder to grow cotton. Engineers tried to build drainage systems, but most efforts were inadequate because it was hard to coordinate across such a large area and the necessary equipment was scarce and poor quality. In order to meet ever-rising cotton quotas, sovkhoz directors compensated by using more water to irrigate and demanding that more canals be built. This made the salinization problem worse.[19] This cycle of hasty construction, soil salinization and immense waste of water was repeated at irrigation projects throughout Central Asia.

The engineers recalled their time leading the "attack on the desert" with pride and pleasure at the adventure of it all.[20] They were not the people who actually grew the cotton. Moscow planners had written out a "complex" method of developing the Hungry Steppe that called for building villages and the roads, schools and hospitals necessary to support them simultaneously with the canals. The inhabitants of these villages were supposed to move voluntarily to the steppe. A 1954 plan for populating the newly irrigated lands called for 40,000 households to be resettled over a four-year period.[21] No part of this plan went smoothly. The idea was to move people from the populous Ferghana Valley to virgin lands in other parts of Uzbekistan, but few families were interested. Under pressure to meet deadlines, local officials resorted to coercion. When unhappy settlers did arrive, they found that the promised villages were primitive clusters of shacks on dirt roads, if indeed any houses had been built at all. Conditions were so miserable that many families left as soon as possible.[22] As with earlier shock campaigns, Moscow was unable to provide the resources necessary to realize its plans. Because of the combined problems with water, logistics, and population, the Hungry Steppe project in the end opened only about 100,000 hectares for cultivation rather than the projected 380,000.

Resettling populations to grow cotton also had profound social consequences, nowhere more so than in Tajikistan. The Tajik government had been transferring populations from mountain villages to cultivate lowlands since the 1920s. After the war the central state expanded this practice, but its motivations had become more complicated. The target populations lived high in the mountains where the Zerafshan River originated, isolated from other parts of Tajikistan and hard for the Communist Party to reach. In 1948 the Tajik party explained that it was necessary to transfer whole communities to the southeast corner of the Hungry Steppe in order both to increase cotton production and to modernize the economic and cultural lives of the people. This was a more ambitious and coercive plan than pushing individual households to move to the steppe in Uzbekistan a few years later. In its early phase over one hundred kolkhozes containing approximately 18,000 households were forced to move. In the early 1950s, as the Farkhod and Qayraqqum reservoirs were built in northwest Tajikistan to irrigate the Hungry Steppe, the party needed to resettle not only the 2400 families flooded out by the dams, but find another 2400 families to work the new lands. Party leaders decided to move the entire district of Macha, some 3400 households, to the steppe.[23]

The resettlement was carried out in stages over a few years; it was theoretically voluntary but brutally coercive in reality. State documents recorded some families being moved out of Macha several times, which indicates they had immediately returned to their original homes. An unrecorded, but apparently high, number of vulnerable elderly people and young children died during the process.[24] A kolkhoz in this region could be made up of four or five villages. As the kolkhozes relocated, the villages were sometimes split up, whether deliberately or accidentally is unclear. Breaking up villages not only separated communities, it undermined the basis for people's identity. Village neighborhoods were organized along lines of kinship, which were marked by religious rites at common ancestors' tombs and communal prayer at neighborhood mosques.[25] Removal of these communities from the network of relationships that connected the past with the present, the living with the dead, was a major component of the hardship that forced migrants endured.

Like many Uzbek families who went to the Hungry Steppe, the Tajiks of Macha did not have the promised housing ready for them when they arrived. For the first few years they were settled with Uzbek host families on established kolkhozes. Imposing miserable people who had lost most of their worldly goods on none-too-wealthy families who did not speak their language would seem to have been asking for conflict, but the moral imperative to provide hospitality (*mehmondo'stlik* in Uzbek) to strangers in need kept friction to manageable levels.[26] Eventually the Tajiks established villages of their own in an area they called New Macha, but the resettlement permanently altered their social identities and religious practice. The settlers mixed and sometimes intermarried with a larger Uzbek community. They built new mosques and graveyards, but had lost a connection with their ancestral holy places that could not easily be replaced. The mixing and resettlement also broke up the old networks of clergy and Sufi brotherhoods.[27]

Life on the Cotton Collectives

The global Green Revolution meant that more crops could be grown with less labor. The decrease in demand for rural labor, combined with the enticements of better-paying jobs in exciting cities, led to mass migration to cities all over the world. The Soviet Union's population also urbanized, at a slower pace and despite the fact that peasants did not receive internal passports until 1975. At some point in the early 1960s the USSR crossed the line from being a predominately rural society to being a predominately urban one. However, union-wide statistics masked significant differences among the republics and regions. Soviet urbanization was largely a phenomenon of the Slavic, western parts of the country. Central Asia remained majority rural, as Table 8.1 shows.[28]

The table shows several shifts in population composition developing over a twenty-year period. Urban areas were growing in all of the republics, and they were becoming less European. In Uzbek towns Uzbeks surpassed the Slavic population by 1959; Turkmen and Tajiks reached that milestone by

Table 8.1 Urban and rural populations in the postwar period

UZBEK SSR

Census Year	Urban			Rural		
	Total	Slavic	Uzbek	Total	Slavic	Uzbek
1959	2,728,580	986,681	1,015,480	5,377,124	201,494	4,022,793
1970	4,362,013	1,434,289	1,777,548	7,597,569	193,898	5,955,993
1979	6,281,636	1,676,080	3,023,782	9,107,671	122,477	7,545,225

TURKMEN SSR

Census Year	Urban			Rural		
	Total	Slavic	Turkmen	Total	Slavic	Turkmen
1959	700,797	269,913	242,895	815,578	16,941	680,829
1970	1,034,199	333,034	448,872	1,124,681	19,888	967,828
1979	1,309,673	367,762	623,475	1,455,075	14,815	1,268,222

TAJIK SSR

Census Year	Urban			Rural		
	Total	Slavic	Tajik	Total	Slavic	Tajik
1959	646,178	252,852	205,516	1,333,719	39,472	845,648
1970	1,076,700	355,621	416,001	1,822,902	24,192	1,213,919
1979	1,315,827	409,695	563,459	2,490,393	26,362	1,673,598

KYRGYZ SSR

Census Year	Urban			Rural		
	Total	Slavic	Kyrgyz	Total	Slavic	Kyrgyz
1959	696,207	415,874	91,804	1,369,630	349,332	745,027
1970	1,097,498	629,994	185,955	1,835,307	352,890	1,098,818
1979	1,348,761	695,471	308,770	2,174,071	333,232	1,378,612

KAZAKH SSR

Census Year	Urban			Rural		
	Total	Slavic	Kazakh	Total	Slavic	Kazakh
1959	4,067,224	2,695,720	678,531	5,242,623	2,148,103	2,116,435
1970	6,498,242	4,403,603	1,105,218	6,350,331	2,223,973	3,055,946
1979	7,855,220	5,068,160	1,634,796	6,829,063	2,002,500	3,654,553

Source: "Demoskop Weekly," Institute of Demographics at the Higher School of Economics (census data), accessed 8 June 2018, http://demoscope.ru/weekly/ssp/emp_lan_97_uezd .php?reg=799.

1970. In rural areas Slavs dwindled to 1 per cent of the population. Kyrgyzstan and Kazakhstan, however, still showed the effects of earlier waves of Slavic settlement and famine. Slavs declined from 25 to 15 per cent of Kyrgyzstan's rural population, making up the second-highest percentage in Central Asia. The highest was in Kazakhstan, where Slavs declined from 41 to 29 per cent of the rural population. Kazakhs did not reach the 50 per cent mark of the rural population until the mid-1970s. Slavs maintained big majorities in urban areas in both republics. The 1979 census recorded that on average 72.4 per cent of Central Asians lived in rural areas, ranging from Turkmenistan's 67 per cent to Kyrgyzstan's 81 per cent.[29]

All the republics contained significant minority populations from elsewhere in Central Asia and other parts of the USSR. In Uzbekistan's towns Tatars (exiled Crimeans as well as Volga Tatars) outnumbered Kazakhs and Tajiks combined. Korean exiles gradually moved from the countryside into cities, where they made up 1.8 per cent of the population. In Tajikistan Uzbeks rose from 28 to 42 per cent of the rural population, while in Kyrgyzstan they stayed at a steady 10–11 per cent in both urban and rural areas. In Kazakhstan Germans consistently made up 5 per cent of the urban and 7–8 per cent of the rural population. Uzbeks made up 7–9 per cent of Turkmenistan's population, evenly divided between urban and rural. These minority communities continued to have schools, newspapers, and books in their native languages provided by the state, although in urban areas Russian was becoming the *lingua franca* for educated people of all nationalities. Despite Khrushchev's declaration that all Soviet citizens were merging into one people, state policy continued to maintain national distinctions, while a new divide was opening up between urban and rural lifeways.

The kolkhozes and sovkhozes provided for all the needs of the rural majority. Where Stalin had treated peasants as slaves of the state, Khrushchev believed that happy farmers were more productive farmers. He ordered the central and republican governments to increase investment substantially in schools, healthcare, and modern recreation on the collectives. The republics in turn passed much of the responsibility for funding and organizing these social institutions to *raislar* (farm directors). This system made being a rais a much bigger, if less dangerous, job than it had been under Stalin.[30] While cotton was always the top priority, farms continued to cultivate grain, fruit and vegetables, and animal products; the apricots of the Ferghana Valley were beloved in fruit-starved Russia. Families were allowed to have private garden plots, on which they lavished more care than on collective property because they earned significant income from selling their produce.[31] Some farms added craft shops to produce ceramics, carpets, and wood-carving. Each farm was meant to be self-contained. A rais supervised a full staff of accountants, mechanics, veterinarians, doctors, agronomists, and many other specialized workers. In the post-Stalin decades these specialists were drawn from the local population, creating a rural professional elite.

For ordinary peasants, work life centered around the brigade. The brigade was a unit of roughly thirty people (the size varied) that was responsible for growing a particular crop or maintaining a particular section of the farm. Brigades helped determine what and how farmers were paid and their conditions of work.[32] Brigades were social units in themselves: in Turkmenistan they could be made up of members from one tribe, in Tajikistan they could be made of migrants from a particular mountain village. Brigade leaders might provide their poorer members with food, or money for a wedding.[33] Brigades were also vehicles for marking social status: a rais might give a brigade made up of his relatives lighter work for more pay, or conversely could show disfavor by assigning a brigade to a particularly disagreeable job. One should note that, in principle, the Soviet Union had neither poverty nor social inequality. This was just one of many ways in which everyday life diverged from state prescriptions.

Rural life did modernize, but the effects were not always what the state intended. Educating the populace was one of the Soviet Union's genuine success stories, but the unevenness of its success was exemplary of the entire modernization campaign. By the mid-1960s the number of primary schools in rural Central Asia had more than doubled from the pre-war period. It is impossible to be more precise than that because Soviet statistics, while not entirely fictional, cover up a great deal. The statistics never show what percentage of all children were in fact attending school, for example. They also never explain anomalies such as an apparent major decline in school construction in the mid-1950s or why there seem to have been 66,400 children in Kyrgyz elementary schools in 1950 but only 35,400 in 1962.[34]

Nevertheless, publications such as the Uzbek *O'qituvchilar gazetasi* (*Teachers' Newspaper*) and *Sovet maktabi* (*Soviet School*) show the increasing reach and ambitions of Central Asian schools. Teachers were instructed to follow a rather daunting curriculum that included science, mathematics, and world history in local languages, plus Russian language and literature. Schools began classes in folk music and dance, art, and physical education. After school clubs and sports teams proliferated for girls as well as boys. Beginning in 1958 schools finally got textbooks for Uzbek and other Central Asian national histories, a crucial tool in building modern national identities.[35] The publications showcased exemplary teachers whose students created in-school history museums or helped with archeological digs, but they also provided forums for teachers to complain about poor conditions and inadequate supplies. In 1963 a group of pedagogical students in Andijan wrote: "In principle it is clear to all that textbooks are as necessary as air and water for teaching students.... But the required textbooks and literature are nowhere to be found."[36] Other teachers reported that textbooks in chemistry, history, and literature were in such short supply that it was almost impossible to do their jobs.[37]

Another new feature of Central Asian schools was vocational tracking. In 1958 Khrushchev called for all young people to be trained in some form of labor to maintain the proletarian nature of Soviet culture.[38] Collective farm children spent at least half their school time learning agricultural and technical skills, while children from designated working class families would spend part of their day in factories doing things like hand-stitching *do'ppis* (traditional embroidered hats).[39] Republican governments struggled to get rural parents to keep their children in school beyond the elementary level, but parents had more economic incentives to start their children in useful work. There was also strong social pressure on girls to leave school and get married in their teen years. Providing vocational training was one way to keep kids in some form of schooling, but it also may have restricted social mobility and widened the distance between rural and urban life.

Agricultural labor became an increasingly fraught issue in the post-Stalin decades. Who would do what kind of work, and who would control the labor supply? The central state, republican governments, farm directors, and men and women on the collectives all contested with each other over these questions through actions in the cotton fields as well as words. The biggest point of contention was over manual versus mechanized harvesting of cotton. Khrushchev enthusiastically promoted harvesting cotton by machine, and was baffled and frustrated by Central Asians' reluctance to adopt the practice. Furthermore, Moscow ministers were appalled by collective farms' reliance on conscripted labor, much of it by children, to pick cotton by hand. The fact that the central state could force Central Asia to grow cotton but fail to control how that cotton was produced not only signaled that the balance of power between center and periphery was changing, but that local actors also wielded power that had to be recognized.

From Moscow's vantage point, mechanizing the cotton harvest would free up labor, increase efficiency, and modernize village life. In 1948 the giant Tashkent Agricultural Machinery plant (Tashselmash) opened—agricultural equipment was one of the few industries the central state allowed in Uzbekistan. The production of mechanical cotton pickers stumbled in the mid-1950s when Khrushchev decided to increase yields by narrowing the rows of plants, which required that the harvesters Tashselmash had just produced be scrapped in favor of a new design. However, by 1960 several thousand pickers were being produced every year.[40] From the collective farm directors' viewpoint, these machines were more trouble than they were worth. The pickers required fuel, spare parts, and trained mechanics, all of which were expensive and in short supply. In Tajikistan the pickers struggled over rolling terrain.[41] Between the government's increasing demands that farms provide a complete social welfare structure, higher harvest quotas, and reluctance to raise the rates it paid for raw cotton, farm directors could not afford to mechanize no matter how much Khrushchev yelled at them.[42]

Picking cotton by hand is hard physical labor, and male peasants found many ways to avoid it. Even when Stalin was still alive the Uzbek Central Committee complained that a large percentage of rural men were hiding behind desk jobs to avoid fieldwork, and the rapid growth of rural administrative needs under Khrushchev made that tactic easier. To make up for the loss, farms relied on women, children, retirees, and imported adults to work through the September–November harvest season. According to state media, urban workers, soccer stars, and university students voluntarily went to the fields in a spirit of patriotism. The reality was that this was a coercive and highly disruptive practice. Khairiniso Ganieva, a Tashkent doctor, recalled:

> I was born and educated up to the 11th Class [grade] in Chimkent, Kazakhstan. School standards were significantly higher than in Tashkent—a fact which surprised me when I went there to study at the medical college. I think the reason was that school children were sent out to the fields one to two months to pick cotton, and had to abandon their studies.... In those days, standards at the medical college in Tashkent were high.... But here too, involvement in cotton production disrupted our studies quite a lot. The medical college was the first to "voluntarily" start a cotton picking brigade and the first to terminate it. In 1969 we picked cotton for three to five months.... We lost so much—both knowledge and strength—during this period.[43]

Not only university students, but children under the legal working age of sixteen picked cotton for little pay, and the practice only grew despite direct government opposition.[44] In 1975 Kyrgyz middle-schoolers in Ak Su raion (near Lake Issyk Kul) were informed by the local sovkhoz director that they would be spending May to December working in the fields. They wrote an angry letter to the newspaper *Komsomolets Kirgizii* complaining that their school lacked heat and for three years they had held physical education classes in the road because the gymnasium was in such bad repair it was unusable. Furthermore, "We all work, from the fourth to the tenth grades." The special correspondent who responded to the students' complaint noted that when she first read this letter she assumed the children were exaggerating. Upon investigation, she changed her mind.[45]

The combination of high state demand for cotton with an inability to control how that cotton was produced led to widespread fraud and abuse. Men came to think of picking cotton as a low-status job, since low-status people like women and children were forced to do it. This reinforced men's refusal to pick, even as rural unemployment rates rose through the 1970s. It also reinforced the gender hierarchy despite the government's regular proclamations of the equality of women with men. Farm directors learned that they could lie to the state about the cotton harvest with few consequences. Exaggerating the amount harvested and how it was harvested became a normal part of doing business; the numbers grew slightly bigger at every stage of the bureaucracy between a farm and Moscow.

The Green Revolution was driven by chemicals derived from petroleum and mineral sources, and modern cotton production relies heavily on those chemicals. Uzbekistan produced some of its own superphosphate fertilizer, but Central Asians mostly relied on imports from other Soviet republics. Whatever agricultural chemicals farms received, they applied generously and asked for more. Aside from fertilizers, farms needed insecticides to protect plants and seed treatments to keep disease at bay. Because mechanical cotton pickers worked more efficiently when the plants were stripped of leaves first, it became common to spread defoliants on the fields before harvest.[46] This was done regardless of the fact that most cotton was harvested by hand, and with no consideration for the health of the people doing the picking.

Possible damage to public health by these practices was masked by explosive growth in Central Asia's population. The central and republican governments built networks of clinics, hospitals, and medical schools that, as with education, finally fulfilled the promises of the 1930s. Little research has been done on public health in this period, but census figures suggest notable success in cutting child mortality. In 1959, Kyrgyzstan recorded 609,901 children age 0–9 but only 313,343 in the 10–19 age group; the figures for Uzbekistan were 2,446,614 and 1,260,819.[47] These are not child mortality rates *per se* (number of deaths per 1000 births according to age brackets), which the USSR did not publish at the time. However, that the older group was only 51 per cent of the size of the younger suggests a high death rate, partly attributable to wartime damage. By 1979 the ratios had improved considerably: Kyrgyzstan had 907,976 children age 0–9 and 819,618 children age 10–19, while Uzbekistan had 4,397,374 and 3,818,808, less than a 20 per cent difference. The laggards in this respect were Tajikistan and Turkmenistan, which averaged a 23 per cent difference between their younger and older cohorts of children.

Reductions in child mortality were overshadowed by the huge increase in births in all the republics, as a 1976 cartoon from the Uzbek women's magazine *Saodat* wryly illustrated (see Figure 8.1). In the early 1960s the Slavic population of the USSR reached a plateau in life expectancy and birth rates, averaging nine more births than deaths per year, then began a slow decline. Meanwhile, the Uzbek population had an average of thirty-one more births than deaths per year.[48] As the cartoon suggests, social services struggled to keep up with such a rapid growth rate. The communist command economy had been good for building industry from practically nothing, but was revealing itself to be poor at responding to the changing demands of a consumer society.

MATURE SOCIALISM

By the fall of 1964 Khrushchev's erratic behavior and policy blunders (especially the Cuban Missile Crisis of October 1962) snapped the party's patience with him. A group of Politburo members led by Leonid Brezhnev (r. 1964–82) forced him to retire. Khrushchev had lost the confidence of Central Asian as well as Slavic communists: while Mukhitdinov had rallied to defend Khrushchev in previous crises, now no one came to his aid.[49] Where Khrushchev had been quick to demote people when his plans did not go well, which was often, Brezhnev's watchword was "stability of cadres." This meant that party apparatchiks could settle in and cultivate their positions in the elaborate client-patron networks that regulated political and economic power. It was under Brezhnev that Central Asian leaders became the true

FIGURE 8.1 Director of the daycare center: "You requested places for only two children?" Mother: "By the time my turn came I had three children, my dear ..." Source: *Saodat* no. 10 (1976): 31. Cartoonist: A. Xoliqov.

governors of their republics, within the boundaries set by Moscow's demands for cotton and other commodities.

More than money, access to goods and services was the key to getting things done in the Soviet Union. Cash alone was not very helpful when faced with a store full of empty shelves, but knowing the sister of the clerk who could snag an item for you the moment it arrived at the store—in exchange for helping her make an appointment with your cousin the dentist—made it possible to live reasonably well. At the political level perpetual defitsit turned republican party leaders into the chief distributors of access, not only to goods, but to nice vacation spots, more lucrative jobs, and to other officials who controlled scarce resources. Client-patron networks functioned on the bases of trust and mutual obligation, similar to the way that pre-Soviet tribal relations had functioned. The new Central Asian "clans" were rooted in family and place, and so bore some resemblance to their predecessors. Extended families made for natural networks of trust. Usubaliev in Kyrgyzstan promoted his relatives from the Naryn region to dominate the bureaucracy. Rashidov in Uzbekistan drew his top deputies from the Samarkand-Bukhara region, relegating other regions to lower status. Rasulov in Tajikistan maintained a network based in Leninobod/Khujand that occupied most party leadership positions. Kunaev in Kazakhstan promoted more Kazakhs into the leadership than ever before, including family members who happened to descend from the old Senior Horde. The principle of stability of cadres allowed town and raion chiefs to spend most of their careers in one region, giving them time to entrench themselves at the top of local networks.[50] However, client-patron networking was a mechanism for coping with economic dysfunction that could be found all over the USSR. It should not be interpreted as a uniquely Central Asian "survival" of the tribal past.

The importance of these networks to everyday economic well-being had surprising effects on the relationship between money and power. The Soviet Union cautiously allowed a handful of Western scholars to conduct research in Central Asia in the late 1970s, for the first time in forty years. Some researchers noted that the highest-paid jobs were in heavy industry and the energy sector, and that these jobs were dominated by Europeans (mostly Russians and Jews). Europeans held most industrial management and engineering positions, and for every Central Asian first secretary of a Communist Party at the republican and oblast levels there was a Russian second secretary. Brezhnev himself had been the second secretary in Kazakhstan from 1954 to August 1955 and then first secretary until March 1956. On the surface, it appeared that Central Asians were colonial subalterns, relegated to lower-income jobs and kept under a watchful Russian eye in government. Social scientist Nancy Lubin, however, based on a year in Tashkent during which she not only did fieldwork but managed to feed herself, argued that in real terms these lower-paid occupations could be much more valuable than prestigious managerial jobs. An "unemployed" mother of nine earned a nice income by making dresses that were impossible to find in stores.[51] A collective farmer could buy first place in line for a car with a lamb where no amount of cash could purchase fresh lamb chops in a state store. A doctor could collect forty times his or her official salary in the form of "tips" (bribes) to guarantee good treatment. Meanwhile a Russian engineer might have an advanced degree and a good salary, but without access to high-demand services or goods he could not parlay those into higher real-world value. The disconnect between salary and value was revealed most starkly in the underground market where people paid bribes to obtain legal access to jobs. A permit to sell lemonade on the streets of Tashkent cost almost 1000 rubles—it gave the vendor opportunities to sell much more than lemonade. Meanwhile, one could buy a place as a skilled air-traffic controller for five hundred rubles or less.[52]

Republican leaders had a stable but distant relationship with Brezhnev and the Moscow apparat. The Russian second secretaries of Central Asian parties did not speak the local languages and had no access to local client-patron networks, and seem to have had little influence. Rashidov became a candidate member of the Politburo in 1961 and Kunaev a full member in 1971, but the central state showed little interest in Central Asia outside of commodities production. In the 1970s the USSR began to fully exploit its oil and natural gas reserves, which Turkmenistan, Uzbekistan, and Kazakhstan had in abundance. However, because Moscow set the prices for commodities the republics did not get an economic windfall from this development. If anything, the scant evidence suggests that Moscow's investments in Central Asia declined somewhat in this period, and that republican leaders' requests in the energy sector changed little.[53]

Showcase to the Former Colonies

The interests of central and republican leaders converged in Central Asia's cities. Both Khrushchev and Brezhnev promoted Central Asia to the newly decolonized countries of Africa and Asia as a model of the benefits of Soviet development. Republican leaders welcomed the attention and investment, and contact with international artists and leaders helped foster the Central Asian intelligentsia. Tashkent was the center of this activity. The city hosted international film festivals, medical conferences, and an International Conference of Writers from Africa and Asia in 1958 that drew hundreds of delegates to affirm the Soviet values of "peace, friendship, brotherhood, and poetry."[54] In 1955 India and the USSR sealed their new friendship with diplomatic meetings in Tashkent and a large open-air banquet in Samarkand hosted by Uzbek party leaders. These public rituals demonstrated Uzbekistan's international importance not only to Jawaharlal Nehru and his daughter Indira Gandhi, but to the crowds of local spectators as well.[55] To be effective showcases the capital cities needed to look clean and modern, so Moscow was willing to pay for broad streets, public transportation, and the model modern district Chilonzar in Tashkent, with its blocks of concrete apartment buildings instead of the traditional extended-family houses built around private courtyards.[56]

That investment was undone on the morning of 26 April 1966, when a massive earthquake and its aftershocks destroyed most of Tashkent. The region is prone to earthquakes; the Turkmen capital Ashgabat had been severely damaged by one in 1948. The Tashkent earthquake left approximately 300,000 people homeless and killed an unrecorded number out of a total population of 1,124,000.[57] The disaster also created an opportunity to rebuild the city on grander terms. People came from all over the Soviet Union to help with the construction, and many of them stayed. By 1979 Tashkent's population had grown to 1,780,002, including a new influx of Europeans who enjoyed the warmer climate. The earthquake enabled Tashkent's transformation into a modern Soviet city, complete with huge open squares, Central Asia's only subway system, and spectacular water fountains that demonstrated the state's mastery over nature in a desert climate. The Old City never disappeared, however, despite plans to raze it, and Uzbeks continued to prefer their traditional courtyard houses to cramped Russian-style apartments.[58]

Central Asia's post-Stalin openness to the world had the greatest effects in its cities. Aside from state-controlled diplomatic and artistic conferences, old media networks of newspapers, magazines, and radio expanded. The new medium of television arrived in Kazakhstan in 1958, although it took many years for television with local-language programming to become widespread in Central Asia. The film industry took off in the 1960s, as each republic acquired its own film studio and began making movies for entertainment in local languages.[59] All of these venues were also subject to censorship, but there were limits to state control over popular culture and how people made use of it. Young Central Asian urbanites participated in the general Soviet youth culture: *stilyagi* (roughly "style-hunters") wearing narrow-leg pants, long coats, and platform shoes (for men) and tight skirts, short jackets, and low-heeled shoes (for women) upset moral guardians in Tashkent as well as Moscow.[60] In the 1970s students at the Kyrgyz State University started their own rock band to play at parties.[61] The magazine *Saodat* was aimed at a more sedate audience of mothers and teenage girls, but assumed its readers were educated enough to follow the latest medical advice on child nutrition and health, a profile of American communist Angela Davis, and a story about the American feminist movement that began with Abigail Adams's admonition to her husband John to "remember the ladies."[62] In a remarkable slip of the censor's attention, the regular column "Girls, this is for you!" interrupted its usual focus on sewing and housekeeping tips to run a straightforward discussion of menstruation (*hayz ko'ra*). The author, a doctor, assured girls that menstruation was normal and healthy and usually began between the ages of thirteen and sixteen. She advised menstruating girls not to ride bicycles, ski, skate, walk long distances, or lift heavy items. Likewise, spicy foods and alcohol were to be avoided, while mineral water and apricots were helpful. Thereafter the column reverted firmly to sewing tips.[63]

A select few Central Asians also had the chance to travel abroad as ambassadors for Soviet modernization. Tajik geologists and engineers worked in Afghanistan, Uzbek irrigation specialists were sent to Egypt. Many republican party leaders served as diplomats in the Middle East and North Africa, both before and after their time in the first secretary post. Companies of traditional dancers and musicians as well as writers and film makers performed all over the world, showing off cultural achievements that were national and Soviet in equal measure. Uzbek gymnast Elvira Saadi won gold medals on the 1972 and 1976 Soviet Olympic teams.[64] Clergy in the SADUM played an important role as Islamic representatives in Saudi Arabia, partly because the USSR did not have formal diplomatic relations with that country. The Soviets allowed only a dozen or so people to make the annual pilgrimage (hajj) to Mecca, carefully vetting them to make sure they were well-spoken, learned, and healthy-looking representatives of a respectable Soviet Islam. SADUM clergy studied in Middle Eastern madrasas, hosted international conferences in Tashkent, and exchanged correspondence and religious literature with their counterparts.[65] These contacts with the larger world were limited by their small scale and close state supervision, but educated Central Asians participated in global cultural currents as much as any Soviet citizens did.

The Afghan Invasion

Central Asians also participated in the last, disastrous, military action of the Brezhnev regime: the invasion of Afghanistan. Afghanistan had been the largest single recipient of Soviet foreign aid *per capita* since the Khrushchev years. The Soviets built flour mills, roads, airports, irrigation infrastructure, and sent teachers and doctors. In 1973 the Afghan monarchy was overthrown by an internal coup. The USSR treated the successor People's Democratic Party of Afghanistan as a client government, but did not try to control it as closely as it did the satellite states of Eastern Europe. Afghanistan's stability began to unravel in 1978, when radical communists seized power and began a coercive shock modernization campaign. The leader of the 1978 coup was himself killed in September 1979 by Hafizullah Amin, who initiated Stalinist purges and rapidly earned popular hatred for his corruption. Brezhnev's Politburo seems to have decided to invade with the limited goal of restoring order.[66] Brezhnev probably had little to do with the decision, since by that time he had had several heart attacks and strokes and was no longer shown live on television, as he had a tendency to drool on himself.

On 27 December 1979, Soviet troops invaded from Termez, a military base on the Uzbek-Afghan border, which gave Uzbek and Tajik units a forward role. They overthrew and killed Amin and replaced him with Babrak Karmal, but Karmal could not establish legitimacy because most Afghans saw him as a Soviet puppet.[67] Northern Afghanistan is home to several million Tajiks, Uzbeks, and Turkmen, including descendants of people who had fled the USSR in the 1920s and 1930s. In addition, the Shiite Hazaras and the Pashtun majority in the south both speak Iranian languages related to Tajik. At the time of the invasion American journalists got very excited at the possibility that Soviet Muslims would turn against their atheist government rather than fight fellow believers, but very few incidents of that kind occurred. Instead the Soviet army used Central Asian soldiers and hundreds of civilian Tajik translators to help win the trust of Afghans and restore orderly government with their knowledge of local lifeways. The problems that developed stemmed from the flawed assumption of the entire operation, that Afghans would peaceably accept military occupation until the USSR gave its stamp of approval to a new government. As Afghan anti-communist *mujahidin* armies multiplied with CIA help, Central Asian soldiers suffered along with their Slavic comrades. Mujahidin were not the only source of trouble, however. Corruption, abuse, and alcoholism were profound problems within the Soviet military before the invasion, and the pressures of a war that was turning out to be anything but short and simple exacerbated those problems. Central Asian soldiers were targets of Slavic ethnic prejudice, although the full extent of racism in the military is not clear. Some Central Asians came out of their war experience just as disgusted by corruption and the needless deaths of civilians as some Slavic soldiers did, while others felt confirmed in their Soviet patriotism. Relations with Afghan peoples also turned out to be more fraught than originally anticipated. Central Asian soldiers generally got along well with Afghan Tajiks and Uzbeks, but the Pashtuns regarded them simply as enemies. By 1981 Soviet popular opinion on the war was turning sour. Mothers of dead and wounded soldiers staged a major public protest in Tashkent that summer, which may have contributed to a policy of replacing most Central Asian soldiers with Slavic ones by 1983.[68] The change in personnel did not make solutions to the Afghanistan problem any clearer, however.

SUMMARY

When Brezhnev died in November 1982 the USSR appeared to be stable and strong; in the US President Ronald Reagan was calling it the "evil empire." Central Asians had become full citizens of this "empire" and generally appeared to be content with it. The five republics now had the complete apparatus of modern nationhood: native-language literature, film, and art; school systems that reached almost all children with narratives of their national histories and cultures; governments run by local authorities who used a well-developed symbolic language of Soviet and Central Asian identity. For citizens who were willing to stay within state-prescribed boundaries, life was not bad and continued to improve. Collective farmers welcomed rural electrification and social development projects by opting to stay on the farm rather than move to cities as central planners hoped they would.[69] Even those interested in a more religious life usually found prayer spaces and Islamic teachers, although most Central Asians below retirement age were too busy trying to get day-to-day tasks done to bother with such things. There were certainly problems, first and foremost the inability of the Soviet economy to deliver basic goods, much less the promised communist abundance. The persistence of coerced manual labor, child labor, and a wide gap between available workers and jobs they were willing to do frustrated and worried economists. The cotton monoculture created environmental and public health problems that, by the late 1970s, became impossible to ignore. The new leaders in Moscow were well aware of widespread fraud and corruption in the system and hoped to root it out. Their goal was the same as Khrushchev's had been: to make the USSR a country where theory and reality matched.

Chapter 9

FROM REFORM TO INDEPENDENCE

Yuri Andropov, chairman of the KGB since 1967, succeeded Brezhnev as General Secretary of the Communist Party of the Soviet Union (CPSU) in November 1982. Andropov suffered from advanced kidney and liver disease when he took office, but had the support of party members who liked his hostility to corruption. Andropov also understood that the party leadership needed new blood, and promoted younger communists whose formative years had been under Khrushchev rather than Stalin. One of his closest protégés was Mikhail S. Gorbachev (b. 1931), secretary for agriculture on the Central Committee and a member of the Politburo since 1980. When Gorbachev became General Secretary in March 1985, he had already given speeches about the need for far-reaching economic reforms. Over the next two years he began a series of reforms he called *perestroika* (economic restructuring) and *glasnost'* (openness to discussing past and present problems). As General Secretary, Gorbachev was unusual not only in his relative youth and reformist zeal but in that he was the only Soviet leader who had no working experience outside the RSFSR. His early writings and speeches made few references to the multi-national nature of the Soviet state, and he did not anticipate that national or ethnic tensions might become factors in his reform program.

The non-Russian republics had many rude surprises in store for Gorbachev. In February 1986, at the 27th Party Congress, Gorbachev berated the Uzbeks for their anger over the arrests of hundreds of local officials in the "Cotton Affair," a product of Andropov's anti-corruption campaign.[1] Uzbeks responded by complaining about Russian arrogance. On 26 April the nuclear reactor at Chernobyl, Ukraine, blew up and dropped radiation on neighboring Belorussia. In December Gorbachev removed Dinmukhammed Kunaev from his position as First Secretary of the Communist Party of Kazakhstan for corruption and replaced him with a Russian. Instead of welcoming reform, Kazakh students protested the insult to their national honor. The following year the Baltic republics of Estonia, Latvia, and Lithuania began to push for legal and economic autonomy. In 1988 Armenia and Azerbaijan erupted in a nasty war over disputed territory, and Georgia unleashed an aggressive nationalism against its minority Abkhaz and Ossete communities. By the end of 1990 all the republics, including the RSFSR, had joined the Baltic states in asserting the sovereignty of their laws and languages. In 1991 Gorbachev felt forced to negotiate a new "Union Treaty" to re-write the terms of the Union of Soviet Socialist Republics (USSR) on a non-socialist, genuinely voluntary basis. However, six of the fifteen Soviet republics refused to attend the talks. The treaty was the last straw for conservatives in the military and the KGB, who staged a thoroughly inept coup on 19 August 1991. The failed coup led to the dissolution of the USSR. Over the following four months the republics declared themselves independent, even though most Central Asian governments had supported the anti-Gorbachev coup. On 8 December the leaders of Russia, Ukraine, and Belorussia announced the end of a state that had already ceased to exist.

Central Asians defended their national interests during these tumultuous years, but did not organize powerful nationalist movements. Central Asian leaders, except for Kyrgyzstan's Askar Akaev, did not support Gorbachev's reforms, but they participated in the new union treaty negotiations and clearly did not want the USSR to fall apart. When it did anyway, they faced a host of unforeseen challenges: How should they handle their economies, suddenly torn from the larger Soviet economic world? What kind of societies did they want to live in, now that the Soviet communist template had disintegrated? How should the republics relate to each other, and to other countries? Uzbekistan, Turkmenistan, and Kazakhstan followed the path of continuity with Soviet practice and became strongman dictatorships. Tajikistan and Kyrgyzstan, which were the poorest republics in the USSR, fell into war and political instability.

WATER, COTTON, AND NATIONALISM

By the late 1970s decades of cotton monoculture had depleted the soil and water of all the republics, but Uzbekistan and Turkmenistan were particularly hard hit. The state did not charge collective farms for water and built new irrigation canals with no covers or linings to prevent leakage and evaporation, which encouraged massive waste. So much water was being drawn off the Amu Darya for irrigation that the Aral Sea began to shrink noticeably in the 1960s. As of the mid-1970s the river no longer reached the sea at all. The former fishing village of Mo'ynaq, Uzbekistan, found itself stranded amid sand dunes.[2] The depletion of water sources damaged cotton yields, which declined in both quantity and quality. Clean drinking water was critically scarce. Most people got their household water from rivers and canals, which were full of chemical run-off from the cotton fields, salts, and untreated sewage from human and animal sources. The USSR had laws requiring water purification plants, but the money to maintain those plants was siphoned off into the shadow economy.[3] True to the Soviet faith that technology could overcome all obstacles, Central Asians eagerly awaited the implementation of a bold plan to divert the mighty Ob and Irtysh rivers of Siberia down a canal to restore the Aral Sea and provide all the irrigation water they could want.[4] Anticipation of this grandiose solution from Moscow allowed local officials to avoid taking responsibility for conserving water themselves.

For centuries farmers had alternated alfalfa with cotton to rejuvenate soil nutrients, but from the 1960s collective farms were under such pressure to produce cotton that they stopped rotating crops. To compensate for the resulting soil depletion, they applied astounding amounts of chemicals to their fields. Where the average Soviet farm applied 30 kg of fertilizers per hectare annually, Uzbek farms used 480 kg. Where the average farm used 1 or 2 kg per hectare of pesticides and herbicides, Uzbek farms used 54.4 kg, including defoliants.[5] As the Amu Darya delta leading to the Aral Sea dried up, the winds blew toxic dust clouds for hundreds of miles; women in the area were found to have high levels of salt in their breast milk. The combination of the lack of clean drinking water with massive exposure to toxic chemicals created public health problems that Brezhnev's government ignored. According to statistics published during Gorbachev's glasnost' campaign, infant mortality rates were rising: from 1970 to 1986 Uzbekistan's rate increased from 31 to 46.2 infant deaths per thousand births. Turkmenistan's rate increased from

46.1 to 58.2 during the same period. Diseases of the lungs and other internal organs were significantly higher in Central Asia than in the rest of the USSR, and the Karakalpak region reported that 8–10 per cent of infants were born with birth defects.[6]

None of these problems attracted concern from Moscow after Brezhnev's death. What did get Andropov's attention was the discovery that Uzbekistan had been falsifying its cotton statistics for years. Exactly how the central government suddenly became alarmed by an open secret is still unclear, but Andropov as KGB chief had more information than anyone on the extent of corruption.[7] He also seems to have harbored a particular dislike for Uzbekistan's party leader Sharaf Rashidov. In early 1983 Andropov sent a pair of investigators to Bukhara, who quickly and very publicly began to arrest hundreds of Uzbek party and collective farm officials. The "Cotton Affair" (or "Uzbek Affair" as some Russians called it) turned into a milder version of the Stalin-era show trials, with televised proceedings showing Uzbek officials weeping as they confessed their guilt.[8] Moscow's narrative of the scandal set the Uzbeks up as a mafia nation, complete with secret payoffs in gold, jewels, and "billions" of rubles, as well as prurient tales of the Ferghana Valley party boss Akhmadzhan Adylov/Ahmadjon Odilov, who allegedly kept a personal dungeon and a harem like a latter-day khan.[9] There is solid evidence for Odilov's corruption, but stories of Odilov torturing his sheep-like subjects are also reminiscent of nineteenth-century orientalist horror tales of the Bukharan emirs, and should be treated with caution. Given that officials in all the cotton-growing republics were guilty of the same offenses, it is puzzling why the Uzbeks were singled out. The image of a fat, corrupt Uzbek man had been a common trope in the Soviet press for decades, so one factor may have been that the Cotton Affair fit with a familiar stereotype.[10]

Andropov initiated a purge of thousands of Uzbeks, a few of whom were sentenced to death. On 31 October 1983 Rashidov died, officially of a heart attack, but according to rumor he committed suicide rather than face arrest.[11] He was replaced by Inamjon Usmanxo'jaev (1983–88), who acquiesced as a majority of the Uzbek Central Committee was removed and Rashidov was vilified as the embodiment of a corrupt system. Gorbachev broadened the purges to the other republics; between 1982 and 1986 all of the long-standing Central Asian party leaders retired, died, or were replaced. Notably, however, Gorbachev approved new leaders who had first been chosen by republican elites rather than imposing his own candidates. The one exception to this pattern, Kazakhstan, blew up in his face.

It is not clear what Gorbachev expected to result from the purges, but his behavior showed that he had a poor understanding of the forces that created the cotton scandal. While Central Asian communists had no choice but to cooperate with the process, they frustrated Gorbachev with their open anger at what they regarded as an insult to their national honor and sovereignty. Gorbachev compounded that anger not only by removing local officials, which destroyed the livelihoods of entire families, but by replacing many of them with Russians. He also supported a proposal by the Politburo member in charge of party organization, Egor Ligachev, to transfer communist bureaucrats across republican borders. If the CPSU had really been a party of equals united by proletarian internationalism that might have worked. What Gorbachev could not see was that decades of korenizatsiia on the one hand and Russian chauvinism on the other had created a party of hierarchical tiers, wherein non-Russians could console themselves for their lack of power at the center with power in their republics. Moving party officials interchangeably among republics would have disrupted the client-patron networks that were vital to economic and political functioning, and would have made the officials dependent on Moscow for what power they had. That may have been Gorbachev's intention, in which case he should not have been surprised when Central Asians quietly but firmly resisted these plans. Russian apparatchiks sent to the region discovered that they could do little without the cooperation of locals, and Ligachev's proposal to exchange party cadres among republics never got off the ground.[12]

Gorbachev also did not seem to comprehend that Moscow's obsession with "cotton independence," not Central Asian greed, was the root cause of the problem. In August 1986 the Central Committee in Moscow canceled the Siberian river diversion project, due not only to its immense cost but to strong opposition from environmental groups. Instead the committee instructed cotton farms to reduce water consumption by 15–20 per cent, while also expanding the amount of irrigated land a projected 23–27 per cent by the year 2000. When Uzbek First Secretary Rafiq Nishanov (1988–89) and others urged Gorbachev to help the republic diversify its economy away from cotton, he showed no interest. In the midst of a hectic reform program that was already veering out of control, Gorbachev did not have the resources to invest in new economic development. His goal was to improve what they already had.[13]

Kazakhstan was not as deeply involved in getting payments from the state for non-existent cotton, but First Secretary Dinmukhamed Kunaev had found plenty of other ways to enrich himself and his family through the shadow economy.[14] Gorbachev pressured him into retiring "for health reasons" in December 1986, but then could not find a Kazakh replacement he regarded as trustworthy. Instead he installed a Russian, Gennady Kolbin, who was new to Kazakhstan. For more than half of its existence the Kazakh republic had been run by a Russian, but Kunaev had been so successful at "kazakhizing" the governing apparat that Kolbin's appointment ignited unprecedented nationalist outrage. Thousands of Kazakh university students protested in Alma-Ata and were violently attacked by police. A shocked Gorbachev had to send in soldiers to restore order. Almost 2000 people were injured and 168 killed. Kolbin stayed in office until May 1989, but just kept the seat warm. Gorbachev replaced him with Nursultan Nazarbaev (r. 1989–2019), who had served as chair of the Kazakh Supreme Soviet under both Kunaev and Kolbin. Nazarbaev allowed commemorations of the riot victims, but also prevented the Kazakh youth group *Zheltoqsan* (December) from turning into an independent political movement by co-opting it into his administration. By making himself the voice of Kazakh grievances, Nazarbaev was able to control the boundaries of political agitation.[15]

RE-STRUCTURING/UNRAVELING

After these public displays of nationalism, Central Asians did little. In 1987 and 1988 the Baltic states lead the way by pushing for economic and legal autonomy and developing "popular front" movements that agitated for linguistic and cultural self-determination. Groups in Ukraine, Belorussia, Moldavia, Georgia, Armenia, Azerbaijan, and Russia formed their own popular fronts and began to coordinate their activities.[16] Delegations of Uzbek and Tajik cultural activists visited Estonia to observe the popular front at work, and an Uzbek cultural movement called *Birlik* (Unity) organized in November 1988. Turkmen intellectuals held meetings in 1989 to encourage greater use of the Turkmen language, and Tajiks formed the *Rastakhez* (Renaissance) movement with similar aims.[17] However, none of these groups was able to spark national independence movements as the other popular fronts did. The other potential source of anti-Soviet agitation, Islam, also failed to rear its head as some Western scholars predicted it would.[18] Why were Central Asians so conspicuously inactive while the rest of the USSR was exploding with nationalist passions?

A word of caution before proceeding. This time period falls into a scholarly gray area, where journalists and political scientists made a first pass at analyzing these complex and fast-moving events, but historians have had little opportunity to examine archival sources in depth. There is still a tremendous amount that we do not know about how the Central Asian communist parties dealt with perestroika and glasnost', and we know even less about how ordinary citizens engaged with the disintegration of their country. What follows can only be a surface sketch.

None of the republics seems to have enacted any of Gorbachev's economic liberalization laws, such as the January 1987 law that opened Soviet markets to joint ventures with foreign companies or the May 1988 law that legalized small cooperative businesses. Nishanov's 1988 plea for a more diversified economy, and Gorbachev's lack of response, suggests that Central Asian conservatism alone is not a sufficient explanation for the lack of economic reform. When in 1987 Gorbachev freed industrial producers to pursue business contracts on their own rather than simply fulfill state orders, he destabilized the union-wide system of goods distribution. For example, whereas a lumber mill in Siberia had been obligated to fulfill orders from Tajikistan regardless of whether it got paid adequately, now the mill would be free to reject Tajik requests in favor of orders from other enterprises that could pay higher rates. This partial freeing of the industrial market was especially damaging to the Central Asian republics. Their economies were based on the production of raw commodities that were shipped to other republics for finishing into more profitable products. They earned little tax revenue from manufactured goods and did not earn enough from commodities to pay for all of the social projects that Moscow required. To maintain fiscal equality among the republics the central state sent cash subsidies, but Gorbachev substantially cut those subsidies and demanded budgetary discipline. However, Moscow did not reduce its demands for cotton.[19]

The result was spiraling economic chaos. The Soviet system did not function well but it functioned as a unit: the republican economies were organized to complement each other. Central Asia did not produce enough meat and milk for its own needs, but that did not matter so long as it could import food from other republics. When Central Asians could not purchase industrial inputs from elsewhere they could not produce the commodities or goods that generated the cash to buy what they did not make themselves. As shortages deepened, all the republics responded by hoarding their resources, which made the shortages worse. Because the Central Asian republics were the poorest in the USSR, they faced a steep competitive disadvantage with few tools of their own. By 1989 shortages of food and basic goods were becoming a serious problem. Their poverty also affected their political options. Estonia was the wealthiest Soviet republic on a *per capita* basis, and in 1987 used its wealth to declare economic autonomy: the Estonian government would decide how much of its tax revenue to pass on to Moscow, not Moscow ministers. Latvia and Lithuania soon followed suit. The Central Asian republics depended on Moscow to supplement their inadequate tax revenue, so economic autonomy would have hurt them.

As the USSR unraveled, Central Asian governments by and large kept political agitation under control, although Tajikistan and Kyrgyzstan were less successful in this. Each republic saw the rise of a "popular front" cultural/political movement, of which Uzbekistan's Birlik was the most prominent. Uzbekistan had been put together from the three cultural centers of old Transoxiana: Bukhara, Khiva, and Kokand. It claimed the lion's share of historical Central Asian achievements and produced most of the Soviet Central Asian literature, music, film, and art that had attracted international attention. In 1988 the poet Muhammad Solih and scientist Abdurahim Po'latov formed Birlik to agitate for more pride and creativity in Uzbek language and culture. The group attracted hundreds of members, mostly from the urban intelligentsia, who were also deeply concerned about the Aral Sea crisis and the devastating health effects of the cotton monoculture. At its peak Birlik brought tens of thousands of Uzbeks out to demonstrate for greater cultural and political freedom, but it threatened the Uzbek Communist Party's hold on power. In June 1989 an opportunity to contain Birlik presented itself when bloody riots erupted in the Ferghana Valley between Uzbeks and Meskhetian Turks, descendants of a "collaborator nation" that Stalin had deported from Georgia in 1944. The violence caused Uzbek party elites to turn against Nishanov and nominate a new first secretary, Islam A. Karimov, who did not have strong ties to any of the regional clans. Karimov contrived to blame the violence, the causes of which were disputed, on "outside agitators" who were at minimum encouraged by Birlik's political demonstrations.[20] He also was able to split Birlik's leadership by allowing them to form a legal political party in exchange for working with the government on common interests. Some Birlik members preferred an oppositional relationship to a government that they felt unjustly blamed them for ethnic unrest, while others wanted to work within the system. In November 1989 Solih founded a break-away party *Erk* (Freedom), which had the effect of fragmenting opposition to the government. Karimov had given an early demonstration of the political skills that would enable him to rule Uzbekistan for twenty-seven years.

Karimov's cunning was not the only, or even the most formidable, obstacle that Birlik faced. The movement became overtly political and focused on abstractions such as democracy and national independence at a time when citizens were feeling more threatened by chaos and impoverishment than communist oppression. Karimov encouraged this fear in order to portray Birlik as an agent of unrest and his government as the protector of order. In 1990 police attacked a Birlik demonstration and arrested its leaders with only murmurings of protest. Activists had misjudged the Uzbek public's mood: people feared disorder more than they desired a new and unknown political system.[21]

The situation in Turkmenistan was similar: a small group of intellectuals confronted a new party first secretary, Sapurmurad Niyazov (r. 1985–2006), who was not interested in changing the power structure he had just taken over. Gorbachev appointed Niyazov during the cotton scandal purges, possibly agreeing to him because, as an orphan, his primary loyalty would presumably be to the party that gave him his career.[22] Certainly Niyazov protected the Soviet order until all was lost. The Turkmen equivalent to Birlik, *Agzybirlik*, focused on language, education, and environmental issues. However, the group could get little traction in a country where only 1 per cent of Turkmen spoke Russian as their first language, and Niyazov had no difficulty squelching the one public demonstration they mounted in 1991.[23]

In Tajikistan different political forces were at work. The Tajik party apparat had been dominated for decades by a client-patron network based in Leninobod/Khujand. This "clan" had promoted economic development in its northern territory to the neglect of the south and especially the eastern Badakhshan region, high in the Pamir Mountains. The blatant imbalance in economic and political power fostered regional resentments that grew worse as perestroika disrupted the economy. The Tajik popular front movement, Rastakhez, found itself trying to promote a national "renaissance" in a country that was fracturing along regional lines. Party head Kakhor Makhkamov (r. 1985–91), possibly following Karimov's example, used a 1990 riot to implicate Rastakhez in promoting ethnic violence. Makhkamov succeeded in marginalizing Rastakhez, but as regional tensions took on an explicitly political character Rastakhez's place was taken by two opposition parties, the Democratic Party of Tajikistan and the Islamic Revival Party of Tajikistan (IRPT).[24]

Islamic Culture, Not Politics

The IRPT was the only political organization of the perestroika period to make Islam a part of its platform. After some sixty years of atheist oppression, with the mujahidin of Afghanistan still battling Soviet occupation, many Western observers expected that Soviet Muslims would start pushing to replace secular law with Islamic law as soon as they had the opportunity. Instead, while believers welcomed the greater freedom that glasnost' provided, they did not use religion as a vehicle for politics.

Islamic institutions and believers had a complicated and often incongruous relationship with the state in post-Stalin Central Asia. When the party tacitly gave up on trying to eradicate religion during World War II, it turned to co-optation by creating the SADUM, based in Tashkent. The administration was intended to be a unified authority for all Muslims, something that had never before existed in Central Asia. The party understood that SADUM could not function effectively without the trust of believers, and so took care to choose a scholar of respectable saintly lineage, Eshon Boboxon (1863–1957), as the first mufti.[25] The clergy who staffed SADUM came from the educated stratum that had always disapproved of popular practices like pilgrimages to saints' tombs and prayers at sacred trees, which aligned their definition of a "civilized" Islam with that of the state. SADUM's efforts to assert its authority over all mosques and clergy, and their revenue, led to fights with locally revered authorities that the muftiate did not always win.

Despite the deep damage that Stalin had inflicted, local Islamic authorities and institutions survived. Most collective farms had communal prayer spaces (often the farm's social club), someone who knew how to lead prayers, and/or acknowledged shrines and Sufi ishans. Otins, women who taught prayers and texts mostly to girls, were generally regarded as unimportant by party activists and left alone. More learned male teachers lead underground study groups called *hujras* (from the residential cells in a madrasa) throughout the Soviet period. SADUM was supposed to register and guide all clergy and teachers, but it regularly found its efforts thwarted by a surprising opponent: the Soviet state itself. This strange situation was a result of incoherent policies in Moscow. Part of Nikita Khrushchev's de-Stalinization campaign was a new emphasis on the rule of law, including a 1954 decree that forbade harassing citizens simply because they were believers. The USSR Council on the Affairs of Religious Cults (CARC) both supervised SADUM and took its legal responsibilities very seriously. This led to occasions where SADUM staff tried to close down unregistered shrines or Sufi groups, only to have a CARC official rush in to defend the rights of believers.[26] The confusion was compounded in 1959, when Khrushchev launched a renewed militant atheist campaign. Although the campaign was short-lived, it reduced SADUM's staffing and budget and empowered the republican governments to close thousands of mosques and shrines. SADUM never recovered its strength, the principle of rule of law withered, and republican governments assumed more authority over religious life.

Life for believers was hardly more consistent during the Brezhnev period, although the causes of inconsistency were different. Brezhnev's government reined in the cultural "thaw" that Khrushchev had permitted and resumed arresting people for expressing dissenting political views. It never brought back the Gulag or mass executions, but it did institute a frightening new practice of locking dissidents in psychiatric institutions on the grounds that they suffered from a disease called "social schizophrenia." In Central Asia police once again arrested people for "crimes of everyday life" such as child marriage or payment of bride price, and sent a few religious teachers to jail for instructing children. Students in hujras reported feeling real fear as they gathered in basements to study.[27] At the same time, as Moscow let republican governments run most of their own internal affairs, anti-Islamic actions were left to local party organizations to undertake. This delegation of responsibility opened up space for believers, but their freedom was dependent on the chance factors of where they were and who they had to deal with. Some collective farms in Tajikistan supported multiple mosques for "native" and resettled communities that engaged in open religious activities. The major shrine complex in southern Kyrgyzstan called *Taxt-i Suleiman* (Solomon's Throne) was always an active center for pilgrims, healers, and mystics despite the fact that both the party and SADUM disapproved of it. By and large people were able to believe and pray if they wanted to, although they always had to watch out for clear red lines (such as printing underground religious literature) or a zealous party official with something to prove.[28]

Learning to survive within the Soviet system changed Islamic culture. Bukhara had been the intellectual center of Central Asian Islam for 1000 years, but the Soviets allowed only one madrasa, the Mir-i Arab, to continue functioning there. Instead Mufti Eshon Boboxon, his son Ziyovuddin Boboxonov (1908–82), and his grandson Shamsuddin Boboxonov (1937–2003) made Tashkent the headquarters of state-approved Islam. In 1971 Ziyovuddin was allowed to open the Imam al-Bukhari Islamic Institute in Tashkent as a university-level center of study. The clergy who ran SADUM learned to be comfortable speaking Russian and developed closer ties with the Arab Islamic centers than had Central Asian clergy in the past. SADUM's Islam was intellectual, focused on finding ways to make the legal and philosophical traditions compatible with communist modernity, what historian Eren Tasar calls "Islamically informed Soviet patriotism."[29]

This form of Islam had little emotional resonance with most people. The Boboxonov family, while respected, never made themselves the sole religious authorities in Central Asia. As republican governments asserted more control over their own Islamic institutions, SADUM lost any ability to enforce its will on personnel and practice outside Uzbekistan. Even within Uzbekistan, if a mulla outside the Tashkent region enjoyed the support of local officials there was little SADUM could do to discipline even egregious behavior. There were so many unregistered teachers, Sufi ishans, and itinerant healers with devoted local followings that in the 1970s SADUM began to attach them formally to registered mosques as a way to keep them under some supervision.[30] This was one of many ways in which the "official" and "unregistered" religious communities were intertwined with each other.

One of the most influential teachers of the mid-twentieth century, Muhammadjon Rustamov Hindustonyi (1892–1989), studied in Bukharan and Indian madrasas, spent years in the Gulag, served in the Red Army during World War II, and after the war taught in both registered mosques and unregistered hujras.[31] His students also served inside and outside the formal establishment. Hindustonyi provided a more traditional training than the SADUM madrasas did, with an emphasis on medieval Central Asian texts that SADUM regarded as obsolete. He also taught that religion and politics should stay separate. This quietist attitude was certainly a practical response to Soviet circumstances, but in the late 1970s a younger cohort of hujra students became impatient with his approach. The challengers looked to contemporary Arab practice as a purer model for Central Asian Muslims, and seem to have been influenced by anti-Soviet rhetoric coming from Afghanistan. Hindustonyi derided them as "Wahhabis" (Saudi-style puritans) who were unjustly condemning the traditions of their ancestors. Arguments over whether or not Muslims had a duty to oppose Soviet rule grew heated under glasnost', but remained confined to small groups. As the USSR stumbled toward its demise, very few Central Asians saw a political alternative in Islam.[32]

Through the second half of 1990 all the republics declared themselves to be sovereign within the Soviet Union, and the first secretaries of their communist parties re-named themselves presidents of their republics. After the failed coup of August 1991 it rapidly became clear that the president of the Russian republic, Boris Yeltsin, had snatched true political authority away from Gorbachev and the CPSU. Even though four of the five Central Asian leaders had supported the coup, they realized that it was now time to focus on protecting themselves. Beginning with Uzbekistan on 1 September and ending with Kazakhstan on 16 December, all five Central Asian republics declared themselves independent. More than 120 years of Russian rule had come to an end.

NOW WHAT?

In 1992 it was very hard for people to absorb the idea that they now lived in independent states. The Central Asian governments wanted to maintain stability: all of them joined the Commonwealth of Independent States when it formed in December 1991 to preserve common economic interests among former Soviet republics, and all of them made a point of encouraging their Slavic citizens to stay. All of them also had to deal with a flood of outside advisors, from Saudi Arabian missionaries to Turkish businessmen to American democracy advocates, each urging them to transition from communism to a different version of modernity. The political and cultural legacies of Russian/ Soviet rule were not so easily shed, however, and Central Asia remains both a part of and distinct from the Slavic and Turko-Persian cultural complexes.

Politically, Uzbekistan, Turkmenistan, and Kazakhstan adapted and tightened Soviet authoritarian practices while Kyrgyzstan developed a more pluralist system and Tajikistan collapsed in civil war. These developments came directly out of late Soviet political currents. In Kyrgyzstan the core issues were similar to those elsewhere: resentment over power imbalances among regional client-patron networks was exacerbated by economic chaos. A small intellectual movement, led by Chingiz Aitmatov, the most internationally famous Central Asian writer at the time, agitated for cultural self-determination.[33] The government of Absamat Masaliev (1985–90) also had to contend with competition for resources between the Kyrgyz and Uzbek populations around the southern town of Osh. Osh was on the eastern end of the Ferghana Valley, an area where Kyrgyz, Uzbek, and Tajik communities were so imbricated with each other that the border delimitations of the 1920s had never been finalized (see Map 9.1).[34] In June

MAP 9.1 The Ferghana Valley.

1990 a land dispute between Kyrgyz and Uzbeks exploded in violence, killing several hundred people.[35] As in Uzbekistan and Tajikistan, the violence provided a reason for governing elites to remove the unpopular Masaliev and replace him with a leader acceptable to all factions, but in this case they chose a non-party man, Askar Akaev (r. 1990–2005). Akaev was a physicist who had spent most of his career in Leningrad and openly supported perestroika. Gorbachev approved his appointment just in time for Kyrgyzstan to declare itself sovereign, allowing Akaev to become the republic's first president in August 1990. He immediately legalized a multi-party system. However, in October 1991 Akaev ran unopposed as independent Kyrgyzstan's president.[36]

Akaev was alone in fostering a democratic political structure in post-Soviet Central Asia, but good intentions were not sufficient. Western-style democracies depend on rule of law that regulates checks and balances among power centers. These concepts, much less their realization in practice, were alien to most Central Asians. It is likely that Akaev's political pluralism lasted as long as it did because Kyrgyzstan was so poor that it depended on Western financial aid, and the price of Western aid is at least surface conformity with democratic legal norms. However, while communist ideology evaporated pretty quickly, established Soviet Central Asian political practice was stronger than new-fangled Western standards. Local elites had their own norms that had worked well for them for decades. It would have taken much more than economic development aid to persuade those elites to give up their bases for economic and political control.[37] After ten years in power Akaev was widely viewed as corrupt, and many Kyrgyz suspected he was grooming his children to succeed him. Democratic ideals had taken just enough root that angry citizens staged what came to be called the "Tulip Revolution" in March 2005 that forced the Akaev family to flee Kyrgyzstan.[38] The fundamental problems of poverty and network rivalries that are not adequately governed by law have remained, making political stability elusive.

The other volatile republic, Tajikistan, was even poorer than Kyrgyzstan. In 1989 Tajikistan had the highest population growth and the lowest *per capita* income in the USSR; the collapse sent Tajikistan over an economic cliff. From 1992 to 1997 the republic was torn apart by a war that killed 40,000–100,000 people and created more than one million refugees, many of whom fled into Afghanistan.[39] The causes of this bitter war are still the subject of vigorous debate among historians.[40] Political, regional, economic, and religious factors cannot be disentangled to outline clear targets for blame. One coalition was based on an alliance between the northern Khujand and southern Kulob client-patron networks, which overlapped with the established Soviet political elite. This side was headed by Emomli Rahmonov, who had been elected chair of the Supreme Soviet in November 1992—the old guard was clinging to power so tightly that Tajikistan still had a Supreme Soviet. The opposition came from the southern and eastern Gharm and Badakhshan regional networks, which overlapped with the nationalist democratic parties and the Islamic Revival Party. This group did not have a single dominant leader.

There were few clear lines in this war, however. While many observers at the time painted the war as a conflict between communism and Islam, the head of the Islamic bureaucracy in Tajikistan, *qazikalon* Hajji Akbar

Turajonzoda, supported the government that paid him while pushing just as hard as the IRPT did to re-establish Islam as the basis for Tajik society.[41] Uzbekistan and Russia sent military aid to Rahmonov's government partly to support the minority Uzbek and Slavic populations, which exacerbated ethnic tensions. On the local level where the battles were fought, the conflict could take on very different appearances: in some places fighting raged between kolkhozes dominated by re-settled communities and those dominated by long-term inhabitants. In some cases groups attacked each other not for political reasons, but to seize control over land. Historian Tim Epkenhans spotlights the role of organized crime bosses, whom he calls "the men of disorder."[42] These bosses turned themselves into militia leaders to fight for the economic networks they had controlled since the 1980s. They also defended a violent form of masculine honor that became a new template for Tajik identity, to the detriment of Tajik women. Some of these militiamen became important powerbrokers among the various factions, changing their political identification as needed. The fighting dragged to an end with the General Peace Accord of June 1997, which established an uneasy coalition made up of representatives from Rahmonov's government and the IRPT. Since then Rahmonov (now Rahmon) has made himself the sole ruler of Tajikistan.

Post-Soviet Authoritarians

Political continuities were simpler in the other three republics: the communist parties changed their names to variants on "people's democratic party of ..." and continued to rule much as before, except more harshly. These republics had more economic resources to draw on than did Kyrgyzstan and Tajikistan: Turkmenistan has significant natural gas reserves, Kazakhstan has gas and oil in its southwest, and Uzbekistan has gas and oil in addition to becoming the world's fourth-largest exporter of cotton in 1991.[43] The former communist apparats took control over these resources and used them to mitigate the effects of the 1990s economic collapse, although they could not completely compensate for the loss of Soviet subsidies (see Figure 9.1). Post-Soviet economic reforms have generally preserved the core of old structures, especially in Uzbekistan and Turkmenistan. The collective farms were disbanded and replaced with cooperative land-leasing schemes, but state control over commodities production continued. Former collective farm families lost the social infrastructure that communism had provided but were not freed from the state procurement

FIGURE 9.1 Despair in a bus station, Tashkent 1992. The Soviet collapse disrupted supply lines for spare parts, with devastating effects on public transportation. Source: Author, 1992.

system that set prices. This left many worse off than before.[44] Similarly, while the retail business sector has been legalized and foreign businesses invited to invest, real economic power remains with client-patron networks that focus on enriching themselves. The most spectacular case of a well-connected Mafioso of this type has been Gulnara Karimova, the eldest daughter of Islam Karimov. Through the 2000s until her downfall in 2014, Karimova amassed a lucrative collection of businesses and contracts, with interests in hotels, telecommunications, and her own line of cosmetics. When she saw a profitable business that interested her, she allegedly used bribes, threats, and violence to acquire it. She became "the most hated woman in Uzbekistan," according to an American diplomat. Her father, under unknown circumstances, allowed her to be taken into custody and stripped of her assets, but international legal actions are still ongoing.[45] This scale of corruption and the absence of secure legal contracts have left Uzbekistan economically isolated.

Turkmenistan is even more isolated. Niyazov, the self-styled *Turkmenboshi* (head Turkmen), sustained his apparat on income from natural gas and allowed very few foreigners into the country except for tourists.[46] His successor Gurbanguly Berdimukhammedov has followed in his footsteps, calling himself the *Arkadag* (the protector) and managing to spark a fight with Iran, formerly one of Turkmenistan's biggest gas customers.[47] While most Central Asian states continued the communist practice of generating loyalty by creating a cult of The Leader, none has carried it quite so far as Turkmenistan. To international amusement, Niyazov had a gold statue of himself erected in the capital Ashgabat that rotated so that the Turkmenboshi always faced the sun. The Arkadag goes on television to sing to his people while critical shortages of food and medicine create a public health crisis of unknown dimensions.[48]

Kazakhstan has been the most open to engagement with foreign countries and companies. In 1989 Kazakhstan's population of 16.5 million was 39 per cent Kazakh, 44 per cent Slavic, and 5 per cent German. Nazarbaev initially projected the image of a state where all nationalities had equal language and political rights.[49] The Kazakh government cooperated with international organizations and accepted assistance from the United States and the Russian Federation in removing the 1400 nuclear warheads that it had inherited from the USSR. It reached an agreement with Russia for continued use of the Baikonur Cosmodrome. Nazarbaev welcomed foreign direct investment and foreign workers to develop Kazakhstan's oil and natural gas fields, and invited foreigners to work in the country's new capital as of 1998, Astana (the former Akmolinsk).[50] However, tens of millions of dollars in foreign direct investment, mostly from the major oil companies, has flowed primarily to a *rentier* class of Soviet-era elites. The Kazakh economy is highly dependent on fossil fuel revenues not only for direct state income, but to fund many of the social services that the communist system used to provide. The state demands that foreign companies pay for schools and hospitals and maintain larger work forces than are strictly necessary, which keeps the peace for the most part, as does the country's relatively high *per capita* GDP. At the same time, stark economic inequality and declining life expectancy have remained stubborn problems.[51]

If Islamist groups did not organize strong political opposition during perestroika, they did so in independent Uzbekistan and Tajikistan, and to a lesser extent in Kyrgyzstan. The reason for this is not any kind of primordial Muslim propensity toward violence, but because Islam provided the most easily available and understandable language for political opposition in increasingly oppressive dictatorships. The best illustration of this process is Uzbekistan. In the 1990s Karimov's government allowed Saudi Arabia, Iran, and the Turkish

Gülen network of private Islamic schools to fund mosques and schools and distribute literature under Uzbek state supervision. However, Karimov was perpetually suspicious of foreign intentions and never established stable alliances with any foreign countries. He expelled all foreign Islamic organizations by 2000. He also showed a Soviet apparatchik's disdain for ordinary citizens' concerns. In a November 1991 incident he refused to meet with civic groups in Namangan, which provoked public anger that in turn infuriated him.[52] In February 1999 six large bombs exploded in Tashkent that killed sixteen people and injured hundreds, and narrowly missed Karimov himself. The perpetrators of this attack have never been identified, but Karimov was quick to blame an Islamic opposition group that had formed in the wake of the 1991 incident, the Islamic Movement of Uzbekistan (IMU).[53] Karimov used the Soviet police apparatus that he had inherited and improved to arrest thousands of suspected oppositionists, many of whom were subject to tortures at which Stalin would have balked. In the wake of the Al-Qaeda attack on the United States in September 2001, Karimov eagerly allied himself with the US in the "war on global terrorism." This gave the Uzbek government access to American assistance in suppressing political opposition in exchange for allowing the US military to use the former Soviet Karshi-Khanabad air base as a vital supply center for its invasion of Afghanistan.[54]

The Uzbek government revitalized Islamic institutions and Karimov made a point of publicly performing the role of a pious Muslim, but Muslims who wanted a religious life outside the state structure were persecuted much more harshly than they had been during Soviet rule. To the surprise of no one except perhaps Karimov himself, the combination of brutal police oppression and ostentatious elite corruption created enraged, armed opposition groups that used Afghanistan and Pakistan as bases for training and weapons. The connections that the IMU made with Al-Qaeda and the Taliban in this period created a conduit for a modern, jihadist Islamic ideology to enter Central Asia. However, while the IMU was able to carry out several more bombings in Uzbekistan it was not able to do any real damage to Karimov's government. The Uzbek police state was too strong and too brutal for small groups making their own bombs to dent, and most Uzbeks did not see this version of Islam as a realistic alternative. The founders of the IMU were killed in Afghanistan and Pakistan in the 2000s, fighting for the Taliban rather than themselves.[55]

The full extent of Karimov's viciousness did not become widely apparent until the Uzbek army massacred hundreds of people in the Ferghana Valley city of Andijan in May 2005. A group of businessmen had organized a mutual financial aid association, based on Islamic principles of fiscal and moral responsibility. They also apparently were influenced by the work of a self-taught religious activist named Akrom Yo'ldoshev. The association ran afoul of local government officials who may have resented a successful business group that they did not control—there is much that is still uncertain about this tragedy. A number of the association's members were arrested and convicted in court of Islamic extremism. Their angry relatives then staged an armed jailbreak that killed a number of guards. The next day large crowds gathered on the streets to protest the government, and troops in armored personnel carriers opened fire indiscriminately on them, killing anywhere from 187 to more than 800 people, most of them unarmed.[56] The massacre drew a mild rebuke from the United States, and Karimov expelled the Americans from the Karshi-Khanabad airbase. He also expelled almost all other foreign organizations, including scholarly exchanges, from Uzbekistan. This began a long period of isolation for the country that only began to change after Karimov's death in September 2016.

Relations between the Central Asian states and the Russian Federation have been neither close nor hostile. All the republics had made their own languages the official language of state business in 1990, although independent Kazakhstan called Russian its "language of inter-ethnic communication."[57] Central Asian governments wrote history texts and opened museums that discussed their sufferings under communism, but that also conspicuously did not blame Russians as an ethnic group for Soviet abuses. Russian and Central Asian security services have found common ground in their fight against "Islamic terrorism." Nonetheless, at the community level instances of anti-Russian anger erupted in public spaces throughout the region, and without their protector in Moscow, Russians felt increasingly uncomfortable and began to leave. The most noticeable declines were in the republics with the largest Russian populations, Kazakhstan and Kyrgyzstan. After 2001 Russians dropped to 23.7 per cent of the population in Kazakhstan and 6 per cent in Kyrgyzstan; they made up less than 5 per cent of the population in the remaining three republics.[58] Russian remains an important *lingua franca* for the intelligentsia across the former USSR, but it is increasingly being replaced by English.

The post-Soviet economic crash, political oppression, and the Tajik war succeeded in doing what decades of Soviet efforts to balance population and labor needs had not: pushed millions of Central Asians to migrate to Russia in search of work.[59] Most of these migrants are unskilled men from rural areas who fill the construction jobs and other undesirable but necessary labor that a sharply declining Russian population cannot. They are often subject to terrible working conditions and attacks by racist gangs, but they can still earn much more money than they could at home. They send vital cash—Kyrgyzstan and Tajikistan get over 30 per cent of their GDPs from personal remittances.[60] Technically they are temporary workers; their legal position within the Russian Federation is less clearly defined than it was in either the Russian Empire or the Soviet Union. However, as long as there is demand for their labor in Russia they will stay and form new communities. Symbiotic economic structures have transformed, but not vanished, in the post-colonial period.

EPILOGUE: FROM COEXISTENCE TO COEXISTENCE

For more than a thousand years the peoples of Central Eurasia have lived together, mostly peacefully, sometimes at war, but always connected. While sharing the steppes between the Dniepr and Volga rivers, Turkic nomads and Kievan Rus' fought, traded, and intermarried across religious and linguistic borders. Turkic peoples and Slavs were common heirs to Mongol political and military structures even as they diverged in religious and cultural terms. As Muscovy gained strength in the fifteenth and sixteenth centuries the grand princes maneuvered to make themselves the central power brokers among the Mongol successor states, at first west and then east of the Volga. Muscovy hosted rival Tatar khans and aristocratic Kazakh hostages, established its own client khanate at Kasimov, and traded with the Uzbek khanates of Khorezm/Khiva and Bukhara. Russian and Tatar elites continued to intermarry, as long as the Tatars converted from Islam to Orthodoxy.

Coexistence slowly turned into Russian conquest from the sixteenth to the eighteenth centuries. In part this was because the Muscovite state created a strong central administration while the Central Asian polities did not. The Kazakh Khanate broke into three separate hordes, which were squeezed between the Zunghar state and China from the east, the Bukharan emirate from the south, and the Russian Empire from the west and north. Kazakh leaders tried to create some independent space for themselves by playing the larger powers off against each other. The Junior Horde Khan Abulkhayr encouraged Cossacks to build fortress lines to protect his people from Kalmyk raids, only to find that the fortresses cut Kazakhs off from grazing lands while providing inconsistent protection at best. The thickening Slavic presence in the steppe also deepened trade and cultural interactions, both friendly and hostile. In the early nineteenth century the Russian government began to incorporate the western Kazakhs into its administration. While most Kazakhs were deeply unhappy about this development, understanding Russian governing practices and language became a necessity for the elite.

The Uzbek khanates also increased trade and diplomatic contacts with the Russian Empire, but did not perceive Russia as a serious threat. Until the mid-nineteenth century most of the Slavs in Transoxiana were slaves, while the attacks by Bekovich-Cherkasskii and Perovskii ended in disaster for the Russians. Instead the khanates of Kokand, Khiva, and Bukhara contended with each other for dominance of Transoxiana. The three khanates were so evenly balanced that no one could decisively win, nor could they find a way to merge ruling houses peacefully. The fighting left them vulnerable when in the 1860s the Russians decided to secure their southern border by conquering Tashkent, setting off a process that ended with the crushing of the Yomut and Tekke Turkmen in 1881.

Military conquest meant that Central Asians and Russians were not just coexisting, but living together. The extent and nature of interactions between the two groups varied tremendously. Kazakhs and Kyrgyz lost land to millions of Slavic settlers, who regularly beat and abused them. Nomads sometimes fought back, but from a weak position. Kazakh aristocrats now served the Russian state as local administrators and judges, enforcing Kazakh law within limits set by Russia. Some of them, like the Valikhanov family, became highly assimilated. A minority of lower-level Kazakhs became settled farmers, lived in Russian towns, and sent their children to school with Russians. Relations in the Russian province of Turkestan were usually less tense, in no small part because settlers avoided the area. Enterprising merchants in Turkestan and Bukhara learned how to profit from the railroad and cash-crop production. Turkestani families pushed more than did Russian officials to establish Russian-language schools for Muslims. Tashkent, Bukhara, and Samarkand developed into dual cities with "European" and "Asian" sections that shared water and food infrastructure but also regarded each other with suspicion and disdain. The rural majority rarely encountered a European in the flesh. Russian officials had to accommodate themselves to local tax and irrigation practices even as they imposed modern documentary standards on personal identities. Meanwhile small groups of educated Kazakhs and Turkestanis sought ways to use the Western idea of "nation" to re-imagine what their communities should be so that one day they could free themselves from Russian rule.

The revolutions of 1917 brought down the old order of rule by khans, emirs, and Russian governors-general, but intensified a multi-level process of cultural convergence between Russians and Central Asians. Russian communists initially thought of themselves as the vanguard of an international revolution that would re-shape human economic relations and moral values. They sought first to transform Russian culture along modern European communist lines, while promising the non-Russian peoples of the Soviet Union that they would both see their nations flourish and prepare to dissolve those nations into the international proletarian dictatorship. Russians, Central Asians, and workers all over the world would emerge from this process as selfless, practical, and scientific atheists who always put the needs of the whole ahead of the needs of the individual. The Bolsheviks found Central Asian allies in the Jadid reformers and young revolutionaries, even though the Central Asians were more interested in nation-building than in international class solidarity.

The transformations of the Soviet period bound Central Asians and Russians together as victims and builders. The central state decided how to create a modern communist society, but relied on local actors to carry out those decisions. Central Asians determined the borders of their new republics and the alphabets in which their languages were written; did much of the groundwork in unveiling women, destroying Islamic institutions, and creating the cotton monoculture; enrolled in schools to become doctors, agronomists, and artists; ran their local governments, collective farms, and the shadow client-patron networks that made the economy function. They endured unfathomable suffering during Stalin's famines and purges just as Ukrainians and Russians did. Even then, many of the agents who confiscated livestock from starving Kazakhs, arrested and shot the first generation of Central Asian leaders, and kept religious life under close government control were themselves Central Asian. During the decades of post-Stalin stability Central Asians enjoyed a more humane Soviet culture that was merging with global trends in mass communication, leisure, and assumptions of mutual obligation between citizens and their governments. The degree of cultural convergence across the late USSR was highly uneven: a university-educated Uzbek might have been completely comfortable speaking Russian, dancing to rock music, and drinking vodka at a wedding discreetly conducted by a mulla. Not far away collective farmers spoke only their local language and the farm chairman had several wives, often passed off as secretaries.

The collapse of the Soviet Union returned Central Asians and Russians to coexistence in Central Eurasia. Their political, economic, and cultural ties have changed but not dissolved, even as the republics have developed in different directions. The Russian presence in Central Asia is much diminished, but more Central Asians live in Russia than ever before. Migrant worker remittances and Russian aid, including military bases in Kyrgyzstan, Kazakhstan, and Tajikistan, keep economies connected. Similar political cultures mark all the post-Soviet countries, generally to the detriment of their citizens. Central Asians retain well-justified pride in their artistic achievements and cultural heritage, which were deeply formed and transformed by Soviet national policies. As Central Asians stake out an independent presence in the world, they bring with them a distinctive way of being, drawn from the entwined histories of all the peoples of Central Eurasia.

NOTES

INTRODUCTION

1 David Christian, *A History of Russia, Central Asia and Mongolia: Inner Eurasia from Prehistory to the Mongol Empire* (London: Blackwell, 1998), xv–xvii distinguishes between "Inner" and "Outer" Eurasia, the latter defined as "well-watered coastal sub-continents that lie in a great arc from Europe, to the Middle East, to India, and to South and Southeast Asia."

2 David Sneath, *The Headless State: Aristocratic Orders, Kinship Society, and Misrepresentations of Nomadic Inner Asia* (New York: Columbia University Press, 2007), 4.

3 Owen Lattimore, "The Geographical Factor in Mongol History," in *Studies in Frontier History* (London: Oxford University Press, 1962), 257 (original lecture given in 1936). In the essay "Inner Asian Frontiers: Chinese and Russian Margins of Expansion," in the same volume, Lattimore argues that nomadic pastoralism arose after and as a consequence of settled agriculture, 141–43.

4 Tim May, *The Mongol Conquests in World History* (London: Reaktion, 2012), 7.

5 In fact historians now would mostly agree that a nation-state—a contiguous patch of land over which a clearly marked ethnic group has sovereignty for a long period of time—has never existed anywhere. The literature on the rise of nations is vast, but the classic works include: Benedict Anderson, *Imagined Communities: Reflections on the Origin and Spread of Nationalism* (London: Verso, 1991); Geoff Eley and Ron Grigor Suny, eds., *Becoming National* (Oxford: Oxford University Press, 1996); and Eric Hobsbawm and Terence Ranger, eds., *The Invention of Tradition* (Cambridge: Cambridge University Press, 1983).

6 The Turkic word "darya" means "river," so to say "the Syr Darya River" is to say "the Syr River River." For an excellent and comprehensive overview of the environment and geography of Central Eurasia, see Peter Perdue, *China Marches West: The Qing Conquest of Central Eurasia* (Cambridge, MA: Harvard University Press, 2005), 14–50.

7   David Anthony, *The Horse, the Wheel, and Language* (Princeton: Princeton University Press, 2007), 102.

8   Anthony, 104–05.

9   This model was first developed by anthropologists studying Indigenous cultures in the early twentieth century. See Clark Wissler, *The American Indian* (New York: Douglas C. McMurtrie, 1917), 204–06; Ruth Benedict, *Patterns of Culture* (New York: Houghton Mifflin, 1934), 41–51.

10 The Mongol component was added to a long-standing Turko-Persian Islamicate "composite society," discussed by Robert Canfield, "Introduction: The Turko-Persian Tradition," in Robert Canfield, ed., *Turko-Persia in Historical Perspective* (Cambridge: Cambridge University Press, 1991), 12–21.

11 There is no commonly approved list of what elements to consider when declaring the boundaries of a cultural complex. Anthropologists use a more finely grained set of elements than I do here, including methods of material production, child-rearing, and food production. I find Julian Steward's caution useful: "The *culture area* is used with least difficulty when it is conceived in terms of elements which have diffused from certain centers." Julian Steward, *Theory of Culture Change: The Methodology of Multilinear Evolution* (Urbana, IL: University of Illinois Press, 1963; original paper presented 1953), 87.

12 Recent considerations of the general idea of empire and how Russia fits in are Jane Burbank, Mark von Hagen, and Anatolyi Remnev, eds., *Russian Empire: Space, People, Power, 1700–1930* (Bloomington, IN: Indiana University Press, 2007); Jane Burbank and Frederick Cooper, *Empires in World History: Power and the Politics of Difference* (Princeton: Princeton University Press, 2010); and Valerie Kivelson and Ronald Suny, *Russia's Empires* (Oxford: Oxford University Press, 2017).

13 Examples of this argument include: Hélène Carrère d'Encausse, "The National Republics Lose Their Independence" in Edward Allworth, ed., *Central Asia: 130 Years of Russian Dominance* (Durham, NC: Duke University Press, 1994, orig. 1967), 254–65; Olaf Caroe, *Soviet Empire: The Turks of Central Asia and Stalinism* (London: Macmillan, 1967); Douglas Northrop, *Veiled Empire: Gender and Power in Stalinist Central Asia* (Ithaca, NY: Cornell University Press, 2004), 22; Benjamin Loring, "Colonizers with Party Cards: Soviet Internal Colonialism in Central Asia, 1917–1939," *Kritika* 15, no. 1 (2014): 77–102.

14 V.I. Lenin, "Deklaratsiia prav narodov Rossii," 2/15 November 1917, in *V.I. Lenin o Srednei Azii i Kazakhstane* (Tashkent: Uzbekistan, 1982), 454.

15 The premise of Joseph Heller's 1961 best-selling novel *Catch-22* was that no matter what action the protagonist took, the structure of the situation guaranteed that he would fail.

16 Joseph Stalin, *Marxism and the National and Colonial Question* (New York: International Publishers, 1935), 163–64. Speech given at the xiith Congress of the All-Russian Communist Party, April 1923.

17 Christian Teichmann, "Canals, Cotton, and the Limits of De-Colonization in Soviet Uzbekistan, 1924–1941," *Central Asian Survey* 26, no. 4 (2007): 501. Other sources for this line of argument include: Yuri Slezkine, "The ussr as a Communal Apartment, or How a Socialist State Promoted Ethnic Particularism," *Slavic Review* 53, no. 2 (Summer 1994): 414–52; Terry Martin, *The Affirmative Action Empire: Nations and Nationalism in the Soviet Union, 1923–1939* (Ithaca, NY: Cornell University Press, 2001); Ron Grigor Suny and Terry Martin, eds., *A State of Nations: Empire and Nation-making in the Age of Lenin and Stalin* (Oxford: Oxford University Press, 2001); Francine Hirsch, *Empire of Nations: Ethnographic Knowledge and the Making of the Soviet Union* (Ithaca, NY: Cornell University Press, 2005).

18 Mark Beissinger, "Soviet Empire as 'Family Resemblance,'" *Slavic Review* 65, no. 2 (2006): 294–303.

19 Adeeb Khalid, "Backwardness and the Quest for Civilization: Early Soviet Central Asia in Comparative Perspective," *Slavic Review* 65, no. 2 (2006): 231–51.

20 Botakoz Kassymbekova, *Despite Cultures: Early Soviet Rule in Tajikistan* (Pittsburgh: University of Pittsburgh Press, 2016), 16. She takes the phrase "repertoires of power" from Burbank and Cooper, *Empires in World History*, 2.

21 "A nation is a historically constituted, stable community of people, formed on the basis of a common language, territory, economic life, and psychological make-up manifested in a common culture. It goes without saying that a nation, like every historical phenomenon, is subject to the law of change, has its history, its beginning and end …" Joseph Stalin, "Marxism and the National Question" [1913], *Works* (London: Lawrence and Wishart, 1953), 2:307.

22 Marlene Laruelle, "The Concept of Ethnogenesis in Central Asia: Political Context and Institutional Mediators (1940–50)," *Kritika* 9, no. 1 (2008): 172.

23 Adeeb Khalid, *Islam after Communism: Religion and Politics in Central Asia* (Berkeley: University of California Press, 2007), 190.

1. EARLY COEXISTENCE

1 Simon Franklin and Jonathan Shepard, *The Emergence of Rus' 750–1200* (London: Longman, 1996), 77.

2 Serge A. Zenkovsky, *The Nikonian Chronicle* (Princeton: Kingston Press, 1984), 1:63; *Povest' vremennykh let* (Moscow: Izd. Akademii Nauk, 1950), 1:47.

3   Serge A. Zenkovsky, *Medieval Russia's Epics, Chronicles, and Tales* (New York: Penguin, 1974), 75.

4   Daniel H. Kaiser, *The Laws of Rus'—Tenth to Fifteenth Centuries* (Salt Lake City, UT: C. Schlacks, 1992), 47.

5   Franklin and Shepard, 326.

6   Robert Mitchell and Nevill Forbes, eds., *The Chronicle of Novgorod, 1016–1471* (Hattiesburg, MS: Academic International, 1970), 64–65; Zenkovsky, *Medieval Russia's Epics*, 194.

7   Willem van Ruysbroeck, *The Journey of William of Rubruck to the Eastern Parts of the World* (London: Hakluyt Society, 1900), 176–77. "William of Rubruck's Account of the Mongols," Silk Road Seattle, Walter Chapin Simpson Center for the Humanities, University of Washington, http://depts.washington.edu/silkroad /texts/rubruck.html#court_christians. See also Lawrence N. Langer, "War and Peace: Rus' and the Mongols in the 13th and 14th Centuries," in Gary Marker, Joan Neuberger, Marshall Poe, and Leila Rupp, eds., *Everyday Life in Russian History* (Bloomington, IN: Slavica, 2010), 192–94.

8   Donald Ostrowski, *Muscovy and the Mongols: Cross-cultural Influences on the Steppe Frontier* (New York: Cambridge University Press, 1998); Damir Z. Khairetidinov, *Musul'manskaia obshchina Moskvy v XIV–nachale XX veka* (Nizhnii-Novgorod: Dukhovnoe uprav. musul'man Nizhnego Novgoroda i Nizhegorodskoi oblast, 2002), 27.

9   *Drevnerusskaia literatura*, "Zadonshchina," accessed 16 June 2016, http://www .drevne.ru/lib/zadon_s.htm.

10 Robert Crummey, *The Formation of Muscovy, 1304–1613* (London: Longman Press, 1987), 53.

11 Tim May, *The Mongol Conquests in World History* (London: Reaktion, 2012), 75–79.

12 Uli Schamiloglu, "Preliminary Remarks on the Role of Disease in the History of the Golden Horde," *Central Asian Survey* 12, no. 4 (1993): 447–57; May, *The Mongol Conquests*, 209.

13 Beatrice Forbes Manz, *The Rise and Rule of Tamerlane* (Cambridge: Cambridge University Press, 1989), 69–70.

14 Janet Martin, "Muscovite Frontier Policy: The Case of the Khanate of Kasimov," *Russian History* 19, no. 1–4 (1992): 169–79.

15 Martin, "Muscovite Frontier Policy" (1992), 174–75; Michael Khodarkovsky, *Russia's Steppe Frontier: The Making of a Colonial Empire, 1500–1800* (Bloomington, IN: Indiana University Press, 2002), 31.

16 Khodarkovsky, *Russia's Steppe Frontier*, 65.

17 Brian Davies, *Warfare, State and Society on the Black Sea Steppe, 1500–1700* (New York: Routledge, 2007), 23–25. The Noghay or Manghit Tatars roamed just east of the Volga; they had emerged as a distinct group within the Jochid Khanate in the late fourteenth century. Vadim V. Trepavlov, "The Formation and Early History of the Manghït Yurt," *Papers on Inner Asia*, no. 35 (Bloomington, IN: Research Institute for Inner Asian Studies, 2001), 12–13.

18 Khodarkovsky, *Russia's Steppe Frontier*, 22. A Tatar raid is dramatically recreated in the first episode of the popular Turkish telenovela *Muhteşem Yüzyıl* (*Magnificent Century*, 2011–2014), directed by Meral Okay and Yilmaz Şahin. The episode, with English subtitles, is available at https://www.youtube.com/watch?v =3qTUTbIN82w.

19 Edward Keenan disputes this argument in "Ivan III, Nikolai Karamzin, and the Legend of the 'Casting Off of the Tatar Yoke' (1480)," in Valerie Kivelson, Karen Petrone, Nancy Kollman, and Donald Flier, eds., *The New Muscovite Cultural History* (Bloomington, IN: Slavica, 2009), 238. Khodarkovsky, *Russia's Steppe Frontier*, 78–81.

20 Edward Keenan, "Muscovy and Kazan, 1445–1552: Some Introductory Remarks on Steppe Diplomacy," *Slavic Review* 26, no. 4 (1967): 548–58.

21 Khodarkovsky, *Russia's Steppe Frontier*, 97–101; Davies, *Warfare, State and Society*, 27.

22 An entry in the *Illustrated Chronicle Compilation* for 1535 shows a young Ivan greeting his mother with the Turko-Arabic "Tabugsalam." *Litsevoi Letopisnei Svod XVI veka. Russkaia letopisnaia istoriia* (Moscow: AKTEON, 2010), 19:482, folio 127 verso.

23 Charles Halperin, *Russia and the Golden Horde* (Bloomington, IN: Indiana University Press, 1985), 98–100; Isabel de Madariaga, *Ivan the Terrible* (New Haven, CT: Yale University Press, 2005), 49–50; Ostrowski, *Muscovy and the Mongols*, 176–82.

24 Matthew P. Romaniello, *The Elusive Empire: Kazan and the Creation of Russia 1552–1671* (Madison: University of Wisconsin Press, 2012), 29–31.

25 Thomas Welsford, *Tūqāy-Timūrid Takeover of Greater Mā Warā al-Nahr, 1598–1605* (Leiden: Brill, 2013).

26 The clearest summary of Chaghatay history can be found in May, *The Mongol Conquests*, 71–75.

27 Lisa Golombek and Maria Subtelny, *Timurid Art and Culture: Iran and Central Asia in the Fifteenth Century* (Leiden: Brill, 1992).

28 Yuri Bregel, *An Historical Atlas of Central Asia* (Leiden: Brill, 2003), 38, 40; Istvan Vasary, "The Jochid Realm," in Nicola Di Cosimo, et al., eds., *The Cambridge*

History of Inner Asia, vol. I, *The Chinggisid Age* (Cambridge: Cambridge University Press, 2009, 2014 [internet]), 81.

29 Joo-Yup Lee, Qazaqliq, *or* Ambitious Brigandage, *and the Formation of the Qazaqs: State and Identity in Post-Mongol Central Eurasia* (Leiden: Brill, 2016), 121–22.

30 "Oirat" was the Mongolian name, "Kalmyk" or "Qalmaq" comes from Islamic sources, and Jungharia or Zungharia was the region where the confederation first formed. Bregel, *An Historical Atlas*, 44; James Millward, *Eurasian Crossroads: A History of Xinjiang* (New York: Columbia University Press, 2007) adds that "Zunghar" refers to the political confederation of Oirat tribes, 88–89.

31 Lee, Qazaqliq, *or* Ambitious Brigandage, 125.

32 Bregel, *An Historical Atlas*, 48.

33 Mirza Muhammad Haidar Dughlat, *History of the Moghuls of Central Asia* (*Tarikh-i Rashidi*) (London: Samson Low, Marston and Co, 1898, reissued Praeger 1970), 171.

34 Bregel, *An Historical Atlas*, 50.

35 Babur, *The Baburnama* (New York: Oxford University Press, 1996), folios 182, 206b.

36 Abolala Soudavar, "The Early Safavids and Their Cultural Interactions with Surrounding States," in Nikki Keddie and Rudi Mathee, eds., *Iran and the Surrounding World: Interactions in Culture and Politics* (Seattle: University of Washington Press, 2002), 95.

37 Scott C. Levi, *The Indian Diaspora in Central Asia and Its Trade* (Leiden: Brill, 2002), 47–48, 61.

38 Arash Khazeni, "The River's Edge: The Steppes of the Oxus and the Boundaries of the Near/Middle East and Central Asia, c. 1500–1800," in Michael Bonine, Abbas Amanat, and Michael Ezekiel Gasper, eds., *Is There a Middle East? The Evolution of a Geopolitical Concept* (Stanford: Stanford University Press, 2012), 141, 145.

39 Bregel, *An Historical Atlas*, 78; Scott Levi, "Turks and Tajiks in Central Asian History," in Jeff Sahadeo and Russell Zanca, eds., *Everyday Life in Central Asia* (Bloomington, IN: Indiana University Press, 2007), 23–24.

40 Millward, *Eurasian Crossroads*, 79.

41 *Istoriia Kazakhskoi SSR* (Alma-Ata: Izd. Akademii Nauk, 1957), 1:223.

42 Audrey Burton, *The Bukharans: A Dynastic, Diplomatic and Commercial History 1550–1702* (New York: St. Martin's Press, 1997), 12; M. Iu. Iuldashev, *K istorii torgovlykh i posol'skikh sviazei Srednei Azii c Rossiei v XVI–XVII vv.* (Tashkent: Izd. Akademii Nauk, 1964), 73.

43 Anthony Jenkinson, "The Voyage of M. Anthony Jenkinson from the Citie of Mosco in Russia to Boghar in Bactria, Anno 1558," in Richard Hakluyt, *The Principal Navigations, Voyages, Traffiques and Discoveries of the English Nation* (Glasgow:

J. MacLehose and Sons, 1903), 11:473. "Crasca" was probably a dyed linen cloth. Jenkinson's account is excerpted, with modernized spelling, in Scott C. Levi and Ron Sela, *Islamic Central Asia: An Anthology of Historical Sources* (Bloomington, IN: Indiana University Press, 2010), 215–21. Russian merchants had been coming to Samarkand since the fifteenth century; see Erika Monahan, *The Merchants of Siberia: Trade in Early Modern Eurasia* (Ithaca, NY: Cornell University Press, 2016), 54.

44 *Istoriia Kazakhskoi SSR*, 224–25.

45 Burton, *The Bukharans*, 463; Monahan, *The Merchants of Siberia*, 259–60.

46 Jenkinson, "The Voyage of M. Anthony Jenkinson," 467, 471–72.

47 Burton, *The Bukharans*, 8–9; Bregel, *An Historical Atlas*, 54–55.

48 *Kazakhsko-Russkie otnosheniia v XVI–XVIII vekakh (sbornik dokumentov i materialov)* (Alma-Ata: Izd. Akademii nauk Kazakhskoi SSR, 1961), 9; *Istoriia Kazakhskoi SSR*, 225; Bregel, *An Historical Atlas*, 54; James Forsyth, *A History of the Peoples of Siberia* (Cambridge: Cambridge University Press, 1992), 30–31.

49 Lee, *Qazaqliq, or Ambitious Brigandage*, 21–23, 41.

50 *Kazakhsko-Russkie otnosheniia*, 5, 12.

51 *Kazakhsko-Russkie otnosheniia*, 3–4, conversations held 20–29 January 1594.

52 1597 letter quoted in George Lantzeff and Richard Pierce, *Eastward to Empire: Exploration and Conquest on the Russian Open Frontier, to 1750* (Montreal: McGill-Queen's University Press, 1973), 117.

53 Donald Ostrowski, "The Replacement of the Composite Reflex Bow by Firearms in the Muscovite Cavalry," in Marker, Neuberger, Poe, and Rupp, *Everyday Life in Russian History*, 203–30.

54 *Kazakhsko-Russkie otnosheniia*, 6–7.

55 *Kazakhsko-Russkie otnosheniia*, 12.

56 The documents printed in *Kazakhsko-Russkie otnosheniia* in 1961 were selected to show that the Kazakhs had freely accepted Russian suzerainty long ago, which legitimized Soviet rule in the twentieth century. The final document in the section (14) suggests that the Muscovite envoy's meeting with Tavvakul did not go well, but the document is apparently badly damaged. From this point the collection leaps ahead to 1694, by which time much had changed for both the Kazakhs and the Russians.

2. THE BALANCE OF POWER SHIFTS

1 Chester Dunning, *Russia's First Civil War* (University Park, PA: Pennsylvania State Press, 2001), chap. 3.

2 George Lantzeff and Richard Pierce, *Eastward to Empire: Exploration and Conquest on the Russian Open Frontier, to 1750* (Montreal: McGill-Queen's

University Press, 1973), 114. The army that founded Fort Tara near the Irtysh River in 1594 was 83 per cent Tatar and Bashkir. The Bashkir are a Turkic-speaking people who remained nomadic pastoralists after the establishment of the Kazan khanate. Their territory was just east of the central Volga River.

3 Svat Soucek, *A History of Inner Asia* (Cambridge: Cambridge University Press, 2000), 183; Lantzeff and Pierce, *Eastward to Empire*, 120–24.

4 Yuri Bregel, *An Historical Atlas of Central Asia* (Leiden: Brill, 2003), 54, 56.

5 More directly, the *atalyk* of Samarkand, Ialangtush, commissioned the Shir-Dor and Tilla-qori madrasas. He ruled Samarkand virtually independently for decades. A.A. Askarov, R.G. Mukminova, eds., *Istoriia Uzbekistana* (Tashkent: Izd. "Fan," 1993), 3:60.

6 Abu'l Ghazi, *Shajara-yi tarakima,* in Scott C. Levi and Ron Sela, *Islamic Central Asia: An Anthology of Historical Sources* (Bloomington, IN: Indiana University Press, 2010), 229.

7 Peter Perdue, *China Marches West: The Qing Conquest of Central Eurasia* (Cambridge, MA: Harvard University Press, 2005), 96–98.

8 Michael Khodarkovsky, *Where Two Worlds Met: The Russian State and the Kalmyk Nomads, 1600–1771* (Ithaca, NY: Cornell University Press, 1992), 90–91, 131–33; Bregel, *An Historical Atlas*, 56–57.

9 Valerie Kivelson, *Cartographies of Tsardom: The Land and Its Meanings in Seventeenth-Century Russia* (Ithaca, NY: Cornell University Press, 2006), 121–23.

10 Peter Bergholtz, *The Partition of the Steppe: The Struggle of the Russians, Manchus, and the Zunghar Mongols for Empire in Central Asia, 1619–1758* (New York: Peter Lang, 1993), 81–82.

11 Bergholtz, 91–93.

12 Perdue, *China Marches West*, 161–67; Russian and English texts are available at the National University of Singapore's Empire in Asia website, last modified 20 November 2014, http://www.fas.nus.edu.sg/hist/eia/documents_archive/nerchinsk.php.

13 Perdue, *China Marches West*, 303–05.

14 Perdue, 282–286.

15 Russians called all merchants from Transoxiana "Bukharans." Allen Frank, *Bukhara and the Muslims of Russia: Sufism, Education, and the Paradox of Islamic Prestige* (Leiden: Brill, 2012), 45–46; Erika Monahan, *The Merchants of Siberia: Trade in Early Modern Eurasia* (Ithaca, NY: Cornell University Press, 2016), chap. 7, 254–301.

16 Audrey Burton, *The Bukharans: A Dynastic, Diplomatic and Commercial History 1550–1702* (New York: St. Martin's Press, 1997), 264.

17 Burton, 343–44; *Materialy po istorii Uzbekskoi, Tadzhikskoi i Turkmenskoi SSR*, Chast' I (Leningrad: Izd. Akademii Nauk SSSR, 1933), 257.

18 Burton, *The Bukharans*, 214, 358.

19 Burton, 206, 420, 425.

20 Ron Sela, "Prescribing the Boundaries of Knowledge: Seventeenth-Century Russian Diplomatic Missions to Central Asia," in Nile Green, ed., *Travel Writing in Central Asian History* (Bloomington, IN: Indiana University Press, 2014), 69–88.

21 Burton, *The Bukharans*, 226, 469.

22 *Materialy po istorii*, 149.

23 Audrey Burton, "Russian Slaves in Seventeenth-Century Bukhara," in Touraj Atabaki and John O'Kane, eds., *Post-Soviet Central Asia* (London: Tauris Academic Studies, 1998), 345–65.

24 Burton, *The Bukharans*, 215, 221.

25 Burton, 293.

26 Stephen Dale, *The Muslim Empires of the Ottomans, Safavids, and Mughals* (Cambridge: Cambridge University Press, 2010), 108–10.

27 Scott C. Levi, *The Indian Diaspora* (Leiden: Brill, 2002), 41.

28 *Cambridge History of Iran* (Cambridge: Cambridge University Press, 1986), 6:449; Burton, *The Bukharans*, 93.

29 Richard Foltz, *Mughal India and Central Asia* (Oxford: Oxford University Press, 1998), 41–43.

30 Burton, *The Bukharans*, 283.

31 Zhuldyz Tulibaeva, *Kazakhstan i bukharskoe khanstvo v XVIII–pervoi polovine XIX v.* (Almaty: Daik-Press, 2001), 84.

32 "Ming" in this case is the Turkic word for 1000, and has nothing to do with the Chinese Ming Dynasty. The name harks back to ancient steppe decimal divisions of military units.

33 Scott C. Levi, "The Ferghana Valley at the Crossroads of World History: The Rise of Kokand, 1709–1822," *Journal of Global History* 2, no. 2 (2007): 222; Scott C. Levi, *The Rise and Fall of Khoqand, 1709–1876* (Pittsburgh: University of Pittsburgh Press, 2017), 16–22.

34 The Manghits in Transoxiana were descendants of the Noghay/Manghit horde of the Jochid Khanate. They had thrived for centuries as top advisers to the khans of several post-Jochid khanates. Vadim V. Trepavlov, "The Formation and Early History of the Manghït Yurt," *Papers on Inner Asia* no. 35 (Bloomington, IN: Research Institute for Inner Asian Studies, 2001), 21–22.

35 Evgenii Anisimov, *The Reforms of Peter the Great: Progress through Coercion in Russia* (Armonk, NY: M.E. Sharpe, 1993), 256–57.

36 Alton S. Donnelly, "Peter the Great and Central Asia," *Canadian Slavonic Papers* 17, no. 2/3 (1975): 212.

37 Bregel, *An Historical Atlas*, 58. The Karakalpaks were a Turkic nomadic tribe that occupied the delta where the Syr Darya flowed into the Aral Sea.

38 Jin Noda, *The Kazakh Khanates between the Russian and Qing Empires* (Leiden: Brill, 2016), 61. Edward Allworth noted that Abulkhayr had earlier pledged loyalty to Russia, that Russians were present in the Kazakh party that journeyed to Khiva, and concluded that this interlude indicated a Russian interest in conquering Khiva. However, Abulkhayr was hoping to use the protection of Nadir Shah to counterbalance Russia. Edward Allworth, *Central Asia: 130 Years of Russian Dominance* (Durham, NC: Duke University Press, 1994, orig. 1967), 49.

39 James Pickett, "Nadir Shah's Peculiar Central Asian Legacy: Empire, Conversion, Narratives, and the Rise of New Scholarly Dynasties," *International Journal of Middle East Studies* 48, no. 3 (2016): 492–95; Levi and Sela, *Islamic Central Asia*, 244.

40 Tulibaeva, *Kazakhstan i bukharskoe khanstvo*, 50, 89.

41 Between 1734 and 1744 the Russians built three fortresses called "Orenburg" in different locations in the southern Urals. The present-day city was their third attempt.

42 Levi, *The Indian Diaspora*, 24–26. Levi, *The Rise and Fall of Khoqand*, 45; Jos Gommans, "Mughal India and Central Asia in the Eighteenth Century: An Introduction to a Wider Perspective," in Scott C. Levi, ed., *India and Central Asia: Commerce and Culture 1500–1800* (Oxford: Oxford University Press, 2007), 39–63.

43 David Christian, "Silk Roads or Steppe Roads? The Silk Roads in World History," *Journal of World History* 11, no. 1 (Spr. 2000): 1–26. The essay deals with the ancient and medieval periods, but Christian's emphasis on the importance of nomads for trans-civilizational and trans-ecological exchanges holds good for the modern period as well.

44 Aleksei Nikishenkov and Iurii Semenov, eds., *Stepnoi zakon: Obychnoe pravo Kazakhov, Kirgizov i Turkmen* (Moscow: Staryi Sad, 2000), 44. Report by Orenburg Frontier Commission, summer 1846.

45 He liked it. Willem van Ruysbroeck, *The Journey of William of Rubruck to the Eastern Parts of the World* (London: Hakluyt Society, 1900), 66–67; "William of Rubruck's Account of the Mongols," Silk Road Seattle, Walter Chapin Simpson Center for the Humanities, University of Washington, http://depts.washington.edu/silkroad/texts/rubruck.html#kumiss.

46 Nikishenkov and Semenov, *Stepnoi zakon*, 42.

47 Beatrice Teissier, ed., *John Castle's Mission to Khan Abulkhayir* (Oxford: Signal Books, 2014), 43, 48; Mambet K. Qoigeldiev, ed. *Istoriia Kazakhstana v russkikh istochnikakh.* Vol. IV, *Pervye istoriko-etnograficheskie opisaniia Kazakhskikh zemel' XVIII vek* (Almaty: Daik-Press, 2007), 37–39.

48 Zhanar Dzhampeisova, *Kazakhskoe obshchestvo i pravo v poreformennoi stepi* (Astana: ENU, 2006), 55–56.

49 Nikishenkov and Semenov, *Stepnoi zakon*, 42; Virginia Martin, *Law and Custom in the Steppe: The Kazakhs of the Middle Horde and Russian Colonialism in the Nineteenth Century* (Richmond, Surrey: Curzon, 2001), 22.

50 Adrienne Edgar, *Tribal Nation: The Making of Soviet Turkmenistan* (Princeton: Princeton University Press, 2004), 20.

51 Mahmud Kashghari, *Diwan Lughat al-Turk,* in Levi and Sela, *Islamic Central Asia,* 70.

52 Abbas Amanat and Arash Khazeni, "The Steppe Roads of Central Asia and the Persian Captivity Narrative of Mirza Mahmud Taqi Ashtiyani," in Green, *Travel Writing,* 123.

53 Arminius Vambery, *Travels in Central Asia* (New York: Harper and Brothers Publishers, 1865), 356.

54 Paul Georg Geiss, *Pre-Tsarist and Tsarist Central Asia: Communal Commitment and Political Order in Change* (London: Routledge, 2003), 97; Anatoly Khazanov, *Nomads and the Outside World* (Madison, WI: Wisconsin University Press, 1994), 175.

55 David Sneath, *The Headless State: Aristocratic Orders, Kinship Society, and Misrepresentations of Nomadic Inner Asia* (New York: Columbia University Press, 2007), 148–49. Sneath's argument is discussed in a forum in Sergei Abashin et al., "Debating the Concepts of Evolutionist Social Theory: Responses to David Sneath," *Ab Imperio* no. 4 (2009): 110–63. See especially Adrienne Edgar's comments in *Ab Imperio,* 153–56.

56 Edgar, *Tribal Nation,* 21–22, 171.

57 Sneath, *The Headless State,* 84–87; Nikolai A. Aristov, *Usuni i kyrgyzy ili kara-kyrgyzy* (Bishkek: Soros–Kyrgyzstan, 2001, orig. 1893), 429.

58 Gulmira Sultangalieva, "The Russian Empire and the Intermediary Role of Tatars in Kazakhstan," in Tomohiko Uyama, ed., *Asiatic Russia: Imperial Power in Regional and International Contexts* (London: Routledge, 2012), 54; Elena Campbell, *The Muslim Question and Russian Imperial Governance* (Bloomington, IN: Indiana University Press, 2015), 65.

59 Possibly a misunderstood version of the man's title, *yaruntishi,* reader of animal bones. Teissier, *John Castle's Mission,* 33, n.35.

60 Teissier, 34–35. The lamb, or the mulla, decided in Castle's favor.

61 Yuriy Malikov surveys this literature in *Tsars, Cossacks, and Nomads: The Formation of a Borderland Culture in Northern Kazakhstan in the 18th and 19th Centuries* (Berlin: Klaus Schwartz, 2011), 88–98. See also Ian W. Campbell, *Knowledge and the Ends of Empire: Kazak Intermediaries and Russian Rule on the Steppe, 1731–1917* (Ithaca, NY: Cornell University Press, 2017), 49.

62 Devin Deweese, *Islamicization and Native Religion in the Golden Horde* (University Park, PA: Penn State Press, 1994), 51.

63 Alexander Morrison, quoted in Teissier, *John Castle's Mission*, 35–36, n38.

64 Pavel P. Ivanov, *Ocherki po istorii Srednei Azii (XVI–seredina XIX v.)* (Moscow: Izd. Vostochnoi literatury, 1958), 154.

65 The word "Sufi" alludes to followers wearing woolen clothes. More directly it derives from the Arabic *tasawwuf*, "purification."

66 The story of a clever person who uses a cow hide this way is ancient and widespread. In Virgil's *Aeneid* Dido claims a large parcel of land on the Mediterranean coast and convinces the locals to make her the queen of Carthage. Stith Thompson, *Motif-index of Folk-literature* (Bloomington, IN: Indiana University Press, 1955), vol. 4, entry K185 cites Turkic, Icelandic, ancient Greek, and Egyptian examples.

67 Jamal Qarshi, *Mulhaqat al-surah*; Mirza Haidar Dughlat, *Tarikh-i Rashidi*, in Levi and Sela, *Islamic Central Asia*, 74–75, 152–53; Deweese, *Islamicization and Native Religion*, 541–43.

68 James Millward, *Eurasian Crossroads: A History of Xinjiang* (New York: Columbia University Press, 2007), 80–83.

69 Tulibaeva, *Kazakhstan i bukharskoe khanstvo*, 43.

70 Martin, *Law and Custom*, 25–28.

71 Nikishenkov and Semenov, *Stepnoi zakon*, 8.

72 Nikishenkov and Semenov, 34, 48–49.

73 Edgar, *Tribal Nation*, 236.

74 Aleksei I. Levshin, *Opisanie Kirgiz-Kazach'ikh ili Kirgiz-Kaisatskikh, ord i stepei* (Almaty: Sanat, 1996, orig. 1832), 367.

75 Teissier, *John Castle's Mission*, 47–50. Castle presented Bopai Khanim with an oil portrait of her son Eraly Sultan and 1000 sewing needles, which were in high demand among Kazakh women.

76 Noda, *The Kazakh Khanates*, 55; Tulibaeva, *Kazakhstan i bukharskoe khanstvo*, 86.

77 Michael Khodarkovsky, *Russia's Steppe Frontier: The Making of a Colonial Empire, 1500–1800* (Bloomington, IN: Indiana University Press, 2002), 150.

78 Noda, *The Kazakh Khanates*, 56–57; *Kazakhsko-Russkie otnosheniia v XVI–XVIII vekakh (sbornik dokumentov i materialov)* (Alma-Ata: Izd. Akademii nauk Kazakhskoi SSR, 1961), 35. My translation of the Russian differs slightly from Noda's.

79 *Kazakhsko-Russkie otnosheniia*, 18–19, instructions to the governor of Tobolsk on conducting trade negotiations with Qaip Khan, October 1716.

80 Khodarkovsky, *Russia's Steppe Frontier*, 152–53.

81 Khodarkovsky, 164–65; Malikov, *Tsars, Cossacks, and Nomads*, 198–209.

82 Noda, *The Kazakh Khanates*, 106; Khodarkovsky, *Russia's Steppe Frontier*, 162.

83 Noda, *The Kazakh Khanates*, 63, 110–11.

84 Perdue, *China Marches West*, 405–06; Noda, 69–72; Allan J. Frank, "The Qazaqs and Russia," *Cambridge History of Inner Asia: The Chinggisid Age* (Cambridge: Cambridge University Press, 2009), 370; Klara Khafizova, *Kazakhskaia strategiia tsinskoi imperii* (Almaty: Taimas, 2007), 41; Campbell, *The Muslim Question*, 18–20.

85 Khodarkovsky, *Russia's Steppe Frontier*, 165, 168–71.

86 Malikov, *Tsars, Cossacks, and Nomads*, 113.

87 Khodarkovsky, *Russia's Steppe Frontier*, 207; Yuriy Malikov, "Disadvantaged Neophytes of the Privileged Religion: Why Qazaqs Did Not Become Christians," in Niccolò Pianciola and Paolo Sartori, eds., *Islam, Society, and States across the Qazaq Steppe (18th–early 20th Centuries)* (Vienna: Verlag der Österreichischen Akademie der Wissenschaften, 2013), 181–212.

88 Malikov, *Tsars, Cossacks, and Nomads*, 203–04.

89 Khodarkovsky, *Where Two Worlds Met*, 230–33. Not every single Kalmyk left. The descendants of those who stayed behind form the core population of today's Republic of Kalmykia within the Russian Federation.

90 Khodarkovsky, *Russia's Steppe Frontier*, 174–77.

91 Geiss, *Pre-Tsarist and Tsarist Central Asia*, 176–77.

92 Nikishenkov and Semenov, *Stepnoi zakon*, 17.

93 Marc Raeff, *Siberia and the Reforms of 1822* (Seattle: University of Washington Press, 1956), 40.

94 Raeff, 45–46. The book was Dominique de Pradt's *Des Colonies et de la Révolution Actuelle de l'Amérique* (Paris: F. Bechet, 1817), which was widely read and translated.

95 Roman Pochekaev, "Rol' 'Ustava ob upravlenii Sibir'skikh Kirgizov' v politiko-pravovom razvitii Kazakhstana," in Burkitbay G. Aiagan, ed., *Materialy mezhdunarodnoi nauchno-prakticheskoi konferentsii "Ot Kazakhskogo khanstva k*

nezavisimomu Kazakhstanu" (Astana: Elorda, 2015), 81. An English-language version of this paper can be found at the Social Science Research Network (accessed 19 August 2016), http://papers.ssrn.com/sol3/papers.cfm ?abstract_id=2530466.

96 *Polnoe sobranie zakonov Rossiiskoi Imperii* (PSZRI), "Ustav o Sibir'skikh Kirgizakh," Law 29127 (St. Petersburg: 1830), 38:417–18, accessed 9 August 2016, http://www.nlr.ru/e-res/law_r/search.php?regim=4&page =417&part=177; Martin, "Muscovite Frontier Policy," 37–39; Virginia Martin, "Engagement with Empire as Norm and in Practice in Kazakh Nomadic Political Culture (1820s–1830s)," *Central Asian Survey* 36, no. 2 (2017): 182.

97 PSZRI, 419.

98 Noda, *The Kazakh Khanates*, 85–86.

99 John W. Slocum, "Who, and When, Were the Inorodtsy? The Evolution of the Category of 'Aliens' in Imperial Russia," *The Russian Review* 57, no. 2 (1998): 177.

3. CONQUEST

1 Yuri Bregel, *An Historical Atlas of Central Asia* (Leiden: Brill, 2003), 62.

2 Pavel P. Ivanov, *Ocherki po istorii Srednei Azii (XVI–seredina XIX v.)* (Moscow: Izd. Vostochnoi literatury, 1958), 127–28. The exceptions tended to be in hostile confrontations, to emphasize difference.

3 Paolo Sartori, "*Ijtihad* in Bukhara: Central Asian Jadidism and Local Genealogies of Cultural Change," *Journal of the Economic and Social History of the Orient* 59 (2016): 208–09.

4 Peter B. Golden, *Central Asia in World History* (Oxford: Oxford University Press, 2011), 50.

5 Scott C. Levi, *The Indian Diaspora in Central Asia and Its Trade* (Leiden: Brill, 2002), 125–28.

6 Jin Noda, "Russo-Chinese Trade through Central Asia: Regulations and Reality," in Tomohiko Uyama, ed., *Asiatic Russia: Imperial Power in Regional and International Contexts* (London: Routledge, 2012), 160–61; Scott C. Levi, *The Rise and Fall of Khoqand: Central Asia in the Global Age, 1709–1876* (Pittsburgh: University of Pittsburgh Press, 2017), 133–35.

7 Egor K. Meiendorf, *Puteshestvie iz Orenburga v Bukharu* (Moscow: Nauka, 1975), 105. French original 1826.

8 Alisher Khaliyarov, "Cash *Waqf* in the Khivan Khanate during the 19th Century," conference paper presented at the Central Eurasian Studies Society conference, November 2016.

9 David Christian, *A History of Russia, Central Asia, and Mongolia* (London: Blackwell, 1998), 217.

10 Ivanov, *Ocherki po istorii Srednei Azii*, 123, 150.

11 Meiendorf, *Puteshestvie iz Orenburga*, 106.

12 Arminius Vambery, *Travels in Central Asia* (New York: Harper and Brothers Publishers, 1865), 469.

13 A.A. Askarov and R.G. Mukminova, eds., *Istoriia Uzbekistana* (Tashkent: Izd. Fan, 1993), 3:85.

14 James Pickett, "Nadir Shah's Peculiar Central Asian Legacy: Empire, Conversion, Narratives, and the Rise of New Scholarly Dynasties," *International Journal of Middle East Studies* 48, no. 3 (2016): 496.

15 Meiendorf, *Puteshestvie iz Orenburga*, 144–45.

16 Mahbuba Qodirova, "Nodira," accessed 15 September 2016, http://www.ziyouz .com/index.php?option=com_content&task=view&id=1043&Itemid=228; Levi, *The Rise and Fall of Khoqand*, 148–55; Laura Newby, *The Empire and the Khanate: A Political History of Qing Relations with Kokand, c. 1760–1860* (Leiden: Brill, 2005), 210–11; Timur Beisembiev, ed., *"Tarikh-i Shakhrukhi" kak istoricheskii istochnik* (Alma-Ata: Nauka, 1987), 110.

17 Devin Deweese, "'Dis-Ordering' Sufism in Early Modern Central Asia: Suggestions for Re-thinking the Sources and Social Structures of Sufi History in the 18th and 19th Centuries," in Bakhtiyar Babajanov and Kawahara Yayoi, eds., *History and Culture of Central Asia* (Tokyo: NIHU Program Islamic Area Studies, 2012), 264–65. She was of Kalmyk origin.

18 Nurten Kiliç-Schubel, "Writing Women: Women's Poetry and Literary Networks in Nineteenth-Century Central Asia," in Ilker Binbaşı and Nurten Kiliç-Schubel, eds., *Horizons of the World: Festschrift for Isenbeke Togan* (Istanbul: Ithaki, 2011), 408–14; Levi, *The Rise and Fall of Khoqand*, 115–19.

19 Dilshod, "Tarixi Muhojiron," in Mahbuba Qodirova, ed., *Dilshod/Anbar Otin* (Tashkent: Fan, 1994), 85. Kiliç-Schubel ("Writing Women," 425) has a somewhat different translation.

20 Douglas Northrop, *Veiled Empire: Gender and Power in Stalinist Central Asia* (Ithaca, NY: Cornell University Press, 2004), 44; Shoshana Keller, "Women in Central Asia: The Modern Period," *Oxford Encyclopedia of Women in World History* (Oxford: Oxford University Press, 2008); e-reference edition http://www.oxford -womenworldhistory.com/entry?entry=t248.e164.

21 Quoted in Tomohiko Uyama, "The Changing Religious Orientation of Qazaq Intellectuals in the Tsarist Period: *Sharia*, Secularism, and Ethics," in Niccolò Pianciola and Paolo Sartori, eds., *Islam, Society, and States across the Qazaq Steppe (18th–early 20th Centuries)* (Vienna: Verlag der Österreichischen Akademie der Wissenschaften, 2013), 97; Qanayuli (1818–81) was one of the "Time of Lament" poets who bewailed Russian rule.

22 Scott C. Levi, "The Ferghana Valley at the Crossroads of World History: The Rise of Kokand, 1709–1822," *Journal of Global History* 2 (2007): 229–30.

23 Zhuldyz Tulibaeva, *Kazakhstan i bukharskoe khanstvo v XVIII–pervoi polovine XIX v.* (Almaty: Daik-Press, 2001), 91–92.

24 Russian administrators called the Kazakhs "Kirgiz" to distinguish them from Slavic Cossacks. They called the Kyrgyz "Kara-Kirgiz" (Black Kyrgyz).

25 Paul Georg Geiss, *Pre-Tsarist and Tsarist Central Asia: Communal Commitment and Political Order in Change* (London: Routledge, 2003), 177–78.

26 Zhanar Dzhampeisova, *Kazakhskoe obshchestvo i pravo v poreformennoi stepi* (Astana: ENU, 2006), 162.

27 Alexander Morrison, "Twin Imperial Disasters: The Invasions of Khiva and Afghanistan in the Russian and British Official Mind, 1839–1842," *Modern Asian Studies* 48, no. 1 (2014): 294–96.

28 Virginia Martin, *Law and Custom in the Steppe: The Kazakhs of the Middle Horde and Russian Colonialism in the Nineteenth Century* (Richmond, Surrey: Curzon, 2001), 64–65.

29 Gulnar Kendirbai, *Land and People: The Russian Colonization of the Kazakh Steppe* (Berlin: Klaus Schwarz Verlag, 2002), 7–8.

30 Salyk Zimanov, *Politicheskii stroi Kazakhstana kontsa XVIII i pervoi poloviny XIX vekov* (Almaty: Arys, 2009, orig. 1960), 176, 184; Dzhampeisova, *Kazakhskoe obshchestvo i pravo*, 177–78.

31 Zimanov, *Politicheskii stroi Kazakhstana*, 224.

32 Zimanov, 202–03, 252–53.

33 Martha Brill Olcott, *The Kazakhs* (Stanford: Hoover Institution Press, 1987), 63.

34 Steven Sabol, "Kazakh Resistance to Russian Colonization: Interpreting the Kenesary Kasymov Revolt, 1837–1847," *Central Asian Survey* 22, no. 2/3 (2003): 239–43.

35 Daniel Prior, *The Sabdan Baatir Codex: Epic and the Writing of Northern Kirghiz History: Edition, Translation and Interpretations, with a Facsimile of the Unique Manuscript* (Leiden: Brill, 2012), 155. Note the extra insult of implying that the Kazakhs were not Muslims.

36 Banu Abdrakhmanova, *Istoriia Kazakhstana: vlast', sistema upravleniia, territorial'noe ustroistvo v XIX veke* (Astana: n.p., 1998), 30–32.

37 Zimanov, *Politicheskii stroi Kazakhstana*, 217–18.

38 Sabol, "Kazakh Resistance to Russian Colonization," 243.

39 Pavel P. Ivanov, *Vosstanie Kitai-Kipchakov v Bukharskom khanstve 1821–1825 gg.* (Moscow: Izdt. Akademiia Nauk, 1937), 28–29; Bregel, *An Historical Atlas*, 62.

40 Tulibaeva, *Kazakhstan i bukharskoe khanstvo*, 60, 93; Arminius Vambery, *History of Bukhara* (London: Henry S. King and Co., 1873), 368–69. One has to be skeptical of any European account from the Imperial era, since blood-curdling tales of "Oriental savagery" sold well, but there is a lot of corroborating evidence for Nasrulla's tyranny.

41 Levi, *The Rise and Fall of Khoqand*, 148.

42 Beisembiev, "*Tarikh-i Shakhrukhi*," 19–23; Levi, 165–67.

43 Levi, *The Indian Diaspora*, 241; Alexander Morrison, "'Nechto eroticheskoe,' 'courir après l'ombre'?—Logistical Imperatives and the Fall of Tashkent, 1859–1865," *Central Asian Survey* 33, no. 2 (2014): 159.

44 Qurban-Ali Khalidi, *An Islamic Biographical Dictionary of the Eastern Kazakh Steppe: 1770–1912*, Alan Frank and Mirkasyim A. Usmanov, eds. (Leiden: Brill, 2004), 5.

45 Muhammadhakimxon To'ra, *Muntaxab at-tavorix (Xo'qand va Buxoro tarixi, sayohat va xotiralar)* (Tashkent: Iangi asr avlodi, 2010), 492 (Persian manuscript completed 1843). Levi, *The Rise and Fall of Khoqand*, 130–31.

46 Muhammadhakimxon To'ra, *Muntaxab at-tavorix*, 496.

47 Muhammadhakimxon To'ra, 505–07.

48 Muhammadhakimxon To'ra, 515. Mawrannahr was the Arabic version of Transoxiana, the land across the Oxus/Amu river.

49 Morrison, "Twin Imperial Disasters," 266; Thomas Barfield, *Afghanistan: A Cultural and Political History* (Princeton: Princeton University Press, 2010), 110–12.

50 Alexander Burnes, *Travels into Bokhara: Being the Account of a Journey from India to Cabool, Tartary and Persia* (Philadelphia: Carey & Hart, 1835).

51 Joseph Wolff, *A Mission to Bokhara* (New York: Praeger Publishers, 1969, orig. 1852), 1. The quote is from Guy Wint's introduction; Bukhara's image had not improved.

52 Meiendorf, *Puteshestvie iz Orenburga*, 137.

53 Barfield, *Afghanistan*, 121–22.

54 Wolff, *A Mission to Bokhara*, 141–42.

55 Aside from Wint's astonishingly lurid introduction to the reprint of Wolff's book, the legend lives on in such recent English articles as David Walton, "Uzbekistan: Murder among Minarets," *The Telegraph*, 15 February 2003, http://www .telegraph.co.uk/travel/726861/Uzbekistan-Murder-among-minarets.html. EurasiaNet.org's blog on Central Asian security issues is called "The Bug Pit" http://www.eurasianet.org/voices/thebugpit.

56 David Schimmelpenninck van der Oye, *Russian Orientalism: Asia in the Russian Mind from Peter the Great to the Emigration* (New Haven: Yale University Press, 2010), 224–26.

57 Morrison, "Twin Imperial Disasters," 284–85, 295.

58 Barfield, *Afghanistan*, 129.

59 Karl Meyer and Shareen Blair Brysac, *Tournament of Shadows: The Great Game and the Race for Empire in Central Asia* (Washington, DC: Counterpoint, 1999); Peter Hopkirk, *The Great Game: On Secret Service in High Asia* (London: John Murray, 1990).

60 Alexander Morrison, "Killing the Cotton Canard and Getting Rid of the Great Game: Rewriting the Russian Conquest of Central Asia, 1814–1895," *Central Asian Survey* 33, no. 2 (June 2014): 133.

61 Tax farming was a pre-modern system in which a government licensed agents to collect taxes on its behalf. In return for their labor, tax farmers got to keep part of the collected taxes.

62 Russia sold Alaska to the United States in 1867. Ilya Vinkovetsky, *Russian America: An Overseas Colony of a Continental Empire, 1804–1867* (New York: Oxford University Press, 2011).

63 Morrison, "Nechto eroticheskoe,'" 162.

64 Morrison, 156, 161–63.

65 Seymour Becker, *Russia's Protectorates in Central Asia: Bukhara and Khiva, 1865–1924* (Cambridge, MA: Harvard University Press, 1968), 25.

66 Timur Beisembiev, *The Life of 'Alimqul: A Native Chronicle of Nineteenth Century Central Asia* (London: Routledge, 2003), 6–7, 76; Levi, *The Rise and Fall of Khoqand*, 193–96.

67 A.M. Malikov, "The Russian Conquest of the Bukharan Emirate: Military and Diplomatic Aspects," *Central Asian Survey* 33, no. 2 (June 2014): 184.

68 Khaidarbek Bababekov, *Istoriia zavoevaniia Srednei Azii Tsarskom Rossiiei v Sekretnykh Dokumentakh* (Tashkent: Inst. Istoriia Narodov Srednei Azii, 2006), 54.

69 Becker, *Russia's Protectorates in Central Asia*, 38–39.

70 Malikov, "The Russian Conquest," 183; Jo-Ann Gross, "Historical Memory, Cultural Identity, and Change: Mirza Abd al-Aziz Sami's Representation of the Russian Conquest of Bukhara," in Daniel Brower and Edward Lazzerini, eds.,

Russia's Orient: Imperial Borderlands and Peoples, 1700–1917 (Bloomington, IN: Indiana University Press, 1997), 211–12.

71 Becker, *Russia's Protectorates in Central Asia*, 42.

72 Quoted in Becker, 32.

73 Becker, 29.

74 Richard Pierce, *Russian Central Asia, 1867–1917* (Berkeley: University of California Press, 1960), 49; Ekaterina Pravilova, *Finansy imperii: den'gi i vlast' v politike Rossiii na natsiional'nykh okrainakh, 1801–1917* (Moscow: Novoe Izd. 2006), 128.

75 Becker, *Russia's Protectorates in Central Asia*, 66.

76 Alexander Morrison, "Military Logistics and Historical Stage-management in the Russian Conquest of Khiva, 1873" conference paper presented at the Central Eurasian Studies Society annual conference, November 2016.

77 Becker, *Russia's Protectorates in Central Asia*, 72.

78 J.A. MacGahan, *Campaigning on the Oxus and the Fall of Khiva* (New York: Harper and Brothers, 1874), 227.

79 Becker, *Russia's Protectorates in Central Asia*, 75–76.

80 A *sotnia* was a unit of one hundred men. MacGahan, *Campaigning on the Oxus*, 359, 364. MacGahan's vivid account made its way into a history of the conquest written forty years later by the Khivan scholar Muhammad Yusuf Bek Bayani. Ron Sela, "Invoking the Russian Conquest of Khiva and the Massacres of the Yomut Turkmen: The Choices of a Central Asian Historian," *Asiatische Studien* 60, no. 2 (2006): 459–77; Scott C. Levi and Ron Sela, *Islamic Central Asia: An Anthology of Historical Sources* (Bloomington, IN: Indiana University Press, 2010), 300–05.

81 Pierce, *Russian Central Asia*, 33.

82 Kwangmin Kim, *Borderland Capitalism: Turkestan Produce, Qing Silver, and the Birth of an Eastern Market* (Stanford: Stanford University Press, 2016), 129–32, 156–61.

83 James Millward, *Eurasian Crossroads: A History of Xinjiang* (New York: Columbia University Press, 2007), 117–20; Beisembiev, *The Life of Alimqul*, 62–63, 70. In 1865 Yaqub Beg sent handsome tribute in Chinese multiples of nine to Alim Qul, but his patron's death shortly thereafter left him free to rule on his own.

84 Ian W. Campbell, "'Our Friendly Rivals': Rethinking the Great Game in Ya'qub Beg's Kashgaria, 1867–77," *Central Asian Survey* 33, no. 2 (2014): 199–214.

85 Bababekov, *Istoriia zavoevaniia*, 29, 50; Sergei Abashin, "The 'Fierce Fight' at Oshoba: A Microhistory of the Conquest of the Kokand Khanate," *Central Asian Survey* 33, no. 2 (2014): 217; Tetsu Akiyama, "Nomads Negotiating the Establishment of Russian Central Asia: Focusing on the Activities of the Kyrgyz Tribal

Chieftains," *Memoirs of the Research Department of the Toyo Bunko* 71 (2013): 154; Levi, *The Rise and Fall of Khoqand*, 204–08.

86 Abashin, "The 'Fierce Fight,'" 220.

87 V.P. Nalivkin, *Polveka v Turkestane* (Moscow: Izd. dom Mardzhani, 2015), 537–38. Originally published as "Moi vospominaniia o Skobeleve," in the newspaper *Russkii Turkestan* 1906, nos. 119 and 120.

88 Bababekov, *Istoriia zavoevaniia*, 63.

89 A minor player in these events was the ruler of the Alai Mountain Kyrgyz, a remarkable woman named Kurmanjan Datka. She understood that fighting the Russians was honorable but futile, and led her people to a peaceful settlement. In 2014 Sadyk Sher-Niyaz directed a fine film about her, *Kurmanjan Datka: Queen of the Mountains* (Trailer, https://www.youtube.com/watch?v=yIjhRQUsj_8); Bruce Pannier, "Who was Kurmanjan Datka and What Does She Mean to the Kyrgyz People?" RFE/RL Qishloq Ovozi, 31 December 2014, http://www.rferl.org/a/qishloq-ovozi-who-was-kurmanjan-datka/26770979.html.

90 Pierce, *Russian Central Asia*, 39–42; Alex Marshall, *The Russian General Staff and Asia, 1800–1917* (London: Routledge, 2006), 137.

4. IMPERIAL RULE

1 Daniel Brower, *Turkestan and the Fate of the Russian Empire* (London: Routledge, 2003), 37–38.

2 From west to east, the Kazakh oblasts were Uralsk, Turgai, Akmolinsk, and Semipalatinsk. Semirechie was added to the Steppe Krai in 1881, then returned to Turkestan in 1898. Virginia Martin, *Law and Custom in the Steppe: The Kazakhs of the Middle Horde and Russian Colonialism in the Nineteenth Century* (Richmond, Surrey: Curzon, 2001), 55; Ian W. Campbell, *Knowledge and the Ends of Empire: Kazak Intermediaries and Russian Rule on the Steppe, 1731–1917* (Ithaca, NY: Cornell University Press, 2017), 63.

3 Brower, *Turkestan and the Fate*, 49; Vahan Barooshian, *V.V. Vereshchagin, Artist at War* (Gainesville: University of Florida Press, 1993).

4 The Library of Congress owns one of the seven extant copies and has digitized it: https://www.loc.gov/rr/print/coll/287_turkestan.html. Heather Sonntag, "Photography & Mapping Russian Conquest in Central Asia: Early Albums, Encounters, & Exhibitions 1866–1876," *Journée d'Etude Centrasiatique*, Atelier 3: *Histoire du Turkestan russe et du Xinjiang*, 26 October 2007, http://www.gis-reseau-asie

.org/article/heather-s-sonntag-photography-mapping-russian-conquest-in-central
-asia-early-albums-encounters-exhib/.

5 Alexander Morrison, *Russian Rule in Samarkand 1868–1910: A Comparison with British India* (Oxford: Oxford University Press, 2008), 104–09. New methods of taxation were simultaneously undermining traditional ways of measuring personal status in Russia proper. In 1865, as part of the Great Reforms, the state began to tax property based on the income it produced rather than the social status of its owner. Yanni Kotsonis, *States of Obligation: Taxes and Citizenship in the Russian Empire and Early Soviet Republic* (Toronto: University of Toronto Press, 2014), 59.

6 Morrison, *Russian Rule in Samarkand*, 128–30.

7 A.K. Abramov. Skobelev had been called away to fight in the 1877–1878 Russo-Turkish war.

8 Sergei Abashin, *Sovetskii kishlak: mezhdu kolonializmom i modernizatsiei* (Moscow: Novoe literaturnoe obozrenie, 2015), 227–28.

9 Beatrice Penati, "Notes on the Birth of Russian Turkestan's Fiscal System: A View from the Fergana Oblast," *Journal of the Economic and Social History of the Orient* 53 (2010): 752–57.

10 Morrison, *Russian Rule in Samarkand*, 39; S.N. Abashin, D. Iu. Arapov, and N.E. Bekmakhanova, eds., *Tsentral'naia Aziia v sostave Rossiiskoi Imperii* (Moscow: Novoe Literaturnoe Obozrenie, 2008), 392, 394.

11 Abashin, Arapov, and Bekmakhanova, *Tsentral'naia Aziia*, 398.

12 Brower, *Turkestan and the Fate*, 28–30.

13 Stefan Kirmse, "Law and Empire in Late Tsarist Russia: Muslim Tatars Go to Court," *Slavic Review* 72, no. 4 (Winter 2013): 779.

14 Martin, *Law and Custom in the Steppe*, 48–57; Campbell, *Knowledge and the Ends of Empire*, 56–57.

15 Vladimir Lenin, *Imperialism, the Highest Stage of Capitalism* (New York: International Publishers, 1939, orig. 1916).

16 Morrison, *Russian Rule in Samarkand*, 293; Ekaterina Pravilova, *Finansy imperii: den'gi i vlast' v politike Rossiii na natsiional'nykh okrainakh, 1801–1917* (Moscow: Novoe Izd. 2006), 275; Kotsonis, *States of Obligation*, 33. Russia only began to systematically track its income and expenditures in the 1860s. Economic statistics from Turkestan and the Steppe Krai should be treated as estimates.

17 Seymour Becker, *Russia's Protectorates in Central Asia: Bukhara and Khiva, 1865–1924* (Cambridge, MA: Harvard University Press, 1968), 127.

18 Becker, *Russia's Protectorates in Central Asia*, 193, lists 12,150; "Demoskop Weekly," Institute of Demographics at the Higher School of Economics (census data),

accessed 31 January 2017, http://demoscope.ru/weekly/ssp/rus_lan_97.php?reg=21; Paul Georg Geiss, *Pre-Tsarist and Tsarist Central Asia: Communal Commitment and Political Order in Change* (London: Routledge, 2003), 225.

19 Adeeb Khalid, "Society and Politics in Bukhara, 1868–1920," *Central Asian Survey* 19, no. 3/4 (2000): 371.

20 Becker, *Russia's Protectorates in Central Asia*, 133.

21 The 1897 census recorded 123 Russians in Khiva, see http://demoscope.ru/weekly /ssp/rus_lan_97.php?reg=22.

22 Scott C. Levi, *The Indian Diaspora in Central Asia and Its Trade* (Leiden: Brill, 2002), 244.

23 Beatrice Penati, "The Cotton Boom and the Land Tax in Russian Turkestan (1880s–1915)," *Kritika* 14, no. 4 (2013): 746. The old argument that Russia conquered Transoxiana because the US Civil War deprived it of cotton does not hold. Cherniaev rode into Tashkent two months after Lee's surrender at Appomattox, and American cotton production surpassed pre-war levels before Turkestani production took off; Julia Obertreis, *Imperial Desert Dreams: Cotton Growing and Irrigation in Central Asia, 1860–1991* (Gottingen: V & R Unipress, 2017), 61–63.

24 Some officials welcomed freeing Russia from dependence on foreign supplies, while others lamented the loss of eight million rubles a year in tariffs; Penati, "The Cotton Boom," 750–52.

25 Paolo Sartori, "Constructing Colonial Legality in Russian Central Asia: On Guardianship," *Comparative Studies in Society and History* 56, no. 2 (2014): 419.

26 Adeeb Khalid, *Making Uzbekistan: Nation, Empire, and Revolution in the Early USSR* (Ithaca, NY: Cornell University Press, 2015), 53.

27 The new textile industry also attracted Europeans. In 1882 a Corsican engineer arrived in Kokand to start modernized silkworm production; Khaidarbek Bababekov, *Istoriia zavoevaniia Srednei Azii Tsarskom Rossiiei v Sekretnykh Dokumentakh* (Tashkent: Inst. Istoriia Narodov Srednei Azii, 2006), 37.

28 Geiss, *Pre-Tsarist and Tsarist Central Asia*, 182; Abashin, Arapov, and Bekmakhanova, *Tsentral'naia Aziia*, 407–08.

29 Martha Brill Olcott, *The Kazakhs* (Stanford: Hoover Institution Press, 1987), 87–89; Geiss, *Pre-Tsarist and Tsarist Central Asia*, 188.

30 Martin, *Law and Custom in the Steppe*, 70–71, 120–22.

31 Banu Abdrakhmanova, *Istoriia Kazakhstana: vlast', sistema upravleniia, territorial'noe ustroistvo v XIX veke* (Astana: n.p., 1998), 53–54.

32 Sarah Cameron, *The Hungry Steppe: Famine, Violence, and the Making of Soviet Kazakhstan* (Ithaca: Cornell University Press, 2018), 38.

33 Robert Geraci, *Window on the East: National and Imperial Identities in Late Tsarist Russia* (Ithaca: Cornell University Press, 2001), 47.

34 Aiganym was a ruler in her own right who requested a personal meeting with the tsar to improve conditions for her people; Virginia Martin, "Using Turki-language Qazaq Letters to Reconstruct Local Political History of the 1820s–1830s," in Paolo Sartori, ed., *Explorations in the Social History of Modern Central Asia (19th–early 20th Century)* (Leiden: Brill, 2013), 223–26, 238.

35 K.Sh. Diiarova, *Chokan Valikhanov: Geograf, Issledovatel', Puteshestvennik* (Almaty: Inst. Geografii, 2011), 16–25.

36 Abdrakhmanova, *Istoriia Kazakhstana*, 48–51.

37 Geraci, *Window on the East*, 127.

38 Wayne Dowler, *Classroom and Empire: The Politics of Schooling Russia's Eastern Nationalities, 1860–1917* (Montreal: McGill-Queen's University Press, 2001), 140–42. For a biography of Altynsarin, see Campbell, *Knowledge and the Ends of Empire*, 63–90.

39 Mukhamedjan Tynyshpaev, *Istoriia Kazakhskogo naroda* (Almaty: Sanat, 2001), 4–5.

40 Dowler, *Classroom and Empire*, 144–45. The curriculum originally included Turki and Farsi, but dropped them after one year.

41 Adeeb Khalid, *The Politics of Muslim Cultural Reform: Jadidism in Central Asia* (Berkeley: University of California Press, 1998), 158–59.

42 Morrison, *Russian Rule in Samarkand*, 70–71.

43 Khalid, "Society and Politics in Bukhara," 375; Becker, *Russia's Protectorates in Central Asia*, 227.

44 "Demoskop Weekly," Institute of Demographics at the Higher School of Economics (census data), accessed 1 February 2017, http://demoscope.ru/weekly /ssp/emp_lan_97_uezd.php?reg=799.

45 Sergei Abashin, "Empire and Demography in Turkestan: Numbers and the Politics of Counting," in Tomohiko Uyama, ed., *Asiatic Russia: Imperial Power in Regional and International Contexts* (London: Routledge, 2012), 131.

46 "Demoskop Weekly," Institute of Demographics at the Higher School of Economics (census data), accessed 1 February 2017, http://demoscope.ru/weekly /ssp/emp_lan_97_uezd.php?reg=930; Abashin "Empire and Demography in Turkestan," 136–38.

47 American censuses also frequently change their categories, as illustrated by this Pew Research Center chart: http://www.pewsocialtrends.org/interactives /multiracial-timeline/; Jennifer Hochschild and Brenna Powell, "Racial Reorganization and the United States Census 1850–1930: Mulattoes, Half-Breeds, Mixed

Parentage, Hindoos, and the Mexican Race," *Studies in American Political Development*, 22, no. 1 (2008): 59–96.

48 Called Kirgiz-kaisatskii in the original. Turgai and Uralsk also had small Bashkir populations.

49 "Demoskop Weekly," Institute of Demographics at the Higher School of Economics (census data), accessed 1 February 2017, http://demoscope.ru/weekly /ssp/emp_lan_97_uezd.php?reg=0.

50 Jeff Sahadeo, *Russian Colonial Society in Tashkent, 1865–1923* (Bloomington, IN: Indiana University Press, 2007), 36–37; Khalid, *The Politics of Muslim Cultural Reform*, 82.

51 Sahadeo, *Russian Colonial Society*, 75–76.

52 Khalid, *The Politics of Muslim Cultural Reform*, 87–89; Geraci, *Window on the East*, 55; Nazira Abduazizova, *Turkiston matbuoti tarixi (1870–1917)* (Tashkent: Akademiia, 2000), 36, 42. See also Tomohiko Uyama, "A Strategic Alliance between Kazakh Intellectuals and Russian Administrators: Imagined Communities in *Dala Walayatining Gazeti* 1888–1920," in Tadayuki Hayashi, ed., *The Construction and Deconstruction of National Histories in Slavic Eurasia* (Sapporo: Slavic Research Center, Hokkaido University, 2003), 237–60.

53 Marianne Kamp, introduction to Vladimir Nalivkin and Maria Nalivkina, *Muslim Women of the Ferghana Valley: A 19th Century Ethnography from Central Asia* (Bloomington, IN: Indiana University Press, 2016), 6–7.

54 Sadriddin Aini, *The Sands of Oxus: Boyhood Reminiscences of Sadriddin Aini* (Costa Mesa, CA: Mazda Publishers, 1998), 38–41.

55 Aini, *The Sands of Oxus*, 241.

56 For more on the maktab curriculum, see Khalid, *The Politics of Muslim Cultural Reform*, 22–24; Marianne Kamp, *The New Woman in Uzbekistan: Islam, Modernity, and Unveiling under Communism* (Seattle: University of Washington, 2006), 78–80.

57 Qurban-Ali Khalidi, *An Islamic Biographical Dictionary of the Eastern Kazakh Steppe: 1770–1912*, Alan Frank and Mirkasyim A. Usmanov, eds. (Leiden: Brill, 2004), xiv; Allen Frank, *Bukhara and the Muslims of Russia: Sufism, Education, and the Paradox of Islamic Prestige* (Leiden: Brill, 2012), 61–62.

58 Tomohiko Uyama, "The Changing Religious Orientation of Qazaq Intellectuals in the Tsarist Period: *Sharia*, Secularism, and Ethics," in Niccolò Pianciola and Paolo Sartori, eds., *Islam, Society, and States across the Qazaq Steppe (18th–early 20th Centuries)* (Vienna: Verlag der Österreichischen Akademie der Wissenschaften, 2013), 100–02.

59 James Meyer, "Immigration, Return, and the Politics of Citizenship: Russian Muslims in the Ottoman Empire, 1860–1914," *International Journal of Middle East Studies* 39, no. 1 (2007): 21–22.

60 Eileen Kane, *Russian Hajj: Empire and the Pilgrimage to Mecca* (Ithaca, NY: Cornell University Press, 2015), 37–38.

61 Kane, *Russian Hajj*, 72, 81.

62 Pravilova, *Finansy imperii*, 283–84; Sartori, "Constructing Colonial Legality," 432.

63 Khalid, "Society and Politics in Bukhara," 372.

64 Olcott, *The Kazakhs*, 80.

65 Sahadeo, *Russian Colonial Society*, 87–88.

66 Sahadeo, 100–03. The Russian mob was backed by soldiers.

67 Brower, *Turkestan and the Fate*, 95–96; Bakhtiyar Babajanov, "Dukchi Ishan und der Aufstand von Andizan 1898," in Anke von Kügelgen, Michael Kemper and Allen J. Frank, eds., *Muslim Culture in Russia and Central Asia from the 18th to the Early 20th Centuries* (Berlin: Klaus Schwarz Verlag, 1998), 2:175–76, 189; Elena Campbell, *The Muslim Question and Russian Imperial Governance* (Bloomington, IN: Indiana University Press, 2015), 91–92.

68 Nodira A. Abdurakhimova and Govkharshod K. Rustamova, *Kolonial'naia sistema vlasti v Turkestane v vtoroi polovine XIX–pervoi chertervti XX vv.* (Tashkent: Universitet, 1999), 64.

69 Kiriak E. Bendrikov, *Ocherki po istorii narodnogo obrazovanie v Turkestane (1865–1924 gody)* (Moscow: Izd. AkPedNauk RSFSR, 1960), 81.

5. REVOLUTIONS

1 A.K. Harrington, "Manifesto of 17 October 1905," Russian History, Durham University, accessed 15 February 2017, http://community.dur.ac.uk/a.k.harrington /Russhist.HTML; Nathaniel Knight, "Manifesto of 17 October 1905," Documents in Russian History, http://academic.shu.edu/russianhistory/index.php /Manifesto_of_October_17th,_1905.

2 Jeff Sahadeo, *Russian Colonial Society in Tashkent, 1865–1923* (Bloomington, IN: Indiana University Press, 2007), 125–32.

3 Martha Brill Olcott, *The Kazakhs* (Stanford: Hoover Institution Press, 1987), 111; Daniel Brower, *Turkestan and the Fate of the Russian Empire* (London: Routledge, 2003), 139–40.

4 Elena Campbell, *The Muslim Question and Russian Imperial Governance* (Bloomington, IN: Indiana University Press, 2015), 139–41.

5 Quoted in Nazira Abduazizova, *Turkiston matbuoti tarixi (1870–1917)* (Tashkent: Akademiia, 2000), 86.

6 Benedict Anderson, *Imagined Communities: Reflections on the Origin and Spread of Nationalism* (London: Verso, 1991), 195–96.

7 Charles Kurzman, *Modernist Islam, 1840–1940: A Sourcebook* (Oxford: Oxford University Press, 2002), 223–26; Adeeb Khalid, *The Politics of Muslim Cultural Reform: Jadidism in Central Asia* (Berkeley: University of California Press, 1998), 90.

8 Khalid, *The Politics of Muslim Cultural Reform*, 167–71.

9 Kurzman, *Modernist Islam*, 228 (original 28 September 1906).

10 Adeeb Khalid, *Making Uzbekistan: Nation, Empire, and Revolution in the Early USSR* (Ithaca, NY: Cornell University Press, 2015), 42–44.

11 Sahadeo, *Russian Colonial Society*, 145.

12 Abduazizova, *Turkiston matbuoti tarixi*, 120–23; Khalid, *Making Uzbekistan*, 51.

13 Paolo Sartori, "*Ijtihad* in Bukhara: Central Asian Jadidism and Local Genealogies of Cultural Change," *Journal of the Economic and Social History of the Orient*, 59 (2016): 215–16.

14 Dilshod, "Tarixi Muhojiron," in Mahbuba Qodirova, ed., *Dilshod/Anbar Otin* (Tashkent: Fan, 1994), 87–88.

15 "The horde of Alash," for the original, and mythical, united Kazakhs.

16 Steven Sabol, *Russian Colonization and the Genesis of Kazak National Consciousness* (London: Palgrave Macmillan, 2003), 73–74.

17 Gulnar Kendirbaeva, "'We Are Children of Alash ...'" *Central Asian Survey* 18, no. 1 (1999): 10–17.

18 Dina A. Amanzholova, *Kazakhskoi avtonomizm i Rossiia: istoriia dvizheniia Alash* (Moscow: Rossiia Molodaia, 1994), 21; Dilyara M. Usmanova, "The Activity of the Muslim Faction of the State Duma and Its Significance in the Formation of a Political Culture among the Muslim Peoples of Russia (1906–1917)," in Anke von Kügelgen, Michael Kemper, and Allen J. Frank, eds., *Muslim Culture in Russia and Central Asia from the 18th to the Early 20th Centuries* (Berlin: Klaus Schwartz Verlag, 1998), 2:417–56.

19 Michael Reynolds, *Shattering Empires: The Clash and Collapse of the Ottoman and Russian Empires 1908–1918* (Cambridge: Cambridge University Press, 2011), 124–25.

20 Campbell, *The Muslim Question*, 198, 202.

21 *Aziatskaia Rossiia* (St. Petersburg: A.F. Marks, 1914), 1:79, 2:277. A similar land law had been passed in the Steppe Krai in 1891. This includes 150,000 desiatinas of cotton in Bukhara and Khiva. Marco Buttino, "Study of the Economic Crisis and Depopulation of Turkestan, 1917–1920," *Central Asian Survey* 9, no. 4 (1990): 60.

22 Faizulla Iskhakov, *Tsentral'naia Aziia i Rossiia v XVIII–nach XX vv.* (Tashkent: OzDavmatbuotliti, 2009), 235.

23 Richard Pierce, *Russian Central Asia, 1867–1917* (Berkeley: University of California Press, 1960), 266.

24 Joshua Sanborn, *Imperial Apocalypse: The Great War and the Destruction of the Russian Empire* (Oxford: Oxford University Press, 2014), 28. The commander of the Russian Second Army, Alexander V. Samsonov, served as governor-general of Turkestan 1909–1914. He committed suicide after the disaster at Tannenburg.

25 Joshua Sanborn, "Unsettling the Empire: Violent Migrations and Social Disaster in Russia during World War I," *The Journal of Modern History* 77, no. 2 (2005): 290–325; Peter Gatrell, *A Whole Empire Walking: Refugees in Russia during World War I* (Bloomington, IN: Indiana University Press, 1999); Sanborn, *Imperial Apocalypse*, 68–69.

26 Sanborn, *Imperial Apocalypse*, 177–79; Marianne Kamp, *The New Woman in Uzbekistan: Islam, Modernity, and Unveiling under Communism* (Seattle: University of Washington, 2006), 54–56.

27 Sanborn, *Imperial Apocalypse*, 181–83; Bruce Pannier, "Remembering the Great Urkun 100 Years Later," Radio Free Europe/Radio Liberty, 29 April 2016, http://www.rferl.org/a/qishloq-ovozi-remembering-great-urkun/27706415.html: Alexander Morrison, "Interpreting and Remembering the 1916 Revolt," EurasiaNet, 19 October 2016, http://www.eurasianet.org/node/80931.

28 Russian documents identify him sometimes as Kyrgyz, sometimes as Kazakh. His status as a chief was more important than his putative ethnic identity. Jörn Happel, *Nomadische Lebenswelten und zarische Politik: Der Aufstand in Zentralasien 1916* (Stuttgart: Franz Steiner Verlag, 2010), 242.

29 Happel, *Nomadische Lebenswelten*, 244–45; Ian W. Campbell, *Knowledge and the Ends of Empire: Kazak Intermediaries and Russian Rule on the Steppe, 1731–1917* (Ithaca, NY: Cornell University Press, 2017), 181–83.

30 The Russian Empire used the medieval Julian calendar, which was 14 days behind the Western Gregorian calendar. The Bolsheviks adopted the Gregorian calendar in 1918, and historians use a dual "Old Style/New Style" dating system for the revolutionary transition.

31   For a fascinating view of the revolution as it unfolded day by day, see https://
     project1917.com/.

32   Adeeb Khalid, "Tashkent 1917: Revolutionary Politics in Muslim Turkestan,"
     Slavic Review 55, no. 2 (1996): 277, 279; Khalid, *Making Uzbekistan*, 70–71;
     Sahadeo, *Russian Colonial Society*, 189–90.

33   Amanzholova, *Kazakhskoi avtonomizm i Rossiia*, 25–27; Sabol, *Russian Coloniza-
     tion*, 94–96, 113.

34   Khalid, "Tashkent 1917," 280; Marco Buttino, *Revoliutsiia naoborot: Sredniaia Aziia
     mezhdu padeniem tsarskoi imperii i obrazovanie SSSR* (Moscow: Zven'ia, 2007; Italian
     original 2003), 123.

35   Khalid, "Tashkent 1917," 286.

36   Sahadeo, *Russian Colonial Society*, 191–95.

37   Seymour Becker, *Russia's Protectorates in Central Asia: Bukhara and Khiva, 1865–
     1924* (Cambridge, MA: Harvard University Press, 1968), 234–36. Junaid Khan had
     Isfendiyar assassinated.

38   Adeeb Khalid, "Society and Politics in Bukhara, 1868–1920," *Central Asian Survey*
     19, no. 3/4 (2000): 387–88.

39   Joseph V. Stalin, "Marxism and the National Question" in J.V. Stalin, *Works*
     (London: Lawrence and Wishart, 1953), 2:307. https://www.marxists.org
     /reference/archive/stalin/works/1913/03.htm.

40   Stalin, "Marxism and the National Question," 2:319.

41   Stalin, "Marxism and the National Question," 2:321.

42   *Dekrety sovetskoi vlasti* (Moscow: GosIzdatPolit, 1957), 1:113–15; Khalid, *Making
     Uzbekistan*, 91.

43   Buttino, *Revoliutsiia naoborot*, 182–83; Khalid, *Making Uzbekistan*,
     71–72.

44   Sahadeo, *Russian Colonial Society*, 200–01; Buttino, "Study of the Economic
     Crisis," 62.

45   Marco Buttino, "Politics and Social Conflict during a Famine: Turkestan Immedi-
     ately after the Revolution," in Marco Buttino, ed., *In a Collapsing Empire:
     Underdevelopment, Ethnic Conflicts and Nationalisms in the Soviet Union* (Milan:
     Feltrinelli, 1993), 258, 260.

46   Khalid, *Making Uzbekistan*, 72–77; Buttino, *Revoliutsiia naoborot*, 243–44.

47   Saidakbar Agzamkhojaev, *Istoriia Turkestanskoi Avtonomii* (Tashkent: Tashkent
     Islom Universiteti, 2006), 223–31.

48   Vladimir Ia. Nepomnin, *Istoricheskii opyt stroitel'stva sotsializma v Uzbekistana
     (1917–1937)* (Tashkent: GosIzdat UzSSR, 1960), 106–07; Julia Obertreis,

Imperial Desert Dreams: Cotton Growing and Irrigation in Central Asia, 1860–1991 (Gottingen: V & R Unipress, 2017), 147.

49 Bakhtiyar Babajanov and Sharifjon Islamov, "*Fatwas* on Land Reform in Early Soviet Central Asia," in Niccolò Pianciola and Paolo Sartori, eds., *Islam, Society, and States across the Qazaq Steppe (18th–early 20th Centuries)* (Vienna: Verlag der Osterreichischen Akademie der Wissenschafte, 2013), 234–38; Buttino, *Revoliutsiia naoborot*, 220–21, 227; Khalid, *Making Uzbekistan*, 94.

50 Amanzholova, *Kazakhskoi avtonomizm i Rossiia*, 34–35. The Bolsheviks did not really understand who Alash's leaders were and what they stood for. For a while in April some Bolsheviks were negotiating with Bukeikhanov while others were trying to arrest him.

51 Amanzholova, *Kazakhskoi avtonomizm i Rossiia*, 38, 42.

52 Amanzholova, *Kazakhskoi avtonomizm i Rossiia*, 129, 187; Russians still called Kazakhs "Kirgiz."

53 Amanzholova, *Kazakhskoi avtonomizm i Rossiia*, 151–52; Dina A. Amanzholova, ed., *Rossiia i Tsentral'naia Aziia, 1905–1925 gg. Sbornik dokumentov* (Karagandy: Karagandiskii gos. universitet, 2005), 184–86.

54 Becker, *Russia's Protectorates in Central Asia*, 265–69; Khalid, "Society and Politics in Bukhara," 390.

55 Quoted in Amanzholova, *Kazakhskoi avtonomizm i Rossiia*, 37–38.

56 The documents from this debate are in Amanzholova, *Rossiia i Tsentral'naia Aziia*, 212–30, 246–74.

57 Shoshana Keller, "The Central Asian Bureau, an Essential Tool in Governing Soviet Turkestan," *Central Asian Survey* 22, no. 2/3 (2003): 282–83.

58 Khalid, *Making Uzbekistan*, 113–16.

59 Becker, *Russia's Protectorates in Central Asia*, 287–89.

60 Khalid, *Making Uzbekistan*, 123.

61 Becker, *Russia's Protectorates in Central Asia*, 294. Emir Alim Khan died in Kabul in 1941.

6. FOUNDING SOVIET CENTRAL ASIA

1 Richard Stites, *Revolutionary Dreams: Utopian Vision and Experimental Life in the Russian Revolution* (New York: Oxford University Press, 1989).

2 The Bolsheviks adopted this cumbersome name after the October Revolution. In 1925 the party became the All-Union Communist Party (bolshevik), abbreviated

VKP(b). This was the beginning of a wild proliferation of ugly acronyms and abbreviations.

3   Georgii Safarov, *Kolonial'naia revoliutsiia* (Moscow: GosIzdat, 1921), 120–21.

4   Vladimir L. Genis, "Deportatsiia russkikh iz Turkestana v 1921 godu ('Delo Safarova')," *Voprosy istorii*, no. 1 (1998): 48.

5   Zailagi Zh. Kenzhaliev and Sof'ia O. Dauletova, *Kazakhskoe obychnoe pravo v usloviiakh sovetskoi vlasti: 1917–1937 gg.* (Almaty: Gylym, 1993), 49; Niccolò Pianciola, "Famine in the Steppe: The Collectivization of Agriculture and the Kazakh Herdsmen 1928–1934," *Cahiers du Monde Russe* 45, no. 1–2 (2004): 145; Alun Thomas, *Nomads and Soviet Rule: Central Asia under Lenin and Stalin* (London: I.B. Tauris, 2018), 58.

6   Dilorom A. Alimova and Rano Ia. Radzhapova, *Turkestan v nachale XX veke: k istorii istokov natsional'noi nezavisimosti* (Tashkent: Sharq, 2000), 391; Adeeb Khalid, *Making Uzbekistan: Nation, Empire, and Revolution in the Early USSR* (Ithaca, NY: Cornell University Press, 2015), 172–73.

7   Shoshana Keller, "The Central Asian Bureau, an Essential Tool in Governing Soviet Turkestan," *Central Asian Survey* 22, no. 2/3 (2003): 286, 290.

8   Khalid, *Making Uzbekistan*, 140.

9   The etymology of basmachi is murky; it refers to the fighters who were led by qurbashi warlords.

10   Botakoz Kassymbekova, *Despite Cultures: Early Soviet Rule in Tajikistan* (Pittsburgh: University of Pittsburgh Press, 2016), 25–27.

11   Jonathan Smele, *Historical Dictionary of Russia's Civil Wars* (Lanham, MD: Rowman and Littlefield, 2015), 501–02; Beatrice Penati, "The Reconquest of East Bukhara: The Struggle against the Basmachi as a Prelude to Sovietization," *Central Asian Survey* 26, no. 4 (2007): 521–538; Khalid, *Making Uzbekistan*, 86–88.

12   Alimova and Radzhapova, *Turkestan v nachale XX veke*, 364–66; Khalid, *Making Uzbekistan*, 143–46.

13   Shoshana Keller, *To Moscow, Not Mecca: The Soviet Campaign against Islam in Central Asia, 1917–1941* (Westport, CT: Praeger, 2001), 40: Dina A. Amanzholova, ed., *Rossiia i Tsentral'naia Aziia, 1905–1925 gg. Sbornik dokumentov* (Karagandy: Karagandiskii gos. universitet, 2005), 345.

14   Alimova and Radzhapova, *Turkestan v nachale XX veke*, 439, 460–63.

15   The ruble became worthless during the war, and Lenin tried to replace it with a gold-backed note called a chervonets. Rubles, chervontsy, and other currencies were in simultaneous use throughout NEP.

16 Gero Fedtke, "How Bukharans Turned into Uzbeks and Tajiks: Soviet Nationalities Policy in the Light of a Personal Rivalry," in Paolo Sartori and Tommaso Trevisani, eds., *Patterns of Transformation in and around Uzbekistan* (Reggio Emilia: Diabasis, 2007), 28–29.

17 Keller, "The Central Asian Bureau," 287–91; Khalid, *Making Uzbekistan*, 154–55.

18 Vladimir Lenin, *V.I. Lenin o Srednei Azii i Kazakhstane* (Tashkent: "Uzbekistan," 1982), 366–68; Amanzholova, *Rossiia i Tsentral'naia Aziia*, 279.

19 Jeremy Smith, "The Georgian Affair of 1922—Policy Failure, Personality Clash, or Power Struggle?" *Europe–Asia Studies* 50, no. 3 (1998): 532.

20 Terry Martin, *The Affirmative Action Empire: Nations and Nationalism in the Soviet Union, 1923–1939* (Ithaca, NY: Cornell University Press, 2001), 9–15.

21 Khalid, *Making Uzbekistan*, 258–61.

22 Benjamin Loring, "Building Socialism in Kyrgyzstan: Nation-Making, Rural Development, and Social Change, 1921–1932," (PhD dissertation, Brandeis University, 2008), 76.

23 Miroslav Hroch, "From National Movement to the Fully Formed Nation: The Nation-Building Process in Europe," in Geoff Eley and Ronald Grigor Suny, eds., *Becoming National: A Reader* (New York: Oxford University Press, 1996), 60–78.

24 Francine Hirsch, *Empire of Nations: Ethnographic Knowledge and the Making of the Soviet Union* (Ithaca, NY: Cornell University Press, 2005), 162–63.

25 Liudmila S. Gatagova, Liudmila P. Kosheleva, and Larissa A. Rogovaia, eds., *TsK RKP(b)–VKP(b) i natsional'nyi vopros* (Moscow: ROSSPEN, 2005), 1:207–22.

26 Keller, "The Central Asian Bureau," 292–93.

27 Russian State Archive of Social-Political History (RGASPI), Fond 62, opis' 1, delo 25, list 26; Abikey Arman Muratuly and Tursun Hazretaly, "S. Khojanov and the Phenomenon of National Communism in Central Asia and Kazakhstan in the 20-Ies XX Century," *Asian Social Science* 10, no. 2 (2014): 97. This article is based on archival sources but poorly translated; use with caution.

28 RGASPI F. 62, op. 2, d. 100, l. 39.

29 RGASPI F. 62, op. 1, d. 22, ll. 81–82.

30 Adrienne Edgar, *Tribal Nation: The Making of Soviet Turkmenistan* (Princeton: Princeton University Press, 2004), 53–56.

31 RGASPI F. 62, op. 2, d. 87, ll. 167–68; Hirsch, *Empire of Nations*, 163.

32 RGASPI F. 62, op. 1, d. 22, ll. 84–85; Edgar, *Tribal Nation*, 61–63.

33 RGASPI F. 62, op. 1, d. 22, ll. 88–89; Hirsch, *Empire of Nations*, 166–68; Arne Haugen, *The Establishment of National Republics in Soviet Central Asia* (Basingstoke: Palgrave Macmillan 2003), 188–94.

34 Hirsch, *Empire of Nations*, 106–07.

35 Laila S. Akhmetova and Vladimir K. Grigor'ev, *Pervye litsa Kazakhstana v stalin- skuiu epokhu* (Almaty: n.p., 2010), 8.

36 Amanzholova, *Rossiia i Tsentral'naia Aziia*, 434–36, 463–64; Viktor M. Usti- nov, *Turar Ryskulov: ocherki politicheskoi biografii* (Almaty: Kazakhstan, 1996), 436.

37 Khalid, *Making Uzbekistan*, 174; Kamil Ikramov, *Delo moego ottsa: roman-khronika* (Moscow: Sovetskii pisatel', 1991), 16–17.

38 Edgar, *Tribal Nation*, 104–05.

39 Loring, "Building Socialism in Kyrgyzstan," 109–15.

40 Khalid, *Making Uzbekistan*, 303–04; Kassymbekova, *Despite Cultures*, 21–22, 49–50.

41 *Sovetskii sport*, 30 August 1957, 3; *Sovetskii sport*, 26 September 1957, 1; Iurii Sholomitskii and Marat Isxakov, *O'zbekistonda fizkul'tura va sport rivojlanishi* (Tashkent: Bilim jamiati, 1974), 6; Amanzholova, *Rossiia i Tsentral'naia Aziia*, 211.

42 Marianne Kamp, *The New Woman in Uzbekistan: Islam, Modernity, and Unveiling under Communism* (Seattle: University of Washington, 2006), 88–90.

43 Edgar, *Tribal Nation*, 230–32.

44 Keller, *To Moscow, Not Mecca*, 93–96.

45 Khalid, *Making Uzbekistan*, 264, 284–85; William Fierman, *Language Planning and National Development: The Uzbek Experience* (Berlin: Mouton de Gruyter, 1991), 69–71, 218–19; Victoria Clement, *Learning to Become Turkmen: Literacy, Language, and Power, 1914–2014* (Pittsburgh: University of Pittsburgh Press, 2018), 54–56.

46 Quoted in Paolo Sartori, "The Tashkent *'Ulama'* and the Soviet State (1920–1938): A Preliminary Research Note Based on NKVD Documents," in Sartori and Trevisani, *Patterns of Transformation*, 161.

47 Virginia Martin, "Barïmta: Nomadic Custom, Imperial Crime," in Daniel Brower and Edward Lazzerini, eds., *Russia's Orient: Imperial Borderlands and Peoples, 1700– 1917* (Bloomington: Indiana University Press, 1997), 251.

48 Kenzhaliev and Dauletova, *Kazakhskoe obychnoe pravo*, 56.

49 Kenzhaliev and Dauletova, *Kazakhskoe obychnoe pravo*, 106. This echoed the complaint of an Imperial official in 1841.

50 Baurdzhan Momysh-uly, "Nasha sem'ia," *Izbrannoe v dvukh tomakh* (Alma-Ata: Jazushy, 1980, orig. 1956), 2:50.

51 Khalid, *Making Uzbekistan*, 233–40; Keller, *To Moscow, Not Mecca*, 40–42.

52 Amanzholova, *Rossiia i Tsentral'naia Aziia*, 420–24; Douglas Northrop, *Veiled Empire: Gender and Power in Stalinist Central Asia* (Ithaca, NY: Cornell University Press, 2004), 75–76.

53 Benjamin Loring, "Rural Dynamics and Peasant Resistance in Southern Kyrgyzstan, 1929–1930," *Cahiers du Monde Russe* 49, no. 1 (2008): 190–91; Edgar, *Tribal Nation*, 175–81; Keller, *To Moscow, Not Mecca*, 86–88.

54 Kassymbekova, *Despite Cultures*, 44.

55 Botakoz Kassymbekova, "Humans as Territory: Forced Resettlement and the Making of Soviet Tajikistan, 1920–38," *Central Asian Survey* 30, no. 3–4 (2011): 357–59; Kassymbekova, *Despite Cultures*, 59–60.

56 Khalid, *Making Uzbekistan*, 312–13; Gatagova, Kosheleva, and Rogovaia, *TsK RKP(b)–VKP(b)*, 619–21.

57 Paul Bergne, *The Birth of Tajikistan: National Identity and the Origins of the Republic* (London: I.B. Tauris, 2007), 102–07.

58 Karl W. Deutsch, *Nationalism and Its Alternatives* (New York: Alfred Knopf, 1969), 3.

7. BREAKING AND BUILDING—THE STALIN ERA

1 *O'zbekiston Kommunisti* 1, no. 1 (1925): 1.

2 Adeeb Khalid, *Making Uzbekistan: Nation, Empire, and Revolution in the Early USSR* (Ithaca, NY: Cornell University Press, 2015), 323–25, 335–37.

3 Matthew Payne, *Stalin's Railroad: Turksib and the Building of Socialism* (Pittsburgh: University of Pittsburgh Press, 2001).

4 Marianne Kamp, *The New Woman in Uzbekistan: Islam, Modernity, and Unveiling under Communism* (Seattle: University of Washington, 2006), 137–39; Douglas Northrop, *Veiled Empire: Gender and Power in Stalinist Central Asia* (Ithaca, NY: Cornell University Press, 2004), 79–81.

5 The excellent documentary series *Red Empire* contains rare footage of a paranji-burning demonstration. Gwyneth Hughes, Mike Dormer, and Jill Marshall, directors, *Red Empire*, Vol. 3, "Class Warriors" (Van Nuys, CA: Vestron Video, 1990).

6 Shoshana Keller, "Trapped between State and Society: Women's Liberation and Islam in Soviet Uzbekistan, 1926–1941," *Journal of Women's History* 10, no. 1 (1998): 22–23; Kamp, *The New Woman in Uzbekistan*, 69–70. The code was formally published in 1928.

7 Adrienne Edgar, *Tribal Nation: The Making of Soviet Turkmenistan* (Princeton: Princeton University Press, 2004), 248–51; Dan Healy, *Homosexual Desire in Revolutionary Russia: The Regulation of Sexual and Gender Dissent* (Chicago: University of Chicago Press, 2001), 185.

8 Kamp, *The New Woman in Uzbekistan*, 186–88, 202.

9 Chiara de Santi, "Cultural Revolution and Resistance in Uzbekistan during the 1920s: New Perspectives on the Woman Question," in Paolo Sartori and Tommaso Trevisani, eds., *Patterns of Transformation in and around Uzbekistan* (Reggio Emilia: Diabasis, 2007), 64–65.

10 Shoshana Keller, *To Moscow, Not Mecca: The Soviet Campaign against Islam in Central Asia, 1917–1941* (Westport, CT: Praeger, 2001), 198–99.

11 Keller, *To Moscow, Not Mecca*, 147–55; Khalid, *Making Uzbekistan*, 343–44.

12 Keller, 152.

13 Keller, 205.

14 Keller, 122–23.

15 Archive of the Office of the President of the Republic of Uzbekistan, Fond 58, opis' 5, delo 85, listy 2–3; Keller, *To Moscow, Not Mecca*, 181–87. Isaac Zelenskii was the chair of Sredazburo.

16 Khalid, *Making Uzbekistan*, 349–50.

17 Keller, *To Moscow, Not Mecca*, 184. The Komsomol was the Communist Party's youth wing.

18 Edgar, "Emancipation of the Unveiled," chap. 8 in *Tribal Nation*, 221–60.

19 Niccolò Pianciola, "Famine in the Steppe: The Collectivization of Agriculture and the Kazakh Herdsmen 1928–1934," *Cahiers du Monde Russe* 45, no. 1–2 (2004): 140–41.

20 Niccolò Pianciola, "Stalinist Spatial Hierarchies: Placing the Kazakhs and Kyrgyz in Soviet Economic Regionalization," *Central Asian Survey* 36, no. 1 (2017): 84–85.

21 Mukhamet Shaiakhmetov, *The Silent Steppe: The Memoir of a Kazakh Nomad under Stalin* (New York: Overlook/Rookery, 2007), 55–57; Sarah Cameron, *The Hungry Steppe: Famine, Violence, and the Making of Soviet Kazakhstan* (Ithaca, NY: Cornell University Press, 2018), 90–93.

22 Pianciola, "Famine in the Steppe," 148–50; Liudmila S. Gatagova, Liudmila P. Kosheleva, Larissa A. Rogovaia, eds., *TsK RKP(b)–VKP(b) i natsional'nyi vopros* (Moscow: ROSSPEN, 2005), 1:528–29.

23 Pianciola, "Famine in the Steppe," 162, 164; Yuri Slezkine, *The House of Government: A Saga of the Russian Revolution* (Princeton: Princeton University Press, 2017), 428–35.

24 Lynne Viola, et al., *The War against the Peasantry, 1927–1930: The Tragedy of the Soviet Countryside* (New Haven: Yale University Press, 2005), 210–11, 219–20; Lewis H. Siegelbaum and Leslie Page Moch, *Broad Is My Native Land: Repertoires and Regimes of Migration in Russia's Twentieth Century* (Ithaca, NY: Cornell University Press, 2014), 296; Manash K. Qozybaev, ed., *Nasil'stvennaia kollektivizatsiia i golod v Kazakhstane v 1931–33 gg: sbornik dokumentov i materialov* (Almaty: Fond XIX vek, 1998), 83–85, 88; Ainuri Saparbekova, J. Kocourkova, and T. Kucera, "Sweeping Ethno-Demographic Changes in Kazakhstan during the 20th Century: A Dramatic Story of Mass Migration Waves, Part I: From the Turn of the 19th Century to the End of the Soviet Era," *Acta Universitatis Carolinae Geographica* 49, no. 1 (2014): 74–77; Cameron, *The Hungry Steppe*, 119.

25 Viktor P. Danilov, Lynne Viola, Roberta Manning, eds., *Tragediia sovetskoi derevni: kollektivizatsiia i raskulachevanie. Dokumenty i materialy, 1927–1939* (Moscow: ROSSPEN, 2000), 2:389.

26 Pianciola, "Famine in the Steppe," 168–70; Cameron, *The Hungry Steppe*, 131–32; Joanna Lillis, "Kazakhstan: A Tale of Famine and Flight," EurasiaNet, 2 June 2017, http://www.eurasianet.org/node/83846; Matthew Payne, "Seeing like a Soviet State: Settlement of Nomadic Kazakhs, 1928–1934," in Golfo Alexopoulos, Julie Hessler, and Kiril Tomroff, eds., *Writing the Stalin Era: Sheila Fitzpatrick and Soviet Historiography* (New York: Palgrave Macmillan, 2011), 75.

27 Edgar, *Tribal Nation*, 205–10.

28 Benjamin Loring, "Rural Dynamics and Peasant Resistance in Southern Kyrgyzstan, 1929–1930," *Cahiers du Monde Russe* 49, no. 1 (2008): 203–07.

29 Qozybaev, *Nasil'stvennaia kollektivizatsiia*, 47–50, 62–64; Cameron, *The Hungry Steppe*, 124–27.

30 Pianciola, "Stalinist Spatial Hierarchies," 83–85.

31 Christian Teichmann, "Canals, Cotton, and the Limits of De-Colonization in Soviet Uzbekistan, 1924–1941," *Central Asian Survey* 26, no. 4 (2007): 505–09; Julia Obertreis, *Imperial Desert Dreams: Cotton Growing and Irrigation in Central Asia, 1860–1991* (Gottingen: V & R Unipress, 2017), 183–84.

32 Marianne Kamp and Russell Zanca, "Recollections of Collectivization in Uzbekistan: Stalinism and Local Activism," *Central Asian Survey* 36, no. 1 (2017): 60–62.

33 Dilorom A. Alimova, ed., *Tragediia Sredneaziatskogo Kishlaka: Kollektivizatsiia, Raskulachivanie, Ssylka, 1929–1955 gg.: Dokumenty i Materialy* (Tashkent: Sharq, 2006), 1:628–29; Rustambek Shamsutdinov, *Qishloq fojeasi: jamoalashtirish, quloqlashtirish, surgun* (Tashkent: Sharq, 2003), 212–15.

34 Oral history interview, Abdullo F., b. 1919, QD 18, transcript p. 5. Interviewed in 2003 in Qashqa Daryo by Yo'sh Olimlar Jamiyati, for "Oral

Histories of Collectivization in Uzbekistan" by Marianne Kamp and Russell Zanca.

35 Sergei Abashin, *Sovetskii Kishlak: mezhdu kolonializmom i modernizatsiei* (Moscow: Novoe literaturnoe obozrenie, 2015), 252–55; Abashin, "Stalin's *rais*: Governance Practices in a Central Asian Kolkhoz," *Central Asian Survey* 36, no. 1 (2017): 140–42.

36 Botakoz Kassymbekova, *Despite Cultures: Early Soviet Rule in Tajikistan* (Pittsburgh: University of Pittsburgh Press, 2016), 84–89; Botakoz Kassymbekova, "Humans as Territory: Forced Resettlement and the Making of Soviet Tajikistan, 1920–38," *Central Asian Survey* 30, no. 3–4 (2011): 358–60.

37 "Gulag" stands for Gosudarstvennoe Upravlenie Lagerei, the State Administration of Camps.

38 The Kazakh party head Levon Mirzoian, an Armenian, was also a full member, while the Russian Jew Grigory Broido was a candidate member for Tajikistan. Evan Mawdsley and Stephen White, *The Soviet Elite from Lenin to Gorbachev: The Central Committee and Its Members, 1917–1991* (Oxford: Oxford University Press, 2000), 49.

39 Christian Teichmann, *Macht der Unordnung: Stalins Herrschaft in Zentralasien 1920–1950* (Hamburg: Hamburger Edition, 2016), 186–87; Oleg Khlevniuk, *Politbiuro: Mekhanizmy politicheskoi vlasti v 1930–e gody* (Moscow: ROSSPEN, 1996), 134.

40 Keller, *To Moscow, Not Mecca*, 224–26.

41 *Kirgiziia v tsifrakh: staticheskii sbornik* (Frunze: Gosstatizdat,1963), 114; *Socialist Construction in the USSR: Statistical Abstract* (Moscow: Soyuzorguchet, 1936), 452–53. Soviet statistics provide a master class in how to use numbers to support propaganda, but close study can yield insights into the messy reality. Turkmenistan provided no data on pupils for 1932–1933, so the compilers simply repeated the figures from the previous year. This suggests serious disorganization in the system.

42 E. Thomas Ewing, *The Teachers of Stalinism: Policy, Practice, and Power in Soviet Schools of the 1930s* (New York: Peter Lang, 2002), 167–71.

43 Peter Blitstein, "Nation-Building or Russification? Obligatory Russian Instruction in the Soviet Non-Russian School, 1938–1953," in Ronald Grigor Suny and Terry Martin, eds., *A State of Nations: Empire and Nation-Making in the Age of Lenin and Stalin* (Oxford: Oxford University Press, 2001), 253–74.

44 Shaiakhmetov, *The Silent Steppe*, 251.

45 Cassandra Cavanaugh, "Backwardness and Biology: Medicine and Power in Russian and Soviet Central Asia, 1868–1934" (PhD dissertation, Columbia

University, 2001), 334, 343; *Kul'turnoe stroitel'stvo v Kirgizii, 1930–1941*
(Frunze: Ilim, 1972), 2:233; *Socialist Construction*, 402; Paula Michaels, *Curative Powers: Medicine and Empire in Stalin's Central Asia* (Pittsburgh: University of Pittsburgh Press, 2001), 77. None of these figures should be taken at face value.

46 Michaels, *Curative Powers*, 79, 84; Cavanaugh, "Backwardness and Biology," 343.

47 Michaels, *Curative Powers*, 138.

48 On the fate of Kho'janov and his family, see Joanna Lillis, *Dark Shadows: Inside the Secret World of Kazakhstan* (London: I.B. Tauris, 2019), 139–41; Hamid Ismailov's novel *The Devil's Dance*, translated by Donald Rayfield (London: Tilted Axis Press, 2018) is a gripping fictional account of the purge period.

49 Khalid, *Making Uzbekistan*, 372–77; Bibi P. Pal'vanova, *Tragicheskie 30-e* (Ashkhabad: Turkmenistan, 1991), 31–32.

50 Anne Applebaum, *Gulag: A History* (New York: Doubleday, 2003), 55.

51 Teichmann, *Macht der Unordnung*, 188; Mikhail B. Smirnov, ed., *Sistema ispravitel'no-trudovykh lagerei v SSSR, 1923–1960: spravochnik* (Moscow: Zven'ia, 1998), 399; Keller, *To Moscow, Not Mecca*, 201–02 on Central Asians in the White Sea Canal camp.

52 Smirnov, *Sistema ispravitel'no-trudovykh lagerei*, 285; Joanna Lillis, "Kazakhstan: Museum Recalls Stalin's Devastating Legacy," EurasiaNet, 25 July 2013, http://www.eurasianet.org/node/67300; Roy Rosenzweig Center for History and New Media's "GULAG: Many Days, Many Lives" has scanned archival documents from Karlag (http://Gulaghistory.org/items/browse/4); and the website *Karlag—NKVD* has history and personal testimonies from Karlag, in Russian, accessed 28 June 2017, http://karlag.kz).

53 James Millward, *Eurasian Crossroads: A History of Xinjiang* (New York: Columbia University Press, 2007), 201–06.

54 Keller, *To Moscow, Not Mecca*, 232.

55 Kate Brown, *A Biography of No Place: From Ethnic Borderland to Soviet Heartland* (Cambridge, MA: Harvard University Press, 2004), 150, 175, 180–81; Terry Martin, "The Origins of Soviet Ethnic Cleansing," *Journal of Modern History* 70, no. 4 (1998): 813–61; Oleg N. Pobol' and P.M. Polian, eds., *Stalinskie deportatsii 1928–1953* (Moscow: Mezhdunarodnyi Fond Demokratiia, 2005), 54–61.

56 Saparbekova, Kocourkova, and Kucera, "Sweeping Ethno-Demographic Changes," 76.

57 Alimova, *Tragediia Sredneaziatskogo Kishlaka*, 2:236–38.

58 Because special settlers were technically not prisoners they had limited rights to economic assistance, although they rarely received what the state promised them.

59 Marco Buttino, "Minorities in Samarkand: A Case Study of the City's Koreans," *Nationalities Papers* 37, no. 5 (2009): 720–23; Jon Chang, *Burnt by the Sun: The Koreans of the Russian Far East* (Honolulu: University of Hawai'i Press, 2016), 167–70; Victoria Kim, *Lost and Found in Uzbekistan: The Korean Story* (2015), https://koreanstory.atavist.com/lost-and-found-in -uzbekistan.

60 J. Arch Getty and Oleg V. Naumov, eds., *The Road to Terror: Stalin and the Self-Destruction of the Bolsheviks, 1932–1939* (New Haven: Yale University Press, 1999), 475–76. Troikas were three-person tribunals: Vladimir N. Khaustov, Vladimir P. Naumov, and N.S. Plotnikova, eds., *Lubianka: Stalin i glavnoe upravlenie gosbezopasnosti NKVD 1937–1938* (Moscow: Mezhdunarodnyi fond Demokratia, 2004), 274–76.

61 Teichmann, *Macht der Unordnung*, 205; Barry McLoughlin, "Mass Operations of the NKVD, 1937–8: A Survey," in Barry McLoughlin and Kevin McDermott, eds., *Stalin's Terror: High Politics and Mass Repression in the Soviet Union* (New York: Palgrave Macmillan, 2003), 124, 141; Ali Iğmen, *Speaking Soviet with an Accent: Culture and Power in Kyrgyzstan* (Pittsburgh: University of Pittsburgh Press, 2012), 99.

62 Rustambek T. Shamsutdinov, N.F. Karimov, E.Iu. Iusupov, eds., *Repressiia, 1937–1938 gody: dokumenty i materialy* (Tashkent: Sharq, 2005), 1:44–50, 54–55, 76.

63 Keller, *To Moscow, Not Mecca*, 232.

64 Teichmann, *Macht der Unordnung*, 204; Khaustov, Naumov, and Plotnikova, *Lubianka*, 268–69, 648.

65 *Report of Court Proceedings in the Case of the Anti-Soviet Bloc of Rights and Trotskyites* (Moscow: Narkomiust, 1938), 212–43, 339–64.

66 Pal'vanova, *Tragicheskie 30-e*, 106; Edgar, *Tribal Nation*, 127–28; Kassymbekova *Despite Cultures*, 197–98.

67 Shamsutdinov, *Qishloq fojeasi*, 31–32.

68 J. Arch Getty, "'Excesses Are Not Permitted': Mass Terror and Stalinist Governance in the Late 1930s," *The Russian Review* 61, no. 1 (2002): 113–38.

69 Teichmann, *Macht der Unordnung*, 214–15; Teichmann, "Canals, Cotton, and the Limits," 511–12; Erika Billeter, *Usbekistan: Dokumentarfotografie/ Documentary Photography 1925–1945* (Bern: Benteli Verlag, 1996), 93–98.

70 Charles Shaw, "Making Ivan-Uzbek: War, Friendship of the Peoples, and the Creation of Soviet Uzbekistan 1941–1945," (PhD dissertation, University of California, Berkeley, 2015), 17, 71, 113.

71 Shaw, 20–22.

72 Shaw, 31–32, 72–73.

73 Shaw, 41; Roberto J. Carmack, "History and Hero-Making: Patriotic Narratives and the Sovietization of Kazakh Front-line Propaganda, 1941–1945," *Central Asian Survey* 33, no. 1 (2014): 95–112; Boram Shin, "Red Army Propaganda for Uzbek Soldiers and Localised Soviet Internationalism during World War II," *The Soviet and Post-Soviet Review* 42 (2015): 39–63; Akrom A'zamov, *Sahifatlarda muhrlangan jasorat* (Tashkent: Uzbekistan, 1995) is a collection of pieces from Uzbek-language wartime newspapers; Rustambek Shamsutdinov, *Ikkinchi jahon urushi va front gazetalari* (Tashkent: Akademnashr, 2017).

74 Shaw, "Making Ivan-Uzbek," 58.

75 Rebecca Manley, *To the Tashkent Station: Evacuation and Survival in the Soviet Union at War* (Ithaca, NY: Cornell University Press, 2009), 186.

76 Manley, 224–26; Shaw, "Making Ivan-Uzbek," 113–16; Paul Stronski, *Tashkent: Forging a Soviet City 1930–1966* (Pittsburgh: University of Pittsburgh Press, 2010), 134–44. In 1962 one of the first notable Uzbek film directors, Shukhrat Abbasov, made a popular movie called *Ty—ne Sirota* (*You Are Not an Orphan*), based on the wartime poem by Ghafur Ghulam "Sen yetim emassan." The film was re-released in 2006 by the Center for Central Asian Cinematography. The complete film, without subtitles, is also available online (accessed 18 July 2017), https://www.youtube.com/watch?v=dNixVYjy7X8.

77 Claus Bech Hansen, "Power and Purification: Late-Stalinist Repression in the Uzbek SSR," *Central Asian Survey* 36, no. 1 (2017): 151.

78 R. Kh. Aminova, ed., *Uzbekistan v gody Velikoi Otechestvennoi Voiny (1941–1945)* (Tashkent: Fan, 1966), 47–49; Shaw, "Making Ivan-Uzbek," 87, 93.

79 Moritz Florin, "Becoming Soviet through War: The Kyrgyz and the Great Fatherland War," *Kritika* 17, no. 3 (2016): 501–03; Timothy Nunan, "A Union Reframed: Sovinformbiuro, Postwar Soviet Photography, and Visual Orders in Soviet Central Asia," *Kritika* 17, no. 3 (2016): 570–574 discusses the imagery of a new Soviet Central Asian identity created by photographers in this period.

80 Hansen, "Power and Purification," 157; Teichmann, *Macht der Unordnung*, 231–32, 237. Ukraine and the new Moldavian SSR suffered from extensive famine right after the war; Stalin did nothing to relieve them.

81 Pobol' and Polian, *Stalinskie deportatsii*, 491–92, 522–33, 541–46; A.Kh. Rakhmankulova, "Natsional'naia politika Sovetskogo Gosudarstva v 1930–1940-e gg.

deportatsiia narodov v Uzbekistan," in N.A. Volynchik and M.A. Ailamazian, eds., *Sovetskie natsii i natsional'naia politika v 1920–1950-e gody* (Moscow: ROSSPEN, 2014), 501–04; Michaela Pohl, "'It cannot be that our graves will be here': The Survival of Chechen and Ingush deportees in Kazakhstan, 1944–1957," *Journal of Genocide Research*, 4, no. 3 (2002): 401–04; Joanna Lillis, "Kazakhstan: Memories of the Chechen Exodus Don't Fade," EurasiaNet, 23 February 2017, http://www.eurasianet.org/node/82551.

82 Adeeb Khalid, *Islam after Communism: Religion and Politics in Central Asia* (Berkeley: University of California Press, 2007), 78–79; Eren Tasar, *Soviet and Muslim: The Institutionalization of Islam in Central Asia* (New York: Oxford University Press, 2017), 47–48.

83 Shaw, "Making Ivan-Uzbek," 225–27; Stronski, *Tashkent*, 193.

84 Shoshana Keller, "The Puzzle of Manual Harvest in Uzbekistan: Economics, Status and Labour in the Khrushchev Era," *Central Asian Survey* 34, no. 3 (2015): 305; Stronski, *Tashkent*, 199; Hansen, "Power and Purification," 152–53.

8. STABILITY AND GROWTH

1 The government re-named its agencies after the war. All the commissariats became ministries: Sovnarkom became the Council of Ministers; the VKP(b), the All-Union Communist Party (bolshevik), became the CPSU, the Communist Party of the Soviet Union; and the NKVD became the MGB, the Ministry of State Security. The Politburo was called the Presidium of the Central Committee from 1952 to 1966.

2 Ainuri Saparbekova, J. Kocourkova, and T. Kucera, "Sweeping Ethno-Demographic Changes in Kazakhstan during the 20th Century: A Dramatic Story of Mass Migration Waves Part I: From the Turn of the 19th Century to the End of the Soviet Era," *Acta Universitatis Carolinae Geographica* 49, no. 1 (2014): 76; Michaela Pohl, "'It cannot be that our graves will be here': The Survival of Chechen and Ingush Deportees in Kazakhstan, 1944–1957," *Journal of Genocide Research* 4, no. 3 (2002): 403.

3 Michaela Pohl, "From White Grave to Tselinograd to Astana: The Virgin Lands Opening, Khrushchev's Forgotten First Reform," in Denis Kozlov and Eleonory Gilburd, eds., *The Thaw: Soviet Society and Culture during the 1950s and 1960s* (Toronto: University of Toronto Press, 2013), 273–74.

4 Laila S. Akhmetova and Vladimir K. Grigor'ev, *Pervye litsa Kazakhstana v stalin-skuiu epokhu* (Almaty: n.p., 2010), 150–53.

5   Pohl, "From White Grave," 293; Oleg Khlevniuk, et al., eds., *Regional'naia politika N.S. Khrushcheva. TSK KPSS i mestnye partiinye komitety, 1953–1964 gg.* (Moscow: ROSSPEN, 2009), 186–88.

6   Gerhard Simon, *Nationalism and Policy toward the Nationalities in the Soviet Union* (Boulder, CO: Westview Press, 1991, German original 1986), 254–55.

7   Nuriddin Mukhitdinov, *Gody, provedennye v kremle* (Tashkent: Izdt. Abdully Kadyri, 1994), 5.

8   Alexander Solzhenitsyn, "The Forty Days of Kengir," *The Gulag Archipelago,* Seventeen Moments in Soviet History: An On-line Archive of Primary Sources, accessed 18 March 2019, http://soviethistory.msu.edu/1954-2/prisoners-return/prisoners-return-texts/the-forty-days-of-kengir/.

9   Michaela Pohl, "The 'Planet of One Hundred Languages': Ethnic Relations and Soviet Identity in the Virgin Lands," in Nicholas Breyfogle, Abby Schrader, and Willard Sunderland, eds., *Peopling the Russian Periphery: Borderland Colonization in Eurasian History* (London: Routledge, 2007), 249.

10 David Holloway, *Stalin and the Bomb* (New Haven, CT: Yale University Press, 1994), 213; Magdalena Stawkowski, "'I am a Radioactive Mutant': Emergent Biological Subjectivities at Kazakhstan's Semipalatinsk Nuclear Test Site," *American Ethnologist* 43, no. 1 (2016): 144; Cynthia Werner and Kathleen Purvis-Roberts, "Unraveling the Secrets of the Past: Contested Versions of Nuclear Testing in the Soviet Republic of Kazakhstan," in Barbara Rose Johnston, ed., *Half-Lives and Half-Truths: Confronting the Radioactive Legacies of the Cold War* (Santa Fe, NM: School for Advanced Research, 2007), 277–98.

11 Mukhitdinov, *Gody, provedennye,* 130.

12 Artemy Kalinovsky, *Laboratory of Socialist Development: Cold War Politics and Decolonization in Soviet Tajikistan* (Ithaca, NY: Cornell University Press, 2018), 35, 38–40. Khlevniuk, *Regional'naia politika,* 353–65.

13 Donald S. Carlisle, "The Uzbek Power Elite: Politburo and Secretariat (1938–83)," *Central Asian Survey* 5, no. 3–4 (1986): 119; Julia Obertreis, *Imperial Desert Dreams: Cotton Growing and Irrigation in Central Asia, 1860–1991* (Göttingen: V & R Unipress, 2017), 247; Simon, *Nationalism and Policy,* 251.

14 Kunaev lost his position in December 1962 but was restored to power in 1964 by his patron Leonid Brezhnev.

15 Eren Tasar, *Soviet and Muslim: The Institutionalization of Islam in Central Asia* (New York: Oxford University Press, 2017), 96.

16 Shoshana Keller, "The Puzzle of Manual Harvest in Uzbekistan: Economics, Status and Labour in the Khrushchev Era," *Central Asian Survey* 34, no. 3 (2015): 297–98.

17 In Tajik the region was known as the Dilwarzin, the "Steppe of Thirst."

18 Obertreis, *Imperial Desert Dreams*, 275–85.

19 Obertreis, 329–33.

20 Obertreis, 286.

21 M.N. Gurevich, ed., KPSS *i Sovetskoe Pravitel'stvo ob Uzbekistane: sbornik dokumentov (1925–1970)* (Tashkent: Izd. "Uzbekistan," 1972), 523.

22 Aleksandr A. Golovanov, "Nekotorye aspekty izucheniia opyta sel'skokhoziaistvennogo stroitel'stva v SSSR (1945–nachalo 60-x godov)," *Obshchestvennye nauki v Uzbekistane* no. 2 (1988): 25; Keller, "The Puzzle of Manual Harvest," 303.

23 Olivier Ferrando, "Soviet Population Transfers and Interethnic Relations in Tajikistan: Assessing the Concept of Ethnicity," *Central Asian Survey* 30, no. 1 (2011): 41–43; Kalinovsky, *Laboratory of Socialist Development*, 186–91.

24 Ariane Zevaco, "From Old to New Macha: Mass Resettlement and the Redefinition of Islamic Practice between Tajikistan's Upper Valleys and Cotton Lowlands," in Stéphane A. Dudoignon and Christian Noack, eds., *Allah's Kolhozes: Migration, De-Stalinisation, Privatisation and the New Muslim Congregations in the Soviet Realm (1950s–2000s)* (Berlin: Klaus Schwartz Verlag, 2014), 164.

25 Ferrando, "Soviet Population Transfers," 44.

26 Ferrando, 46.

27 Zevaco, "From Old to New Macha," 168–69, 178–79.

28 "Demoskop Weekly," Institute of Demographics at the Higher School of Economics (census data), accessed 8 June 2018, http://demoscope.ru/weekly/ssp/emp_lan_97_uezd.php?reg=799. "Slavic" means Russian, Ukrainian, and Belorussian inhabitants.

29 Michael G. Stefany, "Kazakhization, Kunaev and Kazakhstan: A Bridge to Independence," *Orta Asya ve Kafkasya Arastirmalari* 8, no. 16 (2013): 56–57.

30 Sergei Abashin, *Sovetskii Kishlak: mezhdu kolonializmom i modernizatsiei* (Moscow: Novoe literaturnoe obozrenie, 2015), 354–55.

31 Nancy Lubin, *Labour and Nationality in Soviet Central Asia: An Uneasy Compromise* (Princeton: Princeton University Press, 1984), 181–82.

32 Keller, "The Puzzle of Manual Harvest," 301.

33 Beate Giehler, "Maxim Gorki and the Islamic Revolution in the Southern Tajik Cotton Plain," in Dudoignon and Noack, *Allah's Kolhozes*, 132–33; Kalinovsky, *Laboratory of Socialist Development*, 197.

34 *Kirgiziia v tsifrakh* (Frunze: GosStatistIzdat, 1963), 157; *Sovetskii Turkmenistan za 40 let: Staticheskii sbornik* (Ashkhabad: Turkmenskoe izdatel'stvo, 1964), 84; *Uzbekistan za 7 let (1959–1965 gg.): kratkii staticheskii sbornik* (Tashkent: 1966), 132.

Given that the 1959 census reported 272,806 children ages five to nine in Kyrgyzstan, both statistics seem dismally low.

35 Shoshana Keller, "Story, Time and Dependent Nationhood in the Uzbek History Curriculum," *Slavic Review* 66, no. 2 (Summer 2007): 257–77.

36 *O'qituvchilar gazetasi,* 10 January 1963, 4.

37 *O'qituvchilar gazetasi,* 27 January 1963, 2.

38 *Komsomolets Uzbekistana*, 29 November 1958, 2.

39 M. Muhitdinnov and A. Suiumov, "Yoshlarning bilan va tajriba maktabi," *Sovet maktabi* no. 3 (March 1964): 65; Shoshana Keller, "Going to School in Uzbekistan," in Jeff Sahadeo and Russell Zanca, eds., *Everyday Life in Central Asia* (Bloomington, IN: Indiana University Press, 2007), 259.

40 Keller, "The Puzzle of Manual Harvest," 298.

41 Kalinovsky, *Laboratory of Socialist Development*, 185.

42 During Khrushchev's December 1955 visit to Tashkent he mocked and berated the Uzbeks for their slowness to mechanize: Keller, "The Puzzle of Manual Harvest," 305.

43 Marfua Tokhtakhodjaeva and Elmira Turgumbekova, *The Daughters of Amazons: Voices from Central Asia* (Lahore: Shirkat Gah Women's Resource Center, 1996), 128.

44 Keller, "The Puzzle of Manual Harvest," 303–04; Kalinovsky, *Laboratory of Socialist Development*, 192.

45 *Komsomolets Kirgizii*, 29 March 1975, 1. A follow-up story in August showed that many schools were in similarly poor condition: *Komsomolets Kirgizii*, 26 August 1975, 2.

46 Obertreis, *Imperial Desert Dreams*, 344–47.

47 *Kirgiziia v tsifrakh*, 28; "Demoskop Weekly," Institute of Demographics at the Higher School of Economics (census data), accessed 26 June 2018, demoscope.ru/weekly/ssp/census.php.

48 *Uzbekistan za 7 let*, 7; Michael Rywkin, *Moscow's Muslim Challenge: Soviet Central Asia* (Armonk, NY: M.E. Sharpe, 1990), 64.

49 Artemy Kalinovsky, "Not Some British Colony in Africa: The Politics of Decolonization and Modernization in Soviet Central Asia, 1955–1964," *Ab Imperio* no. 2 (2013): 214–15.

50 Carlisle, "The Uzbek Power Elite," 92, 127–28; Kalinovksy, *Laboratory of Socialist Development*, 62–63; Stefany, "Kazakhization, Kunaev and Kazakhstan," 58, 61–62; Edward Schatz, *Modern Clan Politics: The Power of "Blood" in Kazakhstan and Beyond* (Seattle: University of Washington Press, 2004), 98–99; Kathleen Collins, *Clan Politics and Regime Transition in Central Asia* (Cambridge:

Cambridge University Press, 2006), 105–09; James Critchlow, "Prelude to 'Independence': How the Uzbek Party Apparatus Broke Moscow's Grip on Elite Recruitment," in William Fierman, ed., *Soviet Central Asia: The Failed Transformation* (Boulder, CO: Westview Press, 1991), 142.

51   Making and selling items on the private market was legal in the USSR as long as the maker did not hire additional workers, which was defined as "exploiting labor." With nine children on hand, there would have been no need to hire outside labor.

52   Lubin, *Labour and Nationality*, 190–97. For a list of the creative forms that fraud took, see Abdulla D. Davletov, *Predvaritel'noe rassledovanie i preduprezhdenie khishchenii sotsitalisticheskogo imushchestva* (Tashkent: Izdt. "Fan," 1978), 193–94.

53   Donna Bahry, *Outside Moscow: Power, Politics, and Budgetary Policy in the Soviet Republics* (New York: Columbia University Press, 1987), 87–88, 116.

54   Paul Stronski, *Tashkent: Forging a Soviet City, 1930–1966* (Pittsburgh: University of Pittsburgh Press, 2010), 242, 320 n. 24; Rossen Djagalov and Masha Salazkina, "Tashkent '68: A Cinematic Contact Zone," *Slavic Review* 75, no. 2 (Summer 2016): 279–98.

55   Mukhitdinov, *Gody, provedennye*, 149–50; Masha Kiriasova, "'Sons of Muslims' in Moscow: Mediators to the Foreign East, 1955–1962," *Ab Imperio* no. 4 (2011): 112–14.

56   Stronski, *Tashkent*, 220–21.

57   *Uzbekistan za 7 let*, 5; Stronski, *Tashkent*, 252–53, 322 n. 62. Officially the death toll was four, but rumors put it closer to 1000.

58   Nigel Raab, "The Tashkent Earthquake of 1966: The Advantages and Disadvantages of a Natural Tragedy," *Jahrbücher für Geschichte Osteuropas* 62, no. 2 (2014): 273–94.

59   Kristin Roth-Ey, *Moscow Prime Time: How the Soviet Union Built the Multi-Media Empire That Lost the Cultural Cold War* (Ithaca, NY: Cornell University Press, 2011), 228; Michael Rouland, Gulnara Abikeyeva, and Birgit Beumers, eds., *Cinema in Central Asia: Rewriting Cultural Histories* (London: I.B. Tauris, 2013), 15–17.

60   *Komsomolets Uzbekistana*, 13 April 1957, 2–3. Most of these *stilyagi* were probably Slavic, but the article makes clear not all were.

61   *Komsomolets Kirgizii*, 16 May 1978, 4.

62   *Saodat* no. 8 (1971): 21; F. Salimova, "Amrika ayollari kurashmoqda," *Saodat* no. 12 (1971): 24–25.

63   Asolat Qodirova, "Qizlar, sizlar uchun!" *Saodat* no. 3 (1974): 29.

64 Kalinovsky, *Laboratory of Socialist Development*, 204–07; International Gymnastics Hall of Fame, "Class of 2009: Elvira Saadi—Uzbekistan," accessed 9 July 2018, https://www.ighof.com/inductees/2009_Elvira_Saadi.php.

65 Tasar, *Soviet and Muslim*, 256, 262, 277.

66 Oleg Kalugin, "How We Invaded Afghanistan," *Foreign Policy*, 11 December 2009, https://foreignpolicy.com/2009/12/14/how-we-invaded-afghanistan-2/.

67 Thomas Barfield, *Afghanistan: A Cultural and Political History* (Princeton: Princeton University Press, 2010), 237–38.

68 Kalinovsky, *Laboratory of Socialist Development*, 214–18; Jiayi Zhou, "The Muslim Battalions: Soviet Central Asians in the Soviet-Afghan War," *Journal of Slavic Military Studies* 25 (2012): 302–28.

69 Isaac Scarborough, "(Over)determining Social Disorder: Tajikistan and the Economic Collapse of Perestroika," *Central Asian Survey* 35, no.3 (2016): 442–43.

9. FROM REFORM TO INDEPENDENCE

1 *XXVII S"ezd Kommunisticheskoi Partii Sovetskogo Soiuza, 25 fevralia–6 marta 1986 goda: Stenograficheskii otchet* (Moscow: Izdt. Politicheskoi Literatury, 1986), 1:104.

2 For an animated map of the disaster, see "The Shrinking of the Aral Sea," Oriental Express Caucasus & Asia, accessed 24 July 2018, https://orexca.com/aral_sea .shtml.

3 Julia Obertreis, *Imperial Desert Dreams: Cotton Growing and Irrigation in Central Asia, 1860–1991* (Göttingen: V & R Unipress, 2017), 378–80.

4 Philip P. Micklin, "The Fate of 'Sibaral': Soviet Water Politics in the Gorbachev Era," *Central Asian Survey* 6, no. 2 (1987): 69–72.

5 Obertreis, *Imperial Desert Dreams*, 389.

6 Nancy Lubin, "Implications of Ethnic and Demographic Trends," in William Fierman, ed., *Soviet Central Asia: The Failed Transformation* (Boulder, CO: Westview Press, 1991), 57. Only Kyrgyzstan's rate declined: Robert G. Darst, Jr., "Environmentalism in the USSR: The Opposition to the River Diversion Projects," *Soviet Economy* 4, no. 3 (1988): 226; Philip P. Micklin and Andrew R. Bond, "Reflections on Environmentalism and the River Diversion Projects," *Soviet Economy* 4, no. 3 (1988): 266.

7 Kathleen Collins, *Clan Politics and Regime Transition in Central Asia* (Cambridge: Cambridge University Press, 2006), 113–15.

8 See the video series *Red Empire*, vol. 7, "Prisoners of the Past," directed by Gwyneth Hughes, Mike Dormer, and Jill Marshall (Van Nuys, CA: Vestron Video, 1990). A somewhat sensational account of the affair, "Zoloto dlia partii. Khlopkovoe delo," was broadcast by Telekanal Rossiia "Istoriia," directed by Maksim Faitel'berg, 2005 (in Russian), https://www.youtube.com/watch ?v=MUwo-zB3rfs. It includes footage from a documentary about the scandal made by the Uzbekfil'm studio in 1988 called "Plata," directed by Davran Salimov.

9 Boris Z. Rumer, *Soviet Central Asia: A Tragic Experiment* (Boston: Unwin Hyman, 1989), 151–54; "Soviet-Era Corruption-Case Protagonist Dies in Uzbekistan," Radio Free Europe/Radio Liberty, 27 September 2017, https://www.rferl.org/a /uzbekistan-odilov-adylov-dies/28760246.html.

10 "V Tashkente zabyvaiut o zriteliakh," *Sovetskii sport*, 10 October 1957, 2, cartoon by M. Massina. A similar image of a lying Uzbek farm boss was printed in *Komsomolets Uzbekistana*, 25 September 1958, 2. See also Shoshana Keller, "The Puzzle of Manual Harvest in Uzbekistan: Economics, Status and Labour in the Khrushchev Era," *Central Asian Survey* 34, no. 3 (2015): 304.

11 Obertreis, *Imperial Desert Dreams*, 410; James Critchlow, *Nationalism in Uzbekistan: A Soviet Republic's Road to Sovereignty* (Boulder, CO: Westview Press, 1991), 39–44.

12 Critchlow, 138–39.

13 Micklin and Bond, "Reflections on Environmentalism," 261; Darst, Jr., "Environmentalism in the USSR," 230–31.

14 For an over-excited but entertaining account, see Arkady Vaksberg, *The Soviet Mafia* (New York: St. Martin's Press, 1991), 148–50.

15 Mark Beissinger, *Nationalist Mobilization and the Collapse of the Soviet State* (Cambridge: Cambridge University Press, 2002), 73–74; *Conflict in the Soviet Union: The Untold Story of the Clashes in Kazakhstan* (New York: Human Rights Watch, 1990), 27–28; Michael G. Stefany, "Kazakhization, Kunaev and Kazakhstan: A Bridge to Independence," *Orta Asya ve Kafkasya Arastirmalari* 8, no. 16 (2013): 64–66; Bhavna Dave, *Kazakhstan: Ethnicity, Language, and Power* (London: Routledge, 2007), 89–91; Joanna Lillis, *Dark Shadows: Inside the Secret World of Kazakhstan* (London: I.B. Tauris, 2019), 170.

16 Beissinger, *Nationalist Mobilization*, 83–85.

17 Nils R. Muiznieks, "The Influence of the Baltic Popular Movements on the Process of Soviet Disintegration," *Europe-Asia Studies* 47, no. 1 (1995): 8; Victoria Clement, *Learning to Become Turkmen: Language, Literacy, and Power, 1914–2014* (Pittsburgh: University of Pittsburgh Press, 2018), 118.

18 Alexandre Bennigsen, "Unrest in the World of Soviet Islam," *Third World Quarterly* 10, no. 2 (1988): 770–86.

19 Isaac Scarborough, "(Over)determining Social Disorder: Tajikistan and the Economic Collapse of Perestroika," *Central Asian Survey* 35, no.3 (2016): 445–47; Donna Bahry, *Outside Moscow: Power, Politics, and Budgetary Policy in the Soviet Republics* (New York: Columbia University Press, 1987), 55–56.

20 Beissinger, *Nationalist Mobilization*, 258–59; Lawrence Markowitz, "How Master Frames Mislead: The Division and Eclipse of Nationalist Movements in Uzbekistan and Tajikistan," *Ethnic and Racial Studies* 32, no. 4 (2009): 722–23; Collins, *Clan Politics*, 118, 122–23.

21 Markowitz, "How Master Frames Mislead," 724–25.

22 Niyazov was a member of the Tekke tribe, but had lost much of his family in the 1948 Ashkhabad earthquake.

23 Beissinger, *Nationalist Mobilization*, 231–32; Clement, *Learning to Become Turkmen*, 116–18.

24 Collins, *Clan Politics*, 111–12; Markowitz, "How Master Frames Mislead," 728–29; Scarborough, "(Over)determining Social Disorder," 452; Tim Epkenhans, *The Origins of the Civil War in Tajikistan: Nationalism, Islamism, and Violent Conflict in Post-Soviet Space* (Lanham, MD: Lexington Books, 2016), 114–22.

25 Eren Tasar, *Soviet and Muslim: The Institutionalization of Islam in Central Asia* (Oxford: Oxford University Press, 2017), 47–48.

26 Tasar, 99.

27 Tasar, 309–11.

28 Tasar, 318; Stéphane A. Dudoignon and Sayyid Ahmad Qalandar, "'They were all from the Country': The Revival and Politicisation of Islam in the Lower Wakhsh River Valley of the Tajik SSR (1947–1997)," in Stéphane A. Dudoignon and Christian Noack, eds., *Allah's Kolkhozes: Migration, De-Stalinisation, Privatisation and the New Muslim Congregations in the Soviet Realm (1950s–2000s)* (Berlin: Klaus Schwartz Verlag, 2014), 52–53, 73.

29 Tasar, *Soviet and Muslim*, 50; Adeeb Khalid, *Islam after Communism: Religion and Politics in Central Asia* (Berkeley: University of California Press, 2007), 110–12.

30 Tasar, 319, 343–44.

31 Khalid, *Islam after Communism*, 113; Tasar, 353.

32 Hindustonyi wrote a history of "Wahhabism" late in his life to discredit his opponents. See Bakhtiyar Babajanov, Ashirbek Muminov, and Anke von Kügelgen, eds., *Disputaty musul'manskikh religioznikh avtoritetov v Tsentral'noi Azii v XX veke* (Almaty: "Daik-Press," 2007), 105–12; Bakhtiyar Babadjanov, "Debates Over Islam

in Contemporary Uzbekistan: A View from Within," in Stéphane A. Dudoignon, ed., *Devout Societies vs. Impious States? Transmitting Islamic Learning in Russia, Central Asia and China, through the Twentieth Century* (Berlin: Klaus Schwartz Verlag, 2004), 39–60.

33 Aitmatov's novel *The Day Lasts More Than a Hundred Years* was translated and published by Indiana University Press in 1980, earning him international fame.

34 Madeleine Reeves, *Border Work: Spatial Lives of the State in Rural Central Asia* (Ithaca, NY: Cornell University Press, 2014), 3–4.

35 Collins, *Clan Politics*, 118–19.

36 Collins, 178.

37 Eugene Huskey, "Kyrgyzstan: The Fate of Political Liberalization," in Karen Dawisha and Bruce Parrot, eds., *Conflict, Cleavage, and Change in Central Asia and the Caucasus* (Cambridge: Cambridge University Press, 1997), 259–63; Pauline Jones Luong, "Establishing an Electoral System in Kyrgyzstan," chap. 5 in *Institutional Change and Political Continuity in Post-Soviet Central Asia: Power, Perceptions, and Pacts* (Cambridge: Cambridge University Press, 2004), 156–88.

38 Scott Radnitz, *Weapons of the Wealthy: Predatory Regimes and Elite-led Protests in Central Asia* (Ithaca, NY: Cornell University Press, 2010), 132–36.

39 Epkenhans, *The Origins of the Civil War*, 2, 36.

40 Scarborough, "(Over)determining Social Disorder," 448–54.

41 Khalid, *Islam after Communism*, 152.

42 Epkenhans, *The Origins of the Civil War*, 253.

43 Pauline Jones Luong and Erika Weinthal, "Prelude to the Resource Curse: Explaining Oil and Gas Development Strategies in the Soviet Successor States and Beyond," *Comparative Political Studies* 34, no. 4 (2001): 379.

44 Deniz Kandiyoti, "Post-Soviet Institutional Design and the Paradoxes of the 'Uzbek Path,'" *Central Asian Survey* 26, no. 1 (2007): 33–35.

45 Mike Ekel, "Cash Cow for Karimova: Court Documents Assert Shakedown by Daughter of Late Uzbek President," Radio Free Europe/Radio Liberty, 12 October 2017, https://www.rferl.org/a/uzbekistan-karimova-akhmedov-testimony-shakedown/28790227.html.

46 Michael Ochs, "Turkmenistan: The Quest for Stability and Control," in Karen Dawisha and Bruce Parrot, eds., *Conflict, Cleavage, and Change in Central Asia and the Caucasus* (Cambridge: Cambridge University Press, 1997), 312–59.

47 Bruce Pannier, "Iran Offers Turkmenistan New Gas Swap Deal to Pakistan," Radio Free Europe/Radio Liberty, 30 April 2018, https://www.rferl.org/a/iran-offers-turkmenistan-new-gas-swap-deal-to-pakistan-tapi/29201086.html.

48 Laura L. Adams, *The Spectacular State: Culture and National Identity in Uzbekistan* (Durham, NC: Duke University Press, 2010), 5; "Craziest Dictator Ever: Tukmenbashi," *Neatorama* (blog), 11 June 2007, https://www.neatorama .com/2007/06/11/craziest-dictator-ever-turkmenbashi/; Pete Baumgartner, "Spinning Its Wheels: With Turkmenistan in a Skid, Berdymukhammedov Pedals On," Radio Free Europe/Radio Liberty, 13 June 2018, https://www.rferl .org/a/turkmenistan-in-a-skid-berdymukhammedov-pedals-on/29289107.html; Shaun Walker, "Turkmenistan's Singing Dictator Heralds Upcoming Elections," *The Guardian*, 1 February 2017, https://www.theguardian.com/world/2017/feb/01 /turkmenistans-singing-dictator-gurbanguly-berdymukhamedov-heralds -upcoming-elections.

49 "Demoskop Weekly," Institute of Demographics at the Higher School of Economics (census data), accessed 8 October 2018, http://www.demoscope.ru /weekly/ssp/sng_nac_89.php?reg=5. "Slavic" includes Russians, Ukrainians, and Belorussians.

50 Natalie Koch, *The Geopolitics of Spectacle: Space, Synecdoche, and the New Capital of Astana* (Ithaca, NY: Cornell University Press, 2018). As I write this Nazarbaev has just resigned and the Kazakh parliament has voted to re-name the capital "Nur-Sultan," but there's no telling if that change will stick.

51 Richard Carlson, "The Failure of Liberal Democratisation in Kazakhstan: The Role of International Investment and Civil Society in Impeding Political Reform," in Sevket Akyildiz and Richard Carlson, eds., *Social and Cultural Change in Central Asia: The Soviet Legacy* (London: Routledge, 2014), 131–34; Alexander Morrison, "On the Importance of Being Soviet," *EurasiaNet*, 10 August 2018, https://eurasianet .org/s/perspectives-on-the-importance-of-being-soviet; Lillis, *Dark Shadows*, 78–82.

52 Khalid, *Islam after Communism*, 140; Eric McGlinchey, *Chaos, Violence, Dynasty: Politics and Islam in Central Asia* (Pittsburgh: University of Pittsburgh Press, 2011), 119–20.

53 Khalid, 158.

54 "Religious Persecution of Independent Muslims in Uzbekistan from September 2001 to July 2002," Human Rights Watch Briefing Paper, 20 August 2002, https:// www.hrw.org/legacy/backgrounder/eca/uzbek-aug/uzbek-brief0820.pdf; "Uzbekistan: Two Brutal Deaths in Custody," Human Rights Watch, 9 August 2002, https://www.hrw.org/news/2002/08/09/uzbekistan-two-brutal-deaths-custody; Bagila Bukharbayeva, *The Vanishing Generation: Faith and Uprising in Modern Uzbekistan* (Bloomington, IN: Indiana University Press, 2019), 80–87.

55 Bruce Pannier, "IMU Announces Longtime Leader Dead, Names Successor,"
    Radio Free Europe/Radio Liberty, 17 August 2010, https://www.rferl.org/a/IMU
    _Announces_Longtime_Leader_Dead_Names_Successor/2130382.html.

56 Khalid, *Islam after Communism*, 192–97; McGlinchey, *Chaos, Violence, Dynasty*,
    121–123; Sarah Kendzior, "Inventing Akromiya: The Role of Uzbek Propagandists
    in the Andijon Massacre," *Demokratizatsiya* 14, no. 4 (2006): 545–62.

57 Dave, *Kazakhstan*, 101.

58 "Russians in the Ex-USSR: Then and Now," Radio Free Europe /Radio Liberty, 12
    June 2018, https://www.rferl.org/a/russians-in-the-ex-ussr/29287118.html.

59 Sergei Abashin, "Migration from Central Asia to Russia in the New Model of
    World Order," *Russian Politics and Law* 26, no. 6 (2014): 8–23; Jeff Sahadeo, *Voices
    from the Soviet Edge: Southern Migrants in Leningrad and Moscow* (Ithaca, NY:
    Cornell University Press, 2019).

60 "Personal Remittances, received (% of GDP)," The World Bank, accessed 14 August
    2018, https://data.worldbank.org/indicator/BX.TRF.PWKR.DT.GD.ZS.

GLOSSARY

adat nomadic customary law

appanage an autonomous unit consisting of a town and its surrounding countryside, governed by a prince or sultan

apparat the apparatus of Soviet state and party power

apparatchik a Soviet bureaucrat

aq suiek "white bone" aristocratic Kazakhs

ataliq counselor or vizier

aul nomadic Kazakh village or winter camp; Russian plural *auly*

bai in the Soviet period, a rich person

barïmta Kazakh raids on a neighbor's livestock to force resolution of a conflict

basmachi guerilla fighters against the Bolsheviks in the 1920s

bek, beg, or **bey** lord

bii nomadic tribal judge

blat pull—connections that enabled people to acquire scarce goods and services

botir warrior

bytovye prestupleniia "crimes of everyday life" in the Soviet period: veiling, polygyny, paying bride price, child marriage, etc.

caravanserai hostel for traveling merchants and their animals

chachvon women's black face veil

Chinggisid direct descendants of Chinggis Khan, also called the Golden Kin. Only Chinggisids could hold the title of khan

chistka cleansing or purging of the Communist Party

dacha a Russian country retreat; the term encompasses everything from a shack with a vegetable garden to a mansion

desiatina Imperial unit of measure, equivalent to 1.09 hectares or 2.45 acres

distantsiia Imperial administrative unit in the Kazakh steppe, established in the 1830s

do'ppi an embroidered, square skullcap that became a symbol of Central Asian ethnic identity in the Soviet period

frontoviki veteran soldiers from World War II

glasnost' "openness" to discuss past and present problems in the late Soviet Union under Mikhail Gorbachev, 1985–91

Golden Kin direct descendants of Chinggis Khan. They had exclusive right to the title "khan"

hectare a metric measure of land equal to 10,000 square meters or 2.47 acres

hokim Uzbek governor of a province

hujra a cell where students lived in a madrasa; in the late Soviet period an underground Islamic study group

hujum literally "assault"—the Soviet campaign to unveil and liberate women

ignorirovanie Governor-General K.P. von Kaufman's policy of ignoring Islam, 1865–81

inaq chief minister in the Khanate of Khiva

inorodets alien; plural *inorodtsy*

ishan Sufi teacher

Jadids proponents of modern methods of education for Muslims

jut late spring frosts that kill large numbers of herd animals by covering the grass with ice just as the lambs need to graze

Kara-kirgiz "Black Kyrgyz," Imperial Russian name for today's Kyrgyz people

khanqah hostel for traveling Sufis

khojas Sufi spiritual and political leaders; elite families who claimed descent from sacred leaders

Kirgiz-kaisatskii Imperial Russian name for today's Kazakhs

kolkhoz collective farm

kolonizatorstvo "colonizerism," the prejudiced mind-set of Slavic settlers in Central Asia

korenizatsiia Soviet policy requiring that the non-Russian peoples govern their own republics and regions in their own languages

krai a frontier region

kulak a relatively wealthier peasant farmer, defined as an enemy of the state under Stalin

kumiss a lightly fermented mare's milk drink

kun blood price, usually paid in money or livestock

madrasa Islamic higher academy

mahr gift from the groom to the bride

maktab Islamic elementary school

manap Kyrgyz prince

mehmondo'stlik (Uzbek) hospitality

mirza military commander

mujahidin (Arabic, "those who carry out jihad") name of the anti-Soviet Afghan resistance fighters after the 1979 invasion

mulla ordinary, neighborhood Islamic clergy

nachal'nik commandant or chief; plural *nachal'niki*

natsional'nost nationality

oblast district

okrug smaller district

oqsoqol village elder or town official, literally "white beard"

otin female teacher of Islamic prayers and texts

paranji women's long-sleeved cloak

perestroika Gorbachev's program of economic restructuring, 1985–91

perezhitki "survivals" of Islamic culture that confounded Soviet observers post-1945

pir from the Iranian—Sufi teacher

qadi judge of Islamic law

qalin bride price

qara suiek "black bone" commoner Kazakhs

qazikalon the highest clerical office in post-Soviet state Islamic bureaucracies

qurbashi guerilla leaders who fought against the Bolsheviks in the 1920s (see also basmachi)

raion small region, equivalent to a township in the Soviet period

rais chief; official in charge of enforcing Islamic morality in the khanates. In Soviet times the collective farm director was called the rais

Sart town-dweller or settled person, often a merchant. Both Tajiks and Uzbeks could be Sarts

sayyid a direct descendant of the Prophet Muhammad

sheikh from the Arabic—Sufi teacher

soviet literally "council"—a governing party committee

sovkhoz a state farm, where farmers received a regular salary from the state

stilyagi roughly "style-hunters"—teenagers wearing subversive clothes, 1950s and 1960s

tariqa Sufi brotherhood or order

toi feast in celebration of a wedding, circumcision, or other family event

uezd county; plural *uezdy*

ulama scholars; Muslim clergy with higher education

volost township; plural *volosti*

waqf land donated as charity to support shrines, mosques, and other Islamic institutions

zakat obligatory charitable tax; one of the Five Pillars of Islam

zakatchi official in charge of collecting *zakat* in the khanates

ABBREVIATIONS AND ACRONYMS

ASSR	Autonomous Soviet Socialist Republic
BNSR	Bukharan People's Soviet Republic, 1920–24
CARC	Council on the Affairs of Religious Cults, 1944–65
Cheka	the political police, 1917–22. Short for "Extraordinary Committee," the agency was later called the OGPU, NKVD, and the KGB
CPSU	Communist Party of the Soviet Union
Gulag	*Gosudarstvennoe Upravlenie Lagerei*, the State Administration of Camps
IMU	Islamic Movement of Uzbekistan
IRPT	Islamic Revival Party of Tajikistan
KGB	the political police, 1954–91
KhNSR	Khorezm People's Soviet Republic, 1920–24
Komsomol	*Kommunisticheskii soiuz molodezhy*, the youth wing of the Communist Party, for people ages 15–25
KPT	Communist Party of Turkestan, 1918–24
MGB	the political police, 1946–54
NKVD	the political police, 1934–43
OGPU	the political police, 1922–34
RSFSR	Russian Federated Soviet Socialist Republic
SADUM	The Spiritual Administration of the Muslims of Central Asia and Kazakhstan, the state-supervised board of Islamic clergy in the USSR, 1943–91
Sovnarkom	Council of People's Commissars
Sredazburo	the Central Asian Bureau of the Central Committee of the All-Union Communist Party (Bolshevik), 1922–34
SRs	Socialist Revolutionary party; a Russian populist party that formed in 1902

BIBLIOGRAPHY

ARCHIVAL SOURCES

Archive of the Office of the President of the Republic of Uzbekistan, Fond 58, the
 Central Committee of the Communist Party of Uzbekistan.
Russian State Archive of Social-Political History (RGASPI), Fond 62, the Central
 Asian Bureau.

SERIALS

Komsomolets Kirgizii
Komsomolets Uzbekistana
O'qituvchilar gazetasi
O'zbekiston Kommunisti
Saodat
Sovet maktabi
Sovetskii sport

WEBSITES

"Demoskop Weekly." Institute of Demographics at the Higher School of Economics
 (census data). http://www.demoscope.ru/weekly/ssp/census.php.
Harrington, A.K. "Russian History Home Page." Durham University. http://
 community.dur.ac.uk/a.k.harrington/Russhist.HTML.
Human Rights Watch. http://www.hrw.org.
International Gymnastics Hall of Fame. "Class of 2009: Elvira Saadi—Uzbekistan."
 https://www.ighof.com/inductees/2009_Elvira_Saadi.php.

"Khudaybergen Divanov—Father of Uzbek Photography." Uzbek Journeys: Art, Craft & History Tours to Central Asia. 29 May 2012. http://www.uzbekjourneys .com/2012/05/khudaybergen-divanov-father-of-uzbek.html.

Knight, Nathaniel. "Manifesto of 17 October 1905." Documents in Russian History. Last modified 21 February 2009. http://academic.shu.edu/russianhistory/index .php/Manifesto_of_October_17th,_1905.

Kuznetsova, Ekaterina, and Viacheslav Bakharev. Karlag—NKVD. http://karlag.kz.

National University of Singapore. "Empire in Asia, Documents Archive." Last modified 20 November 2014. http://www.fas.nus.edu.sg/hist/eia/historical -texts.php.

Oriental Express Caucasus & Asia. "The Shrinking of the Aral Sea." https://orexca .com/aral_sea.shtml.

"Personal remittances, received (% of the GDP)." The World Bank. https://data .worldbank.org/indicator/BX.TRF.PWKR.DT.GD.ZS.

Polnoe sobranie zakonov Rossiiskoi Imperii (PSZRI). St. Petersburg: 1830. http://www .nlr.ru/e-res/law_r/search.php?regim=4&page=417&part=177.

Roy Rosenzweig Center for History and New Media. "GULAG: Many Days, Many Lives." http://Gulaghistory.org/items/browse/4.

Siegelbaum, Lewis, and James Von Geldern. Seventeen Moments in Soviet History: An On-line Archive of Primary Sources. Michigan State University and Macalester College. http://soviethistory.msu.edu/.

Walter Chapin Simpson Center for the Humanities. Silk Road Seattle. University of Washington. http://depts.washington.edu/silkroad/.

"Zadonshchina." Drevnerusskaia literatura. Translated by L.A. Dmitriev. http://www .drevne.ru/lib/zadon_s.htm.

BOOKS AND ARTICLES

XXVII S"ezd Kommunisticheskoi Partii Sovetskogo Soiuza, 25 fevralia–6 marta 1986 goda. Stenograficheskii otchet. Moscow: Izdt. Politicheskoi Literatury, 1986.

Abashin, Sergei. "Empire and Demography in Turkestan: Numbers and the Politics of Counting." In Asiatic Russia: Imperial Power in Regional and International Contexts, edited by Tomohiko Uyama, 129–50. London: Routledge, 2012.

———. "The 'Fierce Fight' at Oshoba: A Microhistory of the Conquest of the Kokand Khanate." Central Asian Survey 33, no. 2 (2014): 215–31.

———. "Migration from Central Asia to Russia in the New Model of World Order." Russian Politics and Law 26, no. 6 (2014): 8–23.

———. *Sovetskii Kishlak: mezhdu kolonializmom i modernizatsiei*. Moscow: Novoe literaturnoe obozrenie, 2015.

———. "Stalin's *rais*: Governance Practices in a Central Asian Kolkhoz." *Central Asian Survey* 36, no. 1 (2017): 131–47.

Abashin, Sergei, et al. "Debating the Concepts of Evolutionist Social Theory: Responses to David Sneath." *Ab Imperio* no. 2 (2009): 110–63.

Abashin, Sergei N., D. Iu. Arapov, and N.E. Bekmakhanova, eds. *Tsentral'naia Aziia v sostave Rossiiskoi Imperii*. Moscow: Novoe Literaturnoe Obozrenie, 2008.

Abbasov, Shukhrat, dir. *Ty—ne Sirota*. Tashkent, 1962.

Abdrakhmanova, Banu. *Istoriia Kazakhstana: vlast', sistema upravleniia, territorial'noe ustroistvo v* XIX *veke*. Astana: n.p., 1998.

Abduazizova, Nazira. *Turkiston matbuoti tarixi (1870–1917)*. Tashkent: Akademiia, 2000.

Abdurakhimova, Nodira A., and Govkharshod K. Rustamova. *Kolonial'naia sistema vlasti v Turkestane v vtoroi polovine* XIX*–pervoi chertverti* XX *vv*. Tashkent: Universitet, 1999.

Adams, Laura L. *The Spectacular State: Culture and National Identity in Uzbekistan*. Durham, NC: Duke University Press, 2010.

Agzamkhojaev, Saidakbar. *Istoriia Turkestanskoi Avtonomii*. Tashkent: Tashkent Islom Universiteti, 2006.

Aini, Sadriddin. *The Sands of Oxus: Boyhood Reminiscences of Sadriddin Aini*. Costa Mesa, CA: Mazda Publishers, 1998.

Aitmatov, Chingiz. *The Day Lasts More Than a Hundred Years*. Bloomington, IN: Indiana University Press, 1980.

Akhmetova, Laila S., and Vladimir K. Grigor'ev. *Pervye litsa Kazakhstana v stalinskuiu epokhu*. Almaty: n.p., 2010.

Akiyama, Tetsu. "Nomads Negotiating the Establishment of Russian Central Asia: Focusing on the Activities of the Kyrgyz Tribal Chieftains." *Memoirs of the Research Department of the Toyo Bunko* 71 (2013): 141–60.

Alimova, Dilorom A., ed. *Tragediia Sredneaziatskogo Kishlaka: Kollektivizatsiia, Raskulachivanie, Ssylka, 1929–1955 gg.: Dokumenty i Materialy*. Tashkent: Sharq, 2006.

Alimova, Dilorom A., and Rano Ia. Radzhapova. *Turkestan v nachale* XX *veke: k istorii istokov natsional'noi nezavisimosti*. Tashkent: Sharq, 2000.

Allworth, Edward, ed. *Central Asia: 130 Years of Russian Dominance*. Durham, NC: Duke University Press, 1994, orig. 1967.

Amanat, Abbas, and Arash Khazeni. "The Steppe Roads of Central Asia and the Persian Captivity Narrative of Mirza Mahmud Taqi Ashtiyani." In *Writing

Travel in Central Asian History, edited by Nile Green, 113–32. Bloomington, IN: Indiana University Press, 2014.

Amanzholova, Dina A. *Kazakhskoi avtonomizm i Rossiia: istoriia dvizheniia Alash.* Moscow: Rossiia Molodaia, 1994.

———, ed. *Rossiia i Tsentral'naia Aziia, 1905–1925 gg. Sbornik dokumentov.* Karagandy: Karagandiskii gos. universitet, 2005.

Aminova, R. Kh., ed. *Uzbekistan v gody Velikoi Otechestvennoi Voiny (1941–1945).* Tashkent: Fan, 1966.

Anderson, Benedict. *Imagined Communities: Reflections on the Origin and Spread of Nationalism.* London: Verso, 1991.

Anisimov, Evgenii. *The Reforms of Peter the Great: Progress through Coercion in Russia.* Armonk, NY: M.E. Sharpe, 1993.

Anthony, David. *The Horse, the Wheel, and Language.* Princeton: Princeton University Press, 2007.

Applebaum, Anne. *Gulag: A History.* New York: Doubleday, 2003.

Aristov, Nikolai A. *Usuni i kyrgyzy ili kara-kyrgyzy.* Bishkek: Soros—Kyrgyzstan, 2001, orig. 1893.

Askarov, A.A., and R.G. Mukminova, eds. *Istoriia Uzbekistana*, Vol. 3. Tashkent: Izd. "Fan," 1993.

A'zamov, Akrom. *Sahifatlarda muhrlangan jasorat.* Tashkent: Uzbekistan, 1995.

Aziatskaia Rossiia. St. Petersburg: A.F. Marks, 1914.

Bababekov, Khaidarbek. *Istoriia zavoevaniia Srednei Azii Tsarskom Rossiiei v Sekretnykh Dokumentakh.* Tashkent: Inst. Istoriia Narodov Srednei Azii, 2006.

Babadjanov, Bakhtiyar. "Debates over Islam in Contemporary Uzbekistan: A View from Within." In *Devout Societies vs. Impious States? Transmitting Islamic Learning in Russia, Central Asia and China, through the Twentieth Century*, edited by Stéphane A. Dudoignon, 39–60. Berlin: Klaus Schwartz Verlag, 2004.

Babajanov, Bakhtiyar. "Dukchi Ishan und der Aufstand von Andizan 1898." In *Muslim Culture in Russia and Central Asia from the 18th to the Early 20th Centuries*, edited by Anke von Kügelgen, Michael Kemper, and Allen J. Frank, 2:167–91. Berlin: Klaus Schwarz Verlag, 1998.

Babajanov, Bakhtiyar, Ashirbek Muminov, and Anke von Kügelgen, eds. *Disputaty musul'manskikh religioznikh avtoritetov v Tsentral'noi Azii v XX veke.* Almaty: "Daik-Press," 2007.

Babajanov, Bakhtiyar, and Sharifjon Islamov. "*Fatwas* on Land Reform in Early Soviet Central Asia." In *Islam, Society, and States across the Qazaq Steppe (18th–early 20th Centuries)*, edited by Niccolò Pianciola and Paolo Sartori, 233–66. Vienna: Verlag der Osterreichischen Akademie der Wissenschafte, 2013.

Babur. *The Baburnama*. New York: Oxford University Press, 1996.

Bahry, Donna. *Outside Moscow: Power, Politics, and Budgetary Policy in the Soviet Republics*. New York: Columbia University Press, 1987.

Barfield, Thomas. *Afghanistan: A Cultural and Political History*. Princeton: Princeton University Press, 2010.

Barooshian, Vahan. *V.V. Vereshchagin, Artist at War*. University of Florida Press, 1993.

Baumgartner, Pete. "Spinning Its Wheels: With Turkmenistan in a Skid, Berdymukhammedov Pedals On." Radio Free Europe/Radio Liberty, 13 June 2018. https://www.rferl.org/a/turkmenistan-in-a-skid-berdymukhammedov -pedals-on/29289107.html.

Becker, Seymour. *Russia's Protectorates in Central Asia: Bukhara and Khiva, 1865–1924*. Cambridge, MA: Harvard University Press, 1968.

Beisembiev, Timur, ed. *"Tarikh-i Shakhrukhi" kak istoricheskii istochnik*. Alma-Ata: Nauka, 1987.

———. *The Life of 'Alimqul: A Native Chronicle of Nineteenth Century Central Asia*. London: Routledge, 2003.

Beissinger, Mark. *Nationalist Mobilization and the Collapse of the Soviet State*. Cambridge: Cambridge University Press, 2002.

———. "Soviet Empire as 'Family Resemblance.'" *Slavic Review* 65, no. 2 (2006): 294–303.

Bendrikov, Kiriak E. *Ocherki po istorii narodnogo obrazovanie v Turkestane (1865–1924 gody)*. Moscow: Izdt. AkPedNauk RSFSR, 1960.

Benedict, Ruth. *Patterns of Culture*. New York: Houghton Mifflin, 1934.

Bennigsen, Alexandre. "Unrest in the World of Soviet Islam." *Third World Quarterly* 10, no. 2 (1988): 770–86.

Bergholtz, Peter. *The Partition of the Steppe: The Struggle of the Russians, Manchus, and the Zunghar Mongols for Empire in Central Asia, 1619–1758*. New York: Peter Lang, 1993.

Bergne, Paul. *The Birth of Tajikistan: National Identity and the Origins of the Republic*. London: I.B. Tauris, 2007.

Billeter, Erika. *Usbekistan: Dokumentarfotografie/Documentary Photography 1925–1945*. Bern: Benteli Verlag, 1996.

Blitstein, Peter. "Nation-Building or Russification? Obligatory Russian Instruction in the Soviet Non-Russian School, 1938–1953." In *A State of Nations: Empire and Nation-Making in the Age of Lenin and Stalin*, edited by Ronald Grigor Suny and Terry Martin, 253–74. Oxford: Oxford University Press, 2001.

Bregel, Yuri. *An Historical Atlas of Central Asia*. Leiden: Brill, 2003.

Brower, Daniel. *Turkestan and the Fate of the Russian Empire*. London: Routledge, 2003.

Brown, Kate. *A Biography of No Place: From Ethnic Borderland to Soviet Heartland.* Cambridge, MA: Harvard University Press, 2004.

Bukharbayeva, Bagila. *The Vanishing Generation: Faith and Uprising in Modern Uzbekistan.* Bloomington, IN: Indiana University Press, 2019.

Burbank, Jane, and Frederick Cooper. *Empires in World History: Power and the Politics of Difference.* Princeton: Princeton University Press, 2010.

Burbank, Jane, Mark von Hagen, and Anatolyi Remnev, eds. *Russian Empire: Space, People, Power, 1700–1930.* Bloomington, IN: Indiana University Press, 2007.

Burnes, Alexander. *Travels into Bokhara: Being the Account of a Journey from India to Cabool, Tartary and Persia.* Philadelphia: Carey & Hart, 1835.

Burton, Audrey. *The Bukharans: A Dynastic, Diplomatic, and Commercial History 1550–1702.* New York: St. Martin's Press, 1997.

———. "Russian Slaves in Seventeenth-Century Bukhara." In *Post-Soviet Central Asia,* edited by Touraj Atabaki and John O'Kane, 345–65. London: Tauris Academic Studies, 1998.

Buttino, Marco. "Minorities in Samarkand: A Case Study of the City's Koreans." *Nationalities Papers* 37, no. 5 (2009): 719–42.

———. "Politics and Social Conflict during a Famine: Turkestan immediately after the Revolution." In *In a Collapsing Empire: Underdevelopment, Ethnic Conflicts and Nationalisms in the Soviet Union,* edited by Marco Buttino, 257–77. Milan: Feltrinelli, 1993.

———. *Revoliutsiia naoborot: Sredniaia Aziia mezhdu padeniem tsarskoi imperii i obrazovanie SSSR.* Moscow: Zven'ia, 2007, Italian original 2003.

———. "Study of the Economic Crisis and Depopulation of Turkestan, 1917–1920." *Central Asian Survey* 9, no. 4 (1990): 59–74.

Cambridge History of Iran. Vol. 6. Cambridge: Cambridge University Press, 1986.

Cameron, Sarah. *The Hungry Steppe: Famine, Violence, and the Making of Soviet Kazakhstan.* Ithaca: Cornell University Press, 2018.

Campbell, Elena. *The Muslim Question and Russian Imperial Governance.* Bloomington, IN Indiana University Press, 2015.

Campbell, Ian W. *Knowledge and the Ends of Empire: Kazak Intermediaries and Russian Rule on the Steppe, 1731–1917.* Ithaca, NY: Cornell University Press, 2017.

———. "'Our Friendly Rivals': Rethinking the Great Game in Ya'qub Beg's Kashgaria, 1867–77." *Central Asian Survey* 33, no. 2 (2014): 199–214.

Canfield, Robert. "Introduction: The Turko-Persian Tradition." In *Turko-Persia in Historical Perspective,* edited by Robert Canfield, 1–34. Cambridge: Cambridge University Press, 1991.

Carlisle, Donald S. "The Uzbek Power Elite: Politburo and Secretariat (1938–83)." *Central Asian Survey* 5, no. 3–4 (1986): 91–131.

Carlson, Richard. "The Failure of Liberal Democratisation in Kazakhstan: The Role of International Investment and Civil Society in Impeding Political Reform." In *Social and Cultural Change in Central Asia: The Soviet Legacy*, edited by Sevket Akyildiz and Richard Carlson, 127–44. London: Routledge, 2014.

Carmack, Roberto J. "History and Hero-Making: Patriotic Narratives and the Sovietization of Kazakh Front-line Propaganda, 1941–1945." *Central Asian Survey* 33, no. 1 (2014): 95–112.

Caroe, Olaf. *Soviet Empire: The Turks of Central Asia and Stalinism*. London: Macmillan, 1967.

Carrère d'Encausse, Hélène. "The National Republics Lose Their Independence." In *Central Asia: 130 Years of Russian Dominance*, edited by Edward Allworth, 254–65. Durham, NC: Duke University Press, 1994, orig. 1967.

Cavanaugh, Cassandra. "Backwardness and Biology: Medicine and Power in Russian and Soviet Central Asia, 1868–1934." PhD dissertation, Columbia University, 2001.

Chang, Jon. *Burnt by the Sun: The Koreans of the Russian Far East*. Honolulu: University of Hawai'i Press, 2016.

Christian, David. *A History of Russia, Central Asia and Mongolia: Inner Eurasia from Prehistory to the Mongol Empire*. London: Blackwell, 1998.

———. "Silk Roads or Steppe Roads? The Silk Roads in World History." *Journal of World History* 11, no. 1 (Spr. 2000): 1–26.

Clement, Victoria. *Learning to Become Turkmen: Literacy, Language, and Power, 1914–2014*. Pittsburgh: University of Pittsburgh Press, 2018.

Collins, Kathleen. *Clan Politics and Regime Transition in Central Asia*. Cambridge: Cambridge University Press, 2006.

Conflict in the Soviet Union: The Untold Story of the Clashes in Kazakhstan. New York: Human Rights Watch, 1990.

Critchlow, James. *Nationalism in Uzbekistan: A Soviet Republic's Road to Sovereignty*. Boulder, CO: Westview Press, 1991.

———. "Prelude to 'Independence': How the Uzbek Party Apparatus Broke Moscow's Grip on Elite Recruitment." In *Soviet Central Asia: The Failed Transformation*, edited by William Fierman, 131–56. Boulder, CO: Westview Press, 1991.

Crummey, Robert. *The Formation of Muscovy, 1304–1613*. London: Longman Press, 1987.

Dale, Stephen. *The Muslim Empires of the Ottomans, Safavids, and Mughals*. Cambridge: Cambridge University Press, 2010.

Danilov, Viktor P., Lynne Viola, and Roberta Manning, eds. *Tragediia sovetskoi derevni: kollektivizatsiia i raskulachevanie. Dokumenty i materialy, 1927–1939.* Vol. 2. Moscow: ROSSPEN, 2000.

Darst, Robert G. Jr. "Environmentalism in the USSR: The Opposition to the River Diversion Projects." *Soviet Economy* 4, no. 3 (1988): 223–52.

Dave, Bhavna. *Kazakhstan: Ethnicity, Language, and Power.* London: Routledge, 2007.

Davies, Brian. *Warfare, State and Society on the Black Sea Steppe, 1500–1700.* New York: Routledge, 2007.

Davletov, Abdulla D. *Predvaritel'noe rassledovanie i preduprezhdenie khishchenii sotsitalisticheskogo imushchestva.* Tashkent: Izdt. "Fan," 1978.

Dekrety sovetskoi vlasti. Vol. 1. Moscow: GosIzdatPolit, 1957.

de Santi, Chiara. "Cultural Revolution and Resistance in Uzbekistan during the 1920s. New Perspectives on the Woman Question." In *Patterns of Transformation in and Around Uzbekistan*, edited by Paolo Sartori and Tommaso Trevisani, 51–90. Reggio Emilia: Diabasis, 2007.

Deutsch, Karl W. *Nationalism and Its Alternatives.* New York: Alfred Knopf, 1969.

Deweese, Devin. "'Dis-Ordering' Sufism in Early Modern Central Asia: Suggestions for Re-thinking the Sources and Social Structures of Sufi History in the 18th and 19th Centuries." In *History and Culture of Central Asia*, edited by Bakhtiyar Babajanov and Kawahara Yayoi, 259–79. Tokyo: NIHU Program Islamic Area Studies, 2012.

———. *Islamicization and Native Religion in the Golden Horde.* University Park, PA: Penn State Press, 1994.

Diiarova, K. Sh. *Chokan Valikhanov: Geograf, Issledovatel', Puteshestvennik.* Almaty: Inst. Geografii, 2011.

Dilshod. "Tarixi Muhojiron." In *Dilshod/Anbar Otin*, edited by Mahbuba Qodirova, 75–91. Tashkent: Fan, 1994.

Djagalov, Rossen, and Masha Salazkina. "Tashken '68: A Cinematic Contact Zone." *Slavic Review* 75, no. 2 (Summer 2016): 279–98.

Donnelly, Alton S. "Peter the Great and Central Asia." *Canadian Slavonic Papers* 17, no. 2/3 (1975): 202–17.

Dowler, Wayne. *Classroom and Empire: The Politics of Schooling Russia's Eastern Nationalities, 1860–1917.* Montreal: McGill-Queen's University Press, 2001.

Dudoignon, Stéphane A., and Sayyid Ahmad Qalandar. "'They were all from the Country:' The Revival and Politicisation of Islam in the Lower Wakhsh River Valley of the Tajik SSR (1947–1997)." In *Allah's Kolkhozes: Migration, De-Stalinisation, Privatisation and the New Muslim Congregations in the Soviet Realm (1950s–2000s)*, edited by Stéphane A. Dudoignon and Christian Noack, 47–122. Berlin: Klaus Schwartz Verlag, 2014.

Dughlat, Mirza Muhammad Haidar. *History of the Moghuls of Central Asia (Tarikh-i Rashidi)*. London: Samson Low, Marston and Co, 1898, reissued Praeger 1970.

Dunning, Chester. *Russia's First Civil War*. University Park, PA: Pennsylvania State Press, 2001.

Dzhampeisova, Zhanar. *Kazakhskoe obshchestvo i pravo v poreformennoi stepi*. Astana: ENU, 2006.

Edgar, Adrienne. *Tribal Nation: The Making of Soviet Turkmenistan*. Princeton: Princeton University Press, 2004.

Ekel, Mike. "Cash Cow for Karimova: Court Documents Assert Shakedown by Daughter of Late Uzbek President." Radio Free Europe/Radio Liberty, 12 October 2017, https://www.rferl.org/a/uzbekistan-karimova-akhmedov -testimony-shakedown/28790227.html.

Eley, Geoff, and Ron Grigor Suny, eds. *Becoming National*. Oxford: Oxford University Press, 1996.

Epkenhans, Tim. *The Origins of the Civil War in Tajikistan: Nationalism, Islamism, and Violent Conflict in Post-Soviet Space*. Lanham, MD: Lexington Books, 2016.

Ewing, E. Thomas. *The Teachers of Stalinism: Policy, Practice, and Power in Soviet Schools of the 1930s*. New York: Peter Lang, 2002.

Faitel'berg, Maksim, dir. "Zoloto dlia partii. Khlopkovoe delo." Telekanal Rossiia "Istoriia," 2005. https://www.youtube.com/watch?v=MUwo-zB3rf.

Fedtke, Gero. "How Bukharans Turned into Uzbeks and Tajiks: Soviet Nationalities Policy in the Light of a Personal Rivalry." In *Patterns of Transformation in and around Uzbekistan*, edited by Paolo Sartori and Tommaso Trevisani, 11–42. Reggio Emilia: Diabasis, 2007.

Ferrando, Olivier. "Soviet Population Transfers and Interethnic Relations in Tajikistan: Assessing the Concept of Ethnicity." *Central Asian Survey* 30, no. 1 (2011): 39–52.

Fierman, William. *Language Planning and National Development: The Uzbek Experience*. Berlin: Mouton de Gruyter, 1991.

Florin, Moritz. "Becoming Soviet through War: The Kyrgyz and the Great Fatherland War." *Kritika* 17, no. 3 (2016): 495–516.

Foltz, Richard. *Mughal India and Central Asia*. Oxford: Oxford University Press, 1998.

Forsyth, James. *A History of the Peoples of Siberia*. Cambridge: Cambridge University Press, 1992.

Frank, Allan J. "The Qazaqs and Russia." *Cambridge History of Inner Asia: The Chinggisid Age*. Cambridge: Cambridge University Press, 2009. 363–79.

Frank, Allen. *Bukhara and the Muslims of Russia: Sufism, Education, and the Paradox of Islamic Prestige*. Leiden: Brill, 2012.

Franklin, Simon, and Jonathan Shepard. *The Emergence of Rus' 750–1200*. London: Longman, 1996.

Gatagova, Liudmila S., Liudmila P. Kosheleva, Larissa A. Rogovaia, eds. *TSK RKP(b)–VKP(b) i natsional'nyi vopros*. Vol. 1. Moscow: ROSSPEN, 2005.

Gatrell, Peter. *A Whole Empire Walking: Refugees in Russia during World War I*. Bloomington, IN: Indiana University Press, 1999.

Geiss, Paul Georg. *Pre-Tsarist and Tsarist Central Asia: Communal Commitment and Political Order in Change*. London: Routledge, 2003.

Genis, Vladimir L. "Deportatsiia russkikh iz Turkestana v 1921 godu ('Delo Safarova')." *Voprosy istorii* no. 1 (1998): 44–58.

Geraci, Robert. *Window on the East: National and Imperial Identities in Late Tsarist Russia*. Ithaca: Cornell University Press, 2001.

Getty, J. Arch. "'Excesses Are Not Permitted': Mass Terror and Stalinist Governance in the Late 1930s," *The Russian Review* 61, no. 1 (2002): 113–38.

Getty, J. Arch, and Oleg V. Naumov, eds. *The Road to Terror: Stalin and the Self-Destruction of the Bolsheviks, 1932–1939*. New Haven: Yale University Press, 1999.

Ghazi, Abu'l. *Shajara-yi tarakima*. In *Islamic Central Asia: An Anthology of Historical Sources*, edited by Scott C. Levi and Ron Sela, 227–29. Bloomington, IN: Indiana University Press, 2010.

Giehler, Beate. "Maxim Gorki and the Islamic Revolution in the Southern Tajik Cotton Plain." In *Allah's Kolhozes: Migration, De-Stalinisation, Privatisation and the New Muslim Congregations in the Soviet Realm (1950s–2000s)*, edited by Stéphane A. Dudoignon and Christian Noack, 123–47. Berlin: Klaus Schwartz Verlag, 2014.

Golden, Peter B. *Central Asia in World History*. Oxford: Oxford University Press, 2011.

Golombek, Lisa, and Maria Subtelny. *Timurid Art and Culture: Iran and Central Asia in the Fifteenth Century*. Leiden: Brill, 1992.

Golovanov, Aleksandr A. "Nekotorye aspekty izucheniia opyta sel'skokhoziaistvennogo stroitel'stva v SSSR (1945–nachalo 60-x godov)." *Obshchestvennye nauki v Uzbekistane* no. 2 (1988): 21–26.

Gommans, Jos. "Mughal India and Central Asia in the Eighteenth Century: An Introduction to a Wider Perspective." In *India and Central Asia: Commerce and Culture 1500–1800*, edited by Scott C. Levi, 39–63. Oxford: Oxford University Press, 2007.

Gross, Jo-Ann. "Historical Memory, Cultural Identity, and Change: Mirza Abd al-Aziz Sami's Representation of the Russian Conquest of Bukhara." In *Russia's Orient: Imperial Borderlands and Peoples, 1700–1917*, edited by Daniel Brower and Edward Lazzerini, 203–26. Bloomington, IN: Indiana University Press, 1997.

Gurevich, M.N., ed. *KPSS i Sovetskoe Pravitel'stvo ob Uzbekistane: sbornik dokumentov (1925–1970)*. Tashkent: Izdt. "Uzbekistan," 1972.

Halperin, Charles. *Russia and the Golden Horde*. Bloomington, IN: Indiana University Press, 1985.

Hansen, Claus Bech. "Power and Purification: Late-Stalinist Repression in the Uzbek SSR." *Central Asian Survey* 36, no. 1 (2017): 148–66.

Happel, Jörn. *Nomadische Lebenswelten und zarische Politik: Der Aufstand in Zentralasien 1916*. Stuttgart: Franz Steiner Verlag, 2010.

Haugen, Arne. *The Establishment of National Republics in Soviet Central Asia*. Basingstoke: Palgrave Macmillan, 2003.

Healy, Dan. *Homosexual Desire in Revolutionary Russia: The Regulation of Sexual and Gender Dissent*. Chicago: University of Chicago Press, 2001.

Hirsch, Francine. *Empire of Nations: Ethnographic Knowledge and the Making of the Soviet Union*. Ithaca, NY: Cornell University Press, 2005.

Hobsbawm, Eric, and Terence Ranger, eds. *The Invention of Tradition*. Cambridge: Cambridge University Press, 1983.

Hochschild, Jennifer, and Brenna Powell. "Racial Reorganization and the United States Census 1850–1930: Mulattoes, Half-Breeds, Mixed Parentage, Hindoos, and the Mexican Race." *Studies in American Political Development* 22, no. 1 (2008): 59–96.

Holloway, David. *Stalin and the Bomb*. New Haven, CT: Yale University Press, 1994.

Hopkirk, Peter. *The Great Game: On Secret Service in High Asia*. London: John Murray, 1990.

Hroch, Miroslav. "From National Movement to the Fully-Formed Nation: The Nation-Building Process in Europe." In *Becoming National: A Reader*, edited by Geoff Eley and Ronald Grigor Suny, 60–78. New York: Oxford University Press, 1996.

Hughes, Gwyneth, Mike Dormer, and Jill Marshall, directors. *Red Empire*, video series. Van Nuys, CA: Vestron Video, 1990.

Huskey, Eugene. "Kyrgyzstan: The Fate of Political Liberalization." In *Conflict, Cleavage, and Change in Central Asia and the Caucasus*, edited by Karen Dawisha and Bruce Parrot, 242–76. Cambridge: Cambridge University Press, 1997.

Iğmen, Ali. *Speaking Soviet with an Accent: Culture and Power in Kyrgyzstan*. Pittsburgh: University of Pittsburgh Press, 2012.

Ikramov, Kamil. *Delo moego ottsa: roman-khronika*. Moscow: Sovetskii pisatel', 1991.

Iskhakov, Faizulla. *Tsentral'naia Aziia i Rossiia v XVIII–nach. XX vv*. Tashkent: OzDavmatbuotliti, 2009.

Ismailov, Hamid. *The Devil's Dance*. Translated by Donald Rayfield. London: Tilted Axis Press, 2018.

Istoriia Kazakhskoi SSR. Alma-Ata: Izd. Akademii Nauk, 1957.

Iuldashev, M. Iu. *K istorii torgovlykh i posol'skikh sviazei Srednei Azii c Rossiei v XVI–XVII vv.* Tashkent: Izd. Akademii Nauk, 1964.

Ivanov, Pavel P. *Ocherki po istorii Srednei Azii (XVI–seredina XIX v.).* Moscow: Izd. Vostochnoi literatury, 1958.

———. *Vosstanie Kitai-Kipchakov v Bukharskom khanstve 1821–1825 gg.* Moscow: Izd. Akademiia Nauk, 1937.

Jenkinson, Anthony. "The Voyage of M. Anthony Jenkinson from the Citie of Mosco in Russia to Boghar in Bactria, Anno 1558." In *The Principal Navigations, Voyages, Traffiques and Discoveries of the English Nation*, edited by Richard Hakluyt, 449–80. Glasgow: J. MacLehose and Sons, 1903.

Jones Luong, Pauline. *Institutional Change and Political Continuity in Post-Soviet Central Asia: Power, Perceptions, and Pacts.* Cambridge: Cambridge University Press, 2004.

Jones Luong, Pauline, and Erika Weinthal. "Prelude to the Resource Curse: Explaining Oil and Gas Development Strategies in the Soviet Successor States and Beyond." *Comparative Political Studies* 34 no. 4 (2001): 367–99.

Kaiser, Daniel H. *The Laws of Rus'—Tenth to Fifteenth Centuries.* Salt Lake City, UT: C. Schlacks, 1992.

Kalinovsky, Artemy. *Laboratory of Socialist Development: Cold War Politics and Decolonization in Soviet Tajikistan.* Ithaca, NY: Cornell University Press, 2018.

———. "Not Some British Colony in Africa: The Politics of Decolonization and Modernization in Central Asia, 1955–1964." *Ab Imperio* no. 2 (2013): 191–222.

Kalugin, Oleg. "How We Invaded Afghanistan." *Foreign Policy*, 11 December 2009. https://foreignpolicy.com/2009/12/14/how-we-invaded-afghanistan-2/.

Kamp, Marianne. *The New Woman in Uzbekistan: Islam, Modernity, and Unveiling under Communism.* Seattle: University of Washington, 2006.

Kamp, Marianne, and Russell Zanca. "Recollections of Collectivization in Uzbekistan: Stalinism and Local Activism." *Central Asian Survey* 36, no. 1 (2017): 55–72.

Kandiyoti, Deniz. "Post-Soviet Institutional Design and the Paradoxes of the 'Uzbek Path.'" *Central Asian Survey* 26, no. 1 (2007): 31–48.

Kane, Eileen. *Russian Hajj: Empire and the Pilgrimage to Mecca.* Ithaca, NY: Cornell University Press, 2015.

Kassymbekova, Botakoz. *Despite Cultures: Early Soviet Rule in Tajikistan.* Pittsburgh: University of Pittsburgh Press, 2016.

———. "Humans as Territory: Forced Resettlement and the Making of Soviet Tajikistan, 1920–38." *Central Asian Survey* 30, no. 3–4 (2011): 349–70.

Kazakhsko-Russkie otnosheniia v XVI–XVIII vekakh (sbornik dokumentov i materialov). Alma-Ata: Izd. Akademii nauk Kazakhskoi SSR, 1961.

Keenan, Edward. "Ivan III, Nikolai Karamzin, and the Legend of the 'Casting Off of the Tatar Yoke' (1480)." In *The New Muscovite Cultural History*, edited by Valerie Kivelson, Karen Petrone, Nancy S. Kollman, and Donald Flier, 237–51. Bloomington, IN: Slavica, 2009.

———. "Muscovy and Kazan, 1445–1552: Some Introductory Remarks on Steppe Diplomacy." *Slavic Review* 26, no. 4 (1967): 548–58.

Keller, Shoshana. "The Central Asian Bureau, an Essential Tool in Governing Soviet Turkestan." *Central Asian Survey* 22, no. 2/3 (2003): 281–97.

———. "Going to School in Uzbekistan." In *Everyday Life in Central Asia*, edited by Jeff Sahadeo and Russell Zanca, 248–65. Bloomington, IN: Indiana University Press, 2007.

———. "The Puzzle of Manual Harvest in Uzbekistan: Economics, Status and Labour in the Khrushchev Era." *Central Asian Survey* 34, no. 3 (2015): 296–309.

———. "Story, Time and Dependent Nationhood in the Uzbek History Curriculum." *Slavic Review* 66, no. 2 (Summer 2007): 257–77.

———. *To Moscow, Not Mecca: The Soviet Campaign against Islam in Central Asia, 1917–1941*. Westport. CT: Praeger, 2001.

———. "Trapped between State and Society: Women's Liberation and Islam in Soviet Uzbekistan, 1926–1941." *Journal of Women's History* 10, no. 1 (1998): 20–44.

———. "Women in Central Asia: The Modern Period." *Oxford Encyclopedia of Women in World History*. Oxford: Oxford University Press, 2008, e-reference edition http://www.oxford-womenworldhistory.com/entry?entry=t248.e164.

Kendirbaeva, Gulnar. *Land and People: The Russian Colonization of the Kazakh Steppe*. Berlin: Klaus Schwarz Verlag, 2002.

———. "'We Are Children of Alash ...'" *Central Asian Survey* 18, no. 1 (1999): 5–36.

Kendzior, Sarah. "Inventing Akromiya: The Role of Uzbek Propagandists in the Andijon Massacre." *Demokratizatsiya* 14, no. 4 (2006): 545–62.

Kenzhaliev, Zailagi Zh., and Sof'ia O. Dauletova. *Kazakhskoe obychnoe pravo v usloviiakh sovetskoi vlasti: 1917–1937 gg*. Almaty: Gylym, 1993.

Khafizova, Klara. *Kazakhskaia strategiia tsinskoi imperii*. Almaty: Taimas, 2007.

Khairetidinov, Damir Z. *Musul'manskaia obshchina Moskvy v XIV–nachale* xx *veka*. Nizhnii-Novgorod: Dukhovnoe uprav. musul'man Nizhnego Novgoroda i Nizhegorodskoi oblast, 2002.

Khalid, Adeeb. "Backwardness and the Quest for Civilization: Early Soviet Central Asia in Comparative Perspective." *Slavic Review* 65, no. 2 (2006): 231–51.

———. *Islam after Communism: Religion and Politics in Central Asia*. Berkeley: University of California Press, 2007.

———. *Making Uzbekistan: Nation, Empire, and Revolution in the Early USSR*. Ithaca, NY: Cornell University Press, 2015.

———. *The Politics of Muslim Cultural Reform: Jadidism in Central Asia*. Berkeley: University of California Press, 1998.

———. "Society and Politics in Bukhara, 1868–1920." *Central Asian Survey* 19, no. 3/4 (2000): 367–96.

———. "Tashkent 1917: Revolutionary Politics in Muslim Turkestan." *Slavic Review* 55, no. 2 (1996): 270–96.

Khalidi, Qurban-Ali. *An Islamic Biographical Dictionary of the Eastern Kazakh Steppe: 1770–1912*, edited by Alan Frank and Mirkasyim A. Usmanov. Leiden: Brill, 2004.

Khaliyarov, Alisher. "Cash *Waqf* in the Khivan Khanate during the 19th Century," conference paper presented at the Central Eurasian Studies Society conference, November 2016.

Khanykov, Nikolai V. *Opisanie Bukharskogo khanstva*. St. Petersburg: Imp. Akademii Nauk, 1843.

Khaustov, Vladimir N., Vladimir P. Naumov, and N.S. Plotnikova, eds. *Lubianka: Stalin i glavnoe upravlenie gosbezopasnosti NKVD 1937–1938*. Moscow: Mezhdunarodnyi fond Demokratia, 2004.

Khazanov, Anatoly. *Nomads and the Outside World*, 2nd ed. Madison, WI: Wisconsin University Press, 1994.

Khazeni, Arash. "The River's Edge: The Steppes of the Oxus and the Boundaries of the Near/Middle East and Central Asia, c. 1500–1800." In *Is There a Middle East? The Evolution of a Geopolitical Concept*, edited by Michael Bonine, Abbas Amanat, and Michael Ezekiel Gasper, 139–51. Stanford: Stanford University Press, 2012.

Khlevniuk, Oleg. *Politbiuro: Mekhanizmy politicheskoi vlasti v 1930–e gody*. Moscow: ROSSPEN, 1996.

Khlevniuk, Oleg, et al., eds. *Regional'naia politika N.S. Khrushcheva. TsK KPSS i mestnye partiinye komitety, 1953–1964 gg*. Moscow: ROSSPEN, 2009.

Khodarkovsky, Michael. *Russia's Steppe Frontier: The Making of a Colonial Empire, 1500–1800*. Bloomington, IN: Indiana University Press, 2002.

———. *Where Two Worlds Met: The Russian State and the Kalmyk Nomads, 1600–1771*. Ithaca, NY: Cornell University Press, 1992.

Kiliç-Schubel, Nurten. "Writing Women: Women's Poetry and Literary Networks in Nineteenth-Century Central Asia." In *Horizons of the World: Festschrift for Isenbeke Togan*, edited by Ilker Binbaşı and Nurten Kiliç-Schubel, 405–40. Istanbul: Ithaki, 2011.

Kim, Kwangmin. *Borderland Capitalism: Turkestan Produce, Qing Silver, and the Birth of an Eastern Market*. Stanford: Stanford University Press, 2016.

Kim, Victoria. *Lost and Found in Uzbekistan: the Korean Story* (2015). https://koreanstory.atavist.com/lost-and-found-in-uzbekistan.

Kirgiziia v tsifrakh. Staticheskii sbornik. Frunze: Gos. Statischeskoe Izdat., 1963.

Kiriasova, Masha. "'Sons of Muslims' in Moscow: Mediators to the Foreign East, 1955–1962." *Ab Imperio* no. 4 (2011): 106–32.

Kirmse, Stefan. "Law and Empire in Late Tsarist Russia: Muslim Tatars Go to Court." *Slavic Review* 72, no. 4 (Winter 2013): 778–801.

Kivelson, Valerie. *Cartographies of Tsardom: The Land and Its Meanings in Seventeenth-Century Russia.* Ithaca, NY: Cornell University Press, 2006.

Kivelson, Valerie, and Ronald Suny. *Russia's Empires.* Oxford: Oxford University Press, 2017.

Koch, Natalie. *The Geopolitics of Spectacle: Space, Synecdoche, and the New Capital of Astana.* Ithaca, NY: Cornell University Press, 2018.

Kotsonis, Yanni. *States of Obligation: Taxes and Citizenship in the Russian Empire and Early Soviet Republic.* Toronto: University of Toronto Press, 2014.

Kul'turnoe stroitel'stvo v Kirgizii, 1930–1941, Vol. 2. Frunze: Ilim, 1972.

Kurzman, Charles. *Modernist Islam, 1840–1940: A Sourcebook.* Oxford: Oxford University Press, 2002.

Langer, Lawrence N. "War and Peace: Rus' and the Mongols in the 13th and 14th Centuries." In *Everyday Life in Russian History,* edited by Gary Marker, Joan Neuberger, Marshall Poe, and Leila Rupp, 187–202. Bloomington, IN: Slavica, 2010.

Lantzeff, George, and Richard Pierce. *Eastward to Empire: Exploration and Conquest on the Russian Open Frontier, to 1750.* Montreal: McGill-Queen's University Press, 1973.

Laruelle, Marlene. "The Concept of Ethnogenesis in Central Asia: Political Context and Institutional Mediators (1940–50)." *Kritika* 9, no. 1 (2008): 169–88.

Lattimore, Owen. *Studies in Frontier History.* London: Oxford University Press, 1962.

Lee, Joo-Yup. *Qazaqliq, or Ambitious Brigandage, and the Formation of the Qazaqs: State and Identity in Post-Mongol Central Eurasia.* Leiden: Brill, 2016.

Lenin, Vladimir. *Imperialism, the Highest Stage of Capitalism.* New York: International Publishers, 1939, orig. 1916.

Lenin, Vladimir Ilyich. *V.I. Lenin o Srednei Azii i Kazakhstane.* Tashkent: Uzbekistan, 1982.

Levi, Scott C. "The Ferghana Valley at the Crossroads of World History: The Rise of Kokand, 1709–1822." *Journal of Global History* 2, no. 2 (2007): 213–32.

———. *The Indian Diaspora in Central Asia and Its Trade.* Leiden: Brill, 2002.

———. *The Rise and Fall of Khoqand: Central Asia in the Global Age, 1709–1876*. Pittsburgh: University of Pittsburgh Press, 2017.

———. "Turks and Tajiks in Central Asian History." In *Everyday Life in Central Asia*, edited by Jeff Sahadeo and Russell Zanca, 15–31. Bloomington, IN: Indiana University Press, 2007.

Levi, Scott C., and Ron Sela, eds. *Islamic Central Asia: An Anthology of Historical Sources*. Bloomington, IN: Indiana University Press, 2010.

Levshin, Aleksei I. *Opisanie Kirgiz-Kazach'ikh ili Kirgiz-Kaisatskikh, ord i stepei*. Almaty: Sanat, 1996, orig. 1832.

Lillis, Joanna. *Dark Shadows: Inside the Secret World of Kazakhstan*. London: I.B. Tauris, 2019.

———. "Kazakhstan: A Tale of Famine and Flight." EurasiaNet, 2 June 2017. http://www.eurasianet.org/node/83846.

———. "Kazakhstan: Memories of the Chechen Exodus Don't Fade." EurasiaNet, 23 February 2017. http://www.eurasianet.org/node/82551.

———. "Kazakhstan: Museum Recalls Stalin's Devastating Legacy." EurasiaNet, 25 July 2013. http://www.eurasianet.org/node/67300.

Litsevoi Letopisnei Svod XVI *veka. Russkaia letopisnaia istoriia*. Moscow: AKTEON, 2010.19:1528–41 gg.

Loring, Benjamin. "Building Socialism in Kyrgyzstan: Nation-Making, Rural Development, and Social Change, 1921–1932." PhD dissertation, Brandeis University, 2008.

———. "Colonizers with Party Cards: Soviet Internal Colonialism in Central Asia, 1917–1939." *Kritika* 15 no. 1 (2014): 77–102.

———. "Rural Dynamics and Peasant Resistance in Southern Kyrgyzstan, 1929–1930." *Cahiers du Monde Russe* 49, no. 1 (2008): 183–210.

Lubin, Nancy. "Implications of Ethnic and Demographic Trends." In *Soviet Central Asia: The Failed Transformation*, edited by William Fierman, 36–61. Boulder, CO: Westview Press, 1991.

———. *Labour and Nationality in Soviet Central Asia: An Uneasy Compromise*. Princeton: Princeton University Press, 1984.

MacGahan, J.A. *Campaigning on the Oxus and the Fall of Khiva*. New York: Harper and Brothers, 1874.

Madariaga, Isabel de. *Ivan the Terrible*. New Haven, CT: Yale University Press, 2005.

Malikov, A.M. "The Russian Conquest of the Bukharan Emirate: Military and Diplomatic Aspects." *Central Asian Survey* 33, no. 2 (June 2014): 180–98.

Malikov, Yuriy. "Disadvantaged Neophytes of the Privileged Religion: Why Qazaqs Did Not Become Christians." In *Islam, Society, and States across the Qazaq Steppe*

(18th–early 20th Centuries), edited by Niccolò Pianciola and Paolo Sartori, 181–212. Vienna: Verlag der Österreichischen Akademie der Wissenschaften, 2013.

———. *Tsars, Cossacks, and Nomads: The Formation of a Borderland Culture in Northern Kazakhstan in the 18th and 19th Centuries.* Berlin: Klaus Schwartz, 2011.

Manley, Rebecca. *To the Tashkent Station: Evacuation and Survival in the Soviet Union at War.* Ithaca, NY: Cornell University Press, 2009.

Manz, Beatrice Forbes. *The Rise and Rule of Tamerlane.* Cambridge: Cambridge University Press, 1989.

Markowitz, Lawrence P. "How Master Frames Mislead: The Division and Eclipse of Nationalist Movements in Uzbekistan and Tajikistan." *Ethnic and Racial Studies* 32, no. 4 (2009): 716–38.

Marshall, Alex. *The Russian General Staff and Asia, 1800–1917.* London: Routledge, 2006.

Martin, Janet. "Muscovite Frontier Policy: The Case of the Khanate of Kasimov." *Russian History* 19, no. 1–4 (1992): 169–79.

Martin, Terry. *The Affirmative Action Empire: Nations and Nationalism in the Soviet Union, 1923–1939.* Ithaca, NY: Cornell University Press, 2001.

———. "The Origins of Soviet Ethnic Cleansing." *Journal of Modern History* 70, no. 4 (1998): 813–61.

Martin, Virginia. "Barïmta: Nomadic Custom, Imperial Crime." In *Russia's Orient: Imperial Borderlands and Peoples, 1700–1917*, edited by Daniel Brower and Edward Lazzerini, 249–70. Bloomington, IN: Indiana University Press, 1997.

———. "Engagement with Empire as Norm and in Practice in Kazakh Nomadic Political Culture (1820s–1830s)." *Central Asian Survey* 36, no. 2 (2017): 175–94.

———. *Law and Custom in the Steppe: The Kazakhs of the Middle Horde and Russian Colonialism in the Nineteenth Century.* Richmond, Surrey: Curzon, 2001.

———. "Using Turki-language Qazaq Letters to Reconstruct Local Political History of the 1820s–1830s." In *Explorations in the Social History of Modern Central Asia (19th–early 20th Century)*, edited by Paolo Sartori, 207–45. Leiden: Brill, 2013.

Materialy po istorii Uzbekskoi, Tadzhikskoi i Turkmenskoi SSR, Chast' I. Leningrad: Izd. Akademii Nauk SSSR, 1933.

Mawdsley, Evan, and Stephen White. *The Soviet Elite from Lenin to Gorbachev: The Central Committee and Its Members, 1917–1991.* Oxford: Oxford University Press, 2000.

May, Tim. *The Mongol Conquests in World History.* London: Reaktion, 2012.

McGlinchey, Eric. *Chaos, Violence, Dynasty: Politics and Islam in Central Asia.* Pittsburgh: University of Pittsburgh Press, 2011.

McLoughlin, Barry. "Mass Operations of the NKVD, 1937–8: A Survey." In *Stalin's Terror: High Politics and Mass Repression in the Soviet Union*, edited by Barry McLoughlin and Kevin McDermott, 118–52. New York: Palgrave Macmillan, 2003.

Meiendorf, Egor K. *Puteshestvie iz Orenburga v Bukharu*. Moscow: Nauka, 1975. French original 1826.

Meyer, James. "Immigration, Return, and the Politics of Citizenship: Russian Muslims in the Ottoman Empire, 1860–1914." *International Journal of Middle East Studies* 39, no. 1 (2007): 15–32.

Meyer, Karl, and Shareen Blair Brysac. *Tournament of Shadows: The Great Game and the Race for Empire in Central Asia*. Washington, DC: Counterpoint, 1999.

Michaels, Paula. *Curative Powers: Medicine and Empire in Stalin's Central Asia*. Pittsburgh: University of Pittsburgh Press, 2001.

Micklin, Philip P. "The Fate of 'Sibaral': Soviet Water Politics in the Gorbachev Era." *Central Asian Survey* 6, no. 2 (1987): 67–88.

Micklin, Philip P., and Andrew R. Bond. "Reflections on Environmentalism and the River Diversion Projects." *Soviet Economy* 4, no. 3 (1988): 253–74.

Millward, James. *Eurasian Crossroads: A History of Xinjiang*. New York: Columbia University Press, 2007.

Mitchell, Robert, and Nevill Forbes, eds. *The Chronicle of Novgorod*. Hattiesburg, MS: Academic International, 1970.

Momysh-uly, Baurdzhan. "Nasha sem'ia." *Izbrannoe v dvukh tomakh*, Vol. 2. Alma-Ata: Jazushy, 1980, orig. 1956.

Monahan, Erika. *The Merchants of Siberia: Trade in Early Modern Eurasia*. Ithaca, NY: Cornell University Press, 2016.

Morrison, Alexander. "Interpreting and Remembering the 1916 Revolt." EurasiaNet, 19 October 2016. http://www.eurasianet.org/node/80931.

———. "Killing the Cotton Canard and Getting Rid of the Great Game: Rewriting the Russian Conquest of Central Asia, 1814–1895." *Central Asian Survey* 33, no. 2 (June 2014): 131–42.

———. "Military Logistics and Historical Stage-management in the Russian Conquest of Khiva, 1873," conference paper presented at the Central Eurasian Studies Society annual conference, November 2016.

———. "'Nechto eroticheskoe', 'courir après l'ombre'?—Logistical Imperatives and the Fall of Tashkent, 1859–1865." *Central Asian Survey* 33, no. 2 (2014): 153–69.

———. "On the Importance of Being Soviet." EurasiaNet, 10 August 2018. https://eurasianet.org/s/perspectives-on-the-importance-of-being-soviet.

———. *Russian Rule in Samarkand 1868–1910: A Comparison with British India*. Oxford: Oxford University Press, 2008.

———. "Twin Imperial Disasters. The Invasions of Khiva and Afghanistan in the Russian and British Official Mind, 1839–1842." *Modern Asian Studies* 48, no. 1 (2014): 253–300.

Muhammadhakimxon To'ra. *Muntaxab at-tavorix (Xo'qand va Buxoro tarixi, sayohat va xotiralar)*. Tashkent: Iangi asr avlodi, 2010. Persian manuscript completed 1843.

Muhitdinnov, M., and A. Suiumov. "Yoshlarning bilan va tajriba maktabi." *Sovet maktabi* no. 3 (March 1964): 65–69.

Muiznieks, Nils R. "The Influence of the Baltic Popular Movements on the Process of Soviet Disintegration." *Europe-Asia Studies* 47, no. 1 (1995): 3–25.

Mukhitdinov, Nuriddin. *Gody, provedennye v kremle*. Tashkent: Izd. Abdully Kadyri, 1994.

Muratuly, Abikey Arman, and Tursun Hazretaly. "S. Khojanov and the Phenomenon of National Communism in Central Asia and Kazakhstan in the 20-Ies xx Century." *Asian Social Science* 10, no. 2 (2014): 93–101.

Nalivkin, Vladimir P. *Polveka v Turkestane*. Moscow: Izd. dom Mardzhani, 2015.

Nalivkin, Vladimir, and Maria Nalivkina. *Muslim Women of the Ferghana Valley: A 19th Century Ethnography from Central Asia*. Bloomington, IN: Indiana University Press, 2016.

Nepomnin, Vladimir Ia. *Istoricheskii opyt stroitel'stva sotsializma v Uzbekistana (1917–1937)*. Tashkent: GosIzdat UZSSR, 1960.

Newby, Laura. *The Empire and the Khanate: A Political History of Qing Relations with Kokand, c. 1760–1860*. Leiden: Brill, 2005.

Nikishenkov, Aleksei, and Iurii Semenov, eds. *Stepnoi zakon: Obychnoe pravo Kazakhov, Kirgizov i Turkmen*. Moscow: Staryi Sad, 2000.

Noda, Jin. *The Kazakh Khanates between the Russian and Qing Empires*. Leiden: Brill, 2016.

———. "Russo-Chinese Trade through Central Asia: Regulations and Reality." In *Asiatic Russia: Imperial Power in Regional and International Contexts*, edited by Tomohiko Uyama, 153–73. London: Routledge, 2012.

Northrop, Douglas. *Veiled Empire: Gender and Power in Stalinist Central Asia*. Ithaca, NY: Cornell University Press, 2004.

Nunan, Timothy. "A Union Reframed: Sovinformbiuro, Postwar Soviet Photography, and Visual Orders in Soviet Central Asia" *Kritika* 17, no. 3 (2016): 553–83.

Obertreis, Julia. *Imperial Desert Dreams: Cotton Growing and Irrigation in Central Asia, 1860–1991*. Göttingen: V & R Unipress, 2017.

Ochs, Michael. "Turkmenistan: The Quest for Stability and Control." In *Conflict, Cleavage, and Change in Central Asia and the Caucasus*, edited by Karen Dawisha and Bruce Parrot, 312–59. Cambridge: Cambridge University Press, 1997.

Olcott, Martha Brill. *The Kazakhs*. Stanford: Hoover Institution Press, 1987.

Ostrowski, Donald. *Muscovy and the Mongols: Cross-cultural Influences on the Steppe Frontier*. New York: Cambridge University Press, 1998.

———. "The Replacement of the Composite Reflex Bow by Firearms in the Muscovite Cavalry." In *Everyday Life in Russian History*, edited by Gary Marker, Joan Neuberger, Marshall Poe, and Leila Rupp, 203–30. Bloomington, IN: Slavica, 2010.

Pal'vanova, Bibi P. *Tragicheskie 30-e*. Ashkhabad: Turkmenistan, 1991.

Pannier, Bruce. "IMU Announces Longtime Leader Dead, Names Successor." Radio Free Europe/Radio Liberty, 17 August 2010. https://www.rferl.org/a/IMU _Announces_Longtime_Leader_Dead_Names_Successor/2130382.html.

———. "Iran Offers Turkmenistan New Gas Swap Deal to Pakistan." Radio Free Europe/Radio Liberty, 30 April 2018. https://www.rferl.org/a/iran-offers -turkmenistan-new-gas-swap-deal-to-pakistan-tapi/29201086.html.

———. "Remembering the Great Urkun 100 Years Later." Radio Free Europe/Radio Liberty, 29 April 2016. http://www.rferl.org/a/qishloq-ovozi-remembering -great-urkun/27706415.html.

———. "Who Was Kurmanjan Datka and What Does She Mean to the Kyrgyz People?" RFE/RL Qishloq Ovozi, 31 December 2014. http://www.rferl.org/a /qishloq-ovozi-who-was-kurmanjan-datka/26770979.html.

Payne, Matthew. "Seeing Like a Soviet State: Settlement of Nomadic Kazakhs, 1928– 1934." In *Writing the Stalin Era: Sheila Fitzpatrick and Soviet Historiography*, edited by Golfo Alexopoulos, Julie Hessler, and Kiril Tomroff, 59–86. New York: Palgrave Macmillan, 2011.

———. *Stalin's Railroad: Turksib and the Building of Socialism*. Pittsburgh: University of Pittsburgh Press, 2001.

Penati, Beatrice. "The Cotton Boom and the Land Tax in Russian Turkestan (1880s– 1915)." *Kritika* 14, no. 4 (2013): 741–74.

———. "Notes on the Birth of Russian Turkestan's Fiscal System: A View from the Fergana Oblast." *Journal of the Economic and Social History of the Orient* 53 (2010): 739–69.

———. "The Reconquest of East Bukhara. The Struggle against the Basmachi as a Prelude to Sovietization." *Central Asian Survey* 26, no. 4 (2007): 521–38.

Perdue, Peter. *China Marches West: The Qing Conquest of Central Eurasia*. Cambridge, MA: Harvard University Press, 2005.

Pianciola, Niccolò. "Famine in the Steppe: The Collectivization of Agriculture and the Kazakh Herdsmen 1928–1934." *Cahiers du Monde Russe* 45, no. 1–2 (2004): 137–91.

———. "Stalinist Spatial Hierarchies: Placing the Kazakhs and Kyrgyz in Soviet Economic Regionalization." *Central Asian Survey* 36, no. 1 (2017): 73–92.

Pickett, James. "Nadir Shah's Peculiar Central Asian Legacy: Empire, Conversion,

Narratives, and the Rise of New Scholarly Dynasties." *International Journal of Middle East Studies* 48, no. 3 (2016): 491–510.

Pierce, Richard. *Russian Central Asia, 1867–1917*. Berkeley: University of California Press, 1960.

Pobol', Oleg N., and P.M. Polian, eds. *Stalinskie deportatsii 1928–1953*. Moscow: Mezhdunarodnyi Fond Demokratiia, 2005.

Pochekaev, Roman. "Rol' Ustava ob upravlenii sibirskikh Kirgizov' v politiko-pravovom razvitii Kazakhstana." In *Materialy mezhdunarodnoi nauchno-prakticheskoi konferentsii "Ot Kazakhskogo khanstva k nezavisimomu Kazakhstanu,"* edited by Burkitbay G. Aiagan, 80–87. Astana: Elorda, 2015.

Pohl, Michaela. "From White Grave to Tselinograd to Astana: The Virgin Lands Opening, Khrushchev's Forgotten First Reform." In *The Thaw: Soviet Society and Culture during the 1950s and 1960s*, edited by Denis Kozlov and Eleonory Gilburd, 269–307. Toronto: University of Toronto Press, 2013.

———. "'It cannot be that our graves will be here': The Survival of Chechen and Ingush Deportees in Kazakhstan, 1944–1957." *Journal of Genocide Research* 4, no. 3 (2002): 401–30.

———. "The 'Planet of One Hundred Languages': Ethnic Relations and Soviet Identity in the Virgin Lands." In *Peopling the Russian Periphery: Borderland Colonization in Eurasian History*, edited by Nicholas Breyfogle, Abby Schrader, and Willard Sunderland, 238–61. London: Routledge, 2007.

Povest' vremennykh let, Vol. 1. Moscow: Izd. Akademii Nauk, 1950.

Pravilova, Ekaterina. *Finansy imperii: den'gi i vlast' v politike Rossiii na natsional'nykh okrainakh, 1801–1917*. Moscow: Novoe Izd., 2006.

Prior, Daniel. *The Sabdan Baatir Codex: Epic and the Writing of Northern Kirghiz History: Edition, Translation and Interpretations, with a Facsimile of the Unique Manuscript*. Leiden: Brill, 2012.

Qodirova, Asolat. "Qizlar, sizlar uchun!" *Saodat* no. 3 (1974): 29.

Qodirova, Mahbuba. "Nodira." http://www.ziyouz.com/index.php?option=com_content&task=view&id=1043&Itemid=228.

Qoigeldiev, Mambet K., ed. *Istoriia Kazakhstana v russkikh istochnikakh*. Vol. IV, "Pervye istoriko-etnograficheskie opisaniia Kazakhskikh zemel' xviii vek." Almaty: Daik-Press, 2007.

Qozybaev, Manash K., ed. *Nasil'stvennaia kollektivizatsiia i golod v Kazakhstane v 1931–33 gg: sbornik dokumentov i materialov*. Almaty: Fond xix vek, 1998.

Raab, Nigel. "The Tashkent Earthquake of 1966: The Advantages and Disadvantages of a Natural Tragedy." *Jahrbücher für Geschichte Osteuropas* 62, no. 2 (2014): 273–94.

Radnitz, Scott. *Weapons of the Wealthy: Predatory Regimes and Elite-led Protests in Central Asia.* Ithaca, NY: Cornell University Press, 2010.

Raeff, Marc. *Siberia and the Reforms of 1822.* Seattle: University of Washington Press, 1956.

Rakhmankulova, Kh. "Natsional'naia politika Sovetskogo Gosudarstva v 1930–1940-e gg. deportatsiia narodov v Uzbekistan." In *Sovetskie natsii i natsional'naia politika v 1920–1950-e gody,* edited by N.A. Volynchik and M.A. Ailamazian, 497–505. Moscow: ROSSPEN, 2014.

Reeves, Madeleine. *Border Work: Spatial Lives of the State in Rural Central Asia.* Ithaca, NY: Cornell University Press, 2014.

Report of Court Proceedings in the Case of the Anti-Soviet Bloc of Rights and Trotskyites. Moscow: Narkomiust, 1938.

Reynolds, Michael. *Shattering Empires: The Clash and Collapse of the Ottoman and Russian Empires 1908–1918.* Cambridge: Cambridge University Press, 2011.

Romaniello, Matthew P. *The Elusive Empire: Kazan and the Creation of Russia 1552–1671.* Madison: University of Wisconsin Press, 2012.

Roth-Ey, Kristin. *Moscow Prime Time: How the Soviet Union Built the Multi-Media Empire That Lost the Cultural Cold War.* Ithaca, NY: Cornell University Press, 2011.

Rouland, Michael, Gulnara Abikeyeva, and Birgit Beumers, eds. *Cinema in Central Asia: Rewriting Cultural Histories.* London: I.B. Tauris, 2013.

Rumer, Boris Z. *Soviet Central Asia: A Tragic Experiment.* Boston: Unwin Hyman, 1989.

Ruysbroeck, Willem van. *The Journey of William of Rubruck to the Eastern Parts of the World.* London: Hakluyt Society, 1900.

Rywkin, Michael. *Moscow's Muslim Challenge: Soviet Central Asia.* Armonk, NY: M.E. Sharpe, 1990.

Sabol, Steven. "Kazakh Resistance to Russian Colonization: Interpreting the Kenesary Kasymov Revolt, 1837–1847." *Central Asian Survey* 22, no. 2/3 (2003): 231–52.

———. *Russian Colonization and the Genesis of Kazak National Consciousness.* London: Palgrave Macmillan, 2003.

Safarov, Georgii. *Kolonial'naia revoliutsiia.* Moscow: GosIzdat, 1921.

Sahadeo, Jeff. *Russian Colonial Society in Tashkent, 1865–1923.* Bloomington, IN: Indiana University Press, 2007.

———. *Voices from the Soviet Edge: Southern Migrants in Leningrad and Moscow.* Ithaca, NY: Cornell University Press, 2019.

Salimova, F. "Amrika ayollari kurashmoqda." *Saodat* no. 12 (1971): 24–25.

Sanborn, Joshua. *Imperial Apocalypse: The Great War and the Destruction of the Russian Empire.* Oxford: Oxford University Press, 2014.

———. "Unsettling the Empire: Violent Migrations and Social Disaster in Russia during World War I." *The Journal of Modern History* 77, no. 2 (2005): 290–325.

Saparbekova, Ainuri, J. Kocourkova, and T. Kucera. "Sweeping Ethno-Demographic Changes in Kazakhstan during the 20th Century: A Dramatic Story of Mass Migration Waves Part I: From the Turn of the 19th Century to the End of the Soviet Era." *Acta Universitatis Carolinae Geographica* 49, no. 1 (2014): 71–82.

Sartori, Paolo. "Constructing Colonial Legality in Russian Central Asia: On Guardianship." *Comparative Studies in Society and History* 56, no. 2 (2014): 419–47.

———. "*Ijtihad* in Bukhara: Central Asian Jadidism and Local Genealogies of Cultural Change." *Journal of the Economic and Social History of the Orient* 59 (2016): 193–236.

———. "The Tashkent '*Ulama*' and the Soviet State (1920–1938): A Preliminary Research Note Based on NKVD Documents." In *Patterns of Transformation in and Around Uzbekistan*, edited by Paolo Sartori and Tommaso Trevisani, 161–84. Reggio Emilia: Diabasis, 2007.

Scarborough, Isaac. "(Over)determining Social Disorder: Tajikistan and the Economic Collapse of Perestroika." *Central Asian Survey* 35, no. 3 (2016): 439–63.

Schamiloglu, Uli. "Preliminary Remarks on the Role of Disease in the History of the Golden Horde." *Central Asian Survey* 12, no. 4 (1993): 447–57.

Schatz, Edward. *Modern Clan Politics: The Power of "Blood" in Kazakhstan and Beyond.* Seattle: University of Washington Press, 2004.

Schimmelpenninck van der Oye, David. *Russian Orientalism: Asia in the Russian Mind from Peter the Great to the Emigration.* New Haven: Yale University Press, 2010.

Sela, Ron. "Invoking the Russian Conquest of Khiva and the Massacres of the Yomut Turkmen: The Choices of a Central Asian Historian." *Asiatische Studien* 60, no. 2 (2006): 459–77.

———. "Prescribing the Boundaries of Knowledge: Seventeenth-Century Russian Diplomatic Missions to Central Asia." In *Travel Writing in Central Asian History*, edited by Nile Green, 69–88. Bloomington, IN: Indiana University Press, 2014.

Shaiakhmetov, Mukhamet. *The Silent Steppe: The Memoir of a Kazakh Nomad under Stalin.* New York: Overlook/Rookery, 2007.

Shamsutdinov, Rustambek. *Ikkinchi jahon urushi va front gazetalari.* Tashkent: Akademnashr, 2017.

———. *Qishloq fojeasi: jamoalashtirish, quloqlashtirish, surgun.* Tashkent: Sharq, 2003.

Shamsutdinov, Rustambek T., N.F. Karimov, and E. Iu. Iusupov, eds. *Repressiia, 1937–1938 gody: dokumenty i materialy,* Vol. 1. Tashkent: Sharq, 2005.

Shaw, Charles. "Making Ivan-Uzbek: War, Friendship of the Peoples, and the Creation of Soviet Uzbekistan 1941–1945." PhD dissertation, University of California, Berkeley, 2015.

Sher-Niyaz, Sadyk, dir. *Kurmanjan Datka: Queen of the Mountains*. Aitysh Film, Kyrgyzstan, 2014.

Shin, Boram. "Red Army Propaganda for Uzbek Soldiers and Localised Soviet Internationalism during World War II." *The Soviet and Post-Soviet Review* 42 (2015): 39–63.

Sholomitskii, Yurii, and Marat Isxakov. *O'zbekistonda fizkul'tura va sport rivojlanishi.* Tashkent: Bilim jamiati, 1974.

Siegelbaum, Lewis H., and Leslie Page Moch. *Broad Is My Native Land: Repertoires and Regimes of Migration in Russia's Twentieth Century.* Ithaca, NY: Cornell University Press, 2014.

Simon, Gerhard. *Nationalism and Policy toward the Nationalities in the Soviet Union.* Boulder, CO: Westview Press, 1991.

Slezkine, Yuri. *The House of Government: A Saga of the Russian Revolution.* Princeton: Princeton University Press, 2017.

———. "The USSR as a Communal Apartment, or How a Socialist State Promoted Ethnic Particularism." *Slavic Review* 53, no. 2 (Summer 1994): 414–52.

Slocum, John W. "Who, and When, Were the Inorodtsy? The Evolution of the Category of 'Aliens' in Imperial Russia." *The Russian Review* 57, no. 2 (1998): 173–90.

Smele, Jonathan. *Historical Dictionary of Russia's Civil Wars.* Lanham, MD: Rowman and Littlefield, 2015.

Smirnov, Mikhail B., ed. *Sistema ispravitel'no-trudovykh lagerei v SSSR, 1923–1960: spravochnik.* Moscow: Zven'ia, 1998.

Smith, Jeremy. "The Georgian Affair of 1922—Policy Failure, Personality Clash, or Power Struggle?" *Europe–Asia Studies* 50, no. 3 (1998): 519–44.

Sneath, David. *The Headless State: Aristocratic Orders, Kinship Society, and Misrepresentations of Nomadic Inner Asia.* New York: Columbia University Press, 2007.

Socialist Construction in the USSR: Statistical Abstract. Moscow: Soyuzorguchet, 1936.

Sonntag, Heather. "Photography & Mapping Russian Conquest in Central Asia: Early Albums, Encounters, & Exhibitions 1866–1876." *Journée d'Etude Centrasiatique.* Atelier 3: *Histoire du Turkestan russe et du Xinjiang.* 26 October 2007. http://www.gis-reseau-asie.org/article/heather-s-sonntag-photography-mapping-russian-conquest-in-central-asia-early-albums-encounters-exhib/.

Soucek, Svat. *A History of Inner Asia.* Cambridge: Cambridge University Press, 2000.

Soudavar, Abolala. "The Early Safavids and Their Cultural Interactions with Surrounding States." In *Iran and the Surrounding World: Interactions in Culture and Politics*, edited by Nikki Keddie and Rudi Mathee, 89–120. Seattle: University of Washington Press, 2002.

Sovetskii Turkmenistan za 40 let. Staticheskii sbornik. Ashkhabad: Turkmenskoe Izdt., 1964.

Stalin, Joseph. *Marxism and the National and Colonial Question*. New York: International Publishers, 1935.

———. "Marxism and the National Question." [1913]. In J.V. Stalin, *Works* 2:300–81. London: Lawrence and Wishart, 1953. https://www.marxists.org/reference/archive/stalin/works/1913/03.htm.

Stawkowski, Magdalena. "'I am a Radioactive Mutant': Emergent Biological Subjectivities at Kazakhstan's Semipalatinsk Nuclear Test Site." *American Ethnologist* 43, no. 1 (2016): 144–57.

Stefany, Michael G. "Kazakhization, Kunaev and Kazakhstan: A Bridge to Independence." *Orta Asya ve Kafkasya Arastirmalari* 8, no. 16 (2013): 49–72.

Steward, Julian. *Theory of Culture Change: The Methodology of Multilinear Evolution*. Urbana, IL: University of Illinois Press, 1963.

Stites, Richard. *Revolutionary Dreams: Utopian Vision and Experimental Life in the Russian Revolution*. New York: Oxford University Press, 1989.

Stronski, Paul. *Tashkent: Forging a Soviet City 1930–1966*. Pittsburgh: University of Pittsburgh Press, 2010.

Sultangalieva, Gulmira. "The Russian Empire and the Intermediary Role of Tatars in Kazakhstan." In *Asiatic Russia: Imperial Power in Regional and International Contexts*, edited by Tomohiko Uyama, 52–79. London: Routledge, 2012.

Suny, Ronald Grigor, and Terry Martin, eds. *A State of Nations: Empire and Nation-Making in the Age of Lenin and Stalin*. Oxford: Oxford University Press, 2001.

Tasar, Eren. *Soviet and Muslim: The Institutionalization of Islam in Central Asia*. New York: Oxford University Press, 2017.

Teichmann, Christian. "Canals, Cotton, and the Limits of De-Colonization in Soviet Uzbekistan, 1924–1941." *Central Asian Survey* 26, no. 4 (2007): 499–519.

———. *Macht der Unordnung: Stalins Herrschaft in Zentralasien 1920–1950*. Hamburg: Hamburger Edition, 2016.

Teissier, Beatrice, ed. *John Castle's Mission to Khan Abulkhayir*. Oxford: Signal Books, 2014.

Thomas, Alun. *Nomads and Soviet Rule: Central Asia under Lenin and Stalin*. London: I.B. Tauris, 2018.

Thompson, Stith. *Motif-index of Folk-literature*. Bloomington, IN: Indiana University Press, 1955.

Tokhtakhodjaeva, Marfua, and Elmira Turgumbekova. *The Daughters of Amazons: Voices from Central Asia*. Lahore: Shirkat Gah Women's Resource Center, 1996.

Trepavlov, Vadim V. "The Formation and Early History of the Manghït Yurt." *Papers on Inner Asia*, No. 35. Bloomington, IN: Research Institute for Inner Asian Studies, 2001.

Tulibaeva, Zhuldyz. *Kazakhstan i bukharskoe khanstvo v* XVIII–*pervoi polovine* XIX *v.* Almaty: Daik-Press, 2001.

Turkestanskii al'bom. Tashkent: 1872. https://www.loc.gov/rr/print/coll/287_turkestan .html.

Tynyshpaev, Mukhamedjan. *Istoriia Kazakhskogo naroda*. Almaty: Sanat, 2001.

Usmanova, Dilyara M. "The Activity of the Muslim Faction of the State Duma and Its Significance in the Formation of a Political Culture among the Muslim Peoples of Russia (1906–1917)." In *Muslim Culture in Russia and Central Asia from the 18th to the Early 20th Centuries*, edited by Anke von Kügelgen, Michael Kemper, and Allen J. Frank, 2:417–56. Berlin: Klaus Schwartz Verlag, 1998.

Ustinov, Viktor M. *Turar Ryskulov: ocherki politicheskoi biografii*. Almaty: Kazakhstan, 1996.

Uyama, Tomohiko. "The Changing Religious Orientation of Qazaq Intellectuals in the Tsarist Period: *Sharia*, Secularism, and Ethics." In *Islam, Society, and States Across the Qazaq Steppe (18th–early 20th Centuries)*, edited by Niccolò Pianciola and Paolo Sartori, 95–118. Vienna: Verlag der Österreichischen Akademie der Wissenschaften, 2013.

———. "A Strategic Alliance between Kazakh Intellectuals and Russian Administrators: Imagined Communities in *Dala Walayatining Gazeti* 1888–1920." In *The Construction and Deconstruction of National Histories in Slavic Eurasia*, edited by Tadayuki Hayashi, 237–60. Sapporo: Slavic Research Center, Hokkaido University, 2003.

Uzbekistan za 7 let: kratkii staticheskii sbornik. Tashkent: 1966.

Vaksberg, Arkady. *The Soviet Mafia*. New York: St. Martin's Press, 1991.

Vambery, Arminius. *History of Bukhara*. London: Henry S. King and Co., 1873.

———. *Travels in Central Asia*. New York: Harper and Brothers Publishers, 1865.

Vasary, Istvan. "The Jochid Realm." In *The Cambridge History of Inner Asia*, edited by Nicola Di Cosimo, et al., Vol. I, "The Chinggisid Age." Cambridge: Cambridge University Press, 2009 (print), 2014 (internet).

Vinkovetsky, Ilya. *Russian America: An Overseas Colony of a Continental Empire, 1804–1867*. New York: Oxford University Press, 2011.

Viola, Lynne, Viktor Danilov, N.A. Ivnitskii, and Denis Kozlov, eds. *The War against the Peasantry, 1927–1930: The Tragedy of the Soviet Countryside*. New Haven: Yale University Press, 2005.

Walker, Shaun. "Turkmenistan's Singing Dictator Heralds Upcoming Elections." *The Guardian*, 1 February 2017. https://www.theguardian.com/world/2017/feb/01 /turkmenistans-singing-dictator-gurbanguly-berdymukhamedov-heralds -upcoming-elections.

Walton, David. "Uzbekistan: Murder among Minarets." *The Telegraph*, 15 February 2003. http://www.telegraph.co.uk/travel/726861/Uzbekistan-Murder-among -minarets.html.

Welsford, Thomas. *Tūqāy-Timūrid Takeover of Greater Mā Warā al-Nahr, 1598–1605*. Leiden: Brill, 2013.

Werner, Cynthia, and Kathleen Purvis-Roberts. "Unraveling the Secrets of the Past: Contested Versions of Nuclear Testing in the Soviet Republic of Kazakhstan." In *Half-Lives and Half-Truths: Confronting the Radioactive Legacies of the Cold War*, edited by Barbara Rose Johnston, 277–98. Santa Fe, NM: School for Advanced Research, 2007.

Wissler, Clark. *The American Indian*. New York: Douglas C. McMurtrie, 1917.

Wolff, Joseph. *A Mission to Bokhara*. New York: Praeger Publishers, 1969, orig. 1852.

Zenkovsky, Serge A. *Medieval Russia's Epics, Chronicles, and Tales*. New York: Penguin, 1974.

———. *The Nikonian Chronicle*, Vol. 1. Princeton: Kingston Press, 1984.

Zevaco, Ariane. "From Old to New Macha: Mass Resettlement and the Redefinition of Islamic Practice between Tajikistan's Upper Valleys and Cotton Lowlands." In *Allah's Kolhozes: Migration, De-Stalinisation, Privatisation and the New Muslim Congregations in the Soviet Realm (1950s–2000s)*, edited by Stéphane A. Dudoignon and Christian Noack, 148–201. Berlin: Klaus Schwartz Verlag, 2014.

Zhou, Jiayi. "The Muslim Battalions: Soviet Central Asians in the Soviet-Afghan War." *Journal of Slavic Military Studies* 25 (2012): 302–28.

Zimanov, Salyk. *Politicheskii stroi Kazakhstana kontsa XVIII i pervoi poloviny XIX vekov*. Almaty: Arys, 2009, orig. 1960.

INDEX

CPSIA information can be obtained
at www.ICGtesting.com
Printed in the USA
BVHW070308031222
653364BV00004B/5